ELEMENTARY SCHOOL COUNSELING

A COMMITMENT TO CARING AND COMMUNITY BUILDING

Second Edition

John C. Worzbyt, Ed.D.
Department of Counseling
Indiana University of Pennsylvania
Indiana, PA

Kathleen O'Rourke, Ed.D.
Director of Guidance (retired)
Altoona Area School District
Altoona, PA

Claire J. Dandeneau, Ph.D.
Department of Counseling
Indiana University of Pennsylvania
Indiana, PA

Brunner-Routledge

NEW YORK AND HOVE

Published in 2003 by
Brunner-Routledge
29 West 35th Street
New York, NY 10001
www.brunner-routledge.com

Published in Great Britain by
Brunner-Routledge
27 Church Road
Hove
East Sussex BN3 2FA
www.brunner-routledge.co.uk

© 2003 by Taylor & Francis Books, Inc.
Brunner-Routledge is an imprint of the Taylor & Francis Group

This book is a completely revised text of *Elementary School Counseling: A Blueprint for Today and Tomorrow,* published by Accelerated Development in 1989.

Printed in the United States of America on acid-free paper.

10 9 8 7 6 5 4 3 2 1

Library of Congress Cataloging-in-Publication Data

Worzbyt, John C.
    Elementary school counseling : a commitment to caring and community building / John C. Worzbyt, Kathleen O'Rourke, Claire Dandeneau.— 2nd ed.
        p. ; cm.
Includes bibliographical references and index.
    ISBN 1-56032-505-4 (hardback)—ISBN 1-56032-506-2 (pbk.)
1. Counseling in elementary education—United States. 2. Elementary school counselors—Training of—United States. I. O'Rourke, Kathleen, 1941– II. Dandeneau, Claire J. III. Title.

LB1027.5 .W6744 2003
372.14—dc21

2002152019

Contents

List of Figures

List of Activities

**Career and Societal
Caring Activities**

Preface

Elementary School Counseling: A Commitment to Caring and Community Building is a practical and educationally relevant guide for helping elementary school counselors rethink their professional roles and the mission of elementary school counseling programs. We believe that elementary school counseling programs and the counselors who provide leadership are in the people-building business. They are in the business of helping children to acquire the attitudes, knowledge, and skills needed to become caring human beings and builders of caring communities.

Throughout this book, we advocate on behalf of counselors, teachers, administrators, and community supporters, working together to develop elementary school counseling programs that will work in partnership with school academic-instructional programs in providing children with a *balanced education*. A significant quality of a *balanced education* is its focus on academic instruction and people-building and the creation of a caring school community that supports a climate for learning and a commitment to developing human potential. We believe that elementary school counseling programs have a significant role to play in supporting just and caring schools and in developing caring children who do better in school and in life because they are taught how to learn, live, and work in support of themselves, others, and their communities.

A *balanced education* is one that meets society's needs for developing caring and responsible community members while meeting children's developmental and individual needs in helping them to become caring human beings and capable self-managers. A *balanced education* bridges the gap between academic instruction (reading, writing, mathematics, language arts, science, etc.) and people-building (physical, personal/emotional, social, cognitive, and career/societal caring). In the overlap between these two delivery systems (academic-instruction and elementary school counseling) emerges a *balanced education* that emphasizes *school as community, curriculum with coherence, climate for learning, and commitment to character.* A *balanced education* is essential for the growth and prosperity of our nation and good for our children in helping them to become caregivers and builders of caring communities.

We strongly believe that the time is right for elementary school counseling programs to take their rightful place in providing children with a *balanced education.* A complete and comprehensive education contributes to children's understanding of the world and of themselves. These two areas become more relevant and meaningful when taught together as they help children to make the transition between classroom learning and life and living.

In the chapters that follow, we provide readers with a *blueprint for success* in creating and enhancing elementary school counseling programs that work in partnership with school academic-instructional programs in providing children with a quality education. The research cited throughout this text supports the notion that children do better in school and in life when their developmental needs are successfully addressed in a learning climate that supports people and community-building through a coherent curriculum that links learning to living. We believe that we have achieved this balance.

In designing this book, we have relied on our own professional experiences as elementary school teachers, elementary school counselors, community agency service providers, and counselor educators; and from student feedback and practicing elementary school counselors. We have likewise turned to the literature, in particular to the American School Counselor Association's National Standards and the publications detailing their design and implementation. We believe that we have captured the essence of quality, practicality, and applicability in our blueprint for success. Our goal in writing this book has always been to develop a blueprint for success that is caring and community-building in nature and comprehensive, collaborative, and developmental in design. We have strived to provide a framework for success that is present bound, future oriented, and flexible in presentation, allowing for creativity and imagination in developing elementary school counseling programs in support of a *balanced education.* The framework for success, as we have designed it, consists of four parts and 12 chapters. *Part I: Creating a 21st-Century Partnership* focuses on the nature of elementary school education and elementary school counseling in the 21st century and the working relationship between these two programs in providing children with a *balanced education* (see Chapters 1 and 2). Counselor role responsibilities are discussed in helping elementary school counselors foster this partnership and lead and manage a viable and meaningful counseling program that supports caring and community building (see Chapter 3).

Part II: Managing a Responsive Program addresses the importance of strategic planning (see Chapter 4) and decision-making (see Chapter 5) in creating and maintaining a developmental elementary school counseling program that meets children's needs and reflects school district and community values. Readers are provided with detailed directions and examples to follow in conducting a comprehensive strategic plan and a Ternary Decision-Making model to determine the most effective and efficient intervention strategies to be used in meeting children's developmental and individual needs.

Part III: Counseling and the Curriculum addresses child development from a caring perspective. A counseling program curriculum is provided that emphasizes the importance of collaboration and teamwork (school and community) in meeting children's needs in five specific areas to include physical caring (see Chapter 6), personal/emotional caring (see Chapter 7), social caring (see Chapter 8), cognitive caring (see Chapter 9), and career and societal caring (see Chapter 10). These five chapters on developmental caring provide child development information, characteristics of a healthy child, potential risk factors in the absence of caring, ways to enhance personal well-being through caring choices, the counselor's role in caring, and caring activities to enhance children's ability to more effectively care for themselves and others.

Part IV: Challenging the Future emphasizes that today's decisions will influence tomorrow's outcomes. Therefore, today's decisions must not be taken lightly. Counselors are provided with primary, secondary, and tertiary strategies to care for their elementary school counseling programs, keeping them present bound while remaining future oriented (see Chapter 11). Counselors who care for their counseling programs in this manner will have counseling programs that will care for and benefit children, schools, and communities, now and in the future.

Challenging the future is also about forming a circle of care (see Chapter 12) in which all people live, learn, and work together. The *caring circle* consists of a caring physical environment, a caring interpersonal climate, a caring curriculum, and a caring school and community partnership. Collectively, each dimension of care connects to form a circle of caring and community building that serves to strengthen the circle of caring and life itself.

We hope that you will experience as much fun and enthusiasm in designing a caring elementary school counseling program as we did in writing this book. Much success in your todays and tomorrows in helping children to experience full, purposeful, and meaningful lives.

Acknowledgments

Writing *Elementary School Counseling: Strategies for Caring and Community Building* has been a caring and community-building experience. In our quest to produce an elementary school counseling book that would truly touch the lives of children and all who seek to nurture their development, we looked to our own development and what touched our lives. During the six years that it took to write this book, we reached one single, yet deeply felt conclusion. What really mattered was that there were people who cared deeply for us and taught us how to care and to be careful. The care that we receive and pass onto others is what it takes to nurture caring people who become builders of caring communities. The circle of care (Chapter 12) is a lasting tribute to those who give and receive care.

We are especially grateful to caring teachers (parents, family, and friends) and those community members who have shaped our lives and the book that follows. It is these people to whom we owe a debt of gratitude and dedicate this book.

To Drs. Harold L. Munson, George L. Spinelli, and Allan Dye, our mentors, friends, and caregivers, thank you for caring and helping us to become builders of caring communities.

To Barbara J. Rhine, Megan M. Schoenfeld, and Amy Borick, our principal research assistants, typists, and manuscript reviewers, we are deeply indebted. Your friendship, support, enthusiasm, and sense of humor have helped to sustain and enrich our lives throughout this long and involved process.

To Jennifer Hadel, Jana C. Hardee, Nancy Rowse, Heather L. Sakala, Cally L. Scott, Jennifer Lynch, Susan McLean, and Tricia Murin, thank you for your research assistance, typing, and editorial suggestions. And most importantly, we thank you for being a part of our caring circle.

To Emily Epstein, associate editor, Brunner-Routledge, Taylor and Francis, Inc., we are especially indebted. We thank you for your support, patience, and invaluable assistance in helping us to prepare our book for publication.

To Tim Julet, former acquistions editor, Brunner-Routledge, we owe much. Your continued support and encouragement during some difficult times sustained our desire and energy in making this book a reality.

To Susan Sibert and Francine Endler, we express our sincere appreciation for reviewing our manuscript and providing invaluable suggestions that have enhanced the quality and usefulness of our text.

To Dr. Joseph Hollis, founder of Accelerated Development, a member of the Taylor and Francis Group, and a personal friend, we thank you for encouraging us to put pen to paper and to share our ideas. Your guidance and helpful suggestions have helped us to give the best of ourselves to others.

To Richard Rothschild, Print Matters, Inc., thank you for helping us to produce a quality product in a timely manner.

To the many children who have inspired us to care more deeply and live life more fully, we have written this book.

To our families, we are especially grateful. This book, which has truly been a commitment of caring, is a product of a caring community that has at its core those whom we love and appreciate. Thanks for being there.

Caring and community building give life purpose and meaning. Our purpose for being is to teach children to care and to become builders of caring communities. We thank you for helping children to make a life and a living and to take their rightful place in the circle of care.

PART I

CREATING A 21ST-CENTURY PARTNERSHIP

CHAPTER 1

Elementary School Education in the 21st Century

The purpose of this chapter is to introduce elementary school counselors to a new and exciting vision for elementary school education, one that will rely heavily on elementary school counseling programs and their people-building mission of teaching children to care and to build caring communities. The elementary schools of the 21st century will be concerned with not only getting children ready for school, but getting schools ready for children (Boyer, 1995; Houston, 2001). They will accomplish this end by focusing on six crucial Cs designed to build strong cohesive classroom communities, which lay the foundation for successful classrooms (Boyer, 1995; Houston, 2001; Sapon-Shevin, 1999). Those Cs are caring connections, communication, collaboration, community building, a commitment to character (child advocacy), and a curriculum with coherence that relates classroom to life learning (Houston, 2001). Sapon-Shevin (1999) said it best when she stated this simple truth.

All students must feel safe, respected, and valued in order to learn new skills. Fear, discomfort, and anxiety are fundamentally incompatible with the learning process, and make teaching and learning difficult. Successful classrooms are those in which students feel supported in their learning, willing to take risks, challenged to become fully human with one another, and open to new possibilities (xi).

Sapon-Shevin (1999) concluded her thoughts with the following: *"When we teach, we change our students, the world, and ourselves"*

(p. xi). Elementary schools that emphasize the six Cs are destined to shape classrooms, children's lives, and a society that values community, concern for others, and an educational learning experience that teaches children to

- care more deeply,
- manage risks more responsibly, and
- live life more fully in caring communities of their making.

Elementary schools of the 21st century will teach children how to live, learn, and work. They will nurture caring and community building, offer real alternatives to violence and racism, and become proving grounds and models of possibility and hope (Shapon-Shevin, 1999).

EDUCATION IN TRANSITION

Most people would agree that the primary goal of education is to teach young people how to become productive and healthy adults in our society. However, few people agree on what our young people should know and be able to do in fulfilling this goal. Educational reform is a hot topic today and most people agree that educational change is necessary, given the many challenges our society faces. Changing labor markets, a need for more highly skilled workers, the effects of advanced technology, changing family structures, and children and families in crises are but a few of the many societal dynamics affecting children's lives and their education.

However, there is a lack of agreement among educators, politicians, business leaders, and parents as to how education should change, what changes should be made, and who should make them (Herr, 2001). Consequently, the debate continues to escalate regarding educational standards and appropriate student outcomes and, as a result, schools are slow to change. What seems to be certain is that as the list of groups with differing educational agendas rises, the likelihood of identifying a single, one-size-fits-all curriculum that addresses all the essential competencies for life in the 21st century seems unlikely. And perhaps that is as it should be. "The alternative is for local communities to begin working together to answer questions about what they want their children to know and be able to do" (Wagner, 1995, p. 394). This need not be done in a vacuum. Wagner (1995) has advocated a four-element analytical framework to be used in redefining what it means to be an educated adult. Educators and community supporters are asked to think about changes that have taken place in our society in the following focus areas and what educational goals should be developed with respect to

1. education for a changing economy,
2. education for continuing learning,
3. education for citizenship, and
4. education for personal growth and health.

In keeping with Wagner's analytical framework regarding societal changes, the statement on quality education found in chapter 5 of the Pennsylvania State Board of Education Curriculum Regulations provides a prime example of how one state has defined its educational mission (1993).

Quality education prepares students to assume responsible adult roles as citizens, family members, workers and lifelong learners by attending to their intellectual and developmental needs. The overriding mission of public education, in conjunction with families and other community institutions is to elevate all children to the highest level of academic achievement. Public schools will not set achievement levels at the lowest common denominator. Instead, public schools should prepare all students to be: (1) high academic achievers; (2) self-directed; (3) responsible involved citizens; (4) collaborative, high-quality contributors to the economic and cultural lives of their communities; (5) adaptive users of advanced technologies; (6) concerned stewards of the global environment; (7) healthy, continuously developing individuals; (8) caring, supportive family and community members (p. 201).

Communicated a bit more simply, nearly three decades ago, Van Hoose (1975) stated that "The goal of education in a free society is to enable youth to acquire the skills and understandings to be competent and responsible people" (p. 27). Participants of the 1970 White House Conference on Children stated the goal of education in yet another, but similar way when they said:

> *The right to learn is the goal that we seek for the twenty-first century. We want for our children a range of learning opportunities as broad as the unknown range of their talents. We want our children to know themselves and, secure in that knowledge, to open themselves to others. We want them to have freedom, and the order, justice, and peace that the preservation of their freedom demands (United States Department of Health, Education, and Welfare, Office of Child Development, 1970, p. 5).*

Our educational system seeks to develop moral beings with purpose and loyalties that are valuable to the individual and society. Herr (1984) stated it best when he said that ". . . educational reform of any kind must be mindful that at the center of attention are the individual needs for knowledge and skills having general currency in the society that students will occupy" (p. 219).

Despite a nearly thirty-year span in educational reform as reflected in the previous quotes, the goals of education, then and now, have not changed significantly. They have been to elevate all children to the highest level of academic achievement and personal development possible so that they can make a living and a life for themselves and their families in a society that they will leave better off for having contributed to it.

While education is a lifelong endeavor, what happens to children during their elementary school years must be of primary concern and interest to us all. For during those formative years of development, children will experience their first taste of a formal education. As home, school, and community work together, our hope is that this new experience called *school* will be one in which children's developmental and societal needs are met and opportunities for personal growth are commensurate with their potential. With this goal in mind, a look at what elementary education has to offer children in the 21st century will now be addressed.

ELEMENTARY SCHOOL EDUCATION

What follows is a look into our future regarding elementary education, a future that in many respects is already operative in some of our very best elementary schools in the United States. Elementary school education in the 21st century will become more responsive to the needs of children and will enhance our nation's prospects for a better future because our children will receive a more comprehensive and connected education, one that is responsive to the basic building blocks of community, curriculum with coherence, climate, and character (Boyer, 1995). According to Boyer (1995), who was one of this nation's most respected leaders in education and proponent of educational reform:

> *An effective school connects people to create community. An effective school connects the curriculum, to achieve coherence. An effective school connects classrooms and resources, to enrich the learning climate. And an effective school connects learning to life, to build character (p. 8).*

While Boyer would have agreed that public schools can do better, he stated that "We've learned lessons about excellence and quality in the years we've spent researching and talking to teachers" (p. 56). His goal was to reaffirm those practices and to encourage their use in a comprehensive manner in all schools. The *Basic School,* a phrase coined by Boyer, has particular significance in that it focuses on school renewal and educational reform at the elementary school level, embraces local and neighborhood school reform rather than adopting a national reform agenda, gives priority to language and curriculum with coherence, and utilizes proven practices and components of education already in place in our nation's most effective schools.

The *Basic School* by its very design successfully addresses society's need to develop responsible citizens while meeting children's developmental and self-management needs for personal well-being. The building blocks of the *Basic School* (community, curriculum with coherence, climate, and character) are essential for our nation, good for our children, and have particular meaning for elementary school counseling programs because they too share the same building blocks.

The School as Community

Sergiovanni (1995) stated that "communities create social structures that bond people together in a oneness, and that bind them to a set of shared values and ideas" (p. 10). Schools are made up of teachers, children, parents, ideas, materials, equipment, and walls. Without a purpose and focus, little can be accomplished in creating a community for learning. First and foremost, the school must develop a clear vision and mission of what it hopes to achieve. Lacking a sense of oneness, children, parents, and staff alike will drift aimlessly about, accomplishing little. Boyer (1995) and his team of researchers discovered six essential qualities of human interaction that, when applied, facilitate a community for learning. In essence, the elementary school must be a purposeful, communicative, just and disciplined, caring, and celebrative place.

A Purposeful Place

Elementary school educators must focus on the whole child (educationally, socially, emotionally, physically, and morally) and they can accomplish this purpose by meeting four sharply focused goals (Boyer, 1995).

   1. *To communicate effectively.* Language is not addressed as just another subject; rather, it is viewed as a central component to life and living, incorporating all elements of human interaction under one heading: literacy. To be literate, children must be able to read, write, speak, comprehend, listen, use numbers accurately, engage in the arts, and apply all that they know and understand about human nature to interact successfully and sensitively with others.

   2. *To acquire a core of essential knowledge.* Rather than focus on individual subject areas in a traditional sense, this goal not only emphasizes the importance of content, but context as well, in that children are exposed to an integrated curriculum that builds natural and logical connections across disciplines. In doing so, children are able to more readily connect what they are learning to their own lives and to living.

3. *To be a disciplined, motivated learner.* The emphasis is on teaching children the love of learning and how to become a focused and independent learner. Children are taught skills and are provided with the technology and human support to enhance their curiosity and become self-motivated and active learners.

4. *To have a sense of well-being.* The purpose of this goal is to help children develop a sense of right and wrong and an internal guidance system that is fueled by good character, core virtues, and understanding of good citizenship in a teaching/learning environment that models basic decency and goodness. Children with internal guidance systems are better prepared to make decisions that are legally, ethically, and morally sound.

A Communicative Place

A sense of community is further facilitated when children and adults are free to communicate openly, responsibly, and caringly. A free flow of ideas is supported when teachers and children listen to each other; raise educated and provocative questions; share, explore, and reach new levels of understanding; and engage in new ways of behaving. Elementary schools achieve a sense of community in the classroom and in school itself when the learning climate supports genuine understanding.

A Just and Disciplined Place

A community cannot flourish without justice, discipline, and fair play. The elementary schools of the 21st century will need to put forth a concerted effort in supporting the concept of equal opportunity and justice for all and really mean it. While few children and adults seek to be prejudicial, ingrained attitudes and beliefs pertaining to gender, race, religion, skin color, economic status, and related classifications disenfranchise those who are caught in stereotypes that hurt their chances for equal opportunity. By the same token, schools that separate children into winners and losers, engage in rigid teaching systems, and display varying expectations for children based on preconceived notions of capability will want to reassess their position in lieu of supporting schools as *just places* offering equal opportunity for all.

A Caring Place

Teaching children how to care for themselves, others, and their environment is the avenue through which all human needs are met. Caring is the glue that connects us to ourselves and to others with whom we share the planet. As children learn how to build caring connections through their smiles, positive feedback, self-affirmations, and planned acts of kindness, they begin to experience total well-being. They discover their purpose for being—to share with others the very best of themselves. *Teaching children how to care is an action that runs counter to violence, reduces loneliness and human suffering, and increases self-confidence.* Communities become caring places when the people in them become caregivers.

A Celebrative Place

Celebrations give people time to recognize and cherish their small wins. Celebrations foster teamwork and team spirit, and a recognition of, and commitment to, community purpose and values. Elementary school children, parents, and staff need to experience the joy of team accomplishments. The practice of celebrating keeps community values in focus, allows for public recognition of a team effort, and provides an opportunity for all to be personally involved, which further helps to sustain a sense of community.

> *In the end, the* Basic School *is an institution held together by something far more than connecting corridors and a common schedule. It is a community for learning with a shared purpose, good communication, and a climate with justice, discipline, caring, and occasions for celebration (Boyer, 1995, p. 29).*

If elementary schools are to truly embrace the importance of community and meet the six qualities of a learning community, they will need to continually self-assess, asking questions such as the following:

1. Does this school have shared educational goals?
2. Do we speak and listen carefully to each other?
3. Is everyone at our school treated fairly?
4. Do we have reasonable rules that are well known and sensitively enforced?
5. What evidence do we have that we are a caring place?
6. Do we have occasions for celebration?
7. Which school activities strengthen these qualities, and which restrict them? (Boyer, 1995, pp. 30–31)

Only through the building of community in our schools can we hope to strengthen the other communities in which our children live (home, town, state, national, and international communities). As children learn the value of community in their classroom and school, they will be able to apply these same understandings to community service beyond the schoolhouse doors.

A Curriculum with Coherence

". . . We should be aiming to help children become caring adults, builders of communities, sharers of learning, lovers of the printed word, citizens of the world, and nurturers of nature" (Teeter, 1995, p. 360). In order to accomplish this end, elementary schools must organize their curriculum around three goals—content, integration, and relationship to children's lives (Boyer, 1995). A new way of thinking about the existing elementary school curriculum, with its traditional core content areas of social studies, science, language arts, mathematics, and related fields of study, is necessary if these goals are to be addressed. Rather than focus on traditional subjects as isolated units of content, elementary schools can make education more interesting and relevant to children's lives by creating integrated curriculums around universal human experiences that are shared by all people and give meaning to their lives (Boyer, 1995; Noddings, 1995).

In trying to determine what to focus on in developing a meaningful and relevant educational mission and curriculum, Noddings (1995) has suggested that educators (teachers, counselors, and administrators) and parents ask themselves three important questions:

- What do we want for our children?
- What do they need from education?
- What does our society need? (p. 365)

These questions require us to examine the present and envision a brighter future, which we hope to create by actions that we take today in developing a defensible educational mission and curriculum that recognizes human and societal needs. While every elementary school should be encouraged to create its own unique educational mission, most people will come to similar conclusions, namely that our society *". . . needs to care for its children—to reduce violence, to respect honest work of every kind, to reward excellence at every level, to ensure a place for every child and emerging adult in the economic and social world, to produce people who can care competently for their own families and contribute effectively to their communities"* (Noddings, 1995, p. 366).

A curriculum with coherence helps children to move beyond learning fragmented bits of seemingly meaningless information. A curriculum with coherence teaches newly developed attitudes, knowledge, and skills that are relevant to their subjects; promotes self-understanding; and encourages responsible actions that benefit themselves, others, and society.

Noddings (1995) has developed a morally and academically defensible mission for education that addresses the needs of children, society, and the environment; connects all subject matter disciplines; and brings relevancy and purpose to learning. *A curriculum with coherence focuses on matters of human caring.* We need to teach children how to give and receive care and to be careful (risk management). Caring is an all-encompassing concept that some people have described as the ultimate reality of life. To care is to show concern and to demonstrate interest on behalf of oneself, others, and the environment. *Children who care make responsible caring choices in all that they say and do.* They revere the value of life and living. They respect all life forms and make life choices that help to sustain the balance of nature. They understand the nature of risk and risk-taking and practice responsible risk management strategies in all life situations in their quest to care.

Teaching children to care and to be careful is central to all life decisions (Worzbyt, 1998). When children learn how to make responsible and caring choices for themselves, others, and society, everyone will benefit and the results will be evident. *When caring children make caring choices, we will see a kinder and more compassionate world with fewer personal, social, political, economic, and environmental ills* (Williams, Schilling, & Palomares, 1996). The ability to care and to be cared for is at the core of what makes us human and gives life meaning and purpose: *". . . without caring, individual human beings cannot thrive, communities become violent battle grounds, the American democratic experiment must ultimately fail, and the planet will not be able to support life"* (Lipsitz, 1995, p. 95).

Pittman and Cahill (1992) have stated that "caring is something that needs to be conveyed to young people through relationships (nurturing) and environments (structure and settings). It is a way of approaching self, group, and community/society that should be explicitly promoted through example, teaching, and practice. It is something, ultimately, that should be demonstrated by youth through ongoing attitudes and behaviors that transcend the boundaries of specific programs and events" (p. 4).

Teaching children how to give and receive care is the avenue through which all human needs are met. Caring is the glue that connects us to ourselves, others, and our environment. As children learn how to build caring connections, they will experience their humanness and the joys of life and living. They will experience meaning in their lives and discover their purpose for being, which is to share with others the very best of themselves (Worzbyt, 1998).

Teaching children how to give and receive care is an action that runs counter to violence, loneliness, and human suffering. Rather, caring increases thoughtfulness, community building, peacemaking, responsibility, freedom, self-confidence, and self-esteem (Worzbyt, 1998). Communities become safe and caring places when the people in them become responsible and generous caregivers.

Caring is more than a *warm fuzzy,* although many people will tell you that it does feel good knowing in your head and heart that you are doing what is right. Caring requires competent action, although there are no magic formulas to follow in its execution. Caring is often described as a nurturing act and yet it can be a "gut-wrenching" experience filled with pain for the giver and the receiver. How caring is expressed varies from person to person, from situation to situation, and requires differing amounts of time and energy to accept and convey. Caring can be expressed as a relationship and as a virtue to be cultivated. Caring can be a burden, a commitment, and often represents hard work.

As complicated and multifaceted as "caring" appears to be, it can be reduced to a simple guiding principle: *Treat others and the world as you would like to be treated.* The Golden Rule, plus the following themes of care, promote an educational mission and a curriculum with coherence that strive to achieve intellectual competence while producing caring, loving, and loveable human beings. The themes for care (Noddings, 1995) are: (1) caring for self, (2) caring for intimate others, (3) caring for acquaintances and distant others, (4) caring for nonhuman animals, (5) caring for plants and the physical environment, (6) caring for the human-made world of objects and instruments, and (7) caring for ideas. For each theme that has been identified, there are a variety of concepts that can be explored and taught that help children to build caring connections with themselves, others, and their communities. They learn that the purpose of an education is to teach them how to receive and provide responsible acts of caring while being careful. Every academic subject exists for the purpose of shaping caring attitudes, knowledge, and skills (Noddings, 1995; Worzbyt, 1998). When taught from a caring perspective, children experience the relevancy of arithmetic, social studies, language arts, the creative arts, reading, and health and physical education. What follows is a brief description of Noddings's (1995) themes of caring.

Caring for Self

Much of what children learn in school is designed to help them explore the many ways in which they can care for themselves physically, mentally, and spiritually. Every academic discipline influences attitudes, presents knowledge, and teaches children skills that will assist them in making responsible caring choices in promoting their own wellness. In science, children study the life cycle. They learn about their changing bodies, the benefits of exercise, and healthy nutrition. They understand how the choices they make today affect their lives today and tomorrow. Children learn that life has a beginning and an end and a time of growth in which they will discover themselves, create their own essence, experience the value and sanctity of life, and learn how they can make a significant and positive impact in creating a kinder and gentler world. They learn that every academic subject they study offers attitudes, knowledge, and skills that help them to care for themselves because teachers help them to make that connection throughout the teaching-learning process.

Caring for Intimate Others

Children learn that group membership is an important dynamic in their lives. They will belong to many groups over their lifetime and will help to shape these groups and will be shaped by them. This dimension of caring introduces children to the nature of groups, how they effect their lives, the benefits of group membership, the forces that groups can enact on their membership, and how and why people form and join groups. In particular, children learn about family, peer groups, classroom groups, activity-based groups, communities, organizations, and governments.

As children begin to identify with the various groups to which they belong, they are challenged to consider their value, what they stand to gain through membership, and what caring contributions they can make to strengthen these groups. Children understand that they are not only responsible for their own lives, but have a responsibility to insure the safety and well-being of those who care for them. They need to discover how to connect with intimate others (family and friends) through responsible acts of caring.

Children can develop positive caring attitudes, access knowledge, and learn skills that help them to establish and maintain friendships, resolve conflicts when they occur, strive to promote safety practices that affect others, give deserved compliments, practice using caring manners, and listen to and help family and friends in need. The list of caring practices is endless, and the personal caring strengths that children have to share with intimate others only grow stronger with use, as will the relationships that are cultivated through their practice. Children who develop caring strengths through the curriculum and are taught how to use them will cultivate intimate relationships that will last a lifetime.

Language arts, social studies, reading, writing, and the creative arts are subject matter disciplines that teach children how to communicate effectively with others. As they explore different symbols (sound, words, speech, numbers, art), they are studying the history of language, the value of language, "breakdowns" in communication, how to become effective communicators, the role of technology in communication, and the impact of mass communication on human relationships. Children learn that caring for intimate others requires the use of caring choices through body movement, facial expressions, hand gestures, and the use of symbols. They experience the power of language and its ability to inform, persuade, entertain, and inspire. Above all else, they recognize ". . . that integrity is the key to authentic human interaction" (Boyer, 1995, p. 88).

Caring for Acquaintances and Distant Others

Caring for immediate family members and friends is not without effort, but is likely to occur because children have a vested interest in their own well-being and those for whom they care. Children want to belong, be accepted, and loved, and therefore see the benefits of caring for those in their inner circle. However, when it comes to caring for acquaintances and distant others, caring connections are less likely to be fostered. Prejudice, excuses, distrust, misinformation, and distance are all factors that interrupt or diffuse caring for those with whom children share the planet.

Caring for acquaintances and distant others is necessary if we are to survive as a society. When people are threatened (physically and/or psychologically), or believe themselves to be threatened, by individuals or groups outside their inner circle, they often mentally dehumanize them and then give themselves permission to treat them accordingly. This is evidenced by racial tension; crime, violence; stealing from organizations, companies, and governmental agencies; and the distrust held toward people and countries whose beliefs, lifestyles, and customs differ from our own.

One of the greatest challenges facing children and adults in the centuries to come will be working together in the spirit of cooperation and caring. We must strive to build a global family that will address such issues as poverty, war, terrorism, racial unrest, environmental pollution, hunger, illness, and related challenges. If not addressed, these issues will weaken us collectively and individually. Elementary schools of the future will need to help children explore ways in which they can build caring connections with people whom they know little about in order to tackle the more deeply rooted problems that divide humankind.

Caring for Nonhuman Animals

Caring for animals and pets is often the first experience that children have in developing a sense of compassion for those who are unable to care for themselves. And yet an estimated 10 million pets are killed each year at humane societies and shelters (Noddings, 1995). Many more pets are neglected, abandoned, and suffer from physical cruelty and abuse. Responsible parents and caring teachers must teach children to respect their pets and treat them with kindness and affectionate caring. When children truly love their pets, care is given unconditionally and authentically, not out of duty or because of parental demand.

In school, children learn about the value of animals; preserving animals in the wild; and extinction, its causes, and the impact that it can have on the balance of nature. They understand animal care, habitats, and how animals care for their young. They likewise gain knowledge regarding how and why human beings depend on animals for food, clothing, their livelihood, and even their health. Children can learn a great deal about giving and receiving care by reading stories about animals, watching videos, visiting zoos, and raising small animals in their classroom. In addition, literature, science, math, politics, art, history, psychology, music, economics, and religion have much to offer children in their understanding of care and respect for animals.

Caring for Plants and the Physical Environment

An important concept for children to experience is that what they care for will also care for them. Children need to learn that life is a circle and that all things are connected to each other. When plant life is threatened, human life is also affected. Children learn that plants provide people with nourishment, medicines, and oxygen; filter the air which they breathe; and prevent soil erosion. Plants also provide shelter and sustenance for animal and fish life, which helps to support human life. When people destroy plant life, they weaken the ecosystem and jeopardize the quality of human life.

Children are encouraged to raise plants in school. They can discover the value of caring for plants and learn about the various people who earn a living from plants and trees (farmers, foresters, manufacturers, medical specialists, biologists, retailers, etc). They will likewise come to understand that some plants and trees are dangerous in that they cause skin irritations and rashes, produce poisonous fruits and berries, destroy wetlands, and upset the balance of nature in our lakes and ponds.

In studying the physical environment, children understand the importance of caring for the atmosphere, water, and land. Pollution of our natural resources, depletion of the ozone layer, overpopulation, loss of forests, extinction of species and subspecies, and the dumping of toxic and nuclear wastes are but a few of the many assaults upon our planet—our home. Many of these noncaring and hurtful decisions are made in the name of greed, expansion, and progress.

Children need to appreciate the pros and cons associated with harvesting and preserving our forests. A caring balance needs to be achieved between both factions if we are to sustain a healthy environment and a healthy economy. Learning to care while remaining careful requires all children to become sensitive and sensible decision-makers. The decisions that children and adults make today will have far-reaching implications for our planet and its inhabitants tomorrow. *Decisions regarding personal energy consumption, conservation of our natural resources, recycling, and participation in direct hands-on environmental activities should be a part of every child's education.*

Children must fully comprehend what they have to give in caring for their planet and, in return, how their planet will care for them (clean air, water, and land). *Because our resources are limited (economic, natural, and time), children must be taught that laws and personal rights mean little in preserving that which is good if people fail to commit their never-ending human resources (themselves) to living moderately, sensitively, and responsibly* (Noddings, 1992).

Caring for the Human-Made World of Objects and Instruments

While the world of objects and instruments cannot care in a human sense, they must nevertheless be cared for since they do significantly affect children's lives and their environment. Challenging children to examine the various roles that objects and instruments play in their lives can be a fun and eye-opening experience. Since children are living in a world of machines and technology, they need not look beyond their immediate environment to see computers, televisions, VCRs, DVDs, motor vehicles, electrical appliances, heating systems, bicycles, exercise equipment, and so on. In addition to the items listed, there are numerous objects and instruments to be found in our homes, schools, hospitals, and communities. Objects and instruments are relied upon by children and adults for purposes of comfort, entertainment, recreation, safety, travel, health, and expediency. Without them, life would not be the same.

Children learn that objects and instruments have been created for "caring" purposes in that users and those affected by their use are presumably better off for having experienced them. For example, motor vehicles contain many gadgets, gauges, and instruments that are designed to care for and protect drivers, passengers, and the vehicle itself. Seatbelts; airbags; mirrors; adjustable seats; oil, temperature, and electrical gauges; and brakes are just some of the comfort and safety features that, if properly used and maintained (cared for), can make highway travel more enjoyable and safer for all concerned.

Children need to acquire knowledge regarding the value of technology and the objects and instruments that affect their lives. They need to understand how they work, how to use them effectively, and how to care for them so that they can rely on their use. Heat, radon, and carbon monoxide detectors are of little use to families that depend on them if they are defective and are not properly maintained. Protective eye wear, knee pads, gloves, and footwear are of little use unless they are worn. Road signs, traffic lights, and highway pavement markings designed to protect are not likely to save lives if they are ignored or improperly maintained.

Children determine how the use and abuse of objects and instruments can affect their lives and the lives of others. They can be taught how to conduct various safety inspections in their homes, at school, and in their communities and how to maintain and use objects and instruments safely (home appliances, knives, scissors, skateboards, etc.). This is important since objects and instruments that are designed to care can be misused and cause lasting injuries and even death (car radios played too loudly; guns improperly stored; medicines and drugs not taken as prescribed; and household products stored improperly, etc.).

As children understand the human-made world of objects and instruments, they likewise discover that they are part of a larger system of producers and consumers. They explore and experience what it is like to make quality things for others' use and what it means to be a caring and responsible provider of goods and services. They gain information about such concepts as supply and demand, economics, bartering, wages, and what it means to be an informed consumer and a responsible conserver.

Children have an opportunity to study how past economies functioned, why they changed, and the impact of global markets on their lives. They learn about different occupations, the impact of technology and a changing workforce, and the role that education plays in their lives. They recognize the importance in maintaining a prosperous and healthy economy while promoting a caring and healthy society, one with clean air, water, land, and natural resources that are managed with preservation in mind.

Caring for Ideas

When children learn to care for responsible ideas, they exercise care for themselves, others, and the planet. *Ideas shape children's decisions and the way they live their lives.* Children must be challenged to examine their ideas and those of a nation and a global society. Teachers, parents, and community leaders can help children to understand the impact that ideas have had in shaping world events both past and present. Our goal must be to help children cultivate caring ideas and implement them in ways that will improve the circle of life.

By exploring caring ideas, children can examine ideas they wish to call their own. We can help them to develop a moral compass that is based on right, not wrong. They can study moral imperatives like the Golden Rule, fair play, proper etiquette, and good manners.

Children recognize that they live in a society of ideas, values, and virtues. In the absence of sound ideas, beliefs, and values, children will not have a moral compass to follow in making caring decisions. Without sound ideals that people are willing to support, our children will live in a virtueless society with everyone doing what is right according to their own standards.

While most people possess caring ideas, there are many ideas that are hazardous and pose a danger to those who share them and are affected by them. Ideas that promote destruction of our natural resources, prejudice, cruelty toward others, violence, violation of laws and ethical standards, greed, and abuse of power pose real dangers toward maintaining a safe and caring society. Children need to become critically aware of the power of ideas and how they have shaped history and present-day life.

Learning to care and to be careful is everyone's responsibility. Children live in a world of ideas that they help to foster and in turn must help to evaluate. As ideas are evaluated, children must strive to attain a healthy balance between the benefits and potential pitfalls of each. Only when pitfalls are recognized can children learn to contain them while enhancing the benefits that caring ideas offer.

The critical examination of ideas must occur in all fields of study to include health care, journalism, medicine, technology, environmental science, agriculture, genetics, law, government, politics, sociology, and psychology. Every field of study generates ideas that have the potential to do good or evil. By examining all sides of an idea, perhaps the elements of caring and safety will be enhanced, while the potential for danger and destruction will be diminished.

Ideas set the stage for actions and dictate the quality of life experienced by humankind. Children must be taught to examine the soundness of their ideas and those of others, and the risks involved in sharing those ideas. They must be taught to develop the courage to stand up for what is right in a world driven by ideas that have the potential either for doing harm or for providing care.

In summary, the seven core commonalties of caring bring a new perspective to elementary education. They suggest a new way to organize the curriculum, one that adds a fourth "R" to education: *relevancy*. Children will not only become well informed, but will discover some fundamental truths that become apparent in a curriculum with coherence.

- The purpose of an education is to produce competent, caring, loving, and lovable people.
- All life needs and decisions relate to the seven themes of caring.
- An education teaches children how (attitudes, knowledge, and skills) to make caring decisions.
- Caring is central to every academic domain and is the resilient backbone of human life and a strong moral society.

A Climate for Learning

Successful elementary schools must foster a climate for learning, one that brings community and curriculum together in a unified whole. This becomes possible to the extent that they have first developed a sense of community with shared goals, and then have created a curriculum with coherence—two building blocks that have been previously discussed.

Growth-enhancing learning climates, for children attending elementary schools in the 21st century, must be multidimensional if they are to meet children's developmental needs and society's goals for a healthy, caring, and responsible citizenry. Such learning climates must create patterns to fit purpose, resources to enrich, and services for children (Boyer, 1995).

Patterns to Fit Purpose

How elementary schools establish themselves for action will affect their purpose and the outcomes they attain. The physical climate—consisting of conditions such as class size, availability of usable space, attractive surroundings, proper heating and lighting, comfortable and appropriate furniture, educationally sound technology, supplies, and teaching aids—must support the teaching-learning process in ways that encourage children to become disciplined, creative, and well-motivated learners.

In addition to a caring physical climate, successful elementary schools seek to establish sound psychological patterns designed to meet children's developmental needs and society's goals for a healthy, caring, and responsible citizenry. The psychological climate consists of all those interactions between and among teachers, children, parents, counselors, administrators, school board members, and all non-teaching staff that support the interests of children and society.

Learning-friendly climates are ones that are open, communicative, just and disciplined, caring, celebrative of small wins, and flexible; and that adjust class groupings and teaching schedules in ways that satisfy the school's vision and mission.

Resources to Enrich

Elementary schools of the 21st century are an integral part of their communities and the world. They function in a vast resource-rich environment consisting of libraries, parks, museums, zoos, factories, hospitals, entertainment centers, cultural events, and technological advancements that have the potential for making the entire world accessible to all children. Successful elementary schools of the 21st century will utilize all the valuable resources to foster vast networks of knowledge that bring community and curriculum together to enrich the lives of children.

Services for Children

The elementary schools of the 21st century will be dedicated to meeting the needs of the whole child (physical, personal/emotional, social, cognitive, and career and societal) because they understand the connectional relationship between personal wellness and learning potential. Moving beyond effective teaching-learning climates, solid academic programs, and teaching excellence, educators of the

21st century recognize the school's responsibility in providing children with a full range of services (health, counseling, after-school care, family referrals, and enrichment programs) through school and community partnerships that work.

A climate for learning is the third building block for success in helping children to meet their human needs and for society to have a caring, responsible, and responsive citizenry. That is why children in the 21st century must be provided with services, resources, and a fluid environment that will promote learning, strengthen community, build intergenerational and cultural connections, and enrich their lives. The learning climate must be designed to engage every child, stimulate creativity, and instill values that will promote self-disciplined and highly motivated learners.

A Commitment to Character

The fourth and final building block of successful elementary schools in the 21st century is the challenge of connecting learning to life to build character. *Elementary-school education programs that commit to character building will relate lessons of the classroom to life and living, instilling in children a sense of personal and civic responsibility.* Children will be guided in their development of an internal guidance system, one that teaches right versus wrong and responsibility versus reckless abandonment. *They will be taught the same basic core virtues on which our society was founded, namely honesty, respect, responsibility, compassion, self-discipline, perseverance, and giving; all qualities that support excellence in living.*

The core virtues of which we have spoken will be learned through the curriculum, modeled in and outside the classroom, and observed in others' deeds. Children with character will live their lives with meaning and purpose at home, in school, in their communities, and in their relationships and commitments with others.

Boyer (1995) has stated, in reference to elementary school education, that *". . . the* Basic School *is a community, with a coherent curriculum, a climate for learning, and a commitment to character, one that helps students develop the capacity to judge wisely and responsibly in matters of life and conduct. The goal is not only to prepare students for careers, but also to channel knowledge to human ends"* (p. 192).

CONCLUSION

This chapter provides elementary school counselors with a visionary view of elementary schools of the future. Elementary schools that embrace the vision of school as community, a curriculum with coherence, a climate for learning, and a commitment to character are devoted to

- promoting literacy proficiency in all children;
- building caring connections across the disciplines (math, science, social studies, language arts, creative arts, and health and physical education) that relate classroom learning to life;
- creating a climate for learning based on child-centered resources, an array of human services, and a flexible teaching-learning environment; and
- teaching and modeling character-building virtues that give purpose and meaning to life.

Elementary school counselors are sure to have a significant impact when they advocate on behalf of elementary school instructional programs that support the four building blocks of success (community, curriculum with coherence, climate, and character). These same four building blocks also are an integral part of every successful elementary school counseling program. Spirited partnerships are likely to form and grow stronger when a marriage between the school's instructional and counseling programs is built on shared common ground.

BIBLIOGRAPHY

Boyer, E.T. (1995). *The basic school: A community for learning.* Princeton, NJ: The Carnegie Foundation for the Advancement of Learning.

Herr, E.L. (2001). School reform and perspectives on the role of school counselors: A century of proposals for change. *Professional School Counseling, 5,* 220–234.

Herr, E.L. (1984). The national reports on reform in schooling: Some missing ingredients. *Journal of Counseling and Development, 63,* 217–220.

Houston, P. (2001). Superintendents for the 21st century: It's not just a job, it's a calling. *Kappan, 82,* 428–433.

Lipsitz, J. (1995). Prologue: Why we should care about caring? *Kappan, 7,* 665–666.

Noddings, N. (1995). Teaching themes of caring. *Kappan, 7,* 675–679.

Noddings, N. (1992). *The challenge to care in schools: An alternative approach to education.* New York: Teachers College Press.

Pittman, K.J., & Cahill, M. (1992). Youth and caring: The role of youth programs in the development of caring. Commissioned Paper for Lilly Endowment Youth and Caring Conference (February 26–27, 1992). Miami, FL: Center for Youth Development & Policy Research.

Sapon-Shevin, M. (1999). *Because we can change the world: A practical guide to building cooperative inclusive classroom communities.* Boston, MA: Allyn & Bacon.

Sergiovanni, T.J. (1995). *Building community in schools.* San Francisco, CA: Jossey-Bass.

State Board of Education of Pennsylvania (July 1993). Rules and regulations, title 22—education: chapter 5—curriculum. *Pennsylvania Bulletin, 23,* section 5, 201.

Teeter, A.M. (1995). Learning about teaching. *Kappan, 76,* 360–364.

United States Department of Health, Education, and Welfare, Office of Child Development (1970). *Report to the President: White House conference on children.* Washington, DC: Government Printing Office.

Van Hoose, W.H. (1975). Overview: The elementary counselor in the 1970s. *Virginia Personnel and Guidance Journal, 3,* 17–30.

Wagner, T. (1995). What's school really for anyway? And who should decide? *Kappan, 76,* 393–399.

Williams, L.K., Schilling, D., & Palomares, S. (1996). *Caring and capable kids.* Torrance, CA: Innerchoice Publishing.

Worzbyt, J.C. (1998). *Caring children make caring choices.* Harrisburg, PA: Pennsylvania Department of Education.

CHAPTER 2

Elementary School Counseling Programs in the 21st Century

What is an elementary school counseling program and what purpose does it serve? Is there a real need for elementary school counseling programs in today's schools? These questions, and ones like them, have been asked by school professionals, parents, and community leaders for the past 35-plus years (Herr, 2001; Whiston, 2002). In the pages that follow, we will address these questions and provide overwhelming support for elementary school counseling programs and the positive impact they can have on enhancing children's lives and building strong caring communities.

ELEMENTARY SCHOOL COUNSELING: A VISION WITH A CLEAR PURPOSE

Elementary school counseling programs are in the people-building business. They exist for the purpose of helping children to create, package, and market themselves as independent, responsible, and self-managing human beings who are capable of making legal, ethical, and moral decisions that will benefit themselves, others, and society (Campbell & Dahir, 1997; Dahir, 2001). Elementary school counseling programs are in the business of helping children to think critically, communicate their wants and needs thoughtfully, and care for themselves and others unconditionally. Such programs support the teaching of academic skills (reading, writing, and math), but are equally committed to helping children acquire needed information, skills, and attitudes that will enhance all dimensions of their being (physical, personal/emotional, social, cognitive, and career and societal). In particular, elementary school counseling programs support children in their quest to live a wellness lifestyle; socialize with others; develop a sense of personal and civic responsibility; acquire the ability to think, reason, and make decisions; appreciate the values of a work-oriented society; embrace diversity as a positive force in building caring communities; and create a personal identity that gives meaning and purpose to life, living, and caring (Dahir, 2001).

Elementary school counseling programs recognize the unique nature of children; the necessity of meeting their individual and developmental needs; and the importance of providing a humanized, child-centered learning climate where children feel free to question, risk, and grow. Yes, elementary school counseling programs are in the people-building business. They help children to accomplish life tasks and to apply "lessons of the classroom" to their lives in ways that teach them how to live, learn, and work in caring communities that they will help to establish.

Developing a realization and utilization of self is a lifelong learning process. *Helping children to achieve their full potential as caring human beings and builders of caring communities (home, school, and society) is the hallmark of a successful elementary school counseling program and the gold standard of a responsible and meaningful education* (Gysbers & Henderson, 2001).

A BLUEPRINT FOR SUCCESS

Elementary school counseling programs help to create challenging and caring schools and teach children how to become productive and caring people. They teach children the value of investing in themselves, other human beings, and their communities.

The truly successful elementary school counseling programs achieve their success because they are organized for success and because they function in partnership with the school's academic-in-structional program (Gysbers, Lapan, & Jones, 2000). A counseling program that is organized around child development and societal needs, has clearly stated program goals that reflect the behaviors to be learned, and addresses the creation of a positive teaching-learning climate cannot miss in having a significant impact on children's lives and on the society that they will one day inherit. In addition, an elementary school counseling program that functions in partnership with the elementary school's academic mission fosters a collabora-tive working relationship that helps children to learn about them-selves and their world and how to improve both through the caring choices they learn to make (Chapters 6–10).

We will first discuss the organizational structure of successful elementary school counseling programs and then address the im-portance of creating a viable and strong partnership between ele-mentary school counseling programs and the elementary school's academic-instructional program. The *blueprint for success* thus en-compasses having a planned and systematically organized program and a partnership with possibilities.

Organizing for Success

Successful elementary school counseling programs are designed to fulfill their people-building mission. They are organized to

- be proactive,
- serve the developmental needs of all children,
- have an organized and planned curriculum,
- be sequential and flexible,
- function in partnership with the school's academic-instructional program,
- involve the full participation of all people who affect chil-dren's lives,
- embrace a caring theme, and
- provide specialized child-centered services and targeted interventions.

The specific organizational design for elementary school counseling programs will vary from elementary school to elementary school. The different designs will reflect differences in school and community needs, program philosophies, mission statements, program goals, and the availability of program support (resources). Consequently, the success of elementary school counseling programs is not measured in their sameness when compared with other programs, but in the degree to which the organizational structure

- involves an active school-community partnership,
- mirrors the academic-instructional goals of the elementary school,
- reflects the community's values,
- meets the developmental and individual needs of children,
- addresses the community-building needs of society, and
- provides a clear decision-making model for making responsible program decisions that are appropriate, adequate, effective, and efficient (Bowers, Hatch, & Schwallie-Giddis, 2001).

Given all that we have stated about organizing for success, we believe that *comprehensive* (full range of counseling program services), *collaborative* (home, school, and community partnership), and *developmental* (physical, personal/emotional, social, cognitive, career and societal) elementary school counseling programs function best when they address five specific building blocks (see Figure 2.1):

1. Tripartite
2. Program Support
3. Program Caring Goals
4. Program Delivery
5. Service Providers and Recipients

Tripartite

The Tripartite is the heart and soul of effective elementary school counseling programs. Like three legged stools (see Figure 2.2),

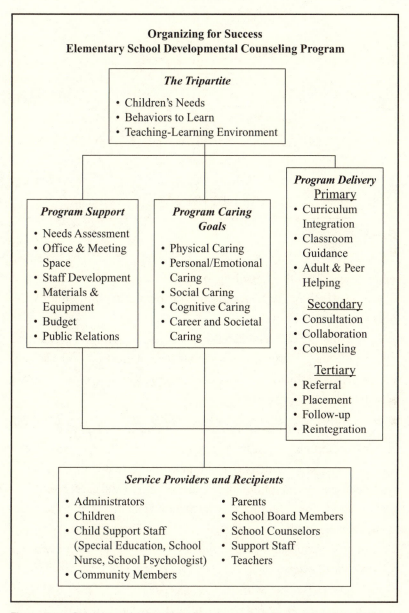

Organizing for Success
Elementary School Developmental Counseling Program

The Tripartite

- Children's Needs
- Behaviors to Learn
- Teaching-Learning Environment

Program Support

- Needs Assessment
- Office & Meeting Space
- Staff Development
- Materials & Equipment
- Budget
- Public Relations

Program Caring Goals

- Physical Caring
- Personal/Emotional Caring
- Social Caring
- Cognitive Caring
- Career and Societal Caring

Program Delivery

Primary

- Curriculum Integration
- Classroom Guidance
- Adult & Peer Helping

Secondary

- Consultation
- Collaboration
- Counseling

Tertiary

- Referral
- Placement
- Follow-up
- Reintegration

Service Providers and Recipients

- Administrators
- Children
- Child Support Staff (Special Education, School Nurse, School Psychologist)
- Community Members
- Parents
- School Board Members
- School Counselors
- Support Staff
- Teachers

Figure 2.1. Organizing for Success: Developmental Elementary School Counseling Program.

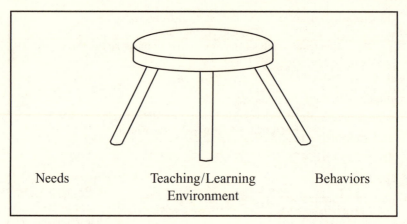

Needs   Teaching/Learning   Behaviors
Environment

Figure 2.2. The Tripartite.

elementary school counseling programs need a firm foundation of support if they are to stand on their own with something valuable to offer children.

The Tripartite consists of children's needs, behaviors to be learned, and the teaching-learning environment. The interaction of these three components facilitates the people-building mission of elementary school counseling programs.

1. *Children's needs.* Of utmost importance is understanding children's developmental nature in response to the educational process. Children are multidimensional human beings with developmental (physical, personal/emotional, social, cognitive, and career and societal) and individual (unique) needs that must be met if they are to become caring, fully functioning, and capable self-managers and community supporters. *Need fulfillment is the pathway through which children learn, achieve their independence, and move in the direction of self-actualization.*

2. *Behaviors to be learned.* Children's developmental and individual needs are met through learned behaviors. Elementary school counseling programs, working in partnership with school academic-instructional programs, are responsible for identifying and teaching the critical behaviors that children must learn. The learning of developmental behaviors enables children to become caring human beings and builders of caring communities.

3. *The teaching-learning environment.* Behaviors are learned in the context of supportive teaching-learning environments. Elementary school counseling programs, working in partnership with school academic-instructional programs, design the most conducive and supportive teaching-learning environments possible. Decisions are made regarding what to teach, when and how to teach it, where teaching should occur, who should be involved, which behaviors should be taught and why, and how best to meet the individual needs of children throughout the teaching-learning process.

Successful elementary school counseling programs are successful because they are focused on their people-building mission of helping children to become caring, responsible, self-managing, and community-minded human beings. This end result can only be achieved in an elementary school counseling program that focuses on children's needs, behaviors to be learned, and caring and supportive teaching-learning environments (Tripartite) that encourage responsible risk-taking and personal and community growth.

Program Support

Successful elementary school counseling programs remain strong and viable when backed by a well-organized and comprehensive support system. While the Tripartite cares for children by teaching them how to care and to make caring choices, Program Support cares for the Tripartite so that it can function best in meeting children's needs.

Program Support consists of six elements, namely needs assessment, office and meeting space, staff development, materials and equipment, budget, and public relations.

1. *Needs Assessment.* By conducting formal and informal assessments of children's needs, the curriculum (instructional and counseling), and the teaching-learning environment (see Chapter 4), elementary school counseling programs can better target ways to strengthen the Tripartite (meet children's needs, target behaviors to teach, and enhance the teaching-learning climate).

2. *Office and Meeting Space.* Adequate and caring space (privacy when needed) is required for parent conferences, teacher-team building, individual and group counseling, large group trainings, and community (home and school) meetings that support the people-building mission of the Tripartite.

3. *Staff Development.* People-building is everyone's business in a caring elementary school. Elementary school counselors will want to work with administrators, community leaders, children, educational specialists, parents, teachers, support staff (cafeteria workers, school bus drivers, secretaries, custodians, etc.), and school board members in developing caring classrooms and caring school-wide communities.

4. *Materials and Equipment.* For the Tripartite to function effectively and efficiently, program materials and equipment are needed to support the fulfillment of program goals and outcomes. This area includes office supplies and materials, office and conference room equipment and furniture, and classroom materials to support the people-building mission of the Tripartite.

5. *Budget.* Financial support is needed to conduct periodic needs assessments; manage staff trainings; purchase materials, supplies, and equipment to achieve counseling program goals; attend professional development seminars and conferences; and enhance the teaching-learning environment of classrooms and the school. Additional funding is needed to build strong home, school, and community partnerships and to fund an active public relations program.

6. *Public Relations.* Elementary school counseling programs not only need to care for children, but they require care as well. Public relations is a caring process that is designed to inform, publicize, promote, and involve all stakeholders in caring for children and the program that makes it all possible—the elementary school counseling program.

Program Caring Goals

Elementary school counseling programs exist to meet children's individual, developmental, and societal needs as addressed in the Tripartite. The specific counseling program goals to be addressed each year are determined through strategic planning (see Chapter 4) and are designed to help children better care for themselves, others, and their communities. The specific developmental caring goal areas addressed throughout this text are:

- Physical Caring
- Personal/Emotional Caring
- Social Caring
- Cognitive Caring
- Career and Societal Caring

We have chosen a people-building theme that emphasizes caring as the core of the school counseling program because caring implies taking charge, being responsible, attending to the needs of others, and providing for the welfare and safety of all people and society (Schaps & Lewis, 1999). Everything that children learn at home, in school, and through community involvement (religion, organizations, and agencies) has the potential for enhancing human caring and community building when taught from a caring perspective (Noddings, 1995). The theme of caring is central to people-building and the work of parents, teachers, counselors, religious leaders, and community supporters. Elementary school counseling programs, because of their people-building mission, can become the unifying force that brings homes, schools, and communities together in their common effort to build caring children. In such a spirit of cooperation, homes, schools, and communities also become stronger caring institutions in their own right. The following five caring goal areas are designed to help children master the developmental tasks of middle childhood:

1. *Physical Caring.* We want our children to learn information, skills, and attitudes that will help them to develop healthy lifestyles through proper nutrition, exercise, and safety (see Chapter 6).

2. *Personal/Emotional Caring.* We want our children to develop caring personalities, build on their strengths, learn self-acceptance, manage their emotions responsibly, and achieve personal independence through responsible self-management (see Chapter 7).

3. *Social Caring.* We want our children to learn caring social skills that will enable them to care for their personal relationships with family, friends, and distant others; value and respect people of diversity; resolve conflicts peacefully; and support their communities (home, school, and community groups) with pride and responsibility (see Chapter 8).

4. *Cognitive Caring.* We want our children to learn information and skills that will enable them to care for their interests as lifelong learners and to apply their thinking, goal-setting, information-processing, problem-solving, and decision-making skills in living caring and responsible lives (see Chapter 9).

5. *Career and Societal Caring.* We want our children to care for themselves, others, and society as volunteers, workers, producers, consumers, family members, and community participants. We want them to become contributors to the economic and cultural lives of their communities, adaptive users of advanced technologies, and concerned stewards of the global environment. We want them to experience and appreciate fully the value of learning, living, and working in a free society and the roles they play in preserving and passing on to others what they have learned (see Chapter 10).

Program Delivery

A comprehensive, collaborative, and developmental elementary school counseling program is designed to address the needs of all children, targets specifically identified people-building goals (needs assessment), and establishes and maintains a caring teaching-learning environment that will support the teaching-learning process as provided for in the Tripartite. A variety of counseling program delivery methods is needed to ensure that a full range of children's needs can be met through *personal growth and child development* (lifestyle enhancement); *prevention* (programs designed to prevent or reduce individual, developmental, and societal dangers); *remediation* (developmental deficits); and *crisis intervention* (school violence, suicide, natural disasters, global unrest, deaths of family members and classmates, etc.).

Given the wide range of children's needs, high children-to-counselor ratios, and limited resources (people, money, and materials), a systematic, appropriate, adequate, effective, and efficient method of resource allocation and distribution of program delivery methods is needed (Adelman & Taylor, 2002). Consequently, we have developed a cost-effective, ternary decision-making model (see Chapter 5) that will assist counselors in carrying out the mission of an elementary school counseling program, which is to meet the needs (developmental, unique, societal) of all children in a caring and responsible manner.

The Ternary Decision-Making Model consists of *primary delivery methods* (academic curriculum integration, classroom guidance, and parent and peer helping) that are developmental and preventative in nature. They are large-group focused and are designed to reach the largest number of children utilizing the full involvement of parents, teachers, peers, and community members as service providers. *Secondary delivery methods* address children's needs (growth enhancing or remedial) that require some additional attention and expertise beyond what primary delivery methods can offer. Secondary methods of intervention include, but are not limited to collaboration, consultation, and counseling (individual and small group). These methods involve the expertise of elementary school counselors and such intermediaries as parents, teachers, administrators, and mental health specialists (school and community). Remediation and growth-enhancement services involve team planning and the delivery of services to small numbers of children in homes and schools.

Tertiary delivery methods are designed to meet children's needs through methods of intervention that often require the combined involvement of school and community resources. Crisis intervention and challenging remediation cases often follow a pathway of child referral, placement, follow-up, and reintegration into the school and classroom. A complete description of the Ternary Decision-Making Model is discussed in Chapter 5. A description of the program delivery methods mentioned in this chapter is presented in Chapters 3 and 5.

Service Providers and Recipients

Elementary school counseling programs could not function without the full participation of school and community service providers and recipients. While we could have included this *building block of success* under *Program Support,* we strongly believe that people are the mainstay of elementary school counseling programs and deserve to be recognized as a central force in their own right. They play a critical role in providing *Program Support,* developing *Caring Program Goals,* and managing the *Delivery Methods,* which help children to care more deeply, manage risk more responsibly, and live life more fully as caring human beings and community participants. Elementary school counseling programs owe their success to those people who shape the lives of others through their people-building efforts.

A Partnership with Possibilities

In 1997, the American School Counselor Association Governing Board adopted the National Standards for School Counseling Programs. In that document, they described the purpose of school counseling programs.

> School counselors work with all students, school staff, families, and members of the community as an integral part of the education program. School counseling programs promote school success through a focus on academic achievement, prevention, and intervention activities, advocacy, and social/emotional and career development (Campbell & Dahir, 1997, p. 8).

During the mid-1960s, elementary school counseling programs were defined in a similar fashion. Elementary school counseling programs were viewed to be comprehensive, collaborative, and developmentally based programs designed to meet the individual, developmental, and societal needs of all children. They were viewed to be an essential and integral part of a child's total educational experience (ACES-ASCA Committee on the Elementary School Counselor, 1966).

While times have changed, the definition of elementary school counseling has remained the same. What has changed is that elementary school counseling programs have drifted away from their primary goal, which has always been to enhance student achievement and accomplishment (Campbell & Dahir, 1997).

More than 35 years later, elementary school counselors are still struggling to find a place for themselves and their programs in the midst of an ongoing educational reform movement that they have done little to shape (Clark & Stone, 2000; Green & Keys, 2001; Lenhardt & Young, 2001, Paisley & McMahon, 2001). Unfortunately, many elementary school counselors do not view themselves and their programs as mainstream contributors and shapers of educational reform. Rather, many view themselves, and are viewed by others (school and community), as support service personnel offering itinerant care to children through crisis intervention, remediation, and prevention. Some elementary school counselors have come to define their role and programs as separate entities, offering services in isolation despite a specific mandate from the American School Counselor Association to function in partnership with the elementary school's academic-instructional program in providing a developmentally appropriate and personally meaningful education (Campbell & Dahir, 1997).

A partnership is formed when two or more people participate together in a joint venture. They share a common interest in the same business and collectively possess the necessary skills and expertise to achieve their shared mission. Following this analogy, parents, teachers, administrators, and elementary school counselors share a common interest in the people-building business. This partnership consists of a joint mission between the elementary school's academic-instructional program and its counseling program to provide children with a *balanced education,* one that seeks "... to encourage the growth of competent, caring, loving, and loveable people who respect honest work, care competently for their families, and contribute effectively to their communities" (Noddings, 1995, p. 366). Figure 2.3 illustrates the academic-instructional and school counseling program partnership and the people who make it all possible.

The partnership provides a planned and *balanced education* that emphasizes a (Boyer, 1995)

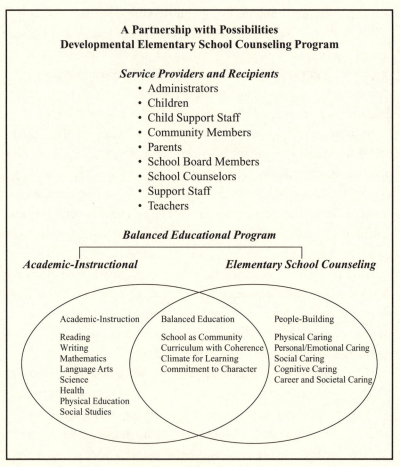

A Partnership with Possibilities
Developmental Elementary School Counseling Program

Service Providers and Recipients
- Administrators
- Children
- Child Support Staff
- Community Members
- Parents
- School Board Members
- School Counselors
- Support Staff
- Teachers

Balanced Educational Program

Academic-Instructional   *Elementary School Counseling*

Academic-Instruction	Balanced Education	People-Building
Reading	School as Community	Physical Caring
Writing	Curriculum with Coherence	Personal/Emotional Caring
Mathematics	Climate for Learning	Social Caring
Language Arts	Commitment to Character	Cognitive Caring
Science		Career and Societal Caring
Health		
Physical Education		
Social Studies		

Figure 2.3. A Partnership with Possibilities.

- school as community,
- curriculum with coherence,
- climate for learning, and
- commitment to character.

While some elementary schools are currently providing children with a quality education, many are not. Those that are may not be doing so in a purposeful and planned manner (see Chapter 4). Elementary school counseling programs with a people-building perspective are committed to addressing the four elements of a *balanced education*. The partnership that we advocate concentrates on academic learning and relies heavily on elementary school counseling programs to provide a network of care that will enable children to be successful at learning and living (Houston, 2001).

School as Community

Elementary school counseling programs care deeply about building a sense of community in classrooms and schools. The purpose of an education goes beyond teaching children merely about the society in which they live. Rather, children must learn to apply the lessons of the classroom to life. If children are to live in communities and contribute to their betterment, schools must provide opportunities for caring and community building in their classrooms and schools.

Elementary school counseling programs, working in cooperation with teachers and the academic-instructional program, can help children to create inclusive, supportive, and cooperative classrooms and school communities in which children experience feelings of connectiveness, belonging, and being a part of something larger than themselves. Caring classrooms and school communities foster a sense of safety and security; support open communication; promote shared goals and objectives; build trust; foster cooperation, courage, and inclusion; and provide a stepping-stone from which to venture forth and become productive and caring members of other communities beyond the schoolhouse door (Sapon-Shevin, 1999).

Building caring school communities is a caring alternative to violence prevention programs, which tend to be more reactive than proactive. Building caring communities is a positive, growth-enhancing, and an all-inclusive approach to supporting diversity in all forms and providing children with a model for living in peace and harmony.

Curriculum with Coherence

Most elementary school academic-instructional programs prepare children to live in society by teaching them a traditional subject matter core curriculum of reading, writing, mathematics, language arts, social studies, science, health, and physical education. Today's children do not live in a world of subject matter labels that communicate distance and a lack of relevancy.

Elementary school counseling programs support teachers and parents in understanding that children live in a world of never-ending life situations that call for their attention and action. Children are looking for ways to embrace life and to make caring and responsible choices that will benefit themselves, others, and their communities. Children do not make subject matter decisions; rather, they make life decisions in the seven themes of caring (Noddings, 1995).

- Caring for self
- Caring for intimate others (family and friends)
- Caring for distant others and acquaintances
- Caring for plants and the environment
- Caring for nonhuman animals
- Caring for objects and instruments
- Caring for ideas (Chapter 1)

Elementary school counseling programs can bring relevancy and coherence to the instructional-academic curriculum by helping teachers to understand how traditional subject matter information, skills, and attitudes relate to people-building, caring, and decision-making in the seven themes of caring. We want children to understand how what they learn in school and home can be used to improve the quality of life for all.

Climate for Learning

Elementary school counseling programs have traditionally been interested in building strong, caring, physical and psychological learning climates that will support the teaching-learning process (Tripartite). In many ways, there is a strong positive relationship between community building and building a positive, caring school climate for teaching and learning (Schaps, 1998). It is no secret that one way to improve education is through a healthy learning climate (Solomon, Watson, Battistich, Schaps, & Delucchi, 1996).

A climate for learning includes such physical conditions as proper lighting; comfortable room temperature; appropriate furniture; instructional equipment and materials; and a building that is safe, secure, and in good repair. It likewise includes a building that is physically attractive and inviting (Sapon-Shevin, 1999).

While the physical climate is important to learning, the psychological climate must be equally attractive and warm. Children must feel connected to their school, classmates, teachers, and the learning process itself if learning is to take place. Children must also feel comfortable from within to risk and grow. Indeed, all who occupy the space called school contribute to the life of the school and its success in teaching children to live, learn, and work in a caring climate (Duke, 1998). Therefore, teachers, parents, administrators, school staff, and community supporters must likewise enjoy a sense of comfort and connectiveness if a caring learning environment is to be established.

Elementary school counseling programs are always looking to improve the teaching-learning climate in ways that will foster human growth and potential through meeting children's individual and developmental needs.

Commitment to Character

Many elementary schools are now focusing on character education as an important aspect of a child's education. We would like to expand this concept from a "commitment to character" to a "commitment to people-building." While a commitment to character is important, and we support it fully, it does not go far enough. People-building encompasses the development of the whole child in growing a caring human being. Elementary school counseling programs thus focus on

- physical caring,
- personal/emotional caring,
- social caring,
- cognitive caring, and
- career and societal caring (Chapters 6–10).

People-building is an ongoing process and is a central component of a *balanced education.* Children learn to become competent, caring, loving, and lovable people who respect hard work, care deeply for their families, and contribute effectively to their communities because they received a quality education (school as community, curriculum with coherence, climate for learning, and a commitment to character).

A truly meaningful education requires the combined efforts of a caring academic-instructional program and a caring elementary school counseling program that provides children with a clear people-building perspective of their potential and how to use that potential to live, learn, and work in ways that will benefit themselves and society. A *partnership with possibilities thus builds caring children and caring communities.* It brings elementary school counseling programs center stage, where people-building can be experienced in every classroom, all day, everyday, throughout the school year. When this happens, elementary school counselors will be able to devote more of their time to the effective delivery of primary, secondary, and tertiary intervention activities (see Chapter 5).

RATIONALE FOR A PARTNERSHIP PERSPECTIVE

Throughout this chapter, we have advocated on behalf of elementary school counseling programs that work in partnership with academic-instructional programs in providing children with a *balanced education*. The purpose of an education is not just to enable children to do better in school, but also to do better in life (Eisner, 2001). In order for children to do better in life, their education must prepare them to be high academic achievers, self-directed learners, responsible and involved citizens, collaborative and high-quality contributors to the economic and cultural lives of their communities, adaptive users of advanced technologies, concerned stewards of the global environment, healthy and continuously developing individuals, and caring and supportive family and community members.

A *balanced education* is one that meets society's needs for developing caring and responsible community members while meeting children's developmental and individual needs in helping them to become caring human beings and capable self-managers. A *balanced education* is essential for the growth and prosperity of our nation and good for our children in helping them to become caring children and builders of caring communities.

A significant quality of a *balanced education* is its focus on people-building and the creation of a caring school community, which supports a climate for learning and a commitment to developing human potential. Model elementary school counseling programs, in support of this mission, help to create just and caring schools and nurture the development of caring children who are taught how to learn, live, and work in support of themselves, others, and their communities. Current writings and research (Boyer, 1995; Ferrandino, 2001; George Lucas Educational Foundation, 2001; Sapon-Shevin, 1999) support the notion that children do better in school and in life when their developmental needs are successfully addressed in a learning climate that supports people and community building through a coherent curriculum that links learning to living.

The model elementary school counseling program of the 21st century, working in partnership with the elementary school's academic-instructional program is designed around a *blueprint for success* containing the following critical components:

- **A Solid Foundation (Tripartite).** A model elementary school counseling program is organized around children's individual, developmental, and societal needs; has clearly stated program goals that reflect the needs to be met; and functions in a caring, teaching-learning climate that supports *caring children building caring communities.*
- **Developmental, Comprehensive, and Collaborative.** A model elementary school counseling program is designed to meet children's developmental needs, is part of a school-wide counseling program initiative that involves all children, and involves the full participation of all people who affect children's lives (school and community).
- **Management-Based.** A model elementary school counseling program is conceived, nurtured, and monitored through a strategic planning process that involves the four management functions of planning, organizing, actuating, and controlling to ensure that children's needs are met through a *balanced education.*
- **Systematic Evaluation Process.** A model elementary school counseling program relies on a continuous, comprehensive, data-based evaluation system designed to measure child learning competencies and the operational strategies of the counseling program in meeting program standards.
- **Comprehensive, Decision-Making–Based Delivery System.** A model elementary school counseling program uses a planned decision-making process in systematically identifying the most appropriate, adequate, effective, and efficient counseling services, delivery systems, and resources to be used in best meeting the individual and developmental needs of all children (growth and development, prevention, remediation, and crisis intervention).

In designing this chapter, we have relied on our own professional experiences as elementary school counselors and counselor educators, and on feedback from former students and practicing elementary school counselors. We have likewise turned to the literature and in particular the American School Counselor Association's 1997 and 1998 publications detailing the National Standards for School Counseling Programs and their implementation. We believe that we have captured the essence of quality in presenting an elementary school counseling program that focuses on children's needs, caring, and community building in the context of a *balanced education.* Our goal in writing this chapter has been to create a *blueprint for success* in developing elementary school counseling programs that are growth enhancing and caring by design, and comprehensive, collaborative, and developmental in nature. We have strived to provide a framework for success while allowing for flexibility and creativity in creating programs that will best address the needs of children and the school and community partnerships that will work in their behalf.

The chapters that follow will provide support to elementary school counselors in their quest to build elementary school counseling programs using a *blueprint for today and tomorrow.* Good luck and much success in your people-building venture, *teaching children to care and to become builders of caring communities.*

BIBLIOGRAPHY

ACES-ASCA Committee on the Elementary School Counselor (1966). Preliminary statement. *Personnel & Guidance Journal, 44,* 659–661.

Adelman, H.S., & Taylor, L. (2002). School counselors and school reform: New directions. *Professional School Counseling, 5,* 235–248.

Bowers, J., Hatch, T., & Schwallie-Giddis, P. (2001). The brain storm. *School Counselor, 39,* 16–19.

Boyer, E.T. (1995). *The basic school: a community for learning.* Princeton, NJ: The Carnegie Foundation for the Advancement of Learning.

Campbell, C.A., & Dahir, C.A. (1997). *Sharing the vision: The national standards for school counseling programs.* Alexandria, VA: American School Counselor Association.

Clark, M.A., & Stone, C. (May 2000). Evolving our image: School counselors as educational leaders. *Counseling Today, 42,* 1–52.

Dahir, C.A. (2001).The national standards for school counseling programs: Development and implementation. *Professional School Counseling, 4,* 320–327.

Duke, D.L. (1998). Challenges of designing the next generation of America's schools. *Kappan, 79,* 688–693.

Eisner, E. (2001). What does it mean to say a school is doing well? *Kappan, 82,* 367–372.

Ferrandino, V.L. (2001). Challenges for 21st-century elementary school principals. *Kappan, 82,* 440–442.

George Lucas Educational Foundation Staff (2001). Educating the heart and mind. *School Counselor, 39,* 25–27.

Green, A., & Keys, S. (2001). Expanding the developmental school counseling paradigm: Meeting the needs of the 21st century student. *Professional School Counseling, 5,* 84–95.

Gysbers, N.C., & Henderson, P. (2001). Comprehensive guidance and counseling programs: A rich history and a bright future. *Professional School Counseling, 4,* 246–256.

Gysbers, N.C., Lapan, R.T., & Jones, B.A. (2000). School board policies for guidance and counseling: A call to action. *Professional School Counseling, 3,* 349–355.

Herr, E.L. (2001). The impact of national policies, economics, and school reform on comprehensive guidance programs. *Professional School Counseling, 4,* 236–245.

Houston, P. (2001). Superintendents for the 21st century: It's not just a job, it's a calling. *Kappan, 82,* 428–433.

Lenhardt, A., & Young. P. (2001). Proactive strategies for advancing elementary school counseling programs: A blueprint for the new millennium. *Professional School Counseling, 4,* 187–194.

Noddings, N. (1995). A morally defensible mission for schools in the 21st century. *Kappan, 76,* 365–368.

Paisley, P.O., & McMahon, H.G. (2001). School counseling for the 21st century: Challenge and opportunities. *Professional School Counseling, 5,* 106–115.

Sapon-Shevin, M. (1999). *Because we can change the world: A parental guide to building cooperative inclusive classroom communities.* Boston, MA: Allyn & Bacon.

Schaps, E. (1998). Risks and rewards of community building. *Trust for Educational Leadership, 28,* 6–10.

Schaps, E., & Lewis, C. (1999). Perils on an essential journey: Building school community. *Kappan, 81,* 215–218.

Solomon, D., Watson, M., Battistich, V., Schaps, E., & Delucchi, K. (1996). Creating classrooms that students experience as communities. *American Journal of Community Psychology, 24,* 719–748.

Whiston, S.C. (2002). Response to the past, present, and future of school counseling: Raising some issues. *Professional School Counseling, 5,* 148–155.

CHAPTER 3

Elementary School Counselors Who Make a Difference

The title of this book, *Elementary School Counseling: A Commitment to Caring and Community Building,* truly reflects the importance of school counseling and of school counselors as key figures in determining the present of, and more significantly, creating a new future for, elementary school counseling programs. The single most important factor contributing to the success of elementary school counseling programs will be the elementary school counselor's ability to forge a positive and strong partnership between academic-instruction and school counseling programs (see Chapters 1 and 2). Only then will elementary schools be able to provide children with an education designed to teach them how to become caring self-managers and builders of caring communities. Education therefore is not just about children doing well academically, but reflects a more holistic view in which educators help all children to achieve success in the classroom and in all areas of life and living.

If elementary school counselors are to truly make a difference in helping all children to attain a balanced education (academic and developmental achievement), they will need to think of themselves first as educators and secondly as counselors (Bemak, 2000; Dahir, 2001; Gysbers & Henderson, 2001; Lenhardt & Young, 2001; Littrell & Peterson 2001; Paisley, 2001). As educators, elementary school counselors will be able to partner with parents, teachers, administrators, school board members, and community volunteers in creating a thriving people-building program that will foster caring children building caring communities. This new educational partnership (Boyer, 1995) will emphasize *a school as community, a curriculum with coherence, a climate for learning,* and *a commitment to character.*

If children are to receive a balanced education, elementary school counselors will need to rethink their job description and expand their professional roles to include those of leader, manager, social change agent, and direct service provider (Bemak, 2000; Clark & Stone, 2000; Koppel, 2001). Traditionally, many elementary school counselors continue to function as direct service providers (Ponec & Brock, 2000). They work quietly and diligently from the sidelines with children, parents, teachers, and administrators, doing what they can to support children and to improve their quality of life. They are well trained and skilled in this role, but are becoming increasingly stressed and frustrated in trying to do more with less. They have more needy children to serve, more classroom guidance lessons to teach, more child study teams to support, more small counseling groups to facilitate, and more consultation meetings to attend. These responsibilities are addressed in the face of increasing time constraints; expanding school program schedules; decreasing professional help and services; decreasing parental involvement; and decreasing operational budgets.

While the role of service provider is still a very important counselor role and will be discussed later in this chapter, it can nevertheless be quite limiting in the absence of other role strategies (leader, manager, and social change agent). With job responsibilities and demands increasing in the presence of educational reform, counselors are limited in what they can accomplish working alone in a role that tends to be more reactionary than proactive (Anderson, 2002).

Elementary school counselors, who are destined to make a positive contribution to their field and to children's lives, see themselves as educators working in partnership with other educators in helping to create a quality education that focuses on people and community building. What follows is an important discussion of elementary school counselors as leaders, managers, social change agents, and service providers. While these critical school counselor roles cannot be separated in practice, their importance to the success of elementary school counseling programs and a balanced education for children requires that they be addressed separately for understanding and suggestions for implementation.

COUNSELORS AS LEADERS

Leadership is a critical counselor role for those who wish to become instrumental players in bringing a balanced education into elementary schools. Unfortunately, the school counselor, as leader, has not been significantly explored or duly emphasized in practice, or taught in school counseling preparation programs (Clark & Stone, 2000).

The leadership challenge is about encouraging people to seize opportunities to lead humankind to greatness by making a positive difference in people's lives and strengthening the communities in which they live (Kouzes & Posner, 1995). A common view of leadership is defined ". . . the art of mobilizing others to want to struggle for shared aspirations" (Kouzes & Posner, 1995, p. 30). The key aspect of this definition is on two words, "want to." Leadership implies a process in which leaders inspire people to contribute their energies, time, resources, and services willingly because they are internally motivated to do so. They follow out of choice, desire, and conviction.

People in positions of authority get others to do what they want because of the power that they hold, but true leaders mobilize others to want to act because of their credibility, honesty, forward-looking perspective, and inspiration (Bennis, 1994; Kouzes & Posner, 1995). Effective leaders approach leadership from the perspective that all people who work with them are volunteers and are at their side because they want to be, not because they have to be.

Elementary school counselors, in many ways, are CEOs of volunteer programs. They wield no specific organizational power with respect to giving orders and commanding obedience to get things done. They must depend upon enlisting the support of others and gaining their confidence and commitment if they are to advocate in behalf of a balanced education.

Elementary school counselors and their school counseling programs are faced with some of the same challenges of volunteer organizations. They must gain the confidence and commitment of children, parents, teachers, administrators, and community members if they are to create and sustain a viable and mainstream elementary school counseling program that is developmental, comprehensive, and collaborative in nature.

EFFECTIVE LEADERSHIP PRACTICES

Leaders must not only have a sense of direction, they must possess the skills and human qualities that move people to action because they are internally motivated to do so. They are people who have developed personal credibility through their actions by challenging, inspiring, enabling, modeling, and encouraging (Kouzes & Posner, 1995). Based on years of leadership research, Kouzes and Posner have concluded that there are five fundamental practices and ten commitments demonstrated by most exemplary leaders in their quest to chart the future of their respective programs, organizations, and businesses. Leaders, by definition, do the following (Kouzes & Posner, 1995, p. 18):

Challenge the Process

1. Search out challenging opportunities to change, grow, innovate, and improve.
2. Experiment, take risks, and learn from the accompanying mistakes.

Inspire a Shared Vision

   3. Envision an uplifting and enabling future.
   4. Enlist others in a common vision by appealing to their values, interests, hopes, and dreams

Enable Others to Act

   5. Foster collaboration by promoting cooperative goals and building trust.
   6. Strengthen people by giving power away, providing choices, developing competence, assigning critical tasks, and offering visible support.

Model the Way

   7. Set the example by behaving in ways that are consistent with shared values.
   8. Achieve small wins that promote consistent progress and build commitment.

Encourage the Heart

   9. Recognize individual contributions to the success of every project.
   10. Celebrate team accomplishments regularly.

These same five practices and ten commitments can place elementary school counselors and their respective programs on the cutting-edge in providing children with a balanced education and a bright future.

Challenging the Process

Elementary school counselors must confront and challenge the status quo if they and their programs are to achieve partnership status and become key players in providing children with a balanced education. Working together, academic-instruction and elementary school counseling programs can challenge outdated ways of think-

ing, which narrowly define an education as solely academic achievement. Counselors, as leaders, can help everyone to understand that a
true education builds people in all areas of their development and
prepares them to care for themselves and their communities in responsible ways.

Search for Opportunities

Elementary school counseling programs can change, grow, and improve when elementary school counselors seek out challenging
opportunities for growing caring children and establishing caring
communities. The following suggestions offer a place to begin.

    **1. *Elementary school counselors are encouraged to view their
school counseling programs from a fresh perspective.*** We encourage counselors to read Chapters 1 and 2 and view their programs as
being in the people-building business, striving to provide children
with a balanced education.

    **2. *Elementary school counselors should ask themselves what it
means to be in the people-building business*** and become possibility thinkers, using brainstorming as a way of generating new ideas.

    **3. *Elementary school counselors are encouraged to examine
all school-related activities,*** from academic-instructional programs
to school counseling programs, and ask themselves, "To what extent
are these programs engaged in people and community building?"

    **4. *Elementary school counselors are to think about ways in
which they can involve administrators, parents, teachers, children,
cafeteria workers, office staff, custodians, bus drivers, and community volunteers as members of a comprehensive people-building
team*** in support of educational renewal efforts.

Experiment and Take Risks

Experimentation and risk-taking are a must if elementary school
counseling programs are to separate themselves from doing what
they have always done (habitual practices). Habit and "in the box"

thinking restrict creativity and new ways of being and doing. Elementary school counselors must assume a leadership role if they are to experiment with the concepts of people-building, partnership formation, and contributing to a balanced education. In support of experimentation and risk-taking, we offer the following suggestions.

1. *Experiment with new ideas.* Rather than instituting a new idea school-wide if they are unsure of the outcome, counselors can ask for volunteers and try it out on a small scale. This is a great way to work out the bugs, solicit feedback, take corrective action, and evaluate the outcome in determining the future of this idea.

2. *Make it safe to experiment and take risks.* Counselors will want all school and community participants to become involved in their elementary school counseling program. For this to occur, elementary school counselors will want to create a safe, secure, and caring environment where all participants feel connected to themselves, others, and the elementary school counseling program. Elementary school counselors who focus on community building, sharing of ideas, cooperation, and inclusion pave the way for people to experiment and take risks in sharing themselves and their ideas.

3. *Provide opportunities to collect innovative ideas.* Breakfast meetings, suggestion boxes, evaluation instruments, brainstorming sessions, and "good idea" clubs stimulate creative thought and breathe new life into existing programs. Encourage people to look beyond their immediate environment for good ideas that relate to people and community building.

4. *Provide for team renewal.* All people need stimulating activity and an occasional change of scenery. Elementary school counselors can help to organize school renewal days where daily routine is altered in some way. They are encouraged to think of different ways to energize and support people in their own growth and utilize them and their community-building ideas to support team renewal.

5. *Honor risk-takers.* The best way to encourage responsible and caring risk-taking is to recognize those school and community doers who care deeply enough, despite personal fears, to make a positive difference in the lives of others and in their communities. All well-intentioned risk-takers and their caring practices need to be recognized regardless of outcome.

6. *Model risk-taking.* Elementary school counselor leaders are role models. Leaders lead by doing. Counselors cannot afford to sit on the sidelines or the centerline if they expect to advocate in behalf of people-building and a partnership status in providing children with a balanced education.

7. *Foster commitment, control, and challenge.* Kouzes and Posner (1995) have stated that to build commitment, one must offer more rewards than punishments. To build a sense of control, choose tasks that require effort but are not overwhelming. To inspire and challenge, encourage others to see change as full of possibilities for a better tomorrow. Counselors must keep these key points in mind when developing a volunteer pool of participants who *want to* become people and community builders in an elementary school counseling program that supports a balanced education.

Inspire a Shared Vision

Visions represent mental images of a preferred future. Leaders are the great dream makers of our time. They are excited about what can be and use their enthusiasm, conviction, and dreams to reinvent the future status of their organizations and programs. Shearson and Lehman Brothers (1984) stated that "Vision is having an acute sense of the possible. It is seeing what others don't see. And when those of similar vision are drawn together, something extraordinary occurs" (pp. 42–43).

Elementary school counselors are challenged with the responsibility of envisioning the future and enlisting the support of others in transforming their dreams into a better, more effective future for elementary school counseling programs. Learning to inspire a shared vision begins with elementary school counselors understanding the nature of their program's business and how that business relates to education (see Chapters 1, 2, and 4).

Envision the Future

Helping children to achieve their full potential as caring and responsible self-managing human beings and builders of caring communities (home, school, and community) is the hallmark of successful elementary school counseling programs and is the gold standard of a balanced education. In order to create this new future, elementary school counselors must reexamine where they and their programs have been and where they see themselves and their programs going in light of educational reform and the ever-changing and expanding responsibilities that they and their programs must address in the years to come. Here are a few ideas for counselors to consider as they envision the future (see Chapters 2, 4 and 11).

1. *Look at the past.* Elementary school counselors must look at their past (programs and roles), present, and future and ask themselves the following questions. To what extent should the past affect the present and the future? Have past practices and programs become comfortable and habitual or do they reflect the changing times in which children live? What changes in past practices and program conceptualization are warranted, given their hopes for the future in helping children to become fully functioning human beings and contributors to the society in which they live? These questions and ones like them will help counselors to reflect on the past and examine future roles that focus on caring, community building, child advocacy, shared goals, staff development, developmental and coherent curriculums linking classroom to life experiences, building climates for learning, and establishing a commitment to character (people-building).

Elementary school counselors who fail to examine their past are likely to continue working in programs that function in the past. Like prehistoric dinosaurs, these programs are likely to become extinct in environments that can no longer sustain their continuation.

2. *Explore your wants.* Elementary school counselors, after reading Chapters 1 and 2, can begin to clarify their vision for a better future. The following questions and suggestions can serve as a starting point in helping counselors to re-create their elementary school counseling programs and themselves.

What do I want my elementary school counseling program to **be?**
(Suggestions: A partner in educational reform; a contributor to a balanced education; developmental, comprehensive, and collaborative.)

What kind of person and counselor do I want to **be?**
(Suggestions: Open, caring, leader, manager, social change agent, and service provider.)

What must my elementary school counseling program **do?** *Doing* leads to *Being.*
(Suggestion: Offer school counseling services in support of a balanced education.)

What must I **do** to become the person and counselor I strive to **be?**
(Suggestions: Become involved in strategic planning, meet with administrators to plan a balanced education, etc.)

What do I want my elementary school counseling program to **have?**
(Suggestions: A good reputation, meaningful services, and the involvement of others.)

What do I want to **have** as a person and counselor?
(Suggestions: A caring attitude, exciting challenges, and opportunities to affect children's lives in a positive direction.)

What do I want my elementary school counseling program to **give?**
(Suggestions: A commitment to caring, a balanced education, and a partnership in educational reform.)

What do I want to **give** as a person and a counselor?
(Suggestions: Caring, inspiration, hope, guidance, etc.)

3. *Write a vision statement.* Elementary school counselors are challenged to write two short vision statements: one that reflects their hopes and dreams for themselves as human beings and counselors, and a second that describes their hopes and dreams for a preferred future state for their elementary school counseling programs.

Counselors are encouraged to seek ideas from the American School Counselor Association, the National Standards for School Counseling Programs, and counseling journal articles and textbooks when writing their vision statements. These ideas will help counselors to create their own "I Have A Dream" statement that can be shared with teachers, administrators, parents, and community members.

4. *Become a reality tester.* Too often people give up on their dreams because they imagine all of the impossible barriers that stand between them and their goals. Elementary school counselors, if they are to succeed in achieving their dreams, must become positive, possibility thinkers and reality testers. Most people are willing to support leaders who are honest, forward moving, inspiring, and competent (Kouzes & Posner, 1995). Counselors who aspire to lead must believe in themselves and the people they serve. They must be willing to challenge their negative assumptions about the future, roll up their sleeves, and go to work in creating pockets of hope and securing the involvement of those who believe in and support their vision for a brighter future.

Enlist Others

On August 23, 1963, a crowd of 250,000 people gathered at the Lincoln Memorial in Washington, DC, to hear an address by Dr. Martin Luther King, Jr. Those who heard the speech watched history in the making and the future unfold. Dr. King uplifted and inspired people of diversity all across our nation as he invited them to go to the mountain top with him and to share in his dream of a nation uplifted and "free at last." That speech and the manner in which it was delivered caught people's attention and inspired a nation to also dream and to follow Dr. King in his quest for caring people to come together in creating a more caring nation and world.

While we do not suggest that counselors must have the speech-writing and oratory skills of a Dr. Martin Luther King, Jr., we do believe that counselors have no choice but to enlist the support of administrators, teachers, parents, children, and community members in turning their vision into reality. To achieve this end, counselors must (1) appeal to a common purpose (a balanced education), (2) communicate expressively, and (3) sincerely believe in what they are saying (Kouzes & Posner, 1995). Leaders need followers, and followers are more likely to follow through dialogue than monologue. Dialogues evolve out of a shared purpose and build commitment and that "want to" spirit discussed earlier in this chapter. To enlist the support of others and a strong volunteer base, we recommend the following actions:

1. *Identify the people to be enlisted in the vision.* Counselors are encouraged to make a list of those people and groups (school and community) who are likely to influence their elementary school counseling programs and will be influenced by them. These are the people and groups that elementary school counselors will want to enlist in building a strong people-building team who will support their counseling programs and a balanced education.

2. *Identify a rallying point.* Once elementary school counselors have identified people and groups whose support they would like to enlist, they need to find that common thread or magnetic field that draws people together (a rallying point). Rallying points can be used by counselors to effectively cement commitment, establish relationships, build enthusiasm, and instill a desire to act. We believe that the two most common threads that motivate and inspire people are people-building and *caring communities.* Most people would agree that caring children building caring communities is good for our children and a necessary prerequisite for establishing civility, cooperation, and inclusion among people of diversity.

3. *Communicate effectively.* Once counselors have identified rallying points, they need to rely on their communication skills to facilitate program change and growth. Counselors are encouraged to use images, word pictures, and relevant examples, and to convey traditional values, appeal to common concerns, convey a sense of being positive and hopeful, focus on "we" rather than "I," and speak with conviction, passion, and emotion. These are the traits that will inspire, build friendly coalitions, and rally the troops to action.

4. *Develop a short presentation.* Elementary school counselors are now ready to develop a high-impact and motivational five-minute presentation that conveys the essence of their vision and can be delivered to anyone at a moment's notice. Counselors can use their message to begin a dialogue about people-building and their desire to partner with the elementary school's academic-instructional program in building a balanced education that will enable children to achieve more in school and to do better in life (Eisner, 2001).

5. *Be realistic, optimistic, and positive.* The future is created by leaders who can instill in others the "I can" consciousness and the "I will" state of mind that moves good ideas from the planning room to the classroom. Counselors need to present the facts and potential rough spots (be realistic) while being hopeful about the future (be optimistic) and supportive of those who stay the course in achieving success (be positive).

When gold miners mine for gold, they focus on the treasure, not on the amount of dirt and rock they will have to remove to succeed. Counselors, like gold miners, must never lose sight of what they are striving to accomplish despite the many roadblocks they will encounter. They must remain realistic, optimistic, and positive in their endeavor to create a balanced education for all children.

Enabling Others to Act

Counselor leaders recognize that they cannot build a developmental, comprehensive, and integrated elementary school counseling program without the support and determination of loyal followers. Having inspired a shared vision, counselors are ready to *foster collaboration* and *strengthen others* through cooperative goal planning, mutual trust, and the sharing of power and information.

Foster Collaboration

Everyone has needs and wants that they seek to meet. Teachers have a need to teach and care for their children. Educational specialists and itinerant instructors have a need to serve the unique attributes of children and address real and potential barriers to learning. Elementary school counselors likewise are working hard to strengthen and enhance people-building through a balanced education. In theory, these people are all educators and should be working together to help children become caring human beings, responsible self-managers, and active community participants. In reality, they often become competitors for time, space, and related resources in their individual attempts to meet their needs and the needs of children they serve. Such competition often creates tension, adversarial relationships, and complacency, rather than the kind of environment that fosters caring and team building.

Elementary school counselors must demonstrate how educational team members can work in collaboration with each other in meeting shared educational goals. What follows are some suggestions that will help counselors foster collaboration.

1. *Always focus on we.* Caring and community building represent a mutual vision that involves all educators. Counselors as leaders are encouraged to speak in terms of "we" and "our" when referring to shared educational goals as a way of emphasizing that we are all educators and people-builders, regardless of professional title.

2. *Increase interactions.* Elementary school counselors are encouraged to partner with elementary school principals and teachers in discussing the value of promoting a balanced education. In addition, opportunities to discuss topics related to caring, people-building, and developing a sense of community need to be provided. These topics become the seeds for building a spirit of oneness among all educators who seek to build caring children and strong communities.

3. *Focus on gains, not losses.* As new ideas in support of caring, people-building, and developing cooperative and inclusive classroom communities emerge, counselors and principals must encourage all educators to try them out, stay focused on their successes, and not become discouraged by those things that do not work.

4. *Form planning and problem-solving partnerships.* High involvement elementary school counseling programs look for ways to engage parents, educators, administrators, and community supporters in planning and problem-solving partnerships that seek to improve all aspects of school life. Topics to address can include building school morale and caring climates, educational reform, people-building, and community service.

5. *Conduct a collaboration audit.* To what extent is collaboration being practiced among school and community participants? This is not only a good question to ask, but one that definitely needs to be answered when planning collaborative opportunities to enhance educational practices. Elementary school counselors and principals, working together, can accomplish this task through an audit that focuses on the degree to which school personnel participate in shared decision-making, openly share ideas and materials, meet together formally and informally to plan teaching strategies, socialize with each other at work, and genuinely enjoy working and playing together.

6. *Go first.* Elementary school counselors and principals must lead the way in fostering collaboration. They can begin this process by presenting an idea for others to consider. The idea becomes the spark that initiates dialogue and later develops into a model for encouraging others to share their ideas, concerns, and suggestions in the spirit of cooperation and collaboration. Counselors also can model collaboration by involving teachers, parents, and community members in problem solving; providing classroom support through team teaching; and demonstrating ways to include people-building concepts through curriculum integration.

Strengthening Others through Power and Information

An old Chinese proverb says that if you want one year of prosperity, grow grain. If you want ten years of prosperity, grow trees. If you want one hundred years of prosperity, grow people. Counselors are in the people-building business, and the way that they grow people is by sharing information, skills, and power with others. While fostering collaboration among people is important, strengthening others is a prerequisite of independent action. Here are some things that counselors can do to strengthen confidence and resolve in other people to become full participants in the people-building enterprise.

1. ***Get to know others.*** Counselors are encouraged to spend time with school staff (bus drivers, cafeteria workers, secretaries, and custodial workers), parents, teachers, administrators, and school board members. This time can be used to share hopes, fears, wishes, talents, hobbies, and ideas for building a better future. Counselors who take the time to understand others will develop new insights as to how they can help to strengthen others and share power with them in helping to meet children's needs.

2. ***Let people know you.*** Counselors need to let people know who they are through their actions. Leaders like Gandhi and Mother Teresa led by example. They cultivated personal power through giving and drew others to a life of giving as well. Counselors have the opportunity to practice caring and people-building in their interactions with others.

3. ***Enlarge people's circle of influence.*** Elementary school counselors are encouraged to help all people develop their gifts and talents and to assist them in sharing what they have to give with others. Enlarging people's circle of influence is empowering for the caregiver and beneficial to those who receive the care.

4. ***Make sure that tasks are relevant.*** All tasks related to elementary school counseling should be consistent with the program's mission. Counselors also have the responsibility of communicating to those who will carry out these tasks what they are expected to do, when to do it, how it is to be done, and why the task is important in meeting the program's mission.

5. ***Educate, educate, educate.*** Without education and coaching, people are reluctant to act, and those who do act are likely to fail in their attempts. People can only *give* what they have to others. If elementary school counselors wish to promote elementary school

counseling through a balanced education, they must educate others about the virtues of a balanced education and the role that elementary school counseling programs play in achieving that end.

6. *Chalk talks and huddles.* Chalk talks are small group paper-and-pencil planning sessions that provide elementary school counselors with the opportunity to discuss their programs with key players in producing a winning team. Huddles represent on-the-spot, informal discussions with team players planning moment-to-moment strategies in achieving small daily wins. Huddles can occur in hallways, cafeterias, counselor's offices, or classrooms, or on playgrounds. Huddles keep people focused on the prize: caring children building caring communities.

7. *Make connections.* Counselors who network with administrators, teacher, parents, civic leaders, business leaders, and school board members are likely to find the support they need to promote a balanced education.

8. *Make heroes of other people.* Elementary school counselors can do the most good for program success and visibility by making heroes of others and what they have given to children. Newspaper articles, e-mails, recognition dinners, personal visits to say thank you, and awards are but a few ways of saying thanks, offering deserved recognition, and showcasing the elementary school counseling program.

Modeling the Way

Leaders create the plans and help to design the road maps that highlight the way and guide people toward desired ends. They help to unravel the bureaucratic entanglements, model the way, and create opportunities for small wins that lead to major victories. Elementary school counselors are sure to enhance their credibility as leaders when they model high performance standards and a caring attitude toward others, and when they instill a sense of program uniqueness and pride.

Set the Example

Modeling the way by setting the example is how elementary school counselors can make their vision for a balanced education a tangible reality. Modeling the way by setting a good example begins with counselors engaging in self-reflection. Counselors must first decide what gives their lives meaning and purpose and then determine the extent to which they model what they believe. If elementary school counselors believe in a balanced education and in forging a partnership relationship with administrators to make it happen, do their actions coincide with their beliefs? The following ideas will help elementary school counselors to engage in a meaningful self-examination, personally and professionally.

1. *Take a look in the mirror.* Counselors who are too busy *doing* have little time to reflect on *being* the person and professional they hope to become. Counselors are encouraged to take frequent daily pauses to reflect on their past activities and future actions and to question how these experiences are defining them and their elementary school counseling programs. Counselors need to understand who they are, what they value, how others see them, and to understand their strengths and weaknesses. Self-reflection takes candor, serious risk-taking, and homework to achieve honest feedback in gaining an objective measure of self.

2. *Write a leadership credo.* Elementary school counselors, after looking into the mirror, are in a good position to clarify their beliefs about themselves and the values they hold regarding their programs. Using this information, a counselor is asked to imagine being away from work for one year. The counselor has been asked by the administration to write a one-page credo spelling out the nature of a quality elementary school counseling program and his or her perspective on leadership as it applies to making this program a reality. This statement will be distributed to all school personnel and will guide program development during the counselor's absence. If you were that counselor, what would you write?

3. *Write a self-tribute.* In this activity, counselors are to imagine that they are to be honored by their state school counselor association as elementary school counselor of the year. They are then asked to pretend to be someone other than themselves who has been chosen to write and deliver one of the speeches praising the counselor's performance and character. If you were selected to write that speech what would you say about yourself?

4. *Audit your actions.* Do counselors practice what they preach? Counselors are encouraged to take a single sheet of paper and draw a vertical line down the middle. On the left side of the paper, they are to write what they preach (vision and mission) and on the right side, what they do. After completing the task, counselors can identify the number of matches they have and how they spend their time. Counselors may discover that they wish to make changes in both columns in clarifying their priorities and actions.

5. *Trade places.* Counselors are encouraged to trade places with school staff, teachers, administrators, civic leaders, and children in order to obtain a fresh perspective in identifying better and different ways to best serve the needs of children. Counselors will become more aware of the strengths, weaknesses, opportunities, and threats that exist and how best to address them.

6. *Be dramatic.* Counselors must be creative in setting examples of leadership and in educating people about their elementary school counseling programs. Abraham Lincoln was an effective storyteller and humorist. He used these attributes to make his points. Counselors can use storytelling, teachable moments, games, activities, songs, and voice inflection as ways to communicate the importance of people-building, caring, and community building.

Plan Small Wins

"Life is a cinch by the inch and hard by the yard," exemplifies the importance of taking small steps and enjoying small wins in pursuit of life goals. Most projects look rather daunting when viewed in their totality. However, when broken down into small manageable steps, the impossible becomes possible. Elementary school counselors are in the people-building business over the long haul. The goal is to begin slowly, involve small numbers of people, and introduce ideas that can be easily managed without causing undo stress. Mistakes will be made, goals will be met, and small wins will energize and strengthen further commitment to elementary school counseling program ideas. Here are a few strategies that will help elementary school counselors plan small wins.

1. *Take it personally.* Elementary school counselors, who want their programs and the people involved in them to experience small wins, must invest themselves in the process of winning. They must take personally the challenge of identifying and implementing task-oriented activities that promote caring learning environments, interpersonal caring, caring curriculums that are relevant to meeting children's and society's needs, and caring beyond the schoolhouse doors.

2. *Make a plan.* Counselors will want to make plans that involve the participation of others. These plans should reflect school and community values, involve service providers and recipients, and focus on caring and people-building strategies that will connect the anticipation of success with the reality of accomplishment.

3. *Create a model.* When implementing plans for change, counselors are encouraged to create a model that can be field tested in the context of a controlled environment. Elementary school counselors can control for small wins by managing the scope of the experience (people involved and resources needed) so that they can give it every chance to succeed.

4. *Ask for volunteers.* Small wins are more likely to occur by using volunteers rather than coercing people to take part who would rather not be involved. School and community volunteers who support the concept of a balanced education are ready, willing, and eager to commit their time, talents, and treasure to that end.

5. *Make programs visible.* Fundraisers, sports teams, and some small businesses keep people informed as to their progress. Scorecards, billboards, and electronic counters placed in visible locations log the progress being made. When progress is made visible, it motivates, energizes, and encourages more effort and determination to succeed. Elementary school counselors can use bulletin boards, newspapers, memos, posters, graphs, charts, and tables to convey progress and small wins to school and community volunteers and interested parties.

6. *Sell the benefits.* Elementary school counselors must first sell the benefits of what they propose before they can claim small wins. Change that is consistent with the school's mission, is user friendly, requires skills common to the population, and is accomplished through training opportunities is likely to be accepted and increases the potential for small wins.

7. *Build community.* Community building is a necessary prerequisite to winning. Sports teams, many small businesses, the military, and religious groups invest in community building to cement caring partnerships, loyalty, and commitment to a common mission. Counselors and administrators who fail to build a caring team are not likely to create a clarity of purpose and the determination needed to succeed.

Encourage the Heart

"When striving to raise quality, recover from disaster, start up a new service, or make dramatic change of any kind, leaders make sure people benefit when behavior is aligned with cherished values" (Kouzes & Posner, 1995, p. 4.). Effective leaders provide the spark that fires up their peak performers and the recognition that energizes their fortitude and will to execute and sustain valued organizational practices.

Encouraging the heart is about celebrating the good works of program volunteers and celebrating the volunteers for the good works that they do. Elementary school counselors have a significant role to play in encouraging the hearts of those people who make elementary school counseling program practices successful.

Recognize Individual Contributions

Leaders help people to develop a winning attitude through their encouragement, clear directions, honest feedback, and positive outlook. They are eager to celebrate small wins, rekindle passion, provide the focus, and set the course that will sustain ongoing commitment and a winning spirit. Elementary school counselors have the opportunity to encourage the heart through their recognition of individual contributors who serve to enhance and strengthen the people-building mission of elementary school counseling programs. Here is how to begin.

1. *Be creative about rewards and give them personally.* Counselors can recognize program volunteers (children, parents, teachers, community members, etc.) for their work performance, for advancing the program's mission, for increasing program visibility, and for promoting program growth. Some ways to personally recognize deserving volunteers are through handshakes, lunches, telephone calls, praise, small parties, certificates, gifts, plaques, cards, and write-ups in the school and town newspapers; and through presenting life savers (candy) and Eveready (battery on a plaque) Battery awards.

2. *Make recognitions public.* Public recognition bolsters personal pride, sets the standards for desired actions, and keeps the counseling program mission and goals in the forefront for others to value.

3. *Design a reward and recognition program collaboratively.* Collaborative development of a recognition program helps to ensure that what is developed is in keeping with the elementary school counseling program mission. For example, a counseling program that is involved in community building needs to be careful in creating a recognition program that fosters inclusion rather than exclusion. Questions to consider in the planning process are:

- Whom can we celebrate?
- What can we celebrate?
- When can we celebrate?
- Where can we celebrate?

- Why should we celebrate?
- How can we celebrate?

4. *Provide real-time feedback.* Real-time feedback is on-the-spot coaching that helps program volunteers recognize their successes and what they can do to improve their people-building skills.

5. *Find people who are doing things right.* Elementary school counselors need to be out and about looking for children, teachers, parents, administrators, and civic leaders who exemplify, through their actions, what elementary school counseling programs seek to accomplish. When counselors catch people-builders in action, they need to celebrate their accomplishments.

6. *Be a coach.* Winning people become winners through coaching. Successful elementary school counselors do not wait for small wins to occur by chance. They make them happen by helping volunteers to become caring and responsible people-builders.

7. *Internal motivators are a must.* Counselors can recognize individuals for their volunteer activities and help them to stay motivated by doing the following:

- Give volunteers an opportunity to do something that helps them to feel good about themselves.
- Help volunteers to accomplish tasks that are worthwhile.
- Provide volunteers with the opportunity to learn new things and new skills.
- Send volunteers to conferences and workshops.
- Involve volunteers in decision-making and program planning.

Celebrate Team Accomplishments

Encouraging the heart is not just about recognizing individual effort; it involves celebrating the efforts of team players as well. Counselor leaders are there to support team accomplishments and to keep their counseling programs center stage at all times. Counselors support team accomplishments through their teaching, coaching, cheerleading, pep rallies, and their presence on the sidelines and frontline.

Sports teams win games because of team effort. Counseling programs win because of the team effort of volunteers who seek to provide a balanced education for children. What follows are some ideas
for celebrating team accomplishments.

1. *Schedule celebrations.* One way to ensure that team effort is
recognized is to schedule specific events worthy of celebration on
the calendar. Here are a few ideas.

- *Founder's day.* Celebrate new beginnings of worthwhile programs and the people who make it happen.
- *Volunteer day.* Celebrate teams of volunteers for the work that
  they do in making the counseling program a success.
- *Project Pride and Respect.* Celebrate school and community
  team efforts that strengthen people- and community-building
  efforts.

2. *Be a cheerleader.* Sports teams, some small businesses, and a
few social service organizations use cheers to recognize and inspire
team effort. Cheerleaders unite, motivate, and energize their teams.
Elementary school counselors can become cheerleaders and can encourage teachers, children, parents, and school administrators to become cheerleaders in helping to celebrate team effort and small wins.

3. *Have fun.* Above all else, counselors, teachers, children, parents, and administrators need to cultivate an atmosphere of fun.
Fun is no longer a luxury, but is a necessary prerequisite to sustaining the intensity and hard work that go into developing and maintaining a balanced education. Counselors must help everyone to
look for good, do good, and celebrate goodness in an atmosphere
of fun and joy.

4. *Identify a social network and strengthen it.* Being an elementary school counselor is a demanding job and difficult to perform in
isolation. Counselor leaders need to take stock of their circle of care
and determine who is in it, how available these people are, when
and how often they connect with others who care, and what relationships need to be strengthened or renewed. Counselors are encour-

aged to build caring connections with a variety of people with whom they can give, take, confide, and celebrate.

5. *Stay in love.* Counselors who make the most effective leaders and celebrators of accomplishment put their heart into their work and their work into their heart. They love who they have become, what they do, and what they give to others. Counselors who are in love with life and living find it easy and rewarding to celebrate team effort.

6. *Plan a celebration today.* Don't wait. Do it today! Plan a celebration to encourage the heart. Write a poem, sing a song, watch a movie, give a hug, share a smile, feed the hungry, and clothe the needy. Do something to celebrate life and living and the people who invest their energies in children, our greatest resource, and our best hope for a caring and peaceful society.

COUNSELORS AS MANAGERS

Successful elementary school counselors must not only be able to lead (get others to want to do what needs to be done), but manage (get things done through people) as well. In more complex terms, management is a process of setting objectives, organizing resources to attain them, and then evaluating the results for the purpose of determining future action. Incumbent in this statement are two distinct, yet overlapping factors. First, management focuses on the fact that there is work to be done if program goals are to be met. Second, equal attention is placed on those who will be doing the work. Since management is a process of getting things done through others, managers must focus their attention on both the objectives to be obtained and the people who will make it possible.

For elementary school counselors, the message is clear. First, counselors must become involved in strategic planning in establishing a detailed plan that identifies the elementary school counseling program vision and mission, program objectives and curriculum, organizational structure, program implementation guidelines, and a systematic method for program control and evaluation (see Chapter

4). Second, elementary school counselors must possess the people-building skills to get things done through people. The definition of management implies that counselors are not responsible for singlehandedly providing all of the program services, but rather are responsible for bringing people, program goals, and resources together so that the program mission can be carried out as intended.

EFFECTIVE MANAGEMENT STRATEGIES

Effective management strategies focus on two overlapping initiatives: strategic planning and people-building (getting things done through people). Since strategic planning strategies are developed in detail in Chapter 4, we will refrain from duplicating that information here, but will identify eight strategic planning questions that counselors and program advisory committee (PAC) members should consider throughout the management process. With respect to counselors' people-building responsibilities, we will identify strategies that counselors can use in helping counseling program volunteers to become successful program contributors.

Strategic Planning Questions

An elementary school counseling program that is not successfully managed will become a costly disappointment and burden to all who are left to pick up the pieces. The strategic planning process discussed in Chapter 4 will enable elementary school counselors to address eight critical questions that affect program development.

1. What new elementary school counseling programs do we need to offer?
2. What programs should be continued without modification?
3. What programs and activities should be modified in terms of what is being taught, how it is being taught, and when it is being taught?
4. What additional resources or modifications in resources will be needed to develop new or modify existing programs?

5. What programs should be discontinued because they no longer support the counseling program mission?
6. What environmental conditions (physical and/or psychological) exist in school that support or threaten program goal attainment?
7. What environmental conditions exist in the community that support or threaten program goal attainment?
8. What societal issues (economic, sociological, medical, demographic, multicultural/ethnic, political, legal, technological, educational) can elementary school counseling programs address in developing a balanced education for children?

People-Building (Managing People)

Strategic planning provides direction and people provide action. Getting things done through people is the hallmark of an effective manager (Bennis, 1994). There is a direct relationship between a manager's actions and an employee's performance. Assuming that counselors have been effective in getting volunteers to want to participate (leadership) in a counseling program does not guarantee that these same volunteers will achieve desired program outcomes. Here is where managing people begins and job performance is defined. Job performance equals motivation plus ability, plus a conducive work environment (Maslow, 1998). Motivation has been defined as the drive to satisfy a want or need. Ability relates to people's assets and strengths, and environment addresses the physical and psychological conditions that support a caring work climate. Most people would assume then, that successful job performance is likely to be attained by people who have the drive and determination to succeed, assets and capabilities to do the job, and a caring and supportive environment in which to work.

Despite all that is known about job performance, many people are not doing what managers want them to do. While most people want to please, do things right, and are cooperative and dependable, they struggle to meet job performance standards (Fournies, 1988).

Fournies has stated (based on years of research), that poor management is the cause of non–job performance. Many managers have to recognize that management is a form of preventative maintenance in which managers do the right things, at the right time, and in the right sequence to shape the desired job performance.

Fournies (1988) identified a number of reasons why employees do not do what they are supposed to do. These same reasons apply to counselor managers and their work with volunteer service providers. What follows are nine barriers to work performance and actions that counselor managers can take to neutralize their effect.

1. *They don't know what they are supposed to do.* Telling is not teaching, and assuming that volunteers know what to do does not make it so. One solution is to be clear in describing performance objectives and tasks to be done. Ask volunteers to describe what they think they are to do so that further explanation can be provided if needed.

2. *They don't know how to do it.* Just because volunteers know what to do is no guarantee that they know how to accurately perform the task. One solution is to break tasks into small steps and model them while giving volunteers a chance to perform the steps and receive feedback.

3. *They don't know why they should do it.* When volunteers do not understand why they are performing certain tasks, they may not take their tasks seriously. One solution is to explain how what they are doing relates to the people-building mission of the elementary school counseling program. Counselors can explain the benefits to those whose behaviors change and the pitfalls likely to be experienced by those who do not learn new ways of behaving.

4. *They receive no positive consequences for doing it.* When volunteers fail to receive positive consequences for doing what they are supposed to do, they are likely to stop what they are doing. One solution is to look for people doing what is right and doing it the right way and positively recognizing their efforts.

5. *They think they are doing what they are supposed to do.* Volunteers who think they are doing what they are supposed to do are not likely to question or second-guess their actions. Any inappropriate behavior will continue. One solution is to give performance feedback specifically and frequently.

6. *They are rewarded for not doing what they are supposed to do.* Sometimes volunteers are rewarded for poor performance. Telling people they are doing a good job when they are not will perpetuate the undesired behavior. One solution is to remove positive reinforcers for poor performance, help others to correct their performance, and reward the change in behavior.

7. *They are punished for doing what they are supposed to do.* Volunteers are sometimes punished for good behavior. Those who do good work are sometimes asked to do more. Volunteers who provide good ideas in a brainstorming session may be asked to implement the idea. Volunteers who are encouraged to share their ideas but are never recognized may cease to contribute their thoughts. One solution is to identify desired people-building behaviors and then examine how those behaviors were treated.

8. *They anticipate negative consequences for doing it.* Fear is a powerful motivator for not doing something. The thought of being criticized is enough to discourage the best intentions. One solution is for counselors to be open with volunteers and to encourage their discussion of fears and apprehensions in participating in the counseling program. Confidence builders, training, and positive feedback help to dissipate the anticipation of negative consequences.

9. *They experience no negative consequences for poor job performance.* Volunteers who perform poorly but are never corrected will continue to perform poorly. One solution is for counselors to assist volunteers in evaluating their performance against well-defined performance criteria. Help them to see what they are doing right, what they are doing wrong, and how they can improve their performance.

Other factors for counselors to consider when evaluating deficits in work performance are the following:

1. They think that your way will not work.
2. They think their way is better.
3. They think something else is more important.
4. Obstacles exist that are beyond the performer's control.
5. Their personal limits prevent them from performing (Founies, 1988, p. 91).

Remember that quality work performance does not occur by accident. It requires the caring attention of effective and responsible counseling program managers.

COUNSELORS AS SOCIAL CHANGE AGENTS

A few years ago, elementary school principal Vincent L. Ferrandino (2001) met with some teachers and parents to develop a mission statement for their elementary school. They were asked to describe their aspirations for their children. The end result was that they wanted their children to be well-rounded, responsible citizens, confident and self-assured, and happy. Little mention was made of standardized tests and high test scores or being academically proficient in all subject areas. This is not to say that these areas were not important to parents and teachers, but that their emphasis was centered on the school's ultimate responsibility, which is to prepare children for life. Children need to develop physical, personal/emotional, social, cognitive, and career and societal (civic) skills if they are to become caring and responsible human beings and builders of caring communities.

Elementary school counselors have a vital role to play as agents for social and educational improvement and reform (Adelman & Taylor, 2002; Herr, 2001; House & Hays, 2002). While lacking in position power, elementary school counselors can become advocates for a balanced education (Chapters 1 and 2) using their skills of persuasion and coalition building to form school and community partnerships and network with caregiving agencies. Most teachers and parents already support an educational mission ". . . to help children create a future where democracy is preserved and the ideals of the nation are moved forward" (Houston, 2001, p. 433).

For elementary school counselors to become active agents for social and educational change, they must view themselves as educators and perceive their elementary school counseling programs as educational programs (Littrel & Peterson, 2001). They must likewise champion a balanced education that emphasizes school as community, a caring curriculum with coherence, a climate for learning, and a commitment to character development (people-building).

Counselors will need to take stands on important educational issues; advocate in behalf of a balanced education for children; challenge and remove barriers that impede academic and personal growth; advocate on behalf of school reform in areas relating to academic assessment, enrichment programs, parent-teacher relations; and network with community organizations that support caring children building caring communities (Clark & Stone, 2000).

EFFECTIVE SOCIAL CHANGE AGENT STRATEGIES

The goal of elementary school counselors and their promotion of a balanced education is to provide children with an education that links classroom learning to life and living and prepares them to make responsible and caring decisions in response to all life situations. To accomplish this end, counselor change agents (Taylor & Adelman, 2000) must first engage parents, teachers, administrators, school boards, and community participants in a serious dialogue about education before designing new elementary school counseling programs or changing existing ones (Chapter 11).

We believe that if elementary school counseling programs are to thrive, elementary school counselors must demonstrate that an effective education is a balanced education, one that integrates academic instruction with "people and community building." How school and community members answer the following questions will determine their stance on this very important subject (Clinchy, 1995, p. 403).

1. What are the purposes of an education? What does it mean to be an educated person in the 21st century?

2. What are the responsibilities of home, family, local communities, business organizations, the media, and cultural groups in strengthening education in our society?

3. How do we know if a school is a good school? How do we hold ourselves accountable, and what kind of assessments do we view as valid and reliable?

4. What is our social responsibility with regard to the increasing disparities in income, health care, and educational opportunities between socioeconomic groups in the United States?

5. How can teachers, parents, students, community members, the clergy, and the local media help to stem the tide of violence in homes, schools, and society? How do we create a safe and civil community?

6. How should schools respond to and draw on the growing diversity of the American population? How should our schools and communities respond to racism, sexism, and ethnic tensions?

7. How do we help our children to feel hope, belief in the future, and a shared sense of purpose?

8. How do we educate for active and informed citizenship in a democratic society?

9. What kind of relationship among schools, families, and community agencies will best enable children to learn?

10. What kind of in-school relationships among students, teachers, parents, administrators, and nonteaching staff enable education to take place? What is a good school climate, and how do we create it?

11. How can we discover and nurture every child's talents and interests?

12. What kind of resources—money, time, and energy—will be needed to enable all children to become lifelong learners?

Based on the focus of this text and the twelve strategic questions posed, we believe that elementary school counseling programs must advocate in behalf of social change and a balanced education that prepares all children to become caring community members and active and concerned citizens (Lenhardt & Young, 2001). In order to achieve this end, Sapon-Shevin (1999) has stated that children should (p. 157).

- be informed and aware of issues and problems in the world. They should approach the world with eyes wide open, noticing things that are wrong or unfair, alert to injustices and inequities.
- feel a commitment to make a difference. They should have a sense that what they do matters, that they can make a difference, and that they must be willing to expend the energy and time to do so.
- have the skills and strategies they need in order to take on problems and issues. They must have communication skills (talking to others, asking questions, and listening), information-gathering skills (reading, data gathering, and ways to sort through confusing or conflicting information), conflict-resolution skills (knowing what to do when people don't agree or are getting angry), and skills in bringing about change (letter writing, lobbying, and advocacy).

Elementary school counselors, as agents for social change and educational reform, can be most effective if they practice and teach to others the skills mentioned by Sapon-Shevin. In particular, counselors, teachers, administrators, parents, and children would do well to follow three specific steps when acting as agents for social and educational reform (Sapon-Shevin, 1999, p. 158).

1. Notice that something is wrong.
2. Have the courage to make a difference.
3. Devise strategies to bring about change.

Notice That Something Is Wrong

Elementary school counselors need to become observant of school policies, educational practices, and social and societal trends that either support or threaten a balanced education. A good place to begin is for counselors to examine the 12 questions posed by Clinchy (1995) and advocate on behalf of strategic planning that supports school and community goals that favor school as community, a caring curriculum with coherence, a climate for learning, and a commitment to character (people-building).

Have the Courage to Make a Difference

Courage is about learning to say yes in the face of fear. Courageous acts occur in response to conviction and in support of strongly held beliefs and values about right and wrong. When counselors recognize that something is wrong and that it goes against the concepts of caring, people-building, and a caring learning community, they must be willing to move from the sidelines to the front lines and muster the courage to make a difference.

Devise Strategies to Bring about Change

Much has been written about change and how to implement it. Change is a constant in life and living and is experienced by all human beings. Sometimes it occurs by chance and other times it is planned. Regardless of how, when, or where it happens, it causes some discomfort until the change is fully experienced and adjustments are made in response to it. That everyone is affected by change does not ensure that they understand the nature of change or how to bring it about so that it is likely to be accepted and supported. While space is limited for an in-depth discussion on this topic, here are a few tips for counselors to consider when advocating in behalf of social change and educational reform.

1. *Invite participation.* Counselors are encouraged to network with people they trust to discuss their ideas regarding change. If others also believe the ideas have merit, a position paper in support of the change can be drafted.

2. *Explain why.* Describe the nature of the present situation and how it runs counter to the school's people-building mission. Provide reasons as to why change in current thinking and actions is desirable.

3. *Describe the benefits.* Explain how children and others affected by the change will benefit from it.

4. *Seek questions.* Invite questions and discussion from those who will implement and be affected by the change.

5. *Acknowledge the rough spots.* Keep people as fully informed as possible. Discuss potential rough spots and what is not known in order to reduce unwanted surprises.

6. *Build confidence.* Move slowly, involve the participation of others, bring in expertise if needed, keep people informed, and provide the necessary resources to support the change process (time, money, staff training, materials, technical support, feedback, etc.).

7. *Create a plan.* Before implementing the change, develop a detailed plan that addresses the following topics.

- Nature of the current situation
- Reason that change is desirable
- Factors enhancing the possibilities for change (people support, availability of resources, time, etc.)
- Possible barriers to change (people, past practice, lack of resources, etc.)
- Strategies to support the change
- A strategy implementation and evaluation plan

With respect to strategy development, we believe that Lewin's (1951) force field analysis model can help counselors to understand and plan a course of action in which change is more likely to be accepted and supported by those affected by it. Using information from the previous steps, counselors should now do the following (see Figure 3.1):

Step 1: *Identify the situation that needs to be addressed.* Example: Community building in school. The problem is that children

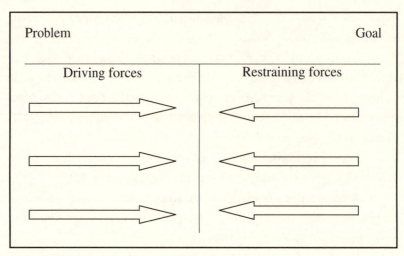

Figure 3.1. Force Field Analysis. When the impact of the two sets of forces is equal, the situation is frozen. However, when the balance in the forces is upset, movement can occur in either direction.

lack a sense of connectiveness within the environment. The goal is to build and strengthen children's sense of connectiveness within the school environment.

Step 2: *Identify the driving and restraining forces affecting this situation.* With every problem to be solved is a goal to be attained. For goal attainment to occur, two sets of forces must be examined. Restraining forces are those environmental conditions (physical and psychological) that support the continuation of the problem, whereas driving forces are those environmental conditions that increase the likelihood that the desired goal will be achieved. A significant driving force in our example could be that teachers support the concept of community building. A possible restraining force might be the lack of teacher training in this area.

Step 3: *After listing the driving and restraining forces, counselors should ask themselves the following questions:*

- Can the effects of any driving forces be increased?
- Can new driving forces be added?
- Can the effects of some restraining forces be reduced?
- Can some restraining forces be eliminated?

The goal is to offset the balance of these two forces in favor of the desired change, which is to build and strengthen children's sense of connectiveness within the school environment.

Step 4: *Having asked these questions, counselors are now ready to identify which driving and restraining forces they wish to address.*

Step 5: *Counselors are now ready to identify specific actions that can be taken to add/or intensify key driving forces and/or to weaken or eliminate key restraining forces.* These strategies need to be clear with respect to who needs to be involved, what will need to be done, what initial steps will need to be taken, and where and how they will be accomplished.

Step 6: *Implement and evaluate the plan.*

Force field analysis is a great way to fully understand the dynamics of change. The process can be taught to anyone contemplating change, but especially to children whom we want to become advocates and supporters of caring and community building.

COUNSELORS AS SERVICE PROVIDERS

Elementary school counselors are best known for and are most visible in their service provider role. They work directly with children in areas of individual and small group counseling and in the classroom facilitating large-group growth enhancement activities (classroom guidance). Counselors also provide indirect services to children through their collaboration, consultation, and coordination efforts with intermediaries such as parents, teachers, educational specialists, administrators, and community agency personnel. The purpose of these indirect functions provides counselors with opportunities to assist third parties in helping children to achieve their full potential as caring children and builders of caring communities. And lastly, elementary school counselors function as trainers and developers of human potential. They help to prepare school and community volunteers to become partners in the delivery of people-building services to children.

As service providers, elementary school counselors play a "hands-on" role in helping children to fulfill their human nature as described by the likes of Erikson, Maslow, Havinghurst, and Piaget. Counselors accomplish this end by nurturing nature through their understanding of human growth and development and assisting others to do the same. Thus, children are supported as their nature unfolds and their full potential is realized.

The focal point around which elementary school counselors function is the Tripartite (Chapters 2 and 4). In nurturing nature, counselors must understand children's developmental, societal, and individual needs. They must understand what behaviors children must learn if they are to attain their true nature and become fully functioning human beings. And, they must understand how to create nurturing teaching-learning environments that will help children to meet their needs through behaviors to be learned (Paisley & McMahon, 2001).

Many books have been written that provide counselors with helpful strategies in developing their service-provider functions. Consequently, it is not our intention to focus on the "how to's" of becoming a service provider, but rather to briefly describe these functions in the context of helping children to become caring human beings and builders of caring communities.

EFFECTIVE SERVICE PROVIDER STRATEGIES

Elementary school counseling programs are people-building programs that are comprehensive by design and developmental in nature. They seek to provide children with information, skills, self-confidence, and opportunities through a balanced education that is proactive and growth oriented in scope and practice. *The ultimate goal is to help all children achieve success in the classroom and in all areas of life and living.* While we believe that this goal is most effectively met through primary intervention methods (curriculum integration, classroom guidance, and peer and parent helping), there are times when the specific expertise of counselors through direct intervention is required in helping children to achieve their full potential. What follows is a brief description of five counselor service-provider functions that we believe are most critical in helping children to become the best they can be: teaching, counseling, collaborating-consulting, coordinating, and training and development.

Teaching

Elementary school counselors perform a teaching function in their work with children in that they conduct guidance lessons with a people-building focus. Large-group teaching sessions with parents, teachers, and children offer counselors a unique opportunity to meet the developmental needs of many children through instructional activities that are in keeping with the school's academic and counseling mission statements. Classroom teaching opens the door for building strong counselor-teacher partnerships and a proactive balanced education with parent and teacher involvement.

Counseling

Counseling is an interpersonal process involving one or more children and a professionally trained and credentialed counselor. The counselor, working in a caring and confidential setting, seeks to help children develop a more effective understanding and utilization of self. Through counseling, children experience a more heightened and accurate sense of awareness (self, others, and the environment); develop new understandings about themselves and the world; and discover more effective, caring, and responsible pathways to success in meeting their needs.

Individual and group counseling are especially helpful in those instances when primary delivery methods are unable to address the unique needs of children (see Chapter 5). Through collaboration and consultation with school and community personnel, counselors are able to identify children who can best benefit from individual and group counseling (crisis, remediation, prevention, growth enhancement counseling).

Collaboration Consultation

Some people use the terms *collaboration* and *consultation* interchangeably. While sharing some similarities, we see some differences as well. Collaboration for us speaks to team planning and participation. Counselors who collaborate with teachers and parents in support of a common cause become full participants in all phases of the activity. Collaboration fosters inclusion, cooperation, and the direct service involvement of all parties in meeting children's needs.

Consultation is a decision-making and problem-solving process that takes place between a consultant and one or more intermediaries (consultees) who seek assistance in meeting the needs of a third party. The consultant does not become directly involved with the consultees in the delivery of services. Should this happen, the consultant now becomes a collaborator on the project.

Counselors often work in partnership with parents and teachers in helping them to best serve the needs of children. Consultation can help parents and teachers to identify and clarify problems and concerns, discuss specific goals and desired outcomes, describe steps that have been taken, evaluate their success, gather and analyze data, redefine the problem, set new goals, create a plan of action, and offer guidance to those who will implement and monitor the plan.

Coordination

Coordination is yet another important service-provider function of counselors. The process involves counselors bringing together people, program goals, and needed resources so that school and community supporters can best serve the needs of children. As coordinators, counselors make sure that all school and community program volunteer service providers possess the training, materials, space, and technical and personal support needed to deliver team-supported people-building services.

In many ways, elementary school counselors function as conductors of large symphony orchestras. They must understand their counseling program and all its parts and be able to convey that understanding to the players. Counselors must know their players and their talents and be able to integrate both into a cooperative, coordinated, and unified whole. The quality of the music (counseling program) rests with the conductor (school counselor).

Training and Development

Elementary school counselors are trainers and developers of human potential. They recognize that people-building and the creation of caring communities is a mission that requires the full participation of teachers, parents, educational specialists, administrators, school board members, and community supporters.

The management task of getting things done through people requires the training and development of counseling program volunteers so that they can perform their people and community building tasks effectively. Volunteers need to know what they are to do and how to do it. A sound training and development program addresses both of these factors. When the process is completed, counseling program volunteers move from a state of dependence to a state of independence in performing their volunteer responsibilities and experience a gradual increase in their self-confidence as well.

Silberman (1990) has developed an eight-step training and development process that we have found to be helpful in assisting elementary school counselors to prepare volunteers for a successful teaching-learning experience.

1. *Screen volunteers.* When working with a volunteer population, counselors are highly encouraged to involve law enforcement in screening people (volunteers) who will interact with children. The safety and security of children is a necessary condition of caring and a prerequisite to training.

2. *Assess volunteers.* Using interviews, questionnaires, or other assessment activities, determine what knowledge, skills, and attitudes volunteers possess regarding the area of training that they are about to receive. For example, how much do teachers know about decision-making (purpose, process, practice) prior to beginning training in this area?

3. *Set general learning goals.* Using assessment data, identify the training goals to be addressed (affective, cognitive, skill-building).

4. *List specific objectives.* Write specific objectives (steps) for each goal identified, which, when followed, will result in goal attainment.

5. *Design training activities.* Objectives are achieved through clearly designed training activities. Identify and develop activities for each training objective. Vary the learning methods and formats used so that there is an effective mixture of teaching-learning methods.

6. *Sequence the training activities.* Review the activities selected and order them in a manner that will best facilitate objective and goal attainment. Some activities may need to be described, modified, or sequenced differently in order to enhance the training experience.

7. *Start detailed planning.* Focus on such details as the clarity of directions, the timing and length of each activity, the availability of needed resources (handouts, materials, equipment, etc.), key points to be made, questions to be asked, and expected outcomes to be attained.

8. *Revise design details.* Mentally rehearse the training before actually going through it. Study its overall design. Question whether or not the training experience will lead to the desired outcomes. Be prepared to make modifications if needed. And lastly, develop a contingency plan that can be used to adjust time constraints, give volunteers additional assistance if needed, and deal with equipment and activity failures.

9. *Review, implement, and evaluate.* Make sure that the training plan gives volunteers an opportunity to *do, use,* and *teach* before working on their own. Volunteers should experience (do) what they will eventually teach. They should be given opportunity to practice (use) what they have learned. And, they should be required to teach others what they have experienced.

The *do, use, teach* training process should be conducted under supervision with appropriate and sufficient coaching and feedback. When training is completed, volunteers will be ready to teach others what they have learned and evaluate their progress. New trainers should be supervised during their first few solo experiences in order to build their confidence and provide feedback as needed.

Parents, teachers, children, and community volunteers are excellent candidates to receive training in a variety of areas that support people- and community-building initiatives. Many schools today have leadership training, peer assistance, and conflict management programs for children. Parents are being trained to facilitate parenting programs, work in school libraries, provide tutorial assistance to children, speak at career fairs, and teach hobbies to children. And, teachers are receiving training and development in character education, peacemaking, diversity enhancement, and community-building programs. The opportunities to expand and strengthen elementary school counseling programs are endless, and the prospects are exciting for counselors who seek to train others as caregivers and community builders.

BIBLIOGRAPHY

Adelman, H.S., & Taylor, L. (2002). School counselors and school reform: New directions. *Professional School Counseling, 5,* 235–248.

Anderson, K. (2002). A response to common themes in school counseling. *Professional School Counseling, 5,* 315–321.

Bemak, F. (2000). Transforming the role of the counselor to provide leadership in educational reform through collaboration. *Professional School Counseling, 3,* 323–331.

Bennis, W.G. (1994). *On becoming a leader.* New York, NY: Addison-Wesley.

Boyer, E.T. (1995). *The basic school: A community for learning.* Princeton, NJ: The Carnegie Foundation for the Advancement of Learning.

Clark, M.A., & Stone, C. (2000, May). Evaluating our image: School counselors as educational leaders. *Counseling Today,* 21–46.

Clinchy, E. (1995). Learning about the real world: Recontextualizing public schooling. *Kappan, 76,* 400–404.

Dahir, C. (2001). The national standards for school counseling programs: Development and implementation. *Professional School Counseling, 4,* 320–327.

Eisner, E. (2001). What does it mean to say a school is doing well? *Kappan, 82,* 367–372.

Ferrandino, V.L. (2001). Challenges for 21st-century elementary school principals. *Kappan, 82,* 440–442.

Fournies, F.F. (1988). *Why employers don't do what they're supposed to do: And what to do about it.* New York, NY: Liberty Hall Press.

Gysbers, N.C., & Henderson, P. (2001). Comprehensive guidance and counseling programs: A rich history and a bright future. *Professional School Counseling, 4,* 246–256.

Herr, E.L. (2001). School reform and perspectives on the role of school counselors: A century of proposals for change. *Professional School Counseling, 5,* 220–234.

House, R.M., & Hayes, R.L. (2002). School counselors: Becoming key players in school reform. *Professional School Counseling, 5,* 249–256.

Houston, P. (2001). Superintendents for the 21st century: It's not just a job, it's a calling. *Kappan, 82,* 428–433.

Koppel, M. (2001). The school counselor's role in restructuring education. *The ASCA Counselor, 38,* 10.

Kouzes, J.M., & Posner, B.Z. (1995). *The leadership challenge.* San Francisco, CA: Jossey-Bass Publishers.

Lenhardt, M.C., & Young, P.A. (2001). Proactive strategies for advancing elementary school counseling programs: A blueprint for the new millennium. *Professional School Counseling, 4,* 187–194.

Lewin, K. (1951). *Field theory in social science.* New York, NY: Harper & Row.

Littrel, J.M., & Peterson, J.S. (2001). Transforming the school culture: A model based on an exemplary counselor. *Professional School Counseling, 4,* 310–319.

Maslow, A.H. (1998). *Maslow on management.* New York, NY: John Wesley & Sons, Inc.

Paisley, P.O. (2001). Maintaining and enhancing the developmental focus in school counseling programs. *Professional School Counseling, 4,* 271–277.

Paisley, P.O., & McMahon, H.G. (2001). School counseling for the 21st century: Challenges and opportunities. *Professional School Counseling, 5,* 106–115.

Ponec, D.L., & Brock, B.L. (2000). Relationships among elementary school counselors and principals: A unique bond. *Professional School Counseling, 3,* 208–217.

Sapon-Shevin, M. (1999). *Because we can change the world: A practical guide to building cooperative, inclusive classroom communities.* Boston, MA: Allyn and Bacon.

Shearson and Lehman Brothers (1984, June 4). *Vision Business Week,* 42–43.

Silberman, M. (1990). *Active training: A handbook of techniques, designs, case examples, and trips.* San Diego, CA: Lexington Books.

Taylor, L., & Adelman, H.S. (2000). Connecting schools, families, and communities. *Professional School Counseling, 3,* 298–307.

PART II

MANAGING A RESPONSIVE PROGRAM

CHAPTER 4

Strategic Planning

Strategic Planning is a process that provides direction and meaning to the daily activities of an elementary school counseling program and involves the examination of the program's values, current status, and operating environment in relationship to the program's desired future (Dahir, Sheldon, & Valiga, 1998; Gysbers, Lapan, & Jones, 2000).

What do Disney World, the NASA space mission, the construction of the Panama Canal, and elementary school counseling programs have in common? They all represent successful accomplishments backed by planning. Regardless of a project's magnitude, large or small, planning is a hidden, and often uncelebrated, process that transforms a dream into reality.

Strategic planning represents a *future inventing process* in which successful organizations create *agendas for excellence.* Their mission is to eliminate or reduce today's problems by spending more time focusing on achieving tomorrow's goals. While there are no guarantees that planning will result in desired outcomes being achieved, it is a sure bet that those who fail to plan are headed for failure (VanZandt & Hayslip, 2001).

WHY DO COUNSELORS FAIL TO PLAN?

Some counselors view planning as a waste of time and a luxury that only a few can afford. These counselors function as firefighters moving from one brush fire (crisis) to another with little time to

101

reflect on creating a future that is developmentally based and growth oriented.

Other counselors fail to plan because they would rather support the certainty and predictability of the status quo than accept risks associated with building an exciting new future for elementary school counseling. The certainty of some discomfort associated with change is enough to stop all but the courageous from venturing forth.

Another reason that strategic planning may not be a high priority for some elementary school counselors is that doing (action) receives more attention than planning in our society. While most people believe that planning helps to ensure successful action, it takes time and is not visible to those who reward action (teachers, parents, administrators, etc.). Consequently, some school counselors engage in lots of daily activity that presumably gives them much attention, but may not be strategically sound in meeting the needs of children and the larger society.

Lastly, some counselors fail to plan because they do not understand the value of strategic planning and are at a loss as to how to do it. We hope that, as this chapter unfolds, readers will

- recognize that strategic planning is a necessary function and not a luxury in developing a successful elementary school counseling program.
- become excited about the prospects of creating a future that better meets the academic, developmental, and societal needs of children.
- recognize that successful elementary school counseling programs are staffed by thinkers (planners) and doers (go-getters).
- surpass their fears of uncertainty and develop the courage to explore and create a desired future state by embracing the strategic planning process that follows.

BENEFITS OF STRATEGIC PLANNING

Bean (1993) has identified 20 benefits emanating from strategic planning, the essence of which are presented in Figure 4.1.

Benefits of Strategic Planning

1. It is visionary, yet realistic.
2. It is supported by a living framework (process of strategic planning).
3. It is a thorough, complete, and coherent plan.
4. It provides a crisp, clear, and precise direction.
5. It is developed by a comprehensive team of active players.
6. It is child driven (needs), not counselor driven.
7. It reflects what is happening inside and outside the school environment.
8. It is driven by opportunity and is productive, not reactive.
9. It reflects the past, present, and future.
10. It is assertive, not passive.
11. It is expansionistic, not protectionistic.
12. It is engaging, synergistic, and creates momentum.
13. It is priority driven, proactive, and focused.
14. It is practical, not academic.
15. It is realistic, not political.
16. It is implementation driven.
17. It is results bound, not bookshelf bound.
18. It is measurable, not vague.
19. It produces measurable program changes.
20. It is ongoing, not episodic.

Figure 4.1.

THE NEED HIERARCHY OF SCHOOL COUNSELING

Bean (1993) has stated that organizations (programs), like people (see Maslow's Needs Hierarchy, 1954), have a hierarchy of needs that must be met in succession if growth is to occur. The basic phases of organizational growth are *Exist, Expand, Establish, Elevate,* and *Elongate.* The strategic planning process is designed to facilitate growth (movement) in an organization regardless of the current phase that it occupies.

Bean's Need Hierarchy as applied to elementary school counseling can be visualized (see Figure 4.2) and explained in the following manner.

Exist

To exist, to survive as a viable program, elementary school counseling programs require carefully planned activity. Strategic planning

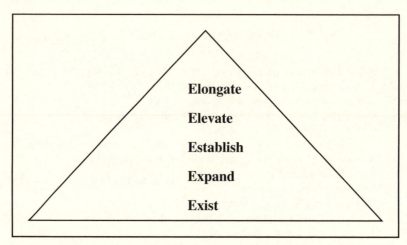

Figure 4.2. Elementary School Counseling Need Hierarchy.

is necessary in helping the counseling program to develop its vision, define its mission, clarify its purpose for being, identify the people who will provide and receive services, specify the services to be provided, and conduct internal and external environmental assessments to make sure that needed and valued services are being provided.

Expand

Elementary school counseling programs are destined for growth, not stagnation. Strategic planning can help elementary school counseling programs assess their strengths, weaknesses, opportunities, and potential threats (SWOT) to their existence. By capitalizing on this valuable information, elementary school counseling programs can build on their strengths, shore up their weaknesses, take advantage of new opportunities, and face potential threats with care, sensitivity, and determination.

Establish

With every period of growth (expansion), time is needed to reflect on these gains and solidify their existence. Long-distance runners cannot sustain a fast pace for an entire race. They must establish a pace that they can sustain following periodic bursts of speed (expansion of potential). While strong elementary school counseling programs are destined for growth, they need to rely on strategic planning to help evaluate, monitor, and control their success and make needed adjustments in program design and delivery in order to *establish* their presence.

Elevate

Elevation of an elementary school counseling program is a process of maximizing its potential and stretching its capacity to achieve the far-reaching fulfillment of all that it has to give. Program elevation is achieved through masterful action plans that are designed to perfect the performance of elementary school counseling programs in providing children and other stakeholders (parents, teachers, administrators, and community) with superior services. The elevation phase contributes to the self-actualization of the elementary school counseling program in achieving its maturity and its purpose for being.

Elongate

After elementary school counseling programs establish and elevate their presence, they must concentrate on developing ways to elongate, to perpetuate their superior performance. Elementary school counseling programs move into and occupy a mode of continuous improvement. While no person or program will ever achieve perfection, both have the capacity for self-improvement. Truly successful and self-sustaining programs rely on their capacity for self-improvement so that they can help the children and the people they serve do the same for themselves.

THE STRATEGIC PLANNING PROCESS

As important as strategic planning is, it is equally important for the process to give way to action. Planning in the absence of movement

```
┌─────────────────────────────────────────────────┐
│              Strategic Planning Process          │
│                                                  │
│   Step 1:  Complete preplanning activities       │
│   Step 2:  Scan the external environment         │
│   Step 3:  Scan the internal environment         │
│   Step 4:  Create a vision for the future        │
│   Step 5:  Define the program mission            │
│   Step 6:  List desired program goals            │
│   Step 7:  Conduct a needs assessment            │
│   Step 8:  Establish priority goals              │
│   Step 9:  Develop program goals/curriculum      │
│   Step 10: Implement the program                 │
│   Step 11: Control for success                   │
└─────────────────────────────────────────────────┘
```

Figure 4.3.

is similar to thinking in the absence of doing—nothing is ever accomplished. What follows is an orderly and carefully thought-out sequence of activities that make up the strategic planning process (see Figure 4.3).

This process is designed to address the tripartite (see Figure 2.2) presented in Chapter 2. Children's needs, the behaviors to be learned, and the teaching-learning environment will be studied and recommendations made to support the healthy growth and development of all children through a comprehensive and developmentally focused elementary school counseling program.

Step 1: Complete Preplanning Activities

Before beginning a lengthy strategic planning process, we recommend that elementary schools

- create a rationale for developing a new elementary school counseling program or modifying an existing one.
- secure school board approval to begin strategic planning.
- identify, select, and train the elementary school counseling Program Advisory Committee (PAC).

Rationale

A Rationale Statement is a marketing tool that is designed to convince the school district, and in particular, the school board, that developing (modifying) an elementary school counseling program is in the best interest of children, the school district, and the community. The Rationale Statement is developed by a small committee (parent, teacher, administrator, and school board member) and chaired by a counselor in the school district's school counseling program. The committee seeks to answer the following questions in creating its Rationale Statement.

1. *Explain why* an elementary school counseling strategic plan is needed and how it can help the elementary school achieve its vision and mission.
2. *List the benefits* that children, teachers, parents, and others will experience if an elementary school counseling program is developed (revised).
3. *Provide evidence* from a variety of valid and reliable sources that speak to the benefits that a well-designed elementary school counseling program can deliver.
4. *Identify support* from within and outside the elementary school to create (revise) an elementary school counseling program.
5. *Acknowledge possible barriers* within and outside the elementary school that may need to be addressed if an elementary school counseling program is to become a reality or to be modified in some way.
6. *Raise questions* that have and are likely to surface from within and outside the school regarding developing (revising) an elementary school counseling program. Respond to these questions to the extent that answers are available.
7. *Outline* the steps to be taken in developing a strategic plan complete with a timetable.
8. *Request endorsements and support* from the administrators and school board to begin the strategic planning process.

School Board Approval

Once completed, the Rationale Statement is submitted to the school board (verbal and written report) for its review. The school board will ask themselves the following four questions and then make their recommendation regarding whether or not to endorse the development (revision) of an elementary school counseling program and to begin strategic planning.

1. How can our children, school district, and community benefit from having a new or improved elementary school counseling program?
2. Can we secure the necessary resources to support a new or modified elementary school counseling program (people, equipment, material, space, and so on)?
3. Do we have sufficient school and community support to initiate a new or modify an existing elementary school counseling program?
4. Are we committed to supporting an elementary school counseling program for the next five years?

Program Advisory Committee

After securing school board support for strategic planning to commence, the board will want to identify, select, and train their elementary school counseling Program Advisory Committee (PAC). The four key areas to consider when developing a PAC are (1) purpose, (2) membership and size, (3) selection, and (4) training and development (Rye & Sparks, 1999).

1. *Purpose.* PAC members will become actively involved in all facets of the strategic planning process. The membership will offer their support, suggestions, and thoughts regarding each draft of the planning document. They will participate in consensus building, help to create a universally supported blueprint for action, and serve as elementary school counseling program advocates in support of funding and programming.

2. *Membership and Size.* The membership should be broad enough in scope to represent the elementary school community and small enough to allow working together to accomplish its purpose. Key people to consider are teachers (K–6), administrators (elementary school principals), pupil support staff (special education, school psychologist, nurse, etc.), parents, and school board members (community representation). A school counselor, or someone very familiar with elementary school counseling programs and strategic planning, should chair the PAC.

3. *Selection.* Committee members can be secured through their response to a written public notice or invited to participate by the PAC chairperson and school administrator. Regardless of the method used, prospective participants will need specific information regarding the PAC's purpose, participant roles, skills sought, and expected time commitment (time frame, length of meetings, meeting dates, and so on).

4. *Training and Development.* PAC training sessions will focus on team building, disseminating needed information, and educating the membership concerning their duties. Four specific tasks should be addressed in training.

- **a.** *Team building:* Activities and experiences are needed that will help the membership bond with each other and function as a cohesive unit.
- **b.** *Understand elementary education:* PAC members will need to understand the vision and mission of elementary school education.
- **c.** *Understand elementary school counseling programs:* PAC members will need information about counseling programs and their purpose. More specifically, they will need to understand how they work in partnership with the school's mission in helping children to become effective self-managers and contributors to the society in which they live (Chapters 1 and 2).
- **d.** *Strategic planning:* PAC members will need information about strategic planning, its purpose, process, and tech-

niques. They will likewise need information about their roles and how they can help to make strategic planning a real success.

Step 2: Scan the External Environment

Elementary school counseling programs are in the people-building business. They are in the business of helping children to become caring human beings who will contribute to the building of caring communities (in and out of school). Community building begins with units of one connecting together to benefit all. Consequently, the PAC, in developing an elementary school counseling program, must consider the social, economic, political, educational, techno-logical, industrial, legal, medical, and environmental influences that either add to or detract from community building.

Quality Assessment

A quality assessment of the external environment seeks to identify the changes that are occurring within a community and what the im-pact of those changes are in facilitating positive human growth and caring or detracting from it. A quality environment assessment will help the PAC to develop an elementary school counseling program that is sensitive to the needs of the community and will help chil-dren to make caring choices that will benefit themselves, others, and their community. Helpful questions for PACs to consider when reviewing community profile data are the following:

- How is our community changing demographically, economi-cally socially, etc?
- What do social service agency statistics reveal about our com-munity? How do poverty, health statistics, crime, population di-versity, and employment patterns affect caring and community building in our community?
- What community needs exist today?
- What needs are anticipated tomorrow?

- What impact (caring or otherwise) is our community having on our children?
- What can a successful elementary school counseling program do to strengthen a sense of community at home, in school, and beyond the schoolhouse doors?

Successful elementary school counseling programs are sensitive to community needs and embrace the opportunity to create caring children building caring communities.

Purpose

The purpose of assessing the external environment is to develop more responsive elementary school counseling programs that will do a better job in people-building, connecting lessons of the classroom to real-life applications. Environmentally sensitive elementary school counseling programs create school environments in which children and communities grow stronger in their care of each other.

Process

PAC members must gather information that accurately reflects the health of their community. They need to assess their community's strengths, weaknesses, opportunities, and threats. This can be done by interviewing community leaders and surveying business people, blue-collar workers, and white-collar professionals regarding what they want their community to become versus what it is now. What must their community do to achieve its desired position? What do they want their community to have in the way of services, recreation, and opportunities? What do they want their community to give to its citizens and youth?

Community information (profile data) can be obtained from school districts, chambers of commerce, courthouses, social service agencies, and through interviews and surveys. This information will help elementary school counseling programs fulfill their people- and community-building missions.

Step 3: Scan the Internal Environment

Whether developing a new elementary school counseling program or breathing new life into an existing program (Chapter 11), a strategic plan needs to include an internal environmental assessment. This assessment is designed to yield information regarding an elementary school's capacity to support a new or sustain an existing elementary school counseling program.

Quality Assessment

A quality internal environmental scan is one that examines the elementary school's vision and mission statements and school profile data. Vision and mission statements that value caring children building caring communities have a people-building focus. Elementary school counseling programs share that same focus and are likely to form a strong, positive partnership with elementary schools that are moving in the same direction (Gysbers & Henderson, 2001).

Purpose

The purpose of conducting an internal environmental scan is to ascertain the degree to which the school community supports the kind of elementary school counseling program described in Chapter 2. This is important information to have when determining the strengths, weaknesses, opportunities, and potential threats that exist in developing an elementary school counseling program that supports caring children building caring communities.

Process

One of the best ways to conduct an internal environmental scan is to give all school personnel a copy of the rationale statement, school vision and mission statements, and a *reaction form,* including the following choices, so they can record their impressions regarding the proposed elementary school counseling program.

- I like this program.
- I have concerns about this program.
- I would suggest the following modifications.
- I would like to know more about this program.

Step 4: Create a Vision for the Future

The vision statement is the heart and soul of strategic planning. It represents the PAC's hopes, dreams, and shared image of a desired future state for its elementary school counseling program. Focused on the future, yet grounded in reality, vision statements enable planners to create a powerful image of what they want to create.

Quality

Scott, Jaffe, and Tobe (1993) have stated the following in reference to the qualities of a well-written vision statement.

- It motivates, inspires.
- It is a stretch, moves toward greatness.
- It is clear, concrete.
- It is achievable, not a fantasy.
- It fits with the highest values.
- It is easy to communicate, clear, and simple (p. 82).

Purpose

An elementary school counseling program vision statement

- sets a desired course of action;
- captures the essence, quality, and values of a desired future state;
- inspires and motivates;
- guides decision-making;
- gets people's attention;
- helps service providers and recipients connect with their purpose in turning the vision into reality; and
- challenges, compels, and instills action.

Writing a Vision Statement

Writing a vision statement for an elementary school counseling program requires the full participation of PAC members. Figure 4.4 outlines this process by presenting guidelines for the PAC chairperson.

A sample vision statement is presented in Figure 4.6. This statement reflects many of the points mentioned in the checklist (Figure 4.5).

Step 5: Define the Program Mission

The mission statement is a declaration of commitment and a call to action designed to operationalize the vision statement.

Quality

A quality mission statement seeks to answer three questions (Haines, 1995, p. 29). We have provided abbreviated responses to these questions as a way of giving some direction in stimulating further discussion.

Writing a Vision Statement

1. Explain the meaning of a vision statement (relate this definition to vision statements made by Dr. Martin Luther King, Jr., John F. Kennedy, etc.).
2. Have PAC members write and share their own personal life vision statements.
3. Explain that businesses, agencies, and companies have vision statements. Read a few examples.
4. Read and discuss your elementary school's vision statement.
5. Ask PAC members to form small groups and discuss what they envision for their children and community (a desired future state).
6. Introduce the idea of writing a vision statement for their elementary school counseling program.
7. Give PAC members a *checklist* of items to consider for inclusion in their vision statement (see Figure 4.5). The list should contain ideas from the American School Counselor Association National Standards, elementary school counseling program textbooks, and related resources.
8. Collect the checklist results and write one or more vision statements for the PAC to review, discuss, and adopt at its next meeting.

Figure 4.4. Writing a Vision Statement for an Elementary School Counseling Program.

Elementary School Counseling Program
Vision Statement Checklist
Sample

Directions: Read the following statements and check those that best describe your vision for a successful elementary school counseling program.

I want an elementary school counseling program that:	Agree	Disagree
1. serves all children.		
2. has an organized, sequential, and planned curriculum.		
3. is a part of our total elementary school program.		
4. offers child-centered services (group and individual counseling).		
5. stresses caring and community building.		
6. involves all school participants (parents, teachers, children, etc.).		
7. maintains a safe and caring school environment.		
8. meets the physical, personal/emotional, social, cognitive, and career and societal needs of all children.		
9. teaches children to become effective self-managers and community builders.		
10. teaches children to make caring choices that will benefit themselves, others, and the environment.		

Figure 4.5.

1. Why do we exist (*to meet children's needs*)?
2. Whom do we serve (*benefactors of services*)?
3. What do we produce (*caring services and caring environments*)?

Purpose

A well-defined mission statement will help the PAC to

- assess counseling programs, policies, and practices;
- make daily programmatic decisions;

Elementary School Counseling Program
Vision Statement
"Caring Children Building Caring Communities"

We envision an elementary school counseling program with a people-building focus in which children learn to create, package, and market themselves as independent, self-managing human beings capable of making legal, ethical, and moral decisions that will benefit themselves, others, and society.

We envision an elementary school counseling program that will meet the developmental and unique needs of all children in a child-centered, humanized, teaching-learning environment. The environment of which we dream will support an equal partnership between academic instruction and our counseling program in teaching children how to apply classroom lessons to life and living.

And lastly, we envision an elementary school counseling program that will involve the full participation of all school personnel and community supporters working together to help "caring children build caring communities."

Figure 4.6.

- identify priority program goals that embody the mission; and
- celebrate individuals, groups, and practices that reflect the mission.

Writing a Mission Statement

Figure 4.7 outlines the procedure to be followed in writing a mission statement.

The following mission statement template can be helpful in writing a short mission statement (Haines, 1995). "Our mission is to serve _____ (benefactors) with the following _____ (services) in order to achieve _____ (why we exist)." Figure 4.8 illustrates a sample elementary school counseling program mission statement that reflects the intent of the elementary school counseling vision statement in Figure 4.6.

Step 6: List Desired Program Goals

The vision and mission statements set the stage for determining the desired elementary school counseling program goals. These goals

---

Writing a Mission Statement

1. Define the meaning and purpose of a mission statement.
2. Explain that mission statements are short, specific, emanate from the vision statement, instill commitment, and provide direction for your elementary school counseling program.
3. Ask PAC members to write their responses to the following three questions after reviewing their elementary school counseling vision statement.
   a. Why do we exist?
   b. Whom do we serve?
   c. What do we produce?
4. Discuss the written responses to these questions and collect the response sheets.
5. Prepare (write) one or more mission statements from the collected information for PAC members to review, discuss, modify, and accept at the next PAC meeting.

Figure 4.7. Mission Statement Writing Guidelines.

are the ones that the elementary school and community feel strongly about and want included in their overall instructional plan for meeting children's needs, teaching desired behaviors, and establishing a safe and caring teaching-learning environment (the Tripartite).

Quality

Goals are the gateway to action. They help elementary school counseling programs focus on what they want to accomplish (caring

---

**Sample
Elementary School Counseling Program
Mission Statement**

We (counselors, teachers, parents, administration, and school board) are committed to providing a developmental elementary school counseling program that serves the needs (developmental, variant, and societal) of all children through a developmental, child-centered program and specialized services and interventions that work in partnership with our academic programs and community in providing classroom-to-life experiences that teach children how to live, learn, and work (caring children building caring communities).

Figure 4.8.

children building caring communities). Desired program goals reflect the five dimensions of development and caring. Those dimensions are physical, personal/emotional, social, cognitive, and career and societal (Part III, Chapters 6–10). These dimensions address all areas of child development and the societal responsibilities that children must learn and practice if they are to live satisfying and productive lives (Paisley, 2001). Desired program goals are of high quality to the extent that they are (Worzbyt, 1991)

- *realistic* (capable of being achieved using available resources),
- *clear and specific* (address the why, what, when, where, and how elements), and
- *value oriented* (fit the value system of the school and community).

Purpose

Desired elementary school counseling program goals provide the foundation for conducting the needs assessment. They reflect the best that elementary schools can hope for in helping children to create, package, and market themselves as capable and responsible human beings. A desired goals list sets the standards for quality and thus provides a benchmark worthy of attainment. Assessing the degree to which these goals are currently being achieved will help the elementary school counseling program eventually identify the priority needs and goals that will be targeted for program development.

Process (Select Desired Program Goals)

Figure 4.9 details the steps to be followed by the PAC chairperson in helping committee members to form their desired list of program goals.

Step 7: Conduct a Needs Assessment

Having developed the desired program goals list (20 goals), the PAC is now ready to assess the gaps that exist between where children

---

Elementary School Counseling Program
Desired Goals List Selection Process

1. Review vision and mission statements and identify the people-building values contained therein.
2. Discuss the four key questions that affect goal selection (see Chapter 2).
   • What do we want our children to **be?**
   • What do we want our children to **do?**
   • What do we want our children to **have?**
   • What do we want our children to **give?**
3. Brainstorm answers to these questions. Make a composite list of the responses.
4. Provide PAC members with a checklist (see Figure 4.10) of quality elementary school counseling goals that reflect the best ideas of the American School Counselor Association (standards), counseling textbooks, child developmental theorists, and state departments of education (Bureau of Elementary School Counseling Certification) have to offer. Arrange these goals according to the five dimensions of development and caring (physical, personal/emotional, social, cognitive, career and societal (see Figure 4.10).
5. Explain how the goals checklist (see Figure 4.10) was developed and ask PAC members to identify their top 20 desired goals.
6. Use the *four key questions* and the initial responses given to aid them in the goal selection process.
7. Collate the data and record the results on a blank checklist.
8. Discuss the results and reach consensus on the 20 most desired goals.
9. Rank order, by discussion and consensus, the top 20 desired goals in descending order from high desire to low desire.
10. Publish the desired goals list and distribute to the PAC.

Figure 4.9.

are in meeting these developmental and societal goals and where they need to be if they are to become caring and fully functioning self-managers and contributors to their communities.

Quality

Quality needs assessments are designed to determine the degree to which children are displaying desired behaviors and meeting their needs as identified in *the desired program goals list.* Asking the right questions is a critical first step in addressing the three legs of

---

Elementary School Counseling Program
Desired Goals Checklist

Physical Caring

What do we want our children to **Be, Do, Have, and Give?** Children have a need to develop positive attitudes, possess valid and reliable knowledge, and learn helpful skills that will enable them to care for their physical well-being and live a safe and healthy lifestyle.

_____ Learn how to be a responsible consumer of health-related information, services, and products (promotes school and community health)

_____ Learn about environmental issues that affect people's health and ways to promote environmental caring

_____ Care of body systems (diet, physical fitness, weight management, etc.)

_____ Understand what it means to be a boy/girl

_____ Accept and appreciate one's physical appearance

_____ Understand physical development and health care (personal appearance, grooming, etc.)

_____ Develop physical skills for playing ordinary games (throwing, catching, hand-eye coordination, balance, etc.)

_____ Practice safe health habits

_____ Assess and manage risk responsibility (learning to be safe)

_____ Other

Personal/Emotional Caring

What do we want our children to **Be, Do, Have, and Give?** Children have a need to develop positive attitudes, possess valid and reliable information, and learn helpful skills that will enable them to understand and care for their personal/emotional needs.

_____ Understand their personal strengths and limitations

_____ Explore their hopes, dreams, and personal aspirations

_____ Learn to understand and express emotions responsibly (emotional intelligence)

_____ Develop personal/emotional self-care strategies

_____ Learn how to use decision-making in choosing responsible, caring choices

_____ Develop core character traits (caring, kindness, honesty, respect, empathy, responsibility, self-discipline, patience, perseverance, and so on)

_____ Learn how to manage and enhance one's own self-esteem

_____ Learn impulse control and anger management strategies

(continued)

Figure 4.10.

***Personal/Emotional Caring* (cont.)**

_____ Practice effective communication skills (I-messages, listening, learning to be assertive)

_____ Learn how to use resistance skills in the face of adversity (saying no, walking away, assertive response, humor, and so on)

_____ Other

Social Caring

What do we want our children to **Be, Do, Have, and Give?** Children have a need to develop positive attitudes, possess valid and reliable information, and learn helpful skills that will enable them to understand and care for their social relationships with others.

_____ Develop caring relationships (manners, sharing, taking turns, compliments, asking for help, greeting others, starting a conversation, etc.)

_____ Learn and practice the power of diversity (understand, accept, and appreciate self and others, explore human differences and cultures, practice peacemaking and community building)

_____ Understand the nature of conflict and how to manage it through caring choices (strategies that resolve conflict peacefully)

_____ Develop and practice healthful family relationships (explore and practice ways to build strong families)

_____ Experience and practice caring and responsible friendship-making strategies

_____ Learn and practice caring strategies for building a sense of community in the classroom and school

_____ Other

Cognitive Caring

What do we want our children to **Be, Do, Have, and Give?** Children have a need to develop positive attitudes, possess valid and reliable information, and learn helpful skills that will enable them to understand and care for their cognitive and educational needs.

_____ Enhance ability to concentrate and pay attention in school

_____ Experience and practice memory strategies that will increase recall and understanding of what is being learned

_____ Develop and practice thinking skills that will enhance children's ability to process information (observing, comparing, classifying, making assumptions, hypothesizing, giving feedback, interpreting, imagining, summarizing, predicting, etc.)

(continued)

Figure 4.10. *(continued)*

Cognitive Caring (cont.)

_____ Explore and practice decision-making and its value in making caring choices

_____ Understand and practice a wide range of study skills and habits to improve learning

_____ Explore and practice strategies to challenge irrational thinking and develop methods to enhance rational thinking

_____ Learn how to set and achieve goals

_____ Learn how to develop and use an internal guidance system in differentiating right from wrong

_____ Other

Career and Societal Caring

What do we want our children to **Be, Do, Have, and Give?** Children have a need to develop positive attitudes, possess valid and reliable information, and learn helpful skills that will enable them to understand and care for themselves and their communities as citizens, workers, caregivers, volunteers, and people of leisure.

_____ Understand the value of work

_____ Develop pride in their work

_____ Learn why people work

_____ Understand how current learnings (self and academic) relate to life inside and outside the classroom

_____ Learn what it means to be a producer and consumer

_____ Experience what it is like to be a volunteer, caregiver, and worker

_____ Participate in hobbies and leisure activities that give purpose and meaning to life and living

_____ Become adaptive users of technology

_____ Contribute to the life of their community

_____ Become concerned stewards of the global environment

_____ Follow rules and laws that promote community living

_____ Other

Figure 4.10.   *(continued)*

the counseling program tripartite. Instruments need to be created that will seek to investigate:

1. Children's acquired developmental and societal behavioral strengths.

2. The academic curriculum (identifying developmental and societal behavioral strengths taught in the classroom).
3. Physical and psychological conditions of the school environment (the degree of environmental support provided to enhance the teaching-learning process).

Purpose

The three-pronged needs assessment process helps the PAC determine what child developmental behaviors have and have not been learned, what behaviors are and are not taught through the academic curriculum, and what kind of environmental supports exist to enhance the teaching and learning of desired behaviors (strengths). This information will help PAC members to:

- identify high need program goals;
- select and develop academic and school counseling experiences and delivery systems to meet these goals;
- enhance the physical and psychological teaching-learning climate to support goal attainment; and
- make targeted programmatic decisions that will affect budget, training, and development; public relations; and resource allocations (material, equipment, etc.) in meeting high-need program goals.

Assessment Instruments

Figures 4.11 through 4.13 represent sample assessment instruments that are designed to assess children's needs and behavioral strengths (see Figure 4.11), the academic curriculum and the behaviors taught (see Figure 4.12), and the school environment and its capacity to support children during the teaching-learning process (see Figure 4.13). These instruments are abbreviated in length due to the availability of space and are meant only to provide the reader with an overview of each assessment instrument (children's needs [Figure 4.11], curriculum [Figure 4.12], and school environment [Figure 4.13]).

Sample Items
Children's Needs Assessment
Grades 5 and 6

Directions: Read each sentence and circle your answer (Yes or No).

Physical Caring

1. I exercise daily.	Yes	No
2. I take care of myself (eat healthy, eye exam, go to dentist, etc.).	Yes	No
3. I like the way I look.	Yes	No
4. I have the physical skills for playing most games at home and school.	Yes	No
5. I feel safe at school.	Yes	No

Personal/Emotional Caring

6. I know my personal strengths and weaknesses.	Yes	No
7. It is okay for me to get angry.	Yes	No
8. I am comfortable with my feelings and emotions.	Yes	No
9. I have a positive self-esteem.	Yes	No
10. I know how to reduce stress in my life.	Yes	No

Social Caring

11. I have close friends at school.	Yes	No
12. I know how to resolve conflict between myself and others peacefully.	Yes	No
13. I get along with all members of my family.	Yes	No
14. I enjoy being around others who are different from me.	Yes	No
15. I feel like my classmates and teachers are like one happy family.	Yes	No

Cognitive Caring

16. I like to think and use my mind.	Yes	No
17. I listen and ask questions in school.	Yes	No
18. I know how to study for tests and receive good grades.	Yes	No
19. I can remember things that I learn (good memory).	Yes	No
20. If asked, I could write the steps used in making a good decision.	Yes	No

Career and Societal

21. I know why people work.	Yes	No
22. I am proud of my work at home and in school.	Yes	No

(continued)

Figure 4.11. Children's Needs (Behavioral Strengths) Assessment (Grades 5 and 6).

Career and Societal (cont.)

23. I have volunteered my time to help people in my
    community (rake leaves, shovel snow, clean up highway,
    collect food for the needy, etc.).   Yes   No
24. I can explain how what I learn in school can help me
    outside of school.   Yes   No

Figure 4.11. *(continued)*

Parallel instruments, using the same statements, can be constructed for teachers, parents, and administrators to use in recording their opinions of children's current behaviors. Here are two examples.

Parents:

My child exercises daily.   Yes   No   Not sure

Teachers/Administrators:

In my opinion, the percentage
of children that exercise daily
in my class is   0%   25%   50%   75%   100%

Parents, administrators, and community members (school board members) would use a parallel form of the teacher instrument. They would be asked to record their opinions concerning each statement as it would apply to their elementary school curriculum (grades K–6).

Process

Figure 4.14 offers some suggestions to PAC chairperson in conducting the following needs assessment activities.

Sample Items
Curriculum Assessment Survey
Teacher Version

Circle the grade level that you teach. K 1 2 3 4 5 6

Directions: The Elementary School Counseling Program Advisory Committee is seeking your assistance in determining the extent to which the following developmental behaviors are being taught at each grade level. Circle the number which best describes what is being taught at your grade level.

Not taught	Taught, but more needs to be done	Adequately taught	Too much is being done	Shouldn't be taught
1	2	3	4	5

Physical Caring

1. Daily exercise   1 2 3 4 5
2. Units on health care.   1 2 3 4 5

Personal/Emotional Caring

3. Emotional management training (feelings and how to express them).   1 2 3 4 5
4. Stress management training (reducing and managing stress safely).   1 2 3 4 5

Social Caring

5. Social skill training (developing peer relationships).   1 2 3 4 5
6. Conflict management training (resolving conflict peacefully).   1 2 3 4 5

Cognitive Caring

7. Thinking skills training (observing, comparing, hypothesizing, etc.).   1 2 3 4 5
8. Decision-making training (steps in making a decision).   1 2 3 4 5

Career and Societal Caring

9. Career awareness training (all about work—why people work, different occupations, importance of work, consumers and producers).   1 2 3 4 5
10. Community service and volunteerism training and practice.   1 2 3 4 5

Figure 4.12.

Sample Items
School Environment Assessment Survey

____ Teacher ____ Parent ____ Administrator ____ School Board Member

Directions: The Elementary School Counseling Program Advisory Committee (PAC) is seeking your assistance in assessing the school environment. This information will help PAC to better meet the needs of our children. Read each statement and write the number of the response which best reflects your opinion.

<u>0</u> Not sure   <u>1</u> No   <u>2</u> Yes   <u>3</u> Yes, but more needs to be done

---

Physical Climate   **# Response**

1. Children feel safe in school.
2. Children have time to exercise daily.
3. The school cafeteria serves healthy food.
4. The playground is a safe environment for children.
5. Our classrooms have adequate lighting.
6. Our classrooms are comfortable (temperature).
7. Our classrooms have adequate ventilation.
8. Our classrooms have adequate resources (videos, books, and materials) to teach people-building skills (items 12–20).

People-to-People Climate

9. Children treat each other fairly and with respect.
10. Our school is a peaceful, caring community.
11. Teachers, administrators, parents, and staff work together, care for each other, and care for children.

People-Building

I support the in-school teaching of:

12. Health care
13. Emotional management training
14. Stress management training
15. Social skills training
16. Conflict management training
17. Thinking skills training
18. Decision-making training
19. Career awareness
20. Community service and volunteer training
21. Diversity appreciation and awareness

(continued)

Figure 4.13.

Elementary School Counseling Program	# Response
22. I know what services our elementary school counseling program provides. 23. I support counselor-led classroom activities. 24. Teachers are people-builders who can help children develop people skills (items 12–21). 25. I would like to be included in our elementary school counseling program. 26. I would like to receive training in people-building (items 12–21).	

Comments: What ideas do you have for teaching children to care and to build caring school communities?

Figure 4.13. *(continued)*

Scoring

The easiest way to score the assessment surveys is to tally the results for each question asked and then convert the results to percentages. The same procedure can be used in scoring the parallel forms. For example, statement one on the Children's Needs Assessment Survey reads, "I exercise daily." If 100 children take the survey and respond to this statement, the distribution of *yes* and *no* responses would be converted to percentages and recorded on a blank form of the survey instrument. This process would be followed for all 24 statements. The 24 statements can now be rank ordered from high need (low percentage of yes responses) to low need (high percentage of yes responses). The same process would be followed when scoring the parallel forms for the Children's Needs Assessment Survey. All of the independent rankings can then be recorded on a Comparison Ranking Form (see Figure 4.15). After a review of the results, the PAC will develop an agreed-upon single ranking of the 24 goals based on need (high need to low need). Once this process is completed, we recommend reducing this list (24 goals) to the top 20 goals based on need.

The PAC should now have two lists of the same 20 goals, one ranked on the basis of desire (high desire—most important—to low

**Elementary School Counseling Program
Needs Assessment Process**

1. Describe the needs assessment process as a way of
   a. identifying gaps or discrepancies that exist between where your elementary school counseling program is now in relationship to where you would like it to be in meeting children's developmental and societal needs.
   b. placing the program goals in descending order from high need to low need.
   c. selecting program goals with the greatest need and targeting them for potential action.
2. Distribute the three needs assessment instruments to be used and discuss the purpose of each.
   a. *Children Needs Assessment Survey* and parallel forms for parents, teachers, administrators, and community members.
   b. *Curriculum Assessment Survey* and parallel forms.
   c. *School Environment Assessment Survey,* parallel forms not needed.
3. Explain that the instruments were developed by school personnel (PAC chairperson and counselors) to assess the status of children's needs in relationship to the 20 desired goals identified in Step 6. Discuss the three instruments, revise as needed, and approve each for distribution.
4. Distribute the assessment surveys to the various groups who will respond to them. Begin with the *Children's Needs Assessment Survey* and end with the *School Environment Assessment Survey.*
5. Collect the survey instruments and score the results.
6. Review the summary data for each survey. Compare the results obtained for each question asked (children, teachers, parents, administrators, and community). Then compare the children's needs assessment data with summary data from the curriculum assessment and the environmental assessment. Discuss the findings.
   a. Which children's needs are being met and which ones are not?
   b. To what degree is the curriculum involved in teaching children the desired behaviors?
   c. To what degree is the school environment giving support to the teaching and learning of the desired developmental behaviors?
7. Using answers to the above questions, conduct a SWOT analysis on the degree to which the desired elementary school counseling program goals are being met.
   S = Program Strengths: What are our strengths? In what areas are we doing well (meeting needs, strong curriculum, supportive environment)?
   W = Program Weaknesses: What are our weaknesses, areas where we are falling below our expectations?

(continued)

Figure 4.14.

O = Opportunities: What opportunities have become apparent in our survey data that can be used to strengthen our program?

T = Threats: What did we learn from the survey data that could threaten our program (lack of resources, people opposed to elementary school counseling, etc)?

8. Using the SWOT assessment information, rank order the 20 program goals in descending order on the basis of need (high need—goals are not being met to low need—goals are being met).

9. The same 20 goals have now been ranked twice. The first ranking was based on desire (Step 6: List Desired Program Goals) and the second ranking is based on need. Keep these lists as they will be used in Step 8 to identify the priority goals list for your elementary school counseling program.

Figure 4.14. *(continued)*

Children's Needs Assessment Survey
Comparison Ranking of Goal Statements Based on Need

KEY: High Need (1) to Low Need (24)

Need Areas	Children	Teachers	Parents	Principal	Final Ranking
Physical Caring					
1. Children exercise daily.	7	4	24	3	
Personal/Emotional Caring					
6. Know personal strengths and weaknesses	10	3	6	2	
Social Caring					
11. Have close friends in school.	3	15	3	5	
Cognitive Caring					
16. Like thinking and using my mind.	1	2	5	1	
Career and Societal Caring					
21. Know why people work.	18	20	20	21	

Figure 4.15.

desire—less critical), and the second list is ranked on the basis of need (high need to low need). These two lists will be used in Step 8 to determine the priority elementary school counseling program goals.

Step 8: Establish Priority Goals

The PAC is now ready to select the elementary school counseling program goals. These goals will become the focal point for program activity.

Quality

We believe that quality program goals are ones that are desirable because they are developmentally and societally sound. They represent what we would like children to Be, Do, Have, and Give. In addition, quality goals also demonstrate an element of need in that there is a proven gap (needs assessment data) between where children are (attitude, skills, and knowledge) and where we would like them to Be. Consequently, quality elementary school counseling programs allocate their time, energy, and resources to program goals that are both desired (educationally sound) and needed (gaps in attainment).

Purpose

When elementary school counseling programs target goals that are desirable and needed, they are making the most of their people-building effort and resources. The purpose of Step 8 is to identify those high-priority goals that reflect desire (developmentally and academically sound) and need (gaps in attainment).

Process

The priority goals selection process is detailed in Figure 4.16.

Once the high-priority program goals have been selected, the PAC will need to make decisions regarding what existing elementary school counseling program services to continue or discontinue and what new programs and services to add. The committee will also need to make

Elementary School Counseling Program
Priority Goal Selection Process

1. Compare the desired program goals list with the needs goal list.

Desired Program Goals List	**Needs Program Goals List**
1. High desire	1. High need
2.	2.
3.	3.
.	.
.	.
.	.
20. Low desire	20. Low need

2. Review the purpose of the two lists. The Desired Goal List is what the PAC believes all children should accomplish to be fully functioning and caring people. The Needs Goal List reflects what is and what is not being accomplished in terms of children acquiring the desired goal outcomes.

3. Create a grid which depicts the interaction of the two goal lists (desire and need).

DESIRE

		High	Low
N High		High Desire (a) High Need	Low Desire (c) High Need
E			
E			
D Low		High Desire (b) Low Need	Low Desire (d) Low Need

4. Arrange the goals from the two lists into four categories
   a. *High Desire—High Need*
      These goals are high-priority goals and warrant the attention of the PAC in allocating needed resources in support of goal attainment.
   b. *High Desire—Low Need*
      These goals are important (high desire) and are being met (low need). The PAC will need to decide if any adjustments in the current allocation of resources are warranted.
   c. *Low Desire—High Need*
      These goals are considered desirable (among the top 20), but are not being met (high need). The PAC will need to decide if they wish to allocate resources to these goals or concentrate their efforts on high desire—high need goals.

(continued)

Figure 4.16.

> d. *Low Desire—Low Need*
>   These goals are considered desirable (among the top 20) and are being met (low need). The PAC will need to evaluate resource allocations to these goals and make adjustments as warranted.
> 5. Select a small number of high-priority goals to target. Conduct a final review of these goals to ensure that they clearly
>   • address children's developmental and societal needs,
>   • support the elementary school's vision and mission,
>   • support the elementary school counseling program vision and mission, and
>   • reflect what the school and community want for their children.
> 6. List the top-priority elementary school counseling program goals.

Figure 4.16. *(continued)*

decisions regarding the allocation and redistribution of needed resources to support the new school counseling program goals.

Step 9: Develop Program Goals/Curriculum

Programs goals give direction, but they do not provide a road map for getting there. Program goals need to be operationalized before their true value can be attained. For that to occur, program goals need resources to support activities, activities to support objectives, and objectives to support goals. What follows is information that will help elementary school counseling programs to develop people-building goals that will teach children how to learn, live, and work from a caring perspective.

Quality

Quality people-building program goals and experiences are designed to support normal growth and development, academic learning, the acquisition of life skills, and classroom-to-life understandings and applications that promote caring and the building of caring communities. Quality people-building program goals and experiences are organized around the five dimensions of development (Chapters 6–9) and those competencies targeted in the needs assessment. And lastly, quality program goals and experiences

- benefit the growth and development of children,
- are part of an organized and planned elementary school counseling curriculum,
- are integrated into the elementary school's instructional program, and
- involve the participants of all people-builders (children, teachers, parents, support staff, administrators, and so on).

Purpose

The purpose of developing program goals is to operationalize the people-building potential that these goals have to offer. Furthermore, the purpose of following a goal-development plan is to enhance the likelihood that all program goals will be well thought out and will yield the desired outcome resulting in a quality elementary school counseling program.

Process

Rye and Sparks (1999) have developed a very comprehensive, yet easy-to-follow process in operationalizing elementary school counseling goals. They begin by stating that there are two basic types of goals that need to be addressed in program development: *program management goals and program outcome goals.* The program outcome goals are those goals that we have referred to as high-priority people-building goals (Step 7: Conduct a Needs Assessment), while the management goals detail prior actions that must be taken to ensure outcome-goal success. For example, the success of program outcome goals hinges on attaining such managerial goals and decisions as the following:

- *Resources:* What resources will be needed (materials, equipment, people, etc.) to achieve the desired goal outcomes?
- *Training:* Will training of service providers be required to achieve the desired goal outcomes?
- *Dates/Time/Location:* What details need to be finalized to achieve the desired goal outcomes?

- *Receivers of Services:* Who will benefit from the goal outcomes? How will the receivers be identified, by whom, by what means, when, and why are these receivers being selected?
- *Cost:* How much will the outcome goals cost in money, time, effort, and resources?
- *Politics:* What steps must be taken, by whom, and under what time frame to obtain the necessary clearances?

Program outcome goals hinge on the successful management of those areas just mentioned. When this occurs, children's developmental and societal needs are more likely to be met through successful goal attainment. The end result is that successful elementary school counseling programs will have a significant role to play in a people-building process that produces caring children building caring communities.

Figure 4.17 illustrates the interaction of *management goals and objectives and outcome goals and objectives* in program development. We have selected as an example the Personal/Emotional Caring Dimension of Development and one priority goal to be addressed in grades K–3. Additional *high-priority program goals* would be developed in the same manner as illustrated.

A format for developing session activities is presented in Chapters 6–10. Other examples of activity outlines can be found in most elementary school counseling activity source books.

Figure 4.18 provides suggested guidelines for PAC members to follow in developing their elementary school counseling program goals. The major role of PAC members in Step 9 of strategic planning will be to review the program curriculum as it is being developed. They can ask questions, offer comments and suggestions, and raise potential concerns regarding specific goals and activities.

The resource audit (see Figure 4.19) is helpful in determining needed resources and identifying program-management goals to be addressed in securing those resources. Completing this step is necessary in helping PAC members to decide the feasibility of being able to achieve specific program goals as designed. When needed

Personal/Emotional Caring
Grades K–3

High Desire and High Need: Children have a need to understand and express their emotions.

Goal: To teach children how to understand and express their emotions.

Management Objectives:

1. By September 1st, materials (children's booklets and teacher manuals) will be purchased for a teacher in-service on *emotional management.*
2. On October 15th, a three-hour, teacher training for all K–3 teachers will be held in the large-group training room (9:00 a.m.–noon).
3. On October 22nd, teachers will teach session 1 in the emotions management program and will conduct weekly sessions until the six-session program is completed.
4. Beginning on October 22nd, the elementary school counselor will collect weekly assessment data (goal outcome surveys) and meet briefly (10 to 15 minutes) with each teacher (6 teachers) to discuss program results and answer questions pertaining to the next weekly session.

Outcome Objectives:

By the end of the six-week emotions management program, 85% of the children (K–3) will be able to

a. Name four feelings (sad, angry, happy, afraid).
b. Match four feeling words with faces expressing these feelings.
c. Identify the feelings of children in their class (by facial expressions).
d. Share one personal experience for each feeling (sad, angry, happy, afraid).
e. Name three things (strategies) they can do to feel better when they are sad, angry, or afraid.

Strategies/Activities:

1. Counselor will conduct a three-hour training session for teachers in grades K–3 on emotions management training (October 15, 9:00 a.m.–noon).
2. Teachers (K–3) will help children to understand and express their feelings using a six-session series on emotions management training.

    Session 1: Introduction: "What Are Feelings?"
    Session 2: Feeling/Words Game
    Session 3: Feelings, Facial Expressions, and Body Signs
    Session 4: Understanding My Feelings
    Session 5: Understanding Others' Feelings
    Session 6: Taking Care of Me: What Can I Do to Feel Better?

Figure 4.17. Elementary School Counseling Program Goal Development.

Elementary School Counseling Program
Steps in Developing High-Priority Goals

1. List the priority program goals that will be targeted for this year.
2. Review these goals to ensure that they reflect the following:
   a. Elementary school program vision and mission.
   b. Elementary school counseling program design and mission.
   c. Children's developmental and societal needs.
   d. Community needs.
3. Develop each goal following the outline in Figure 4.17.
4. Conduct a resource audit (see Figure 4.19) for each goal to be developed.
5. Discuss program goal strengths, potential weaknesses, opportunities, and threats.
6. Review and revise program goals, objectives, activities, and resources to strengthen goal outcomes.

Figure 4.18.

Priority Program Goal
Resource Audit

Goal: To teach children how to understand and express their emotions

Resources	Needed Resources Is this resource needed? Yes/No	Resource Availability Is this resource available? Yes/No	Resource Not Available Is it possible to acquire this resource? Yes/No
Special Training			
Money			
Equipment			
Materials			
Space			
Time			
School Support			
Community Support			
Other			

Figure 4.19.

resources are unavailable, modification in program design will be necessary.

After developing elementary school counseling program goals (resources, activities, objectives, and goals), key program goal information can be transferred to program-planner sheets, one sheet for each goal to be addressed (see Figure 4.20). Program planners are helpful memory aids because they provide counselors with the key information they need for each program priority goal being targeted for that year. The program planner identifies multiple delivery methods that may be utilized to address the same goal, service providers, service recipients, needed resources, budget allocations, and a calendar of activities.

Elementary School Counseling Program Planner

Grade level(s): K–3
Goal Area: Personal/Emotional Dimension
Goal(s): To help children understand and express their emotions.
Intervention: Write the intervention method(s) to be used and provide the information needed: Individual counseling, group counseling, classroom guidance, curriculum integration, other _____.

Goal Support Information	Intervention 1 _____	Intervention 2 _____	Intervention 3 _____
Management Outcome Objectives			
Service Provider(s)			
Service Recipient(s)			
Resources			
Budget			
Calendar			

Figure 4.20.

Information taken directly from the program planners can then be used to create a yearly

- budget,
- calendar, and
- resource list.

Step 10: Implement the Program

Program implementation involves moving the elementary school counseling program from the "drawing room" to the classroom (action). Strategic planning is of little value if elementary school counseling programs never move from a created vision to reality.

Quality

Successful elementary school counseling programs achieve their success through a two-phase process of program implementation. Phase one is *orientation. Orientation* is designed to aid school personnel, children, families, and community volunteers in their understanding and utilization of elementary school counseling programs. Phase two, *training and development,* is designed to prepare school personnel, children, families, and community volunteers to become service providers in the elementary school counseling program.

Purpose

The purpose of program implementation is to help everyone in the school and community to understand that they have something valuable to gain and give as elementary school counseling program service recipients and providers. We want everyone to understand that they have an important role to play as people-builders helping children to learn, live, and work as caring human beings contributing to caring communities. We believe that a successful orientation and training plan will result in

- children succeeding in school and life.
- school and community members using elementary school counseling program services.
- school and community members providing elementary school counseling program services.

Process

We begin with the orientation phase, which involves meeting with children, parents, teachers, administrators, and community members and sharing with them the elementary school counseling program story, what it has to offer, how they can benefit from program services, and steps they can take to receive services. Orientation never ends because there is always more to say about your program, additional people to contact, and new projects and services to promote. A major aspect of program orientation is public relations. Your goal is to keep the public informed, generate enthusiasm and excitement about elementary school counseling, publicize your successes, and encourage the involvement of others as service recipients and providers. Figure 4.21 provides some suggestions for establishing an exciting orientation program.

As with orientation, training also is an important aspect of implementing and maintaining a dynamic and successful elementary school counseling program. All members of the school and community have a significant role to play in shaping the lives of children, including the children themselves. Everyone needs to learn about their people-building potential and how they can contribute to the growth and development of others and especially of children. One aspect of training is sensitizing people to their responsibilities as people-builders and then developing that potential through training. Figure 4.22 provides some suggestions for developing a dynamic training and development plan (Silberman, 1990).

As more people become providers of services, the elementary school counseling program will be able to increase the quantity and

---

Elementary School Counseling Program
Orientation Guidelines

1. Identify your target audience (children, teachers, parents, community members, etc.). Eventually you will want to target all people who are major stakeholders in your program.
2. Review your strategic planning information (community profile, vision and mission statements, needs assessment data, targeted program goals, etc.). Identify your program strengths, weaknesses, opportunities, and threats (SWOT).
3. Decide what you want your message to be for the target audience selected. Your goal is to excite your audience about what your program has to offer. Create, package, and market your program in ways that stimulate audience involvement.
4. Identify the target-audience orientation goals that you most want to achieve now (example: target-audience goals for children):
   a. To inform children who their counselor is.
   b. To inform children what the counselor does.
   c. To demonstrate for children people-building experiences.
   d. To involve children in a people-building experience.
   e. To show children where the counselor's office is located.
   f. To tell children how they can meet with their counselor.
5. Identify activities and secure needed resources to meet your orientation goals.
6. Identify the strategies that you will use to communicate the above goals (audio sound system, activities, puppet show, art work, songs, games, video message, signs)
7. Create a detailed orientation plan consisting of management objectives, outcome objectives, activities, and resources.
8. Establish an orientation calendar of events (6 months to 1 year).
9. Determine your orientation budget and costs.
10. Execute your orientation plan.

Figure 4.21.

quality of its services and expand its visibility, intensity, and energy (Chapter 5).

Step 11: Control for Success

Controlling is a proactive process designed to detect and correct significant deviations between program goal outcomes and program goal standards established during strategic planning.

Elementary School Counseling Program
Training and Development Guidelines

1. Identify your target audience and the active training program to be implemented (e.g., select a core group of children to be trained as peer helpers or study buddies. Children will learn that they have something to give to others as people-builders.
2. Set general outcome goals. (What do you want children to Be, Do, Have, and Give as a result of this training?)
3. Conduct a resource audit and determine management goals to be addressed before the peer-helper training begins.
4. Identify the specific outcome objectives that support each general outcome goal. The objectives are to specify the what, when, where, who, why, and how aspects of goal attainment.
5. Design training activities to support the goals and objectives to be met. These activities (simulation, role plays, games, skill builders, etc.) should be written on index cards as this will provide more flexibility in sequencing learning experiences.
6. Sequence your activities so that they support your training experience.
7. Fill in the details. Describe how each activity will be conducted, what materials will be needed, how the teaching-learning environment should be arranged, set reasonable time limits, and decide how to conclude each experience in order to enhance learning.
8. Rehearse your training agenda and make revisions where necessary.
9. Implement your training package.
10. Evaluate the results. Use role-plays, simulations, and paper-and-pencil assessments to determine participant capabilities in performing the desired training outcomes.

Figure 4.22.

Quality

While each priority program goal has specific and unique criteria to be evaluated, there are five general criteria that apply to all program goals. These long-standing and significant criteria are appropriateness, adequacy, effectiveness, efficiency, and side effects (Craig, 1978). They represent the benchmarks of quality when controlling for program success.

1. *Appropriateness:* This is basically a value-laden category that questions the suitability of chosen resources, activities, objectives, and goals to meet children's developmental and societal needs. The challenge is to offer evidence to support the selected program goal priorities and the methodology being used to achieve the desired results.

2. *Adequacy:* Program goals are likely to be met if they are adequate to the extent that resources, activities, and objectives are sufficient in quantity and quality to produce the desired results.

3. *Effectiveness:* Program resources, activities, and objectives may be appropriate and adequate, but are they effective (capable of producing the desired results)? Ineffective goal plans may need to be modified or replaced to increase their effectiveness (resources, activities, objectives, and goals).

4. *Efficiency:* Program goals may be appropriate, adequate, and effective, but are they efficient in terms of their cost-effectiveness (time, money, personnel required, etc.)? This can be determined by comparing the estimated costs with the actual costs in light of the results obtained. Do the achieved results justify the expenditure of resources, or is there a more efficient process to be explored?

5. *Side Effects:* Every program goal will produce anticipated and unanticipated results, some of which may be considered positive (helpful) and others negative (hurtful). The goal is to take full advantage of positive side effects (anticipated and unanticipated) while minimizing or eliminating the undesirable side effects. This may require some modifications in resources, activities, objectives, and goals.

Purpose

Controlling helps to ensure that children's needs (developmental and societal) are being met through targeted program behaviors and that the teaching-learning process supports the acquisition of these behaviors. Thus the purpose of controlling is to identify the degree to which targeted behaviors are being met so that effective decisions can be made requiring corrective action in keeping the elementary school counseling program on course (Trevisan & Hubert, 2001).

Process

Controlling for program success consists of three definitive steps.

1. Monitor and measure program performance and its impact in meeting children's needs.
2. Compare program performance results with program standards (criteria).
3. Ascertain the difference (acceptable-unacceptable) and implement corrective action if necessary.

The controlling process evaluates what is currently happening in terms of meeting children's needs, the behaviors to be learned, and the teaching-leaning environment (tripartite) and compares these results with what is expected in these areas. This process is depicted in Figure 4.23.

Three types of controlling methods are typically used when conducting an ongoing assessment of elementary school counseling pro-

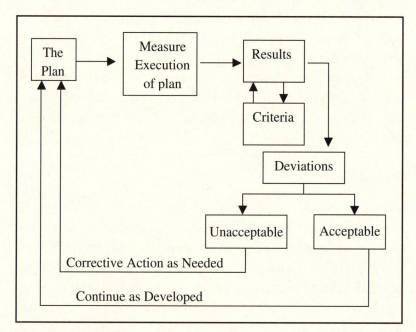

Figure 4.23. The Control Process.

grams. They are preliminary control, concurrent control, and feedback control (Donnelly, Gibson, & Ivancevich, 1981).

- **Preliminary Control:** Preliminary control represents the steps taken by counselors and PAC members to determine if what they are doing programmatically is consistent with their vision and mission statements (academic instruction and school counseling programs). Preliminary control helps elementary school counseling programs to stay focused and goal directed. Any deviations identified will require discussion and corrective actions to be taken.
- **Concurrent Control:** Concurrent control involves the ongoing monitoring and fine-tuning of counseling program plans as they are being implemented. This is done to achieve the desired performance outcomes. Concurrent control recognizes the imperfections that exist in program planning and implementation and allows for minor adjustments to be processed as program goals, objectives, activities, and the use of resources unfold.
- **Feedback Control:** Feedback control occurs after program goals, objectives, and activities have been completed. Participants and service providers can step back from what they have experienced and evaluate what did and did not work. Surveys, observations, and interviews are often used to improve program results (meet counseling program standards).

All three types of control measures are critical to the success of any elementary school counseling program in responding to the following questions:

1. Did our program (priority program goals) satisfy the five general criteria (appropriateness, adequacy, effectiveness, efficiency, and side effects)?
2. Did our program plan have a significant and positive impact on meeting children's needs?
3. Was our program plan in keeping with our vision and mission statements?

4. What corrective actions, if any, are warranted in resources, activities, objectives, and goals to bring our goal performance outcomes and standards in line with each other?

Figure 4.24 outlines controlling guidelines that will assist elementary school counselors and PAC members in controlling for program success.

Elementary School Counseling Program
Controlling for Success

1. Determine what program areas to evaluate.
   - Behaviors to be learned
   - Curriculum assessments (academic and counseling)
   - Environmental assessments (physical and psychological)
2. Identify the questions to investigate.
   - To what degree (in percentages) are children acquiring the desired behaviors (priority program goal standards)?
   - To what degree are academic and counseling program curriculums successful in teaching the behaviors to be learned (resources, activities, objectives, goals)?
   - To what degree is the teaching-learning environment supporting the teaching-learning process?
3. Decide what information needs to be collected, who will collect it, from whom it will be collected, and what methods will be used to collect it. Also, calculate the cost to conduct your assessment.
4. Be sure to use data collected from all three methods of controlling (preliminary control, concurrent control, and feedback control) when assessing counseling program results.
5. Conduct your program assessment and collect your data.
6. Review the collected data and develop a report that answers your program assessment questions.
   - Are children acquiring the behaviors to be learned (performance standards versus performance outcomes for each program goal)?
   - Are the academic and school counseling program curriculums (resources, activities, objectives, and goals) teaching children the behaviors they need to learn?
   - Is the school's teaching-learning environment supporting the behaviors to be learned? Has the school done all it can do to improve the teaching-learning environment?

(continued)

Figure 4.24.

7. Make sure the right information gets to the right people at the right time. Information needs to be presented in a way that increases the probability of its acceptance. Present the data clearly (tables and narration), make specific and objective written recommendations, and indicate the benefits for implementing them and pitfalls if they are not implemented. Report this information to those who have the power to make decisions and act on them. And lastly, timing is everything. Determine when the decision-maker must have this information to make timely and cost-effective decisions.

8. Report what corrective actions need to be taken
   - Identify the people who will be responsible for implementing the corrective actions.
   - Provide a detailed accounting of the corrective actions to be taken to include modifications in resources, activities, objectives, and goals.
   - Submit a timetable for the completion of the corrective actions.
   - Provide a schedule for reporting program actions being taken.
   - Provide a description of the accepted reporting format (verbal feedback, written, and so on) and the names of those individuals who are to receive the feedback.

Figure 4.24. *(continued)*

The controlling function requires the expenditure of time, money, and human resources to keep an elementary school counseling program viable and goal directed in meeting its vision and mission. Often this process must be accomplished using crude assessment measures and incomplete and fragmented data. Despite these imperfections, we believe the time and effort spent trying to help children become caring human beings building caring communities is well worth the struggle.

For school counseling programs and individuals that have neglected controlling for success, the long-standing and timely words of Gilbert Wrenn (1962) may encourage all elementary school counselors to overlook their assessment inadequacies and the problems associated with controlling and take the plunge. *"More mistakes can be made by counselors who assume they know, but never attempt to find out than by counselors who conduct studies, but do so poorly"* (p. 146).

BIBLIOGRAPHY

Bean, W.C. (1993). *Strategic planning that makes things happen: Getting from where you are to where you want to be.* Amherst, MA: Human Resource Development Press, Inc.

Craig, D.P. (1978). *Hip pocket guide to planning and evaluation.* San Diego, CA: Learning Concepts.

Dahir, C.A., Sheldon, C.B., & Valiga, M.J. (1998). *Vision into action: Implementing the national standards for school counseling programs.* Alexandria, VA: American School Counselor Association.

Donnelly, J.H., Jr., Gibson, J.L., & Ivancevich, J.M. (1981). *Fundamentals of management* (4th ed.). Plano, TX: Business Publications.

Gysbers, M.G., & Henderson, P. (2001). Comparing guidance and counseling programs: A rich history and a bright future. *Professional School Counseling, 4,* 246–256.

Gysbers, N.C., Lapan, R.T., & Jones, B.A. (2000). School board policies for guidance and counseling: A call to action. *Professional School Counseling, 3,* 349–355.

Haines, S.G. (1995). *Successful strategic planning: Building a high-performance business.* Menlo Park, CA: Crisp Publications, Inc.

Maslow, H.A. (1954). *Motivation and personality.* New York: Harper & Row.

Paisley, P.O. (2001). Maintaining and enhancing the developmental focus in school counseling programs. *Professional School Counseling, 4,* 271–277.

Rye, R.D., & Sparks, R. (1999). *Strengthening k–12 school counseling programs: A support system approach* (2nd ed.). Philadelphia, PA: Accelerated Development.

Scott, C.D., Jaffe, D.T., & Tobe, G.R. (1993). *Organizational vision, values, and mission: Building the organization of tomorrow.* Menlo Park, CA: Crisp Publications, Inc.

Silberman, M. (1990). *Active training: A handbook of techniques, designs, case examples, and tips.* San Diego, CA: University Associates, Inc.

Trevisan, M.S., & Hubert, M. (2001). Implementing comprehensive guidance program evaluation support: Lessons learned. *Professional School Counseling, 4,* 225–228.

Worzbyt, J.C. (1991). *Beating the odds.* Altoona, PA: R.J.S. Films.

Wrenn, G. (1962). *The counselor in a changing world.* Washington, DC: American Personnel and Guidance Association.

VanZandt, Z., & Hayslip, J. (2001). *Developing your school counseling program: A handbook for systematic planning.* Belmont, CA: Brooks/Cole.

CHAPTER 5

Meeting Program Goals through Effective and Efficient Decision-Making

Elementary school counseling program goals are defined and refined as part of the strategic planning process. The attainment of these program goals ultimately leads to children's attainment of the competencies in the various caring and development domains: physical, personal/emotional, social, cognitive, and career and societal. Since the elementary school counseling program by design is developmental, comprehensive, and collaborative, it is to address the needs of all children and it involves the efforts of all school personnel to achieve its people-building mission. At first glance, such an all-encompassing program can seem overwhelming and labor and time intensive. However, if there is an organized system of program delivery and a defined process that guides counselors and other school personnel in the implementation of these services, it is our belief that an effective elementary school counseling program can achieve its people-building mission with relative ease. In essence, it is possible to maximize the use of program resources and interventions so that the greatest amount of programming and services can be available to the total school population (Adelman & Taylor, 2002).

An organized system of delivery and a defined process that guides counselors in the implementation of services is thus critical to an elementary school counseling program's success. We have developed a systematic and planned process for elementary school counseling programs. The Ternary Decision-Making Model is based on the community mental health prevention model (Caplan, 1964) and is applied to the school setting. The Ternary Decision-Making Model is designed to provide a systematic and structured process that ensures an elementary school counseling program is consistent with its *mission and vision.* It is designed to continuously direct the decision-making process so that all children's *developmental* needs are addressed. It is a *comprehensive* delivery system in that it focuses and directs the resources of the program to enhance or to remediate children's developmental and special needs. It involves multiple service providers in a *collaborative* effort to deliver the best possible interventions to meet children's needs.

THE TERNARY DECISION-MAKING MODEL

The model has a comprehensive organized delivery system and it provides a detailed decision-making guide for the implementation of program services. Elementary school counseling programs that implement such a system and a decision-making process enhance their programs and utilize their resources efficiently.

An Organized System of Delivery

Drawing on the community mental health model, the program divides program service into three intervention categories: primary intervention, secondary intervention, and tertiary intervention. The focus of primary intervention level is developmental. Primary interventions are provided so that there are few to no incidences in which children's learning is disrupted or interrupted. In fact, all primary interventions are designed to foster positive growth for all individuals *before* disruptions in learning can occur. Secondary intervention is designed to provide program services to a child whose learning is being interrupted or disrupted and to a child whose learning could be enhanced by more targeted growth-producing exercises. The last level of intervention is tertiary intervention, and it is imple-

The Ternary Model	
Intervention Level	**Delivery Systems**
Primary	Curriculum Integration Classroom Guidance Curriculum Peer and Parent Helping Programs

Secondary	Collaboration
	Consultation
	Counseling
	    Individual
	    Group

Tertiary	Referral Placement Follow-up Reintegration

Figure 5.1. The Ternary Model—Intervention Levels and Delivery Systems.

mented when the child's learning becomes so compromised that the school can no longer provide the necessary services to maintain active progress in the school setting. In this case, the efforts to assist the child focus on the use of resources available within the community.

Within each of these intervention levels, there are several delivery systems. The delivery systems are the actual strategies that are utilized at that level (see Figure 5.1). How these intervention levels and delivery systems are utilized is the main focal point of the Ternary Decision-Making Model. The decision-making process is detailed in the following section.

A Defined Process of Implementation

The Ternary Decision-Making Model utilizes a simple decision-making process whereby a series of questions can be used to make intervention decisions and thus choose and target interventions (primary, secondary, tertiary) so that they meet both the developmental and unique needs of all children. The questions are:

1. Are the child's needs developmental and are they being served through curriculum integration, the classroom guidance curriculum, and other school-wide programs? (Primary Intervention)

2. Does evidence exist indicating that primary intervention methods are not working? If so, can individualized interventions (collaboration, consultation, or counseling) be used to assist or enhance the child's learning? (Secondary Intervention)

3. Does evidence exist indicating that secondary intervention methods are not working? If so, what other resources (community services) can be tapped to help facilitate meeting the needs of the child? (Tertiary Intervention)

The questions are asked in sequence. If there is an affirmative answer to a question, then the appropriate delivery system (for that level) is implemented. A full presentation of the Ternary Decision-Making Model in action is presented later in this chapter.

THE STRENGTHS AND BENEFITS OF THE TERNARY MODEL

The three intervention levels, a variety of delivery systems, and a broad range of service providers associated with the Ternary Decision-Making Model allow counselors to maximize the utilization of elementary school counseling program resources in achieving the best results in meeting children's developmental and unique needs as described in the tripartite. An examination of the intervention benefits of the Ternary Decision-Making Model follows.

Programmatic Benefits of the Ternary Model

Counseling programs typically favor one of three types of interventions: developmental, remedial, or crisis intervention. The Ternary Decision-Making Model integrates all three types of intervention in varying combinations that will best meet the needs of children. The Ternary Decision-Making Model enables counselors to examine children's needs with respect to selecting the most effective and efficient intervention strategies. It requires counselors to "slow down" their actions and to carefully consider (decide) what level of intervention will best meet the children's needs. The end result of the implementation of the Ternary Decision-Making Model is that children will be served by intervention strategies that are in keeping with an elementary school counseling program that is developmental, collaborative, and comprehensive in nature.

The Ternary Decision-Making Model has a high focus on development and prevention. When implemented as described, the benefits of primary intervention affect the lives of children schoolwide. When primary intervention strategies are implemented, they lessen the need for secondary and tertiary interventions. The following example illustrates this point. Derek enters a school whose counseling program is not based on a Ternary Decision-Making Model. He struggles because he has not been exposed to any cognitive skill-building activities. As he progresses through school, his struggles increase, and he begins to retreat from the learning process. He starts to develop minor behavioral problems. He rarely completes his homework and is lacking in test-taking skills. By the time Derek reaches the sixth grade, he is nearly totally withdrawn from the learning process and school community. His attendance at school is sporadic. Due to the number of absences, his case is now at a crisis state, and he has to be referred to the truant officer for action. Taken to the extreme, Derek is now highly at-risk for eventually dropping out of school.

Let's examine what Derek's school trajectory would have been if he had enrolled in a school with a counseling program based on the Ternary Decision-Making Model. Derek enters the school with the same cognitive needs and deficiencies. However, in grades 1 through 3, Derek receives primary intervention and is taught many cognitive skills. By third grade he has learned how to use a "daily planner" to keep track of his homework, and he has learned various ways to study for tests. His parents attended a special parent program called *Helping Your Child with Homework*. He now has a scheduled time at home when he must finish his homework, and his mother or his father review his assignments each night. By the seventh grade, Derek is involved in his own education and he is also beginning to further understand the connections between his school assignments and the "outside world." He has been bugging his parents for a higher allowance, and they agree that he can take a "job" mowing the lawn and caring for the family vehicles. Using his time management skills, he sets up a schedule for mowing the lawn and vacuuming, washing, and waxing the two family cars. His skills lead to success, and his allowance is increased. Derek builds on this success, and by the time he is in high school, he has a job at a local supermarket. His has developed post–high school plans and is planning on attending a local community college to study computer hardware maintenance.

The differences between the two scenarios regarding Derek's experience are apparent. In the first scenario, Derek's cognitive developmental needs are not addressed through primary intervention strategies and his problems escalate until they reach crisis proportions. In the Ternary Decision-Making Model scenario, all children's cognitive developmental needs are addressed through primary intervention strategies, thus reducing the need for remediation while enhancing the learning experience for all. Derek is successful, and his love of learning is strengthened.

The example that was used to show the benefits of the Ternary Decision-Making Model highlighted the dimension of cognitive caring. If we expand that example and include the other aspects of caring, namely physical, personal/emotional, social, and career and societal caring, then the benefits increase fourfold. As children's physical, personal/emotional, social, cognitive, and career and societal needs are cared for and met through primary intervention strategies, there is less and less need for specialized attention, be it through remediation or crisis intervention. The Ternary Decision-Making Model assists the counselor in strategically meeting the developmental needs of all children. Additionally, when primary intervention strategies are being used, counselors can devote their time and energy to addressing the unique needs of children. The counselor is thus able to provide secondary intervention strategies without sacrificing the primary intervention strategies that are being implemented on a daily basis in every child's classroom and throughout the school.

Multiple Service Providers Increase Efficiency of the Ternary Model

Each of the delivery systems that we have identified has specific resource implications, particularly with respect to the time needed to be invested by service providers. Managing time and allocating personnel is not a new concept, and allocating time to support ideas and goals is not new either. The key aspect of the Ternary Decision-Making Model is to focus on the utilization of time and people resources in order to maximize an effective and efficient delivery of people-building services to those who will benefit from them.

As you may recall from Chapter 4, key personnel and service providers are actually identified within the vision and mission of the counseling program. Thus, based upon vision and mission statements, we can identify who should be tapped to facilitate each of the delivery systems and who should be the recipients of the services. Figure 5.2 illustrates how this can be done.

The Ternary Decision-Making Model moves beyond the "counselor as an island" approach to the delivery of the counseling program. In essence, the program is delivered by a wealth of school and community resources through a multiple service provider system that produces maximum efficiency of the utilization of resources. An example is the best way to illustrate the efficiency of this model. For simplicity's sake, we'll use an example in which a counselor is the sole provider of the counseling program and its services. The counselor has a fixed number of hours that can be devoted to the counseling program. So, in the course of a school day, that time must be allocated across the various services. For the sake of discussion, let's say that the counselor has 7 hours of the school day

The Ternary Model

Intervention Level	Delivery Systems	Service Providers	Service Recipients
Primary	Curriculum Integration Classroom Guidance Curriculum Peer & Parent Programs	T, C, P, SC, CL, CSS	C, P
Secondary	Collaboration Consultation Counseling Individual Group	T, C, P, SC, CSS, CL	C, P, T, A, SC, CSS
Tertiary	Referral Placement Follow-up Reintegration	SC, CSS, P, T, A, CL, SB	C, P

Key: Administrators, (A), Children (C), Child Support Staff (CSS), Community Leaders (CL), Parents (P), School Board Members (SB), School Counselors (SC), Teachers (T).

Figure 5.2. Service Providers and Recipients of the Ternary Model.

that can be allocated. The typical day for the counselor might look as follows:

- 2nd grade curriculum unit on self-esteem—1 hour
- group counseling for children identified for family support— 1 hour
- one-on-one counseling—1 hour
- 3rd grade curriculum unit/friendship—1 hour
- 3rd grade curriculum unit/decision-making—1 hour
- consultation with parents/teachers—1 hour
- lesson planning for next day—1 hour

Clearly, the counselor has devoted time to the delivery of the program for the 7 hours allocated. The time may have been used effectively, but was it used efficiently?

The Ternary Decision-Making Model allows for the counselor to utilize additional service providers to deliver program services. With the addition of service providers, the different program interventions areas that would be "delivered" for a typical day would look *substantially* different from the previous example. The counselor, instead of being just the service deliverer, now works as a both a coordinator and an overseer of the program. This, of course, does not preclude the counselor from providing services. It simply allows for more individuals to be involved in the implementation and caring aspects of the counseling program. This builds on the ideas that school is a community that supports a curriculum with coherence, facilitates a climate for learning, and involves everyone in the people-building process. The participation of all school personnel in meeting children's academic and developmental needs increases the connection between counseling and academic instruction in providing a balanced education. What does this mean in practical terms? The counselor in the earlier example roughly engaged a total of 70 children: 60 in three classroom-guidance lessons, 6 children in group counseling, 1 child in individual counseling, and 3 individuals for consultation. If an elementary school counseling program is being processed through the Ternary Decision-Making Model, decisions are made to make the best use of time and people though primary, secondary, and tertiary strategies with major emphasis being placed on primary interventions methods. What follows is a description of a typical day using a Ternary Decision-Making Model.

- Each teacher conducting a guidance lesson
  15 teachers $\times$ 20 children = 300 children
- Parents Helping Parents Program
  2 parents leading a program for seven parents
  A total of 9 parents involved—their 7 children are being affected
- Special education teachers addressing counseling needs as part of implementing the Individualized Educational Plan

2 teachers × 4 children—affecting 8 children over the course of the day
- Conflict management training program-training for peers and staff
Affected directly: 6 children and 6 teachers
Affected indirectly: approximately 120 children
- The counselor's services (from example above)
70 children

This counselor, in the course of the day, has a program whose impact is effective and is also efficient—a total of (300 + 7 + 8 + 120 + 70) 505 children were affected either directly or indirectly due to the coordination of the program! This equates to a total of 505 additional children receiving the benefit of the counseling program. So, the counselor who implements a ternary model and utilizes multiple service providers cares for the program more effectively and efficiently and has a much greater effect on the learning climate, and thus the total caring community, than the counselor who single-handedly implements a school counseling program without involving the community of stakeholders.

Cost-Efficiency of the Ternary Model

There is a cost (time, money, children served) efficiency factor to be considered when evaluating the Ternary Decision-Making Model

Intervention Level	Cost-Benefit Ratio
Primary	400:1
Secondary	6:1
Tertiary	1:6

Figure 5.3. Cost-Benefit Ratio by Intervention Level.

(see Figure 5.3). The cost for the delivery of services increases as counselors move down the intervention levels from primary to tertiary. An example can be used to illustrate this. Let's compare the cost benefit for: (1) primary intervention (curriculum integration); (2) secondary intervention (group counseling); and (3) tertiary intervention (referral for community counseling). For the primary intervention, the counselor trains 20 teachers to implement the curriculum initiative. These 20 teachers then implement the curriculum into their classrooms with 20 children. A total of 400 children are benefiting from the initiative of the counselor. So, the cost-benefit ratio relative to the provision of services is 400:1. A secondary group-counseling intervention would be more costly. For this secondary intervention, the counselor will be the service provider working with six children. The cost-benefit ratio for this group counseling service is 6:1. With respect to the tertiary intervention referral, the cost-benefit ratio increases even more significantly. In most cases, a referral to community-based outside services involves a team of professionals. These professionals are assembled to assist in the process. The team would most likely consist of the school nurse, a teacher, the school psychologists, two staff from the referral agency, and the school counselor. Here the cost-benefit ratio is 1:6.

It is quite evident that the cost of providing services increases dramatically when moving from primary intervention to tertiary intervention. As the total number of children being served decreases, the cost to provide those services increases.

The goal of the Ternary Decision-Making Model is to provide sufficient curriculum and school-wide programs to meet all children's development needs as they occur rather than wait for remedial and crisis situations to arise. As we have demonstrated here, when remedial or crisis interventions are the major focus of an elementary school counseling program, not only is children's learning potential interrupted, there is also a corresponding dramatic increase in the costs of those services, and the needs of many children go unattended while only the needs of a few are addressed.

TERNARY DECISION-MAKING MODEL IN ACTION

We have provided an overview of the Ternary Decision-Making Model, shown how it is a comprehensive organized delivery system that provides a detailed decision-making guide for the implementation of program services, and examined its strengths and benefits. Building on this understanding, we will now describe in detail the actual implementation of the model. Figure 5.4 provides a diagram

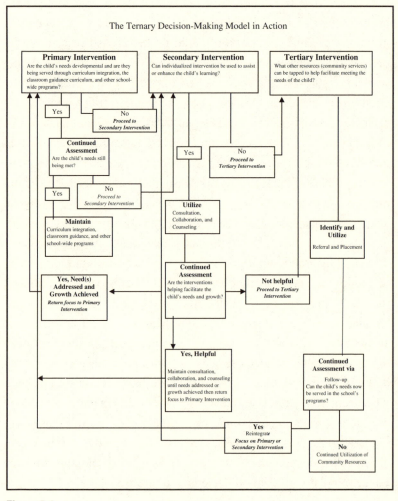

Figure 5.4.

of the model in action with the directional arrows illustrating the actual decision-making processes. In the subsequent sections, the various intervention levels are presented and examples are provided to illustrate the model in action.

Primary Interventions

The goal of the ternary model is to create the necessary conditions to maximize learning and people-building for all children within the school environment. It begins with the implementation of strategies designed to address the question: *Are the child's needs developmental and are they being served through curriculum integration, the guidance curriculum, and other school-wide programs?* This question is answered by establishing an integrated curriculum, a guidance curriculum, and other school-wide programming that facilitate children's, teachers', and parents' understanding of developmental and learning tasks that occur at each grade level and helping children gain competencies in these areas.

Here is an example to illustrate the primary intervention decision-making process. Children who are entering the school community at first grade may be experiencing a wide variety of emotions. They may be unsure of how to make friends, feeling afraid of being in a new environment, and worried about being separated from their parents. Primary intervention is designed to meet the collective needs of *all* first graders who are making the transition into the school community. Targeted curriculum activities can be designed to help children adjust to their new surroundings and to feel safe and secure, and connected to their peers. Lessons designed to help children learn about friendships and the qualities of a good friend can be taught. Additionally, programming can be implemented to help parents address issues of separation. Teachers and counselors can offer a one-night workshop on "helping your child make the transition to school." In this workshop parents can learn how to talk to their children about the first day of school and how to best facilitate the transition process. Primary intervention strategies are designed to promote normal growth and development in all children and to circumvent problems before they occur.

The implementation of the primary intervention level *maintains* and ensures that children's developmental needs are addressed on a continuous basis. Along with the ongoing attention to the developmental needs of each child, the primary intervention level allows for a *continued assessment* of whether the *child's needs are still being met* at the primary level. In essence, the counselor asks, *Are the child's needs still being met?* Given that the child's needs are no longer being addressed at the primary level, this is the counselor's cue that intervention strategies are warranted and to *proceed to the secondary intervention* level.

Secondary Interventions

When the primary intervention strategies are actively implemented, fewer disruptions to learning occur and children develop in healthy and productive ways. The primary-based interventions will not be sufficient to address all children's needs. Some children may benefit from additional attention offered through secondary intervention strategies.

In cases in which the child's learning or the people-building process is becoming compromised or hampered, the secondary level of intervention is implemented. Typically, this starts with the identification of the individual child issue by the teacher or parent(s) or in some cases by the children themselves through self-referral. Knowledgeable school personnel then follow up this identification with an assessment of the disruption. Once assessed, a plan for intervention is adopted. The intervention possibilities at this stage are individualized and can involve consultation, collaboration, and group or individual counseling or a combination of the three. The decision-making question that this level of intervention is designed to address is: *Can an individualized intervention be established to assist or enhance the child's learning?*

Let's look at three different situations that would warrant a secondary intervention. Mary, a third grader, is having difficulty at-

tending in the classroom when the teacher goes to the board to explain a concept. Mary starts talking to other children in the class
and disrupts not only her learning, but that of others as well. Despite
the use of primary intervention strategies by Mr. Jones, the teacher,
to keep all children focused during the teaching-learning process,
Mary continues her disruptive behaviors.

Since primary intervention is not addressing Mary's needs, Mr.
Jones begins a secondary intervention by requesting a consultation
with the counselor. The two of them engage in a discussion designed
to assess Mary's needs. Through consultation, Mr. Jones notes a pattern in Mary's behavior. He notes that except for the time when he is
"lecturing" to the whole class, Mary's behavior is excellent. As a result of their discussion, the counselor and Mr. Jones wonder if this is
what causes the change in Mary's behavior. Mr. Jones decides to talk
with Mary and to investigate the validity of their observation. After
talking with Mary, Mr. Jones learns that she "gets really bored" when
he turns to write on the chalkboard. With this new information in
hand, Mr. Jones renews the consultation with the counselor and they
discuss ways in which he can involve Mary during these "bored"
time periods. Together they develop a plan designed to help Mary.
Mr. Jones decides that he will give Mary responsibilities that relate
to the material being discussed. Mr. Jones asks for Mary's help in
taking notes that he can use to develop handouts and overhead transparencies for use in the future. With the newly defined task, Mary
becomes engaged in class and no longer disrupts the learning environment. In this case, consultation between teacher and counselor
was effective. The child's needs were addressed, and her learning and
that of others was no longer disrupted.

The second case involves Troy. Troy is a fifth grader who has
been acting in an aggressive manner toward other children (he bul-
lies them). The teacher expresses her concern to the counselor, and
they agree that Troy's behavior is a disruption to the learning and
people-building process in the classroom. Troy's behavior has been
an ongoing problem, and he has not responded to the classroom
guidance lessons on conflict management and anger control (primary

interventions). Since Troy's needs were not addressed at the primary level, the counselor decides that it is best to move to the secondary intervention level and calls for a parent-teacher conference. The counselor orchestrates this consultation so that a more in-depth discussion about Troy's needs can occur. The parents confirm that they are having similar troubles with Troy at home as he often tries to bully his younger sister. All parties agree that it would be helpful for the counselor to work with Troy in individual counseling. The counselor arranges to see Troy every other day for 30 minutes. During their time together, the counselor works with Troy on a behavioral modification plan. The counselor involves both the classroom teacher and Troy's parents in monitoring and in evaluating the plan. As Troy becomes successful and he is reinforced for his positive changes, he becomes more involved in the classroom community and uses his new skills to facilitate people-building in others. Here again, the secondary intervention was successful because Troy has now re-entered the learning community.

The third case is of a fourth grader named Juanita. Juanita is an excellent child. In fact, when the counselor presented a guidance unit on physical wellness, Juanita really connected with the concepts being presented, and her personal wellness plan was an outstanding product. She also did a tremendous job of implementing her wellness plan and in six weeks was demonstrating a real command of the concepts of physical wellness. The counselor realizes that Juanita's potential in this area could be enhanced and consults with the physical education teacher about working with her. The teacher, who also coaches the school soccer team, sees a perfect opportunity for Juanita to enhance her skills in the wellness area. The teacher-coach agrees to have Juanita become the wellness "trainer" for the soccer team. Together the teacher-coach and Juanita develop a wellness plan for the team, and Juanita helps the teacher-coach implement the plan. Juanita's involvement with the team helps her actualize her potential. Thus, her enhanced skills are now working to assist in a concerted people-building mission for the soccer team.

Secondary interventions should be monitored for their effectiveness. The counselor should monitor whether the interventions are *helping facilitate the child's needs and growth.* In the secondary level of intervention, the child continues to receive the benefits of primary interventions while receiving the additional attention through secondary intervention strategies. If the secondary level intervention is *helpful,* but has not met the expressed needs of the child, the counselor will *maintain* the intervention until the desired result(s) have been attained. When secondary intervention strategies are *not helpful,* the counselor should *proceed to the tertiary intervention level.* However, the ultimate goal of the Ternary Decision-Making Model is to meet children's developmental needs through primary intervention strategies.

Tertiary Interventions

Tertiary intervention occurs when school-based interventions at the primary and secondary level have both failed. The question asked at this stage is: **What other resources (community services) can be tapped to help facilitate meeting the needs of the child?** The following case study is presented to illustrate a tertiary intervention. Troy is unresponsive to individual counseling provided in that the behavioral plan does not facilitate desired changes in behavior (see previous secondary-intervention case study involving Troy). He continues to exhibit aggressive behavior and, in fact, the behavior begins to escalate. The counselor, in consultation with other school personnel and Troy's parents, decides that his need for counseling is intense and beyond that which the school counselor can offer within the school environment. They decide to *refer* him to outside counseling where a more thorough and comprehensive treatment plan can be designed to meet Troy's specific needs. The whole purpose of the intervention at this stage is to maximize focus on Troy's needs with the ultimate goal of helping Troy become a contributing member of the school and the classroom community. After the *referral* has been made, the counselor's responsibilities are to maintain contact with the outside service provider so as to assess how the child's needs can be served in school while tertiary intervention takes place. In order to do so, it is imperative that school counselors acquire the appropriate consent from the parents to allow tertiary service providers to communicate with them. With consent, the counselor and the tertiary service provider develop an integrated treatment plan for the child. For example, Troy could be receiving intensive individual counseling from a community-agency mental health practitioner and also be involved with an ongoing school psychoeducational group for anger management for *added focus*. As Troy's behavior begins to modify, the intensity of the tertiary and secondary interventions can be adjusted to meet his current needs with the ultimate goal of *returning the focus* solely to the *primary intervention level*.

In the case in which tertiary intervention necessitates a total removal of the child from the school setting, a *reintegration* plan will need to be developed to move the child back into the school community. Let's use the case of Billie. Billie is a fifth grader who was initially identified for secondary intervention because of a drug-related problem. The teacher made the referral to the counselor because she noted that Billie's behavior had become erratic and that Billie often seemed to be "out of it." The counselor began to work with Billie in individual counseling. The counseling was not successful, and Billie was not responding. Subsequently, Billie was arrested with several older children for shoplifting and possession of drugs. This arrest led to Billie's *placement* in a residential treatment facility for six months. The counselor was involved with the *referral* and even was engaged in consultation with the treatment staff at the *placement* facility. Upon completion of the six-month treatment program, Billie is re-entering school. The counselor, in consultation with the treatment staff and Billie's parents, decides that it is best if Billie re-enter the school at the secondary intervention level. The counselor agrees to meet with Billie for individual counseling and to work in consultation with his teachers to facilitate his return to the classroom. Once Billie's needs have been addressed and there is a successful integration into the school and classroom community, he may no longer need secondary intervention, as primary intervention strategies will be sufficient to meet his developmental needs.

In the most severe cases, in which a child has ongoing tertiary intervention needs, a residential placement can be warranted. A residential placement allows for intensive treatment to be targeted to meet the child's unique needs. Counselors need to understand that effective residential placement includes the successful return of children to their home, school, and community. Upon return to the school, counselors should make every effort to insure that the child is given every opportunity to successfully re-engage in the learning process and take full advantage of the balanced education provided.

The Ternary Decision-Making Model ensures that the *mission and vision* of elementary school counseling program can be achieved. It is simplistic yet sophisticated enough in its design that it directs the decision-making process so that all children are cared for and their *developmental* needs are met within a caring community.

BIBLIOGRAPHY

Adelman, H.S., & Taylor, L. (2002). School counselors and school reform: New directions. *Professional School Counseling, 5,* 235–248.

Caplan, G. (1964). *Principles of preventive psychiatry.* New York: Basic Books.

PART III

COUNSELING AND THE CURRICULUM: A CARING APPROACH

CHAPTER 6

Physical Caring

Physical Caring is a process in which children learn what it means to be physically fit and how to use the information, attitudes, and skills they have developed to make healthy choices in promoting and sustaining their own physical well-being.

HUMAN DEVELOPMENT

During the middle childhood years, children experience predictable and gradual changes in their physical growth and development. Sustained growth patterns that were established in the late preschool years with respect to gradual increases in height and weight and improved gross- and fine-motor coordination continue to evolve. Progress also is noted in children's ability to perform more complex skills and master more complex and elaborate motor tasks in such areas as swimming, dancing, bicycle riding, skating, and playing musical instruments.

As children approach their preteen years, they experience more pronounced changes in their growth and development known as puberty. This is a period of very rapid growth and hormonal changes starting as early as eight years and lasting, for some, well into their late teens. During this period, boys and girls are transformed into young men and women. Accompanying these significant physical changes are emotional, social, and cognitive changes that will be addressed in subsequent chapters.

As children evolve in their physical development from ages 5 through 12, three interactive and dynamic elements affect physical development, causing major variations in body size, shape, and ability. These elements are heredity, environment, and behavior (Pollock & Middleton, 1994). Heredity affects the transmission of parent characteristics to offspring. These genetically influenced traits affect such factors as physical size, looks, rate of growth, some talents, and personality.

The environment includes children's total surroundings and consists of such elements as where they live and daily-life experiences that influence physical, social, cognitive, and emotional growth. Together, the environment and heredity become major influencers in shaping children's lives.

And finally, behaviors (people actions) play a significant role in affecting children's growth and development. Human beings have the capacity to think, reason, and make choices regarding the actions they will take in response to life situations. Herein lies the salvation of humankind. For it is in the area of behavior that children can have the most significant impact in managing their own physical well-being. Indeed, children's behaviors are so powerful they can influence, to some degree, the impact that heredity and the environment can have on growth and development. Through the use of learned healthy attitudes, valid and reliable information, and caring skills, children can make informed decisions regarding their physical health, the outcome of which will enhance their physical well-being while reducing their risks to disease, injury, and premature death. Indeed, the outcome of medical research has estimated that more than one-half of all disease is lifestyle related (53 percent), one-fifth is attributed to environmental causes (21 percent), one-tenth (10 percent) is influenced by the health care system, with only 16 percent being attributed to genetic causes (Murphy & Murphy 1987). *The evidence overwhelmingly speaks in favor of prevention as the best medicine for physical well-being.* Healthy lifestyle choices and habits thus have the greatest and most significant impact on lifetime physical fitness and human development. The choices that children make in childhood will have lasting effects in shaping the quality of their lives well into their teenage years and beyond.

THE PHYSICALLY HEALTHY CHILD

Physically healthy children understand the impact of personal choice in developing habits and behaviors that will help them to achieve a healthier, happier, and more productive life. These children tend to be enthusiastic, energetic, and confident in themselves because they have what it takes to care for their physical well-being. More specifically, these children

1. have health knowledge that enables them to develop health literacy, maintain and improve health, prevent disease, and reduce health-related risk behaviors;
2. choose health behaviors that promote health; prevent illness, injury, and premature death; and improve the quality of the environment;
3. choose to participate in healthful situations that promote health and a quality environment;
4. choose to be in healthy relationships that encourage health-enhancing behaviors and that are free of violence and drug misuse and abuse; and
5. make responsible decisions that promote health, increase safety, protect the environment, and show respect for self and others (Meeks, Heit, & Page, 1996).

SIX CATEGORIES OF RISK

Most people would agree that teaching children how to care for their physical well-being is an important dimension of people-building. Not addressing this issue has far-reaching consequences that will adversely affect children's learning potential, emotional stability, interpersonal relationships, susceptibility to illness and life-threatening disease, and exposure to physical injury (intentional and unintentional) and premature death. Equally devastating will be the cost to society in lost human potential, skyrocketing medical bills, and a continued strain on an already weakened health care system, which struggles to remediate the effects of unhealthy lifestyles.

In the not too distant past, the major health risks to children were contagious diseases like tuberculosis, diphtheria, measles, mumps, rubella, and whooping cough (McKenzie & Richmond, 1998). Today, children's physical health is threatened by six categories of risk, most of which are rooted in the context of their behaviors, which account for most of their serious illnesses and premature deaths.

The six categories of risk that threaten children's physical well-being are (Meeks et al., 1996)

1. Unintentional and intentional injuries
2. Risk of tobacco products
3. Alcohol and other drug use
4. Sexual behaviors: infections, disease, and unwanted pregnancies
5. Diet and disease
6. Insufficient physical activity

These risk factors can be reduced through the attainment of accurate information, attitudinal changes regarding the importance of physical self-care and health enhancement, and the development of risk-management strategies that will help children to make healthy caring choices. Our goal must be to help children understand that most serious illnesses, injuries, and premature deaths that occur in their age groups are largely preventable. They have the potential and responsibility to create healthy lifestyles through the daily choices that they make. *Good health is a prerequisite to learning and a life of purpose and meaning.*

Unintentional and Intentional Injuries

Unintentional injuries are injuries that are sustained through high-risk, yet preventable, behaviors that threaten self-esteem, harm health, and increase the likelihood of injury, disease, and premature death

(Meeks et al., 1996). These behaviors are often learned in childhood, persist into adulthood, and contribute to poor health, a less than adequate education, and detrimental social outcomes.

Despite the fact that the unintentional injury-related death rate among children declined by 33 percent from 1987 to 1997, it still remains the leading cause of death among children in the United States (National SAFE KIDS Campaign, 1999). And while the causes and consequences of injury rates vary with a child's age, gender, race, and socioeconomic status, the most recent data reported by the National SAFE KIDS Campaign regarding childhood injury for all children ages 5 to 14 years indicate the following:

- In 1997, unintentional injury resulted in the deaths of 1,524 children ages 5 to 9; for children ages 9 to 14, there were 1,824 deaths.
- Among children ages 5 to 9 years, motor vehicle–occupant injuries were the leading cause of death, followed by pedestrian injuries, drownings, fire and burns, and bicycle injuries.
- Among children ages 10 to 14 years, motor vehicle–occupant injury is the leading cause of death, followed by pedestrian injury, drowning, bicycle injury, and fire and burns.
- Every day, more than 39,000 children are injured seriously enough to require medical treatment, totaling more than 14 million children each year.
- Each year, injuries to children 14 and younger result in 213,000 hospitalizations, nearly 7,900,000 emergency room visits, and more than 11,000,000 visits to physicians' offices. Treatment for injury is the second leading cause for visits to hospital emergency rooms for children in this age group.
- Injury is the leading cause of medical spending for children ages 5 to 14.
- The annual lifetime costs of unintentional injury among children ages 14 and younger is nearly $175 billion in direct medical costs, $16.9 billion in lost future earnings, and $148 billion in quality of life.

Prevention is the key to reducing the devastating and long-lasting effects of unintentional injury to children, to their families, and to society. People working in the field of risk management believe that an estimated 90 percent of unintentional injuries to children are preventable (National SAFE KID Campaign, 1999). In order to reduce the incidence and severity of unintentional injury and disability and the occurrence of premature death due to unintentional injury, it will take a team approach to meet this challenge. Education (academic and counseling programs), environmental improvements and modifications (engineering), enactment and enforcement of safety legislation and regulations, economic incentives, and community involvement projects designed to decrease risk and increase safety will help children to better care for their physical well-being.

Use of Tobacco Products

The use of tobacco products is the leading cause of cardiovascular disease, many cancers, cerebrovascular disease, and chronic obstruction pulmonary disease (Hoeger & Hoeger, 2000). The American Cancer Society (1993) has reported that tobacco use in all forms is considered a major threat to life. Based on current research related to tobacco use, it is estimated that approximately 10 percent of the 5 billion people living on the planet will die as a result of smoking-related diseases, 3 million of whom die each year. Cigarette smoking is the largest preventable cause of illness and premature death in the United States. As frightening as these statistics are, what is even more frightening is that approximately 90 percent of today's smokers began smoking as children, and 3,000 more children will become regular smokers each day (U.S. Department of Health and Human Services, 2000). "The physical addiction to nicotine is six times to eight times more powerful than the addiction to alcohol, and most likely greater than for some of the hard drugs currently used" (Hoeger & Hoeger, 2000, p. 324).

Smokeless tobacco is equally dangerous to children's health and presents its own set of health risks. The use of smokeless tobacco ("spit" or chew tobacco), which contains 2.5 times as much nicotine as a pack of cigarettes, is highly addictive and can lead to gum disease, oral cancer, cardiovascular disease, and changes in heart rate and blood pressure. Despite all that is known about the dangerous effects of smokeless tobacco, some 15 million Americans use tobacco in this form. What is even more alarming is that 20 percent of all boys in grades 9 to 12 use this product, and a third of them started at age 5, with an average starting age of 9 (Kids Health, 2000).

If children are to manage their risks to the damaging effects of tobacco, prevention is the leading risk-management strategy at their disposal. Teaching children the value of making caring choices regarding the hazards and dangers of tobacco use is a goal worthy of attainment.

Alcohol and Other Drug Use

This category of risk behaviors focuses on the misuse and abuse of alcohol and other drugs. "Alcohol is a psychoactive drug that depresses the central nervous system, dulls the mind, impairs thinking and judgment, lessens coordination, and interferes with the ability to respond quickly to dangerous situations" (Meeks, Heit, & Page, 1996, p. 6).

Since 1975, researchers at the University of Michigan, using national surveys entitled *Monitoring the Future,* have tracked drug use among teenagers across the United States and, since 1991, the nationwide surveys have also included eighth and tenth graders. Alcohol remains the drug of choice among middle- and high-school students. The preliminary findings of the 2001 survey indicate that four out of five students (80%) had consumed alcohol by the time they graduated from high school and nearly 50 percent had done so by eighth grade. Even more remarkable is the fact that nearly two-thirds of twelfth graders and a quarter of eighth graders report having been drunk once in their life (Johnston, O'Malley, & Bachman, 2002). There is limited research regarding the drinking patterns of young children. One such study conducted by Van Kammen, Lober, and Stouthamer-Lober in 1991 reported results from a large Pittsburgh, Pennsylvania, study that 7.8 percent of first graders, 12 percent of fourth graders, and 56.6 percent of seventh graders had tried beer at least once.

In *America's Children: Key National Indicators of Well-Being, 2001* (fourth annual report on the condition of our nation's children), the following statistics were offered regarding alcohol use among eighth, tenth, and twelfth graders during 2001. Fourteen percent of eighth graders, 26 percent of tenth graders, and 30 percent of twelfth graders reported having five or more alcoholic beverages in a row during the two weeks prior to taking the survey. Approximately 3 million teenagers are thought to have a drinking problem in the United States (Hoeger & Hoeger, 2000).

In addition to the health problems associated with the illegal use of alcohol among children, America's young people are using illicit drugs like marijuana, cocaine, steroids, heroin, and inhalants with equally devastating health effects. The use of these drugs upsets the balance of every system in the body and is often the cause of dangerous and unpredictable violent behaviors that result in injury and death to users and innocent bystanders alike.

More than one-half of children report having tried one illicit drug before finishing high school, and approximately 35 percent of eighth graders have reported trying at least one illicit drug (Johnston et al., 2002). In *America's Children 2000 Report,* 12 percent of eighth graders, 22 percent of tenth graders, and 26 percent of twelfth graders had indicated illicit drug use in the previous 30 days. Teaching children how to care for their physical well-being in a world of hazards and dangers (alcohol and other drug use) is necessary if they are to live healthy lifestyles.

Sexual Behaviors: Infections, Disease, and Unwanted Pregnancies

This category of risk behavior focuses on sexual behaviors that result in HIV infection, other sexually transmitted diseases, and unwanted pregnancies. The statistics are clear. The sexual behaviors of today's young people are a cause for concern. In a recent national survey of high school students, approximately 50 percent said that they have had sexual intercourse, and 8 percent of them had had sexual intercourse before age 13 (U.S. Centers for Disease Control and Prevention, 2000). The same survey also indicated that only 58 percent report using a condom and only 16 percent reported using birth control pills.

Each year, more than 900,000 pregnancies occur among American teenagers (ages 15–19) and almost 190,000 teens, ages 17 and younger, have children (U.S. Department of Health and Human Services, 1999a). The current birth rate for young teens (15–17 years) is 30.4 births per 1,000 teenagers. Birth rate statistics for teens have shown a steady decline from 1991 to 2000, a decline of 20 percent (Ventura, Mathews, & Hamilton, 2002). These results are attributed to the nation's efforts to help community and nonprofit organizations to establish successful teen pregnancy prevention programs. The messages being communicated to all teens are to postpone sexual activity, to stay in school, and to prepare to work (U.S. Department of Health and Human Services, 1999a).

In addition to unwanted pregnancies, unprotected sexual activity poses an increased risk to HIV infection and AIDS and exposure to other sexually transmitted diseases. The number of 12- to 20-year-olds in the United States infected with HIV has increased 77 percent since 1991, and a significant number of young adults who have AIDS were infected with HIV during their adolescent years as a result of high-risk behavior practices (Kolbe, 1992; Meeks, Heit & Page, 1996). In 2000, 342 adolescents were reported with AIDS nationwide, and 879 adolescents were reported with HIV infection (U.S. Centers for Disease Control and Prevention, 2002). In addition, more than 3 million adolescents are infected each year with one or more sexually transmitted diseases (STDs), some of which are incurable. Left untreated, STDs can produce irreversible damage to various systems of the body (Hoeger & Hoeger, 2000). At what age should children learn about the hazards and dangers associated with high-risk behaviors that can result in unwanted pregnancies, HIV, and other sexually transmitted diseases? When should children be provided with the facts and life skills that will enable them to make responsible caring choices with respect to their own physical well-being? We are of the opinion that children should be given every opportunity to learn and practice those risk-management strategies that will help to ensure their good health.

Diet and Disease

"Scientific evidence has long linked good nutrition to overall health and well-being. Proper nutrition means that a person's diet supplies all the essential nutrients to carry out normal tissue growth, repair, and maintenance . . . and produces the energy necessary for work, physical activity, and relaxation" (Hoeger & Hoeger, 2000, p. 174). Hoeger and Hoeger (2000) have reported that too much or too little of any nutrient can be cause for concern in that serious health problems can develop. The typical diet of people in the United States is too high in calories, sugar, fat, saturated fat, and sodium and not high enough in fiber (fruits, vegetables, and grains). The end result is that diseases of dietary excess and imbalance are among the leading causes of death in the United States (Meeks, Heit, & Page, 1996). Poor diet and nutrition play a significant role in the cause and progression of such chronic diseases as atherosclerosis, coronary heart disease, hypertension, some cancers, obesity, diabetes, and osteoporosis.

The dietary patterns of adults are established during childhood and the news is not good. In 1996, 76 percent of children ages 2 to 5, 88 percent of children ages 6 to 12, and 94 percent of children ages 13 to 18 had a diet that was poor or needed improvement (National Institute of Child Health and Human Development, 2000). The Healthy Eating Index (HEI) as reported in the *America's Children: Key National Indicators of Well-Being, 2001* (Federal Interagency Forum on Child and Family Statistics, 2001) indicates that as children get older, the quality of their diet declines, and this is linked to a decline in fruit and milk consumption. As many as 87 percent of high-school students reported that they do not follow the daily recommended allowance of five or more servings of fruits and vegetables, and two-thirds of all young people indicated that they did not eat a daily breakfast (Devaney, Gorden, & Burghardt, 1995). Approximately 84 percent of young people exceed the national recommendations for fat intake, and more than 90 percent exceed national recommendations for consumption of saturated fats (Lewis, Crane, Moore, & Hubbard, 1994). The end result is that many children and adolescents are experiencing physical health problems such as obesity, eating disorders, high blood pressure, elevated blood cholesterol levels, and stress (physical and psychological) resulting from poor body image, low self-esteem, and peer isolation and rejection (Caldwell, Nestle, & Rogers, 1998). Data from the 1999 National Health and Nutrition Examination Survey (NHANES) related to childhood obesity indicate that an estimated 13 percent of children ages 6 to 11 years and 14 percent of adolescents ages 12 to 19 years are overweight (National Center for Health Statistics, 2000).

In addition to the physical and psychological effects of poor eating habits and nutrition, these children tend to score lower on a wide range of cognitive tests, experience some diminished brain function, and do not perform as well academically as their counterparts who come to school having met healthy nutritional requirements. Eating a balanced, heart-healthy diet is necessary if children are to develop healthy lifestyles, maximize their educational potential, and lower their risk of chronic diseases.

Insufficient Physical Activity

Physical fitness relates to optimal functioning of the heart, lungs, muscles, and blood vessels. In order to be physically fit, physical activity is required. Energy must be expended through bodily movement by skeletal muscles, which, if done on a daily basis, will produce progressive health benefits (Zigler & Stevenson, 1993). People who engage in regular physical activity reduce their risks for developing or dying from heart disease, diabetes, colon cancer, and high blood pressure. Regular physical activity keeps bones, muscles, and joints healthy, and it seems to elevate mood, reduce the symptoms of depression and anxiety, and enhance the ability to perform daily tasks. The expenditure of calories resulting from regular physical activity also helps to maintain a healthy body weight.

Despite the benefits of physical activity, nearly half of all American youth (ages 12 to 21) are not vigorously active on a regular basis (U.S. Department of Health and Human Services, 1999b; Seefeldt, 1998), with only 29 percent of adolescents participating in daily physical education, a decline of 13 percent from 1991 to 1999 (National Center for Chronic Disease Prevention and Health Promotion, 2002). Today's children are less physically active and are generally more obese than children in the 1960s (Zigler & Stevenson, 1993). In fact, the percentage of young people who are obese has doubled over the last 20 years, and about 8 million young people from ages 6 to 17 are overweight (National Center for Chronic Disease Prevention and Health Promotion, 2002). And of even greater concern is the tendency for physical problems such as cardiovascular disease to start as early as first grade (American Academy of Pediatrics, 1985). In more recent studies, evidence exists that demonstrates that many young children exhibit two or more risk factors for cardiovascular disease. These risk factors are physical inactivity, a poor cholesterol profile, high blood pressure, diabetes, obesity, and smoking (Hoeger & Hoeger, 2000).

Physical health is a fundamental dimension of development and is closely linked to academic success and mental well-being. Children who are physically active are more energetic, mentally alert, less stressed, and are generally healthier than their less physically active counterparts (Marx, Wooley, and Northrop, 1998).

Teaching children about the importance of physical activity and providing them with opportunities to be physically active helps to increase the likelihood that they will choose to be physically active throughout their lives.

The Cumulative Effects of Risk

The preceding six categories of risk behavior, taken individually, can have a lasting and significant impact on the quality of life. However, when taken collectively or in combination with one another, the impact of these risk factors is even more devastating. Today, many children are practicing multiple high-risk behaviors that not only threaten their potential to succeed in life, but in time will weaken the very fiber of our country and its ability to grow and prosper as a nation. The good news is that risk behaviors are voluntary actions of choice that can be stopped and replaced with responsible caring choices. *Our children deserve no less than the very best that we have to give in helping them to become the very best that they can be.*

ENHANCING PHYSICAL WELL-BEING THROUGH CARING CHOICES

If children are to succeed in school and in life, their physical needs must be met. However, the most effective approach to take in helping children to become responsible caregivers has often been debated. Some elementary school counseling programs have adopted a purely reactive mentality, waiting for risks to arise and then developing strategies to address them, whereas other programs recommend taking a more proactive stance. We place ourselves in the second camp. People-building is a proactive process that teaches children how to live healthy, successful, and personally satisfying lives. The collective participation of counselors, teachers, parents, and the community is needed if children are to learn physical caring strategies.

We want children to understand what it means to care for their physical well-being and to recognize how what they learn in school can help them to become responsible caregivers. In addition, we want children to understand that their physical well-being not only lies in the personal choices they make for themselves, but how those same choices affect the lives of others and their environment. We want children to relate to the "circle of life" concept, which supports the belief that the balance of life is maintained through responsible decision-making.

Having stated that physical caring has far-reaching implications for children and society, we believe that elementary school counseling programs can have a greater impact by addressing six areas of physical caring.

Growth and Development and Caring

This area focuses on understanding how children grow and develop into young men and women. Children are taught how to care for their body systems; relate to their maleness/femaleness; accept and appreciate their physical appearance; understand how they learn best; achieve appropriate developmental tasks for middle childhood; learn about the life cycle; understand people's needs at various stages of development; learn about the aging process; and discuss thoughts and feelings about death, loss, and grief.

Nutrition Caring

This area focuses on the impact of nutrition and physical well-being. Children are taught the value of making caring choices in response to developing healthy eating habits. In particular, children need to practice caring strategies in planning a healthful diet that includes selecting foods from the Food Guide Pyramid. The guide is based on research from the United States Department of Agriculture and the Department of Health and Human Services and recommends daily guidelines to ensure a balanced diet. Other caring choices include learning how to read and use food labels, making healthy food selections in response to disease prevention and/or reduction, learning how to prepare and store foods safely, maintaining a heart-healthy weight, protecting and maintaining a healthy food chain, and recognizing and responding responsibly to eating disorders.

Personal Health Caring

This area focuses on developing a personal health management plan that includes teaching children how to make caring choices in response to being physically well groomed (skin, hair, nails, feet, posture, and dress), caring for eyes and ears, getting regular physical checkups, practicing healthy dental care, obtaining adequate rest and sleep, participating in daily movement and exercise activities, and improving skill-related fitness.

Risk-Management Caring

This area focuses on helping children to increase their awareness of risk and to measure, judge, and control risk in response to alcohol, tobacco, and other drugs; communicable and noncommunicable diseases; and injury prevention and safety.

Alcohol, Tobacco, and Other Drugs

Children learn how to make caring choices in response to developing a safe and drug-free lifestyle. Children are taught to recognize the value of prescription drugs (medicine) when authorized by a physician. They likewise learn about the dangers associated with drug misuse and abuse and how to resist social pressure that would compromise their physical health. And in those instances when personal or family drug misuse or abuse does occur, children are taught how to access school and community resources for purposes of intervention and treatment.

Communicable and Noncommunicable Disease

Children are taught how they can prevent and lower their susceptibility to disease. More specifically, they learn that some diseases are infectious (communicable) and are caused by pathogens that enter the body through direct and indirect contact with another person. They learn how to keep their immune system healthy, prevent the spread of pathogens, reduce the risk of infection with common communicable diseases, understand their family history for disease, reduce the risk of cardiovascular disease and cancer, and learn ways to manage chronic diseases.

Injury Prevention and Safety

This is the area of physical health that focuses on practicing rules in the home, school, and community; following safety guidelines for different weather conditions and disasters; securing assistance in emergency situations; learning basic first aid; following safety procedures for all recreational and physical activities; staying safe in motor vehicles; becoming a safety-minded pedestrian; reducing the risk of violence; and protecting oneself in dangerous situations. Children learn appropriate risk-management strategies and safety practices designed to enhance their quality of life in a world of hazards and dangers.

Consumer and Community Health and Caring

This area of physical caring focuses on teaching children how to become responsible consumers of health-related information, products and services. More specifically, children learn how to analyze advertising, recognize and report unsafe practices that could jeopardize people's health, use school and community health services when appropriate, and participate in school and community activities that promote school and community health.

Environmental Caring

This is an area of caring that focuses on environmental issues that affect children's physical health. Children have a need to promote environmental caring activities as a way of strengthening the environment and promoting their own self-care and the care of others. In particular, children have a need to address and promote such environmental issues as maintaining clean air and water; protecting plants, trees, and animals; decreasing and eliminating environmental pollutants (indoors and outdoors); protecting themselves from the sun's radiation; encouraging the responsible disposal and recycling of by-products; encouraging population management; and co-operating with environmental agencies that care for our planet. Closer to home, children can make caring decisions that will have a positive impact on their home, school, and community environments, particularly in the areas of safety and risk management.

When people fail to care for their physical environment despite all that they do to care for themselves, the effects of a contaminated and weakened environment will eventually compromise their good health. The old adage of *what you care for will care for you* certainly holds true in this instance.

In reviewing the six areas of physical caring, it becomes evident that the expertise of many people will be needed in helping children to acquire and accumulate information, quality skills, self-confidence, and opportunities to practice what they have learned. Parents, classroom teachers, the school nurse, health and physical education teachers, administrators, community organizations, and the counselor are key team players in this process.

Physical caring strategies and activities can be met through the academic curriculum, school counseling programs, and through various community organizations like the American Red Cross and health and environmental groups that promote physical health. *The elementary school counselor can play a major role in helping team players understand their people-building responsibilities when it comes to helping children achieve a state of physical well-being.*

THE COUNSELOR'S ROLE

The primary role of the counselor is to emphasize the importance of teaching children to care in the context of being careful (risk management). They can help teachers to recognize how what they teach in math, science, language arts, social studies, music, health, and physical education can provide children with information and skills that will enhance their physical well-being. What children learn at home and in school should help them to make caring choices regarding their growth and development, nutrition, and personal health. Children should likewise be prepared to make wise caring choices in response to injury prevention and safety; to select and use health-related information, products, and services; and to be involved in environmental protection activities that enhance physical well-being.

Counselors can work with children in the classroom, in small groups, and individually to explore the value of music, reading, exercise, hobbies, and other choices that children can make to relax, have fun, and generally improve their physical health. Counselors likewise can explore with children the many simple choices they can make each and every day to promote physical caring. Smiling, washing hands, walking (rather than running) in the school hallways, brushing teeth, eating a nutritious breakfast, and picking up paper on the playground are examples of caring choices that require little time yet promote physical well-being.

When counselors are not providing direct service to children, they can be consulting with teachers and parents and helping them to explore ways to promote physical caring strategies at home and in school. As coordinators of school counseling services, counselors can involve organizations and community groups to participate in school activities that are designed to promote community-caring practices. Creating safe streets, playgrounds, and school buildings are projects that require a team effort.

When children recognize the information, skills, and healthy attitudes they have developed to promote physical caring and are given the opportunity to practice what they have learned, *caring children will make caring choices.* What follows are a number of activities and suggestions that are designed to facilitate physical caring. As children explore the many ways in which they can promote physical caring, even more ideas will emerge and more caring choices will be exhibited. Use these activities and other caring ideas to help children experience the positive impact they can have as caregivers (for self, others, and the environment).

PHYSICAL CARING ACTIVITIES

Wellness Graph

Brief Overview of Activity:

This activity will give children an opportunity to think about some wellness behaviors they have learned and to evaluate how they do over time in practicing these behaviors. They also will have a heightened sense of self as a result of the positive practices they have developed.

Objectives:

1. Children will evaluate, on a weekly basis, how they have personally performed in six specific physical caring categories.
2. Children will demonstrate positive growth in at least one of the six areas during a six-week period of time.

Materials Needed:

Graph sheets for each child.

Procedures:

1. Show examples of bar graphs and explain that graphs are used to show progress (or lack of it) over a period of time. Talk with the children about some things that could be graphed in terms of their wellness practices, for example, eating habits, physical exercise, sleep, social activities, responsibility, personal relaxation.
2. Give each child a copy of the Wellness Graph Worksheet (Figure 6.1) and explain that each week, for a six-week period, they will be asked to evaluate their personal wellness practices.
3. Help children to brainstorm two or three things they can evaluate for each category listed on the graph paper. For example, what are some areas that children can evaluate regarding having healthy eating habits?
4. Using a bar graph, ask children to rate themselves using the following categories:

Wellness Graph

Week 1	Poor	Fair	Average	Good	Great
Eating Habits					
Exercise					
Sleep					
Social					
Responsibility					
Taking Time for Me					
Week 2					
Eating Habits					
Exercise					
Sleep					
Social					
Responsibility					
Taking Time for Me					
Week 3					
Eating Habits					
Exercise					
Sleep					
Social					
Responsibility					
Taking Time for Me					

Figure 6.1.   *(continued)*

Wellness Graph					
Week 4	**Poor**	**Fair**	**Average**	**Good**	**Great**
Eating Habits					
Exercise					
Sleep					
Social					
Responsibility					
Taking Time for Me					
Week 5					
Eating Habits					
Exercise					
Sleep					
Social					
Responsibility					
Taking Time for Me					
Week 6					
Eating Habits					
Exercise					
Sleep					
Social					
Responsibility					
Taking Time for Me					

Figure 6.1. (continued)

Great—I'm doing everything I need to do in this area.

Good—I've done a good job, but I could do a bit better.

Average—It's OK, but I could improve a lot.

Fair—I really haven't worked very much at this and it needs lots of work.

Poor—This is one area I definitely need to improve.

5. Collect the graphs and remind children that for the next six weeks, you will be asking them to rate their personal wellness behavior in the six areas.

6. Encourage children to choose at least one area to consciously work on to see if they can improve. Remind them to really work to see if they can make a difference.

7. Continue with this activity (marking the chart) every week for the next six weeks.

Closure:

In closing this activity, provide time for children to discuss what they learned about their motivation to change as a result of working on a particular behavior. Since some children will be more successful than others at developing new habits, encourage conversation about things that were helpful, e.g., exercising with a friend, keeping a food diary, going to bed at the same time every night and getting up at approximately the same time as well, setting aside a specific time for doing something they enjoy, and so on. Process the activity and how they feel—Was it rewarding to show progress in a specific area? Did you have more energy? Did you feel better about yourself? Suggest that they try to continue the new behavior even though they will no longer be evaluating their progress on a weekly basis.

Do You Know Someone Who?

Brief Overview of Activity:

This activity has a twofold purpose in that it can be used as a getting-acquainted mixer for children as well as help them to focus on positive wellness habits. This is a good activity to use in a classroom during the first week or two of the school year. Children will have an opportunity to get to know at least 10 of their classmates.

Objectives:

1. Children will become acquainted with at least 10 of their classmates.
2. Children will gain an increased awareness of wellness habits and personal lifestyles.

Materials Needed:

A *Do You Know Someone Who* worksheet (Figure 6.2) for each child.

Procedures:

1. Talk briefly about ways we become acquainted with each other. What are some things that help you to get to know others? (Similar interest, hobbies, groups, etc.)
2. Give each child a copy of *Do Your Know Someone Who.* Give children five minutes to circulate around the room collecting signatures from classmates who have done the activities listed on the survey. This worksheet is designed for children to identify individuals in the classroom who engage in the healthy behaviors listed. Children are to mingle, gaining signatures of individuals who are making the healthy choices listed.
3. Tell them that they can only have a person sign their survey once.
4. Encourage children to talk with those who sign their sheets as a way of getting to know them better.
5. When children have completed the task, discuss the survey items.
   With whom do you have something in common?
   What did you learn about someone in our class?
   Were you surprised at anything you learned?
6. Allow a few minutes for discussion and then ask children to indicate, by a show of hands, how many of them practice the good health habits in the survey. Reinforce them for their positive habits and remind them that these good practices

Do You Know Someone Who:

1. Eats at least two fruits every day? _____

2. Likes tossed salad? _____

3. Always wears a seat belt when riding in a car? _____

4. Eats three balanced meals each day? _____

5. Wears a helmet while biking or skateboarding? _____

6. Likes him- herself as he or she is? _____

7. Gets eight or more hours of sleep each night? _____

8. Exercises 20–30 minutes at least three times per week? _____

9. Knows how to use relaxation strategies to keep calm? _____

10. Drinks six to eight glasses of water each day? _____

Figure 6.2.

will help them to have good attendance and be well prepared to do their best in school.

7. Encourage children to think about something they will do in the future to help them develop more positive wellness practices.

Closure:

Close this activity by reminding children that today they had an opportunity to get to know at least 10 of their classmates a little better and to also review some positive wellness practices that will help them to have a healthier and more productive school year.

Coat of Wellness

Brief Overview of Activity:

This activity will encourage children to begin to focus on the positive wellness habits they have already developed. It will also help them to consider other habits they think they need to cultivate in order to be optimally healthy.

Objectives:

1. Children will identify at least one positive wellness habit they have developed.
2. Children will identify at least one behavior they feel they need to consider changing in order to be optimally healthy.

Materials Needed:

1. Construction paper
2. Scissors
3. Crayons or markers
4. Rulers

Procedures:

1. Talk with the children about a coat of arms. In ancient times, each family had a personal coat of arms to identify the family. It was also used as a protection in battle.

2. Show examples of some typical shields that have been used. You may want to have some patterns available for children who may need some assistance in making their shield or have a worksheet already made so that children can move directly into the activity (see Figure 6.3, Coat of Wellness).

3. Allow time for children to complete their wellness shields, drawing pictures to illustrate the following:

   a. A positive health habit you practice each day.

   b. A positive health habit you wish you would do every day.

   c. Something about your own "wellness" that concerns you (for example, not getting enough sleep, eating too many sweets, not doing enough exercise).

   d. A wellness goal you would like to achieve this school year.

4. When children have completed their shields, encourage them to show them to their classmates. Place the shields on a bul-

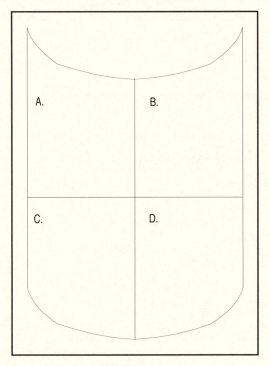

Figure 6.3. Coat of Wellness.

letin board to remind children of the positive habits they have developed or would like to develop.

Closure:

Take a few minutes to remind children of the good feelings they experience when they are proud of their habits and behaviors. Encourage them to continue practicing their positive habits and improve at least one wellness habit during the school year.

Walking for Wellness

Brief Overview of Activity:

In this activity, children will take a 30-minute walk as a way of exploring the potential benefits of participating in a regular walking program. They will be asked to think of things that will make walking interesting and exciting.

Objectives:

1. Children will participate in a 30-minute walking program.
2. Children will identify at least five things they can do during walking to make the exercise program more interesting and exciting.

Materials Needed:

1. Each child will need appropriate walking shoes. This requirement should be discussed with children the day before the activity.
2. Five-inch by 8-inch card for each child.

Procedures:

1. Ask children to choose a partner with whom to walk.
2. Explain the parameters of this activity with respect to safety and the walking path to be followed.

3. Begin the activity with a 5-minute warm-up walk. Then have the children walk quickly for 20 more minutes. Lastly, tell the children to walk slowly for 5 minutes (cool down).

4. When the walk is completed, provide time for sharing of experiences and feelings.

   What did you see?

   How did it feel?

   Would this activity be something you could do regularly to improve your health?

5. Talk about things one can do while walking:

   a. Listen to music.

   b. Watch people.

   c. Enjoy the beauties of nature.

   d. Use your imagination.

6. Describe the benefits of regular exercise.

7. Encourage children to develop a walking (or other type of exercise) program for a six-to-eight week period and stick to it.

8. Give children a 5-inch by 8-inch card and ask them to write down five things they can do while exercising so it does not become boring. Permit time for children to share their ideas with class members.

Closure:

Give children time to talk about their experience. Encourage them to really commit to a regular daily workout for six to eight weeks. Remind them that you will be following their progress and attitudes regarding a regular exercise program.

What Wellness Means to Me

Brief Overview of Activity:

This activity helps children to verbalize a wellness mantra (a personal statement of well-being) and it encourages them to think about their own personal wellness. The activity can be integrated into a language arts or creative writing class. Encourage children to think about their own personal wellness.

Objectives:

1. Children will have an opportunity to think about what wellness means to them and how it relates to their lifestyle.
2. Children will develop their own personal statements of what wellness means to them.

Materials Needed:

1. Chart paper and markers
2. Theme paper and pen or pencil for each child

Procedure:

1. Allow children time to brainstorm some of the health benefits of wellness. Some ideas include:
   a. People who practice positive health and wellness habits have more energy.
   b. People who have good nutrition habits get sick less often.
   c. People who practice good personal hygiene often have more friends. (It's more fun to be around someone who is clean, has no body odor, etc.)
2. Ask children to think about what wellness means to them on a more personal level. As they talk about some of their beliefs, jot down their ideas on chart paper for all to see.
3. Give children paper and pencils and ask them to develop their own personal statement of how wellness plays an important part in their life. Remind them that they can look at wellness in general or focus on one particular aspect of wellness that is important to them such as regular brushing of teeth, getting enough rest, and so on.
4. When children have completed their statements, they can share their ideas.
5. Encourage children to take their statements home and share them with family members.

Closure:

Bring this session to a close by reminding children that they have wellness habits in their life that are important to them. Encourage them to make a lifelong commitment to practice wellness habits.

Take a Wellness Stand

Brief Overview of Activity:

This activity will assist children in evaluating their wellness habits. As they listen to what other children have to say, they will begin to consider wellness changes they can make in their own lives.

Objectives:

1. Children will evaluate their own wellness habits (strengths and weaknesses).
2. Children will set a personal wellness goal.

Materials Needed:

1. Cards with the words "Always," "Usually," "Sometimes," "Seldom," and "Never"
2. Five-inch by 8-inch card for children to write their "Wellness Goals"

Procedure:

1. Place the five cards at different locations in the room.
2. Explain to children that they will be participating in an activity that will help them to examine their personal health habits and decide which ones they can improve.
3. Point to the five cards placed around the room and explain to children that when a statement is read, they are to stand next to the word that best describes their response to the statement.
4. Read the following statements.
   a. I get at least 8 or 9 hours of sleep each night.
   b. I drink at least eight glasses of water each day.

    c. I wear a seat belt when riding in a car.

    d. I eat at least two pieces of fruit each day.

    e. My parent(s) spends at least one-half hour per week talking with me about what's happening in my life.

    f. I find it easy to talk with a friend or counselor about my feelings.

5. Spend time discussing children's responses to the statements. Discuss health habits that everyone should consider practicing.

6. Ask children to name one positive health habit that they would like to develop.

7. Give children 5-inch by 8-inch cards and tell them to write down a wellness goal they would like to achieve. Explain to children that for the next six weeks, they will be practicing their wellness health habit.

8. Each day they are to record (check) their progress on the cards.

9. Check in with your children daily to see how they are doing with their wellness health-habit goal.

Closure:

Explain to children the importance of practicing good health habits. Remind them to record their daily progress. Offer assistance to those who may experience difficulty practicing their new goal. Monitor children's progress daily.

Wellness Auction

Brief Overview of Activity:

This activity will help children to prioritize their wellness goals and discuss how important these goals are to them. They will select one goal and decide what steps they can take to achieve this goal.

Objectives:

1. Children will explore and prioritize their wellness goals.

2. Children will participate in a wellness auction.

3. Children will identify specific steps they can take to reach their wellness goals.

Materials Needed:

1. Play money or tickets representing various amounts of money
2. *Wellness Goal Auction Sheet* for children (Figure 6.4).

Procedure:

1. Talk briefly with children about their experiences with auctions. Ask them if they have ever been to an auction with their parents. Do they know what happens at an auction? Briefly explain the bidding process and how items are sold to the highest bidder.
2. Have children identify specific wellness goals that are important to them. Identify some items to get them started. A few examples might include:
   To have more friends
   To eat a balanced diet
   To get at least eight hours of sleep each night
   To cut down on sweets
   To feel better about myself
   To be kinder to siblings
3. Make a comprehensive list of wellness goals using children's ideas.
4. Auction each goal and let the children bid for the two goals they want. The goals go to the highest bidder.
5. Continue the bidding until each child has two wellness goals.
6. Give each child a *Wellness Goal Auction* form so that they can record one of their goals.
7. Ask children to write three action steps they can take to reach this wellness goal.
8. Give children time to share their goals and the action steps they will take to reach their goals.
9. Explain to children that they are to practice their action steps during the week.

Wellness Goal Auction

The goal I have purchased is:

Action steps needed to reach my goal:

1.

2.

3.

Figure 6.4. Wellness Goal Auction Sheet.

Closure:

To bring closure to this activity, remind children that while bidding was fun, the real value of this activity is practicing their action steps to attain their goals. Remind them that in real life, they do not have to bid on wellness goals. They can choose to practice any wellness goal that will help them to better care for themselves.

My Lifeline

Brief Overview of Activity:

In this activity, children will draw a lifeline of their health, describing preventive measures and good health habits they have practiced to this point in their lives. Then they will identify future health habits they will practice during the next five years.

Objectives:

1. Children will explore personal preventive health habits and record them on a lifeline.

2. Children will share their personal wellness stories.
3. Children will realize the need to care for their physical well-being.

Materials Needed:

Pieces of poster board, cut 4-inch by 36-inch for each child to complete a lifeline. It would be helpful to have the lifeline already pre-drawn, if possible.

Procedure:

1. Show a sample lifeline (timeline) to the children. Talk about some of the events that can go on a wellness lifeline (for example, received immunizations, had tonsils out, started an exercise program, played on a team sport, had regular dental appointments, and so on). The timeline may also include descriptions of things that happened to you to make you feel really good, such as visits from favorite relatives or a trip to Disney World.
2. Provide children with a piece of poster paper (4-inch by 36-inch), and instruct them to create a lifeline allowing one space for each year of life. Ask them to create an additional five spaces for five years into the future.
3. Encourage children to develop their own wellness lifeline by indicating on the line all of the crucial wellness activities they have completed. They can write words or draw pictures to illustrate wellness lifeline events.
4. Ask children to name additional wellness, lifeline events they would like to accomplish during they next five years.
5. Provide children time to share their lifelines in small groups. Display lifelines for all to see.

Closure:

In closing this session, encourage children to share some of their reactions, observations, and insights gained from this activity. Discuss group similarities and differences with regard to how children care for their physical well-being.

ADDITIONAL IDEAS FOR PHYSICAL CARING

In My Bag

Have children bring a bag with one item in it that reflects their commitment to caring for their physical self. Apples, toothbrush, comb, small pillow, and running shoes are examples of items that reflect physical caring. Take turns asking children to share their items and to tell how they relate to physical caring.

I'm a Beautiful Person Collage

Children are asked to create collages to show the things they do to remain physically well. Collages can be posted to make a great bulletin board.

Crystal Ball Activity

Children will be given a crystal ball worksheet that divides the ball into 10 years, 25 years, and 50 years. They are to look into their future and decide what kinds of positive health habits will help them to care for themselves throughout their lives.

10 years	25 years	50 years
Brush my teeth daily	Regular exercise	Regular doctor visits
Wear seat belts	Be kind to family	Keep active

Helping Me Relax

While playing soft, relaxing music, assist children in creating an imaginary, safe place to relax when stressed. Ask children to share their safe, quiet place. Have them describe what it is like (sights, sounds, smells, and so on).

Family Fun Day

Encourage children to have weekly family fun days when all members get together to do something physical and fun. This can have long-lasting positive results to promote good physical health as well as family togetherness.

Healthy Snack Day

Provide children with information that they can share with their family regarding healthy (and easy to prepare) snacks for all.

Home Safety Check

In conjunction with fire prevention week, have children do a home safety check to assure that everyone in the family knows what they should do in the event of a home fire. The local fire department can provide home checklists to help insure home safety.

Food and Personal Needs Drive

Encourage children to bring in food or personal care items (tooth-paste, shampoo, soap, washcloths, etc.) for a local food pantry or domestic abuse shelter. Discuss with them the importance of being a volunteer and helping to care for others who are in need of help.

Food Pantry Volunteer

If there is a food pantry in your area where lunch is served to home-less persons, encourage children to volunteer a few hours to help serve food, wash dishes, and so on.

Charity Walks

Get children involved in some of the walks/runs that are sponsored each year by the community to benefit charities in the area. This activity has a twofold purpose in that it helps children to exercise while helping those in need.

Pet Day

Sponsor a "pet day" at school where children share their pets with classmates. Ask children to identify things they do to care for their pets and things their pets do to care for them.

Humane Society Guest Speaker

Invite a speaker from the local Humane Society to discuss pet care, activities of the Humane Society, and ways that children can become involved in helping the Humane Society care for animals.

Class Pet

Have a class pet (for example, goldfish, hamster, turtle) that can be cared for by children. Chart growth, care and feeding, cage cleaning, etc. Give all children an opportunity to care for the pet during the school year.

My Plant

Give children a plant at the beginning of the school year and encourage them to care for their plant throughout the school year. Use this experience to emphasize the importance of caring for all living things and to show how other living things care for them.

Cleanup Day

Organize children into teams to clean up the schoolyard, neighborhood, and so on. This can be a great public relations tool for school neighborhoods and a wonderful service to the senior citizens of the community.

Spruce Up Our School!

In the fall, have children plant tulip, hyacinth, crocus, and daffodil bulbs in a protected area of the schoolyard. In the spring they will be delighted with the colorful results of their caring for the environment.

Why Recycle?

If the school is in an area that does not have mandatory recycling, children can begin a voluntary program of recycling within the classroom. It may be prudent to just begin with one type of recyclables at a time, for example, newspapers, because it could become a large undertaking to do all types at once. This project can also be a

valuable curricular component in helping children to understand
how recycling can improve the environment.

Bike/Skateboard/In-Line Skating/Scooter Safety Day

Invite the local police officer in to talk with children about why it is
important to care for one's equipment, to wear a helmet and elbow
and kneepads, and to obey road signs and traffic signals. This would
be helpful to do in the fall with a follow-up in the spring. Help children to understand how objects can care for them if they care for
objects by using them properly.

Toy Safety

Have children brainstorm toys and athletic equipment that can be
dangerous if used improperly. Once the list is completed, divide the
class into groups, and have each group choose one toy or piece of
equipment and write a safe-use plan for it.

My Life Guide

Children will make a list of caring ideas from their family value system
that will help them to care for their physical needs. Once completed, the
caring ideas can be posted around the room so that children can gain
new ideas for physical caring and safety. This same activity can be used
to explore other caring ideas that children use in caring for themselves
and others (socially, emotionally, cognitively-academically, and so on).

BIBLIOGRAPHY

Academy of Child and Adolescent Psychiatry (2000). News release (*http://www.
aacap.org/press_release/2000/0522.htm*).

American Academy of Pediatrics (1985). *Getting your child fit: Special report.* Elk
Grove Village, IL: AAP.

American Cancer Society (1993). *World smoking and health.* Atlanta, GA: American Cancer Society.

Caldwell, D., Nestle, M., & Rogers, W. (1998). School nutrition services. In E.
Marx, S.F. Wooley, & D. Northrop (eds.), *Health is academic* (pp. 195–223).
New York, NY: Teachers College Press.

DeHart, G.B., Sroufe, L.A., & Cooper, R.G. (2000). *Child development: Its nature and course* (4th ed.). Boston, MA: McGraw-Hill.

Devaney, B.L., Gordon, A.R., & Burghardt, J.A. (1995). Dietary intakes of students. *American Journal of Clinical Nutrition,* GI (Suppl. 1), 2055–2125.

Federal Interagency Forum on Child and Family Statistics (2001). *America's Children: Key National Indicators of Well-Being, 2001.* Washington, DC: U.S. Government Printing Office.

Hoeger, W.W.K., & Hoeger, S.A. (2000). *Lifetime physical fitness and wellness: A personalized program* (6th ed.). Englewood, CO: Morton Publishing Co.

Johnston, L.D., O'Malley, P.M., & Bachman, J.G. (2002). *Monitoring the future national results on adolescent drug use: Overview of key findings, 2001.* (NIH Publication No. 02-105). Bethesda, MD: National Institute on Drug Abuse.

Kids Health (2000). *Talking to your child about smoking and smokeless tobacco.* Wilmington, DE: Nemours Center for Children's Health Media (*http://kidshealth. org/parent/positive/talk/smoking_p.2.html*).

Kolbe, L.J. (1992). Statement. The risky business of adolescence: How to help teens stay safe—Part 1. Hearing before the Select Committee on Children, Youth, and Families, U.S. House of Representatives, pp. 22–23. Washington, DC: U.S. Government Printing Office.

Lewis, C.J., Crane, N.T., Moore, B.J., & Hubbard, V.S. (1994). Healthy people 2000: Report on the 1994 nutrition progress review. *Nutrition Today, 29* (6), 6–14.

Marx, E., Wooley, S.F., & Northrop, D. (eds.) (1998). *Health is academic: A guide to coordinated school health.* New York, NY: Teachers College Press.

McKenzie, F.D., & Richmond, J.B. (1998). Linking health and learning: An overview of coordinated school health programs. In E. Marx, S.F. Wooley, & D. Northrop (eds.), *Health is academic* (pp. 1–14). New York, NY: Teachers College Press.

Meeks, L., Heit, P., & Page, R. (1996). *Comprehensive school health education* (2nd ed.). Blacklick, OH: Meeks Heit Publishing Co.

Murphy, T.A., & Murphy D. (1987). *The wellness for life workbook.* San Diego, CA: Fitness Publications.

National Center for Chronic Disease Prevention and Health Promotion (2002). *Physical activity and good nutrition: Essential elements to prevent chronic diseases and obesity 2002.* (*http://www.cdc.gov/nccdphp/dnpa/dnpaaag.htm*).

National Center for Health Statistics (2000). *Prevalence of overweight among children and adolescents: United States, 1999.* (*http://www.cdc.gov/nchs/products/ pubs/pubd/hestats/overwght99.htm*)

National Institute of Child Health and Human Development (2001). News release: Fourth annual federal report, America's children: Key national indicators of well-being. Federal Interagency Forum on Child and Family Statistics (*http:// www.childstats.gov/ac2001/toc.asp*).

National Institute of Child Health and Human Development (2000, January 31). NIH news alert: The health behaviors in school aged children. World Health Organization (*http://www.ruhbc.ed.ac.uk/hbsc*).

National SAFE KIDS Campaign (1999). Fact sheet. (*http://www.safekids.org/fact99/trends99.html*).

Pollock, M.B., & Middleton, K.(1994). *School health instruction: The elementary & middle school years* (3rd ed.). St. Louis, MO: Mosby.

Seefeldt, V.D. (1998). Physical education. In E. Marx, S.F. Wooley, & D. Northrop (eds.), *Health is academic* (pp. 1–14). New York, NY: Teachers College Press.

U.S. Centers for Disease Control and Prevention (2000, June 9). CDC Surveillance Summaries, MMWR 2000; 49(No. SS-5).

U.S. Centers for Disease Control and Prevention (1996, September 27). CDC Surveillance Summaries, 1995. MMWR, 45 (ss-4).

U.S. Centers for Disease Control and Prevention, National Center for HIV, STD, and TB Prevention, Divisions of HIV/AIDS Prevention, Surveillance Branch (2002, March 1). (*http://www.cdc.gov/hiv/graphics/adolesnt.htm*).

U.S. Centers for Disease Control and Prevention (1998). 1998 Guidelines for treatment of sexually transmitted disease. MMWR 1998: 47 (No. RR-1): pp 1–118.

U.S. Department of Health and Human Services (1999a). HIV/AIDS surveillance report (year-end edition vol. II, No. 2): Washington, DC: U.S. Department of Health and Human Service–Public Health Service.

U.S. Department of Health and Human Services (1999b). *Physical activity and health: A report of the surgeon general.* Atlanta, GA: U.S. Department of Health and Human Services, Centers for Disease Control and Prevention, National Center for Chronic Disease Prevention and Health Promotion.

U.S. Department of Health and Human Services (2000). *Reducing tobacco use: A report of the surgeon general.* Atlanta, GA: U.S. Department of Health and Human Services, Centers for Disease Control and Prevention, National Center for Chronic Disease Prevention and Health Promotion, Office on Smoking and Health.

Van Kammen, W.B., Lober, R., & Stouthamer-Lober, M. (1991). Substance use and its relationship to conduct problems and delinquency in young boys. *Journal of Youth and Adolescents, 20,* 399–413.

Ventura, S.J., Mathews, T.J., Hamilton B.E. (2002). Teenage births in the United States: Trends 1991–2000, an update. *National Vital Statistics Reports 50* (9). Hyattsville, MD: National Center for Health Statistics.

Zigler, E.F., & Stevenson, M.F. (1993). *Children in a changing world: Developmental and social issues* (2nd ed.). Pacific Grove, CA: Brooks/Cole Publishing Co.

CHAPTER 7

Personal/Emotional Caring

Personal/Emotional Caring is a process of self-care in which children learn to value and manage themselves as capable and self-determining human beings whose success comes from the application of internal attributes and strengths.

PERSONAL/EMOTIONAL DEVELOPMENT

Erik Erikson (1963) has emphasized the importance of the middle childhood years as a time in children's lives when they strive to master adult skills and feelings associated with life's successes and failures. When children initiate activities, seek out learning experiences, and work hard to accomplish goals, they develop a basic belief in their own competence. They view themselves as capable achievers and experience real successes in their academic pursuits, social interactions, and life challenges. Deep feelings of competence and self-worth emerge with repeated successes as children develop a sense of industry through responsible decision-making and goal attainment. The term *industry* captures the essence of what takes place during middle childhood development. Industry is derived from a Latin word meaning "to build." During this stage of development, children are busy building a variety of life skills that will enhance their personal/emotional well-being; skills that will help them to responsibly self-regulate (manage) in caring ways.

Children who fail repeatedly in their attempts to master new life skills and achieve success are often left with feelings of incompetence and inferiority. They tend to devalue themselves and experience a life of discouragement and failure. They fail to satisfy their developmental and personal needs. Maslow (1954) has stated that developmental needs that are not met, or only partially met, jeopardize the fulfillment of higher-order needs and negatively affect a child's ability to self-manage. Children who are to develop a personal/emotional sense of well-being must learn how to meet their physiological, safety and security, love and belonging, and esteem needs in responsible and caring ways if they are to move in the direction of self-actualization (fulfillment of one's human potential).

During middle childhood, children learn to define themselves as their personal sense of self emerges through social interaction and self-introspection. During the elementary school years, children become increasingly more aware of themselves as unique individuals and likewise become more aware of how they view others and how others view them (Zigler & Stevenson, 1993). Personal/emotional development is thus a stage-driven process in which children learn who they are (self-concept) and how they feel about themselves (self-esteem). This process shapes children's attitudes, beliefs, and feelings about themselves and their world and determines the life-long actions they will take in response to the self-perceptions that they have formed (Saarni, Mumme, & Campos, 1998).

Self-Concept: Who Am I?

As children grow and develop, they create mental pictures of themselves (concepts of self). With age and maturity, these pictures become more defined and multifaceted. Young children (preschool) are likely to describe themselves in terms of age and physical characteristics (hair color, size, height, etc.), whereas older children (middle childhood) will present a more complex, mature, and better integrated picture of their *psychological self.* The *psychological self* is referred to as such because children now name psychological characteristics and traits in their self-description to include inner thoughts, feelings, abilities, and character traits (Broughton, 1978;

Harter, 1998; Selman, 1980). For example, John, a third grader, might describe himself as kind, caring, a good artist, and someone who is fearful of making formal presentations in class.

Children are thus able to formulate a *metatheory* of self and others in which they consider a variety of life situations and experiences in bringing together complex and multifaceted descriptions of self in comparison with others. Thus, children are able to view themselves as unique.

By age 8 or 9, children are able to identify and compare similarities and differences between themselves and others. They likewise recognize the nature of an inner, private self that harbors internal thoughts and feelings unknown to others and sometimes to themselves. The emergence of this awareness increases children's insightfulness, self-understanding, and perspective-taking when considering the thoughts, feelings, and actions of others (Akos, 2000).

Self-Esteem: How Do I Feel about Myself?

As children develop a multifaceted view of themselves, they are inclined to evaluate what they have created. They wonder about their value and worth as people and begin to formulate opinions of themselves that will affect their personalities, relationships, academic performance, and general well-being both now and in the future.

Akin et al. (1990) have stated that "Self-esteem is the emotional result of an ever changing collection of accurate and/or inaccurate assessments one continually makes of oneself. The assessments are based on the way one views oneself (self-image) and thinks about oneself (self-concept) relative to numerous personal characteristics such as physical appearance, personality traits, status in various groups, and the like" (p. 2).

Children who feel good about themselves (high self-esteem) view themselves as capable and goal-oriented individuals who are generally successful in achieving their wants and needs. They like people and people like them. They feel valued and accepted by family and friends and perceive themselves to be worthy contributors and caregivers (Akos, 2000).

In contrast, children with low self-esteem believe that they are unloved, do not belong, and are inadequate in comparison to others. Children with low self-esteem are at an increased risk of experiencing anxiety, depression, difficulty in school situations, loneliness, and a sense of powerlessness.

Self-esteem develops gradually throughout middle childhood and represents the feelings that emerge from the beliefs and attitudes that children form as they evaluate their self-concept. Saarni et al. (1998) stated that self-esteem is thus based upon perceived objective information about oneself and the subjective evaluation of that information. Children who develop high self-esteem do so not because of what others do to them, but rather from what they do for themselves. Self-esteem is a by-product of achievement and realistic perceptions and expectations of self in transition. For example, Tom, a fifth grader, sees himself as having athletic ability in football despite some skill deficits that he hopes to address (perceived self). He pictures himself as he would like to be—a skilled football player (ideal self)—and strives to self-improve through realistic goal-setting and hard work. Tom will experience positive self-esteem knowing that he is making progress toward a realistic challenging goal that is based on self-improvement rather than perfection.

Positive self-esteem is therefore contingent upon children possessing a realistic, fact-supported, perceived self and an ideal self that is challenging but not out of reach. Children must be taught how to be reality oriented in setting their goals and in judging themselves based on the outcomes of their actions. How children judge themselves will affect their creativity, integrity, spontaneity, and stability in everything they do. *"Self-esteem is the mainspring that slates every child for success or failure as a human being"* (Briggs, 1975, p. 3).

Emotional Development

While self-esteem is a process of self-judgment in which children decide if they like what they have created, emotional development is a stage-driven process in which children learn to identify, understand, and express their emotions responsibly. Emotional development leads to emotional intelligence, in which children learn to understand the complexities of emotion-arousing situations and how to address them by managing their actions in a responsible and caring manner.

Children during the middle childhood years have already experienced a full range of emotions and are now developmentally ready to begin understanding emotions and their causes (Saarni, Mumme, & Campos, 1998). For children to truly care for themselves and others, understanding emotions and their causes is a necessary prerequisite to making responsible life choices. Kuersten (1999) has stated that, *"Emotional health is one of the bedrocks of success in life. Being able to understand and manage our feelings, and to connect with others in satisfying ways, are crucial to finding personal happiness, stability, and peace"* (p. 1).

Goleman (1996) coined the term "emotional intelligence" to describe a different way of being smart. Emotionally intelligent children, according to Goleman, have learned to manage their feelings in ways that enhance their connections with self (happiness, stability, and peace), with others (fostering meaningful relationships), and with the environment (living a purposeful and meaningful life). These are children who have learned to manage distressing moods, control impulses, motivate themselves, and remain hopeful and optimistic in times of personal setbacks. They have empathy in their relationships with others and are able to delay immediate gratification when pursuing goals.

According to Goleman (1996), emotional intelligence is largely learned even in the presence of genetic factors that influence a variety of temperaments from birth. Consequently, lifelong strengths, contributing to the development of emotional intelligence, can be taught at home and in school. Children who learn empathy, impulse control, persistence, self-motivation, and other fundamentals of emotional competence are likely to make responsible caring choices in pursuit of satisfying and purposeful lives.

THE PERSONAL/EMOTIONAL HEALTHY CHILD

Children who enjoy personal/emotional health possess the attitudes, information, and skills to meet their needs and to make responsible life decisions when caring for themselves. They are in the process of becoming as they strive to achieve an identity and a life of purpose and meaning.

Children who possess personal/emotional health are in the process of creating a psychological self that enables them to rely on their own internal resources in the face of daily life challenges. They are striving to know good, be good, and to do good (responsible caregivers). More specifically, children who have attained personal/emotional health are effective self-managers who

- accept personal responsibility for their own actions;
- accurately assess the effects of their behaviors on others;
- express feelings in an appropriate manner;
- show concern for others' feelings;
- demonstrate remorse when others hurt;
- ask for help when needed;
- gracefully accept the help of others;
- possess caring personality characteristics (kindness, respect, courage, trust, responsibility, etc.);
- understand their personal strengths and limitations;
- identify and discuss their feelings with others;
- demonstrate self-confidence;
- demonstrate enthusiasm for life;
- manage stress responsibly;
- demonstrate effective listening and communication skills;
- have clear values;
- readily accept calculated risks;
- pursue personal interests while maintaining a sense of community;
- recognize that people have choices in how they express their feelings;

- are open to complaints, criticisms, and suggestions for self-improvement; and
- possess meaningful hopes, dreams, and aspirations.

Children who possess these personal qualities and ones like them are well on their way to attaining personal/emotional health (Brooks, 2000). They are learning responsible ways to care for themselves and others. They are able to accurately assess their needs and wants and to stay focused in using their personal/emotional strengths in meeting life's challenges.

UNDERSTANDING THE NEED FOR PERSONAL/EMOTIONAL CARING

During the middle childhood years (6 to 12 years), children face the challenges of mastering adult skills and the feelings that accompany success and failure. Success at meeting the challenges of daily living enhances children's beliefs in themselves and bolsters their self-confidence and motivation in wanting to care for their personal/emotional needs. Perls (1969) believed that children can achieve a sense of unity and integration in their lives to the extent that they are aware of their needs and stay focused in meeting them. In doing so, they will be able to achieve personal/emotional caring based on their own ability to self-regulate in the face of life's challenges.

However, when children experience repeated failures in mastering personal/emotional self-care, lack awareness and focus in meeting their needs, and seek to manipulate others to get what they need and want, they are often left with feelings of incompetence, inferiority, and self-doubt (Barasch, 2000). When this happens, these children are at an increased risk of experiencing the following:

Depression

The Harvard Mental Health Letter (2002) indicated that approximately 2% of children ages 7–12 in the United States suffer from major depression. They also report that similar to adults, children's depression is a recurrent illness and they could experience multiple relapses. More specifically, in the first Surgeon General's report on Mental Health, there is indication that children who suffer from depression will experience a relapse within two years (U.S. Department of Health and Human Services, 1996). In fact, there is evidence that suggests that depression is occurring early, in younger children, than in past decades (National Institute of Mental Health, 2000). This illness is linked to drug and alcohol use, eating disorders, deviant behaviors, and rising suicide rates. Despite the devastation that depression causes, it is one of the most treatable mental illnesses.

Suicide

According to *Suicide Rates in Children: Fact Sheet Report #651* released in July 2000, more than 2,000 young people between the ages of 10 and 19 committed suicide in this country [in 1995]. Suicide is reported to be the third leading cause of death in this age group, surpassed only by motor vehicle crashes and homicide. Suicide attempts reach their peak in midadolescence, and the incidence of mortality increases throughout the teenage years (Grunbaum et al., 1999).

Children as young as five years of age have been reported to make suicide attempts. Why children become suicidal is a complex question at best, but ". . . some researchers believe that suicidal children are highly sensitive, have a low tolerance for frustration, and have feelings of depression, guilt, hostility, and anger that they are unable to express" (reported by Stefanowski-Harding, 1990 and cited in Thompson & Rudolph, 2000, p. 459). Meeks, Heit, and Page (1996) reported the following reasons as to why children and adolescents take their own lives:

- Fighting with parents
- High parental expectations
- Feelings of inferiority
- Difficulty making positive social adjustments
- Friction with peers

- Difficulty at school
- Depression
- Academic failure
- Changes in the family
- Death of a parent
- Breakup (p. 64)

Eating Disorders

The Harvard Eating Disorders Center reports several findings with respect to young children and eating disorders (2002).

- Children aged 8 to 10 are dissatisfied with their size; more specifically approximately one-half of the girls and one-third of the boys were dissatisfied. Most dissatisfied girls wanted to be thinner while about equal numbers of dissatisfied boys wanted to be heavier. Boys wanted to grow into their bodies, whereas girls were more worried about their bodies growing.
- Of girls aged 9 to 12, slightly more than half reported exercising to lose weight, slightly less than one-half reported eating less to lose weight, and approximately 1 out of 20 reported using diet pills or laxatives to lose weight.
- Forty percent of fourth graders report that they diet either "very often" or "sometimes."

The Alliance for Eating Disorder Awareness (2002) reports that eating disorders affect approximately 5 to 10 million American adolescent girls and women and approximately 1 million American boys and that eating disorders can be found in children as young as 3 years old. Berg (1998) has stated that 25 percent of all teenage girls have some type of dysfunctional eating pattern and that eating disorders also are reported to be increasing among children. Berg (1998) has stated that discussions pertaining to this topic should begin as early as fifth and sixth grade.

The effects of dysfunctional eating patterns and disorders take their toll in decreased energy, fatigue, chest and abdominal pain, sleep disturbances, and poor bone health, not to mention emotional disturbances that include moodiness, depression, irritability, and inability to concentrate. In addition to the potentially life-threatening effects of eating problems are those that affect a child's ability to learn and result in loss of social contact with family and friends.

Lowered Self-Esteem

Thompson and Rudolph (2000) view self-esteem as a by-product of children's productive activity, their relationships with others, and their perceptions of how they believe they are doing. Children have a need to develop a sense of autonomy and independence that evolves through setting goals, learning and applying life skills, and developing meaningful social relationships. When these needs are not fulfilled, children feel powerless and often experience physical and emotional pain.

The National Institute of Child Health and Human Development (NICHD, 2000) reported the results of a 1997–1998 survey on the health behaviors of school-age children, ages 11, 13, and 15, in 26 European countries and regions, Canada, and the United States. In the health and well-being portion of the survey, students in the United States and Israel reported the highest frequency of health-related problems and symptoms and were most likely to take medications for these symptoms. Headaches, stomachaches, nervousness, feeling tired, feeling low, and feeling lonely were among the symptoms reported.

Stress

Chandler (1987) defined stress ". . . as a state of emotional tension arising from unmet needs or environmental threats" (p. 4). Nazario (1991) has stated that approximately 35 percent of all children in the United States are experiencing stress.

The reasons for stress are wide and varied, but the most common relate to pressures to excel academically, athletically, and socially. Children also experience stress in relationship to uncertainties that they experience in living (birth of a sibling, death of loved ones, community and school violence, illness, harm to self and others, and fears regarding uncertainty of the future) (Chandler, 1987; Felger, 1992; Mann, 1993; Stepp, 1993).

Children who fail to cope with stress in responsible and caring ways ". . . do not attend well, have trouble concentrating, and receive poor grades. Behaviorally, they seem to have trouble interacting and are hyperactive, withdrawn, hostile, angry, impatient, or irritable" (Jackson & Owens, 1999, p. 75).

Violence

The Children's Defense Fund's division on violence prevention and youth development (Children's Defense Fund, 2002) provides fact sheets about youth and violence. More specifically, they examine gun violence, juvenile justice, and school safety. The following is a brief summary of their 1999–2001 reported findings.

- 3,365 children and teens were killed by gunfire;
- 1,990 children were murdered by gunfire;
- 1,078 children committed suicide using a firearm;
- 214 children died from an accidental shooting;
- 153 children who were killed by a firearm were younger than the age of 10 and 73 were younger than the age of 5;
- and there was a 23 percent decrease in juvenile arrest for violent crime despite population growth; a 56 percent decrease in juvenile homicide; and a 39 percent decrease in juvenile robbery.

While the percentage of juvenile crime is decreasing, it is still abundantly clear that children lives will be affected by violence. Schools are also affected by such violence. The National School Safety Center (2002) provides a report that reviews all school safety surveys. Notable statistics from that summary report include:

- More than one in three students (39 percent of middle schoolers and 36 percent of high schoolers) said they don't feel safe at school.

- Forty-three percent of high-school and 37 percent of middle-school boys believed it is OK to hit or threaten a person who makes them angry. Nearly one in five (19 percent) of the girls agreed.
- During 1998, students aged 12 through 18 were victims of more than 2.7 million crimes at school, including about 253,000 serious violent crimes (rape, sexual assault, robbery, and aggravated assault).
- In 1999, 50 states reported that they expelled a total of 3,523 students from school for bringing a firearm to school; 57 percent of the expulsions by school level were students in high school, 33 percent were in junior high, and 10 percent were in elementary school.

These statistics present a simple fact that in the absence of personal/emotional caring strategies being practiced, violence is often the alternative action exhibited.

The Cumulative Effects of Risk

Children's lives are shaped by the interplay of complex genetic and environmental factors, the effects of which we do not fully understand. And yet despite these unknowns, we do know that teaching children responsible personal/emotional caring strategies can help them to achieve a sense of industry and success.

From time to time, children experience personal/emotional health problems that interfere with their ability to think, feel, and act in responsible and productive ways. We hope that children confronted with these challenges will possess an awareness of self and the surrounding environment and the personal/emotional caring resources needed to self-regulate and get their lives back on track. But many children will not be so fortunate. Lacking in awareness and the personal/emotional caring strategies to meet their needs, some children will experience discouragement resulting in academic failure, family conflicts, low self-esteem, stress, violence, depression, diminished social status, and for some, the greatest tragedy of all: suicide.

The cumulative effects of risk emanating from an inability to care for one's personal/emotional needs in a responsible manner often results in emotional, mental, and behavioral problems (Aronen & Soinen, 2000). One in every five young people, at any given time, is affected by emotional and mental distress and one in 10, or as many as 6 million young people, may have a serious emotional disturbance (United States Department of Health and Human Services, 1996).

All of us want our children to be happy and caring people. We want them to live lives of purpose and meaning and to embrace a world full of opportunities with hope and optimism. This can become a reality despite the risks that present themselves when children's personal/emotional health is threatened. Children who understand how to care for their personal/emotional health are able to handle life's problems and challenges through their ability to make caring choices in support of their needs.

ENHANCING PERSONAL/EMOTIONAL WELL-BEING THROUGH CARING CHOICES

In the domain of personal/emotional caring, children are taught the qualities of humanness, namely the development of caring assets and personality attributes (character traits) that serve them well in their own self-care and in the care of others (Robenson, 2000). We want our children to understand their strengths and weaknesses, likes and dislikes, and hopes and fears. We want them to exercise self-control; experience success in doing things for themselves; express themselves responsibly; set goals; develop initiative; and learn new skills, talents, and abilities that help them to become competent and responsible players in their world. We want them to be active and curious, develop positive and caring peer relationships, engage in successful learning experiences, express their emotions responsibly, care for their hurts and accept the care of others, and be able to delay personal gratification for the greater good when necessary.

When children learn how to care for themselves personally and emotionally, they become caring, lovable, and responsible human beings with a life of purpose and meaning. They know who they are, that they are accepted by others, and most important, that they are acceptable to themselves. They are on their way to developing a self-identity that is based on a realistic, fact-supported, perceived self and an ideal self that is challenging to attain, but not totally out of reach. This helps children to develop positive self-esteem and lives full of hope and encouragement. *Helping children to attain a realistic and confident sense of self is important for it is the mainspring that slates them for a life of success or failure* (Kohn, 1996).

Elementary school counseling programs are in the people-building business and are therefore challenged to promote a sense of caring with a wellness focus. Teachers, parents, counselors, peers, administrators, and community supporters working together must teach children the personal/emotional caring strategies that help them to become caring human beings who love themselves, who are accepted by others, and who develop lifestyles with a "service to others" focus (Sapon-Shevin, 1999).

Children learn to meet their personal/emotional needs first by developing an *awareness* of self and their potential and second by developing a *utilization* of self in which they learn how to use their assets in caring ways to meet their needs, the needs of others, and the needs of their environment. Children are equipped with a wide range of bodily systems and senses that enable them to think, feel, and do. When their systems and senses are working together and children are *aware* of the feedback they are receiving (from self, others, and the environment), they can *utilize* their personal self-caring assets to self-regulate and to enhance their personal/emotional health.

In order for children to achieve personal/emotional well-being, they must develop a sense of awareness (about self, others, and the environment), learn personal/emotional caring strategies, and be able to use these strategies in the context of making caring choices. We can help children to maximize their personal/emotional health through an elementary school curriculum and school counseling program partnership that will teach children how to

- enhance their awareness skills,
- make responsible choices,
- develop positive character attributes,
- build positive self-esteem,
- express feelings in caring ways,
- communicate with others in caring ways,
- practice stress management strategies, and
- use resistance skills.

Self-Awareness and Caring

A realization of self must precede a utilization of self. Children must first become aware of themselves, of others, and of the environment before they can apply the feedback that they receive from these sources. Children who are tuned in to their five senses, to others, and to the environment will become more sensitive to their needs, strengths, limitations, emotions, thoughts, and actions. The feedback that they receive will help them to more effectively manage their lives in caring and responsible ways.

When children listen to music that calms their soul, they can turn to this type of music in the future for its pleasing and calming effect. The more children learn about themselves in relation to others, the more capable they become in developing healthy relationships as well as maintaining a sense of safety in the presence of interpersonal conflict. Likewise, the more children learn about themselves in relationship to their environment, the more successful they become in managing themselves and the environment in ways that foster personal/emotional health.

Elementary school counseling programs can increase children's awareness of their personal/emotional selves by helping them to

- identify their personal strengths and limitations;
- explore their dreams, hopes, and aspirations;

- develop a feelings vocabulary; and
- learn personal/emotional self-care strategies.

These awareness goals can be accomplished through art, music, role plays, observations, and activities that challenge their five senses. As a result, children will learn that they can trust their bodies to provide them with accurate information in understanding themselves, others, and the environment. Possessing this information, children are better equipped to make caring choices in meeting their personal/emotional needs while caring for others and their world. Only those children who are self-aware are capable of using what they know and understand to choose, change, and reinvent themselves in caring and responsible ways (Barasch, 2000).

Decision-Making and Caring

Personal/emotional caring is a proactive process requiring disciplined goal setting and action-oriented decision-making. A decision is a choice. Decision-making is a process to be followed that results in responsible choices being made. Choices are made in response to life situations as they are experienced. A life situation represents anything that children do in life. For example, experiencing a headache, taking notes in class, interacting with friends, and participating in a group discussion are all examples of life situations. Within all life situations are goals to be attained, problems to be solved, and choices to be identified and evaluated in arriving at caring and safe choices that will result in goal attainment.

To illustrate the value of decision-making, consider the following life situation. Jim, a sixth grader, finds a wallet containing a $100 bill. The name and address of the person losing the wallet and money are found in the wallet. The next step is to help Jim frame this life situation in the context of a decision-making process. The goal in this life situation is for Jim to care for himself and the person who lost the wallet and money. The problem is stated as a question to be addressed, "What should Jim do?" Choices are then generated and examined. Only those choices that are considered to be of a responsible and caring nature will be considered in helping Jim to meet his goal. How Jim resolves this life situation will have a defining impact on his character and respect for others.

Elementary school counseling programs can help children to identify life situations and to view them from a decision-making perspective. In so doing, children will be better able to meet their personal/emotional needs through safe, caring, and responsible actions. More will be said about decision-making and the presentation of an easy-to-use three-step decision-making model in Chapter 9, *Cognitive Caring.*

Character Building and Caring

Elementary school counseling programs are in the people-building business and exist to promote excellence in living and learning. Personal/emotional caring helps children to develop people qualities and attributes that help them to like themselves and be liked by others. We want our children to ". . . not only become knowledgeable, but socially and ethically responsible as well" (Boyer, 1995, p. 173).

The goal of teaching and school counseling programs is to provide children with an education that focuses on their mind, body, and spirit. If children are to become caring and responsible human beings who are personally and emotionally fit, elementary school counseling programs must help children to develop such core character traits as caring, kindness, honesty, respect, responsibility, self-discipline, patience, perseverance, and giving. These traits, and ones like them, can be developed in the home, places of worship, and in schools. A team effort can be deemed successful when children discover that what they learned about character really does make a positive difference in their personal/emotional health and how they conduct their lives. *Through character building, children learn that what they become is based on what they do.* As children define themselves, giving meaning and purpose to their lives, they discover that building character with a caring focus helps them to apply the lessons of the classroom to their daily lives.

Self-Esteem and Caring

Teaching children how to enhance their self-esteem is critical if they are to achieve personal/emotional well-being. Self-esteem relates to how children feel about themselves and those dimensions of self that they value (family, bodily self, academic self, social self, etc.). Self-esteem is that emotional sense of self that children experience when they evaluate their self-concept. They either generally like what they have created or do not like the selves they have become. Life is certainly more pleasant and valued when children have good feelings about themselves and enjoy life. Consequently, a positive and healthy self-esteem is worth attaining for oneself.

For children to earn self-esteem, they must understand what it is and what it is not. We will begin by identifying and dispelling some of the myths that surround this concept.

Myth 1: Children with high self-esteem feel good about themselves all the time.

Myth 2: Positive self-esteem can be given to children by caring adults.

Myth 3: Children are either born with high self-esteem or they are not.

Myth 4: Children who experience emotions of sadness, anger, or fear do not have high self-esteem.

The truth about self-esteem is that it is not a constant state of emotional bliss. Children, like adults, have emotional ups and downs in response to daily life challenges. Children with high self-esteem are generally up more than they are down, but they do experience fluctuations in their self-esteem.

When children are down, many adults want to cheer them up with positive and caring statements in hopes of raising their self-esteem. The truth is that children and adults cannot raise the self-esteem of other children by bombarding them with positive statements, sayings, or songs that communicate platitudes of good will. The way that children develop positive self-esteem is based on what they do for themselves. Self-esteem is a by-product of success and must be earned.

Self-esteem is not a genetically based trait. All children can learn how to enhance their state of emotional well-being by virtue of the goals they set and the actions they take in achieving success and taking time to enjoy the fruits of their labor.

Lastly, all human beings are capable of displaying a wide range of emotions, including sadness, anger, and fear. Displaying a full range of emotions is healthy and actually supports the development of a high self-esteem. Children who are open to life and are able to meet their wants and needs through self-expression and effective communication are managing their lives in a responsible manner. They experience the personal freedoms and successes that emanate from caring and responsible action. Self-esteem relates to children's emotional sense of self and is quite stable over time, whereas emotional expression enhances communication and is quite variable in accordance with current life events and children's perceptions of them.

Children who develop a positive emotional sense of self (self-esteem) are self-confident, willing to take moderate and calculated risks, foster caring and satisfying relationships with others, deal effectively with stress, set goals, and make responsible decisions. Parents, teachers, and counselors can help children to raise their self-esteem by addressing four conditions that Bean (1992) has stated are central to achieving personal/emotional wellness. The four conditions are

- connectiveness,
- uniqueness,
- power, and
- models.

First, children must achieve a sense of *connectiveness* with themselves, others, and the environment. They must feel a part of the world, appreciated by others, and comfortable in their surroundings. Being connected helps to ensure a sense of safety, security, and predictability in children's lives. Being connected is a need that must be satisfied for self-esteem to be achieved.

Second, children must experience a sense of *uniqueness* that is fulfilled when children feel they possess the human qualities that define their personhood, qualities that are appreciated and valued by others. These qualities represent strengths, assets, personality characteristics, and attributes that define children as having the potential to build meaningful life connections. When children feel underappreciated for their unique qualities, qualities that define them in caring and responsible ways, their self-esteem goes down. Children need to be aware of their unique qualities and be recognized for them if they are to understand what gives them value.

Third, children must experience a sense of *power,* feelings of competence and mastery over their own destiny. The utilization of children's unique attributes is what gives them the power to build satisfying and caring connections within themselves, others, and the environment. When children feel powerless, their self-esteem will go down. Consequently, children need to be encouraged and reinforced for using their unique qualities to build important connections in their lives and to enhance their self-esteem.

Fourth, children must develop a sense of *models.* Models provide children with the "how to's" of life and living. They help them to discern right from wrong and to organize themselves and their environment in ways that enable them to accomplish tasks that are consistent with their values and beliefs. Models are used to teach children how to build connections. When children lack appropriate and caring models, they are at a loss of what to do and how to do it. When children are lacking in needed models their self-esteem goes down. With responsible and caring models, children have the confidence and self-esteem to care for their personal/emotional well-being.

Elementary school counseling programs teach children that life is about building connections, maintaining connections, and addressing life's disconnections (divorce, death, and losses of all kind). Children can become successful in building connections when teachers, parents, and counselors *model* the *unique* attributes that children need to develop. When children develop a sense of *uniqueness* and use their attributes in caring ways, they derive *power* from what they have learned to build responsible and caring *connections*. Building connections will help children to develop a sense of industry and positive self-esteem.

Emotional Management and Caring

According to Goleman (1995), author of the best seller *Emotional Intelligence,* emotional well-being is a strong predictor of academic achievement and success, employment, marriage, and physical health. Children and adults with emotional intelligence are able to successfully and responsibly manage their emotions, relationships, and learning. Goleman (1995) has pointed out that children lacking in emotional intelligence skills such as self-control, zeal, persistence, and the ability to motivate oneself are directly related to the blatant disrespect of others, high incidence of fighting, and loneliness among children in our schools. *Current research has suggested that most children are experiencing deficits in all areas of emotional health* (U.S. Department of Health and Human Services, 1996).

Emotional intelligence is believed to be the bedrock upon which all other intelligences are built and it is more closely linked to lifelong success than IQ (Goleman, 1995). Recent studies have demonstrated that emotional intelligence predicts about 80 percent of a person's success in life. Despite everything that we know about emotional competence, it has been dropping for the past two decades. Children and teenagers are more impulsive, more disobedient, more lonely, more depressed, and more anxious than they were 20 years ago (Goleman, 1995).

Perhaps what is more relevant than the decline in emotional intelligence is that children can be taught emotional skills that enhance their ability to care for themselves and others. The good news is that emotional intelligence does not mature until a child is 15 or 16 years old, giving parents, teachers, and counselors ample opportunity to develop and enhance their emotional competence in daily living. Teaching children to become effective emotional self-managers involves the development and integration of emotional caring programs into school counseling and academic curriculums that are supported by a caring and challenging school climate (Herring, 1990). The following emotional caring strengths are the core of most successful emotional education programs.

- Empathy training
- Impulse control
- Decision-making
- Anger management training

Empathy Training

Children need training in identifying and experiencing the feelings of others. Children who are empathic are sensitive to other's needs, can relate to multiple points of view, and are more likely to understand and tolerate the behaviors of others. Beland (1992) identified the following objectives that can help children to develop a sense of empathy.

- Develop a feelings vocabulary.
- Increase children's awareness of their own feelings.
- Help children to identify others' feelings using contexture cues (facial expressions and body signs).
- Recognize that children may have different feelings regarding the same situations.
- Recognize that people's feelings can change and why this is so.
- Learn to recognize others' feelings through perspective taking.
- Understand that children may have different likes and dislikes.
- Teach children to differentiate intentional acts from unintentional acts (motives).
- Learn to apply rules of fairness and equality in life situations.
- Communicate feelings using "I" messages, and practice active listening with others.
- Learn to express care and concern for others.

Impulse Control

Children who are impulsive tend to act before they think. They fail to consider the options open to them and the consequences of each. "Children who learn how to control their impulses and delay gratification are better able to concentrate, deal with frustration, make plans, and follow through on them" (Hutter, 1999, p. 81). Elementary school counseling programs can teach children impulse control strategies and how to use them in developing self-discipline and in controlling their impulses through delayed gratification. The following strategies have proven to be useful in this regard.

- Thought-stopping strategies
- Relaxation training
- Positive imagery
- Self-talk exercises
- Goal-setting and time management

These techniques, and others like them, help children to delay immediate gratification and to break the cycle of impulsive behaviors using time as a variable so that children have the opportunity to think before acting.

Decision-Making

While impulse control methods help children to break the cycle of impulsive behaviors, decision-making helps them to consider their goals and to explore choices and their consequences in arriving at a course of action that is based on rational thought. Decision-making is discussed and described in detail in Chapter 9, *Cognitive Caring.*

Anger Management Training

Children have a need to understand anger, anger cues, and those factors that trigger anger responses in them. They likewise have a need to develop strategies that will help them to calm themselves in times of anger, head off situations that provoke anger in them when possible, and channel their anger in productive and caring ways when it occurs. The following sequence of steps outlines an anger management process that children can learn and use in caring for themselves and others (Beland, 1992; O'Rourke & Worzbyt, 1996; Schmidt, 1993).

1. Help children to recognize when they are angry.
2. Help children to accept their anger.
3. Assist children in deciding if their problem is something they can or cannot change.
4. Help children to think out loud in solving their problem (Stop, Think & Go Decision-Making, Chapter 9).
5. Help children to study their options and to evaluate them based on Right, Reality, and Responsibility (Chapter 9).
6. Help children to create and implement their plan of action.
7. Help children to evaluate how they handled their anger (evaluate plan).

The more children understand about anger and how to manage it in a caring and responsible manner, the better prepared they will be to accept and express it in ways that will enhance their personal/ emotional health.

Communication Skills and Caring

The way children care for themselves and others is based on how they express their feelings, thoughts, and actions with others. Children who are open to their own feelings and are able to express them openly with others are behaving in healthful ways. They likewise are open to the needs and wants of others and are equally successful in attending to their own needs and wants as well.

Children who have difficulty communicating are often unable to express their feelings, thoughts, needs, and wants openly. They have unfinished business, unresolved pain, and regrets in their quest to cope with blocked feelings and unmet needs. They strive to self-maintain in ways that intensify their pain (physical and psychological) rather than resolve it.

When responsible and caring communications are blocked, children often resort to tactics such as minimizing their problems; blaming others for their problems; making excuses; pretending that everything is okay; and avoiding people, feelings, thoughts, and situations that are at the root of their problems. Such excuses and defensive behaviors often result in feelings of anger, anxiety, fear, frustration, and jealousy.

Children can be taught effective and caring ways of expressing their true feelings. More specifically, children can learn how to improve their communications with others through the expression of

- I-messages,
- active listening,
- nonverbal communication, and
- assertiveness.

I-messages include specific behaviors or events, the effect(s) that these messages or events have on an individual, and the feelings that result. An example of an I-message is "Because you cut in front of me in the lunch line, I will have to wait longer to get my lunch and I am angry with what you did." When children learn to give I-messages, they take ownership for their feelings, thoughts, and actions and give others a chance to do the same.

Active listening shows others that you are interested in what they have to say. By maintaining eye contact, facing the person, using facial and other nonverbal forms of communication, and repeating back the essence of the message, the listener can confirm, clarify, or summarize what was heard.

And lastly, children can enhance their communications by learning to use assertive behaviors. Children who are assertive stand up for their rights and let others know in an honest, thoughtful, and respectful manner what has happened to them, how they feel about it, and what they would like done to correct the situation. For example, Billy says to John, "You took a book off my desk without asking. I am upset with your behavior. I want you to return my book to me today." Learning to be assertive is a way that children can learn to care for themselves while being respectful of others' needs.

Stress Management and Caring

"Stress management is a process that teaches children about the meaning of stress, how stress affects their lives, and how best to manage stress in a responsible manner" (O'Rourke & Worzbyt, 1996, p. 437). Stress is the response of the body as it attempts to cope with the demands of life and living. Stressors are physical, mental, and social factors that children experience that cause changes in the body. These changes can be physical or emotional or both.

Stress can be beneficial to the extent that it motivates people to action and energizes their resolve to complete a task. However, stress can be harmful if it takes over people's lives and manages them rather than they managing it. If children do not learn to manage stress, their health may be affected. To help children manage stress and their personal/emotional wellness, they can learn a variety of stress management techniques such as the following (Meeks et al., 1996).

1. Using responsible decision-making skills.
2. Getting enough rest and sleep.
3. Participating in physical activities.
4. Using a time management plan.
5. Writing a journal.
6. Having close friends.
7. Talking with parents and trusted adults.
8. Helping others.
9. Expressing affection in appropriate ways.
10. Caring for pets.
11. Changing one's outlook.
12. Keeping a sense of humor (pp. 163–164).

These actions will help children to relieve anxiety and tension in their lives. They will help them to relax and feel more comfortable while meeting their daily responsibilities. Other useful techniques to consider are diaphragmatic breathing, muscle relaxation training, imagery and visualization exercises, cognitive restructuring, self-instruction training, thought stopping, and the development of behavioral strengths that enhance social relationships.

Resistance Skills and Caring

Sometimes children's personal/emotional health is jeopardized when peers or adults pressure them into doing something that they do not want to do or know is wrong. When children are asked to violate the law or compromise their values against their will, they experience a range of emotions that includes fear, anxiety, frustration, guilt, anger, disappointment, resentment, disrespect, depression, and a host of stress-induced physical symptoms.

Unfortunately, many children find themselves giving in to the demands of their peers even when they know that what they are doing is wrong. Elementary school counseling programs can help children to stand up to peer pressure and teach them how to say "no" by using one or more of the following methods.

- Humor
- Walking away
- Assertive messages
- Avoiding situations or people that might exert pressure
- Behavior rehearsal (practice plans to stop or avoid peer pressure)

Using resistance skills when needed will help children to care for their personal/emotional well-being.

THE COUNSELOR'S ROLE

Just as children are responsible for managing their physical and social health, so they are equally responsible for maintaining and enhancing their personal/emotional health. The elementary school counselor must first teach children the value of the following health-preserving ideas.

- Teach children the "golden rule" and its value in promoting self-worth. "Do unto others as you would have them to unto you."
- Teach children that fear melts away with patience, persistence, and a plan.
- Teach children the value of *self-improvement* and how it differs from striving for *perfection.*
- Teach children to disregard the old adage that says, "If something is worth doing, it is worth doing well" and replace it with, "If something is worth doing, it is worth doing poorly until you get to do it well."
- Teach children to treat themselves with love and kindness and there will be sunshine in their hearts the year around.
- Help children to understand that the most common weakness of humankind is to allow themselves to be influenced by their own negative thoughts and the negative thoughts of others.
- Help children to see that failure is never permanent for those who see value in their own potential.
- Teach children that they are the creators of their own destinies and the architects of their own successes.
- Encourage children to develop a sense of humor and to cherish the value of laughter.
- Teach children the value of taking time on each busy day to relax, play, and nurture their childhood ways.
- Teach children to be optimistic and to value each new day.
- Help children to enhance their capacity for self-awareness and to apply what they learn about themselves and their environment in ways that will enhance their personal/emotional health.
- Teach children that they are responsible for their lives and the choices they make.

Simple truths shape destinies and give meaning and purpose to life and living. If children are to succeed in school, their personal/ emotional needs must be met. We need only look to the growing number of children who are using drugs and alcohol, experiencing depression, suffering from psychosomatic illnesses, perpetrating acts of violence, and running away from home in response to life's stressors to understand the importance of helping them to achieve and maintain sound personal/emotional health.

We want children to understand what it means to make caring choices in response to managing their personal/emotional well-being. We want them to understand the relationship between academic learning and how this relates to their own self-care. Ultimately, we want our children to develop the personality attributes, life skills, and caring attitudes that will enable them to achieve and sustain personal/emotional health. Elementary school counselors assume a major responsibility for orchestrating a school-wide effort in providing children with the tools to become knowledgeable, responsible, and caring people. They can help to accomplish this end by focusing on the following:

1. Address the "whole child." A child's personal/emotional development will affect their learning and social adjustment.
2. Encourage the implementation of a coordinated and systematic personal/emotional education curriculum that addresses such areas as character education, development of self-esteem, self-awareness, emotional intelligence, communication skills, decision-making, and resistance training. These skills can be integrated into the academic curriculum.
3. Create a supportive and safe school environment that draws upon the cooperation of all school personnel and community supporters in developing a comprehensive school personal/ emotional health program for children.
4. Teach school personnel to recognize the warning signs, troubled feelings, and changes in behavior that children exhibit when their personal/emotional health is threatened.

5. Teach parents what steps they can take to enhance the personal/emotional health of their children.

6. Develop child care teams and a caring network of service providers and families working as partners to help children with personal/emotional problems.

7. Emphasize the importance of building on children's strengths and providing support that respects the ethnic and cultural values of those being served.

8. Bring the school and community together in developing a caring community partnership that embraces people-building and connects adults with children who are striving to develop personal/emotional health.

Elementary school counselors have a significant role to play in creating a caring school climate that embraces and contributes to the personal/emotional growth of children. What follows are a number of activities that counselors can share with teachers and parents that will help them in their quest to develop and strengthen the personal/emotional lives of children.

PERSONAL/EMOTIONAL CARING ACTIVITIES

You Are Unique

Brief Overview of Activity:

In this lesson, children will have an opportunity to see that each person is unique.

Objectives:

1. Children will learn one way that each person is unique.
2. Children will be able to identify at least three areas of personal uniqueness.

Materials Needed:

1. White paper (for outlining hands), markers, crayons, ink pad
2. Water, soap, and towels for cleanup

Procedure:

1. Explain to children that no two people have the same fingerprints—that is why fingerprints are used for identification. Making an ink fingerprint is even better than signing your name to show who you are.
2. Distribute paper and crayons or markers to all children. Tell them to outline their hands on the paper.
3. Using the inkpad, have children make fingerprints in their hand tracings.
4. Have children compare their fingerprints with those of their classmates.
5. Pose the following questions:
    a. Could you tell the difference between your fingerprints and those of your classmates?
    b. Was there anyone in class whose fingerprints looked like yours?

    c. How were your fingerprints different from those of other
       classmates?

    d. What did you learn about yourself by doing this activity?

NOTE: It may be interesting to enlist the help of a school security
officer in doing this activity.

Closure:

Talk about being unique. Since no two persons are exactly alike, fingerprints are one example of our uniqueness. Ask children to share,
in groups, three additional ways that they are unique or special.

Venn Diagrams

Brief Overview of Activity:

In this session, children will begin to identify connections they have
with other members of their class.

Objectives:

1. Children will identify their special interests and talents.
2. Children will begin to connect with others in class as a result
   of comparing interests and hobbies, likes and dislikes.

Materials Needed:

1. Venn Diagram for each child
2. "Things About Me" worksheet for each child
3. Pencils or pens

Procedure:

1. Ask children if they have anything in common with anyone in
   class. No doubt, they will say things such as "Sandy and I like to
   play Barbies together," or "Mark and I are on the soccer team."
2. Tell them that we are going to do an exercise in which they
   will begin to identify connections with other members of the
   class as well.

Things about Me

1. My favorite color is _____.
2. My birthday is in the month of _____.
3. My favorite day of the week is _____.
4. My shoe size is _____.
5. My favorite TV show is _____.
6. My favorite sport is _____.
7. My favorite food is _____.
8. My favorite holiday is _____.
9. My favorite season of the year is _____.
10. I have _____ brothers.
11. I have _____ sisters.
12. My hobby is _____.
13. My favorite song is _____.
14. My best school subject is _____.
15. My worst school subject is _____.

Figure 7.1.

3. Distribute copies of the "Things about Me" worksheet (Figure 7.1) and provide time for children to complete their sheet.

4. Group children into pairs and have them share their answers with one another. Give them a Venn Diagram (Figure 7.2) on which to record their answers. Remind them that each one has a part of the circle in which to record answers that don't match with their partner. However, if their answers match, they record them in the space where the circles overlap. Provide about 5 minutes for children to compare answers and complete their diagrams.

5. Discuss commonalities. Identify the pair in the group that had the most answers in common. Talk about connections we make with others as a result of interests or hobbies.

6. If time permits, allow children to pair up with someone else and complete another diagram to identify commonalities with another classmate.

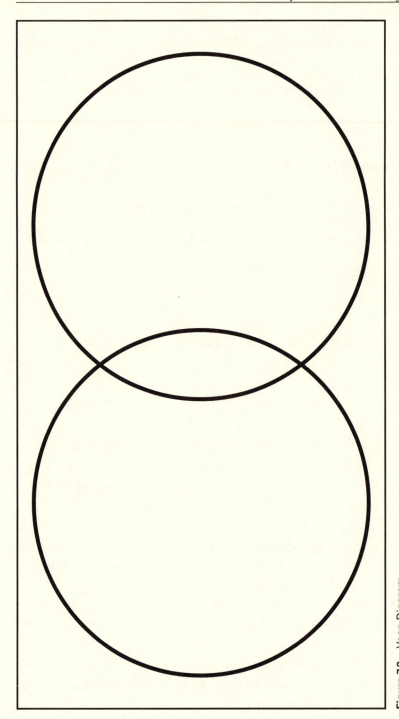

Figure 7.2.   Venn Diagram.

7. Remind children that they use their unique qualities (hobbies, interests, skills, and personality characteristics) to build connections with others.

Closure:

As a way of bringing closure to this activity, remind children that it may be interesting to begin some hobby groups based upon information obtained from the surveys. If interest seems high, it may be advantageous to plan a "Hobby Day" sometime in the near future as a way of helping children to make more social connections within their classroom.

"Me" Shirt

Brief Overview of Activity:

This session will provide children with an opportunity to really think about who they are and what makes them special. It will also give them a nonthreatening arena to share their special "selves" with others.

Objectives:

1. Children will be able to identify at least five special characteristics about themselves.
2. Children will have a "keepsake" to remind them of the things that make them unique and worthwhile people.

Materials Needed:

1. A plain white t-shirt for each child (or have children bring in a plain white t-shirt for the activity)
2. T-shirt paint (may be bought at craft store)

Procedure:

1. Introduce the topic of personal characteristics by asking children to describe one characteristic that makes them special. If any children have difficulty thinking of something, invite class members to share something they think is special about that child.

2. Demonstrate the project by showing a sample "me" shirt that has been made by a teacher or counselor. Note the self-descriptors this person has used (words, pictures, etc.) on his shirt.

3. Provide paper t-shirts for children to design their shirts. Remind them that each shirt must identify at least five unique characteristics.

4. Demonstrate the use of t-shirt paint before children begin to transfer their t-shirt designs onto their cloth shirts.

5. Give ample time for children to complete and share their "me" shirts. (If possible, hang a clothesline across the room to display the shirts for a short time before children take them home.)

6. Point out the fact that everyone is different and special and that we should all be proud of our uniqueness.

Closure:

As children begin to share their unique characteristics, encourage them to use these characteristics as a way of connecting with their peers. For example, remind them to frequently compliment their classmates when they have accomplished something special or unique.

Conditions of Self-Esteem

Brief Overview of Activity:

This session will acquaint children with the four conditions of self-esteem and make them aware of how they should be able to identify their personal traits for each of the conditions.

Goals:

1. Children will be able to identify the four conditions of self-esteem.

2. Children will identify a personal response for each of the four conditions of self-esteem.

Materials Needed:

1. "Conditions of Self-Esteem" worksheet (Figure 7.3)
2. Crayons, markers, pencils

Procedure:

1. Begin by talking with children about some of the conditions needed for a plant to be healthy. Most will be able to identify

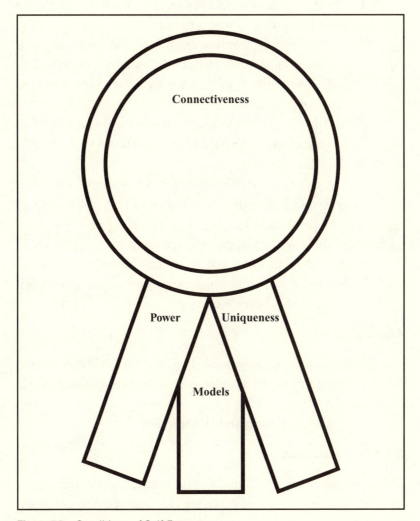

Figure 7.3. Conditions of Self-Esteem.

water, sunshine, nutrients, good soil, etc. Then relate this discussion to the conditions needed for a person to have a healthy self-esteem. Most likely, the answers will not be as clear-cut.

2. Present the four conditions of self-esteem and briefly describe each condition.

    a. Connectiveness—being connected to persons, groups

    b. Uniqueness—something that makes one special or different in some way

    c. Power—using unique attributes to build a connection (smiling to connect with a friend)

    d. Models—sayings, rules, examples, and demonstrations that show "how to do something." Models give direction and allow children to practice what they have observed (i.e., seen modeled).

3. Allow time for children to talk among themselves in small groups regarding at least one of the conditions—for example, What makes you unique?

4. Provide a copy of the "Conditions of Self-Esteem" worksheet and allow sufficient time for children to write their personal traits on the worksheet.

5. Talk briefly with children about the kinds of things they have written. Remind them that if we can identify someone or something in each area, chances are that we are able to feel pretty good about ourselves.

Closure:

Bring this session to a close by reminding children to cultivate each of the four areas of self-esteem in order to be the best persons they can be.

Caring and "Characters"

Brief Overview of Activity:

In this session, children will look at their favorite Disney "characters" and begin to identify some of the caring characteristics that are shown by these characters in stories, cartoons, and videos they have seen.

Objectives:

1. Children will identify specific caring acts that they see in their favorite Disney "characters."
2. Children will work together to create a school-wide display of "Disney (Caring) on Parade."
3. Children will identify at least one caring character trait that they will work to develop during the next month.

Materials Needed:

1. Pictures of Disney characters
2. Videos featuring the Disney characters
3. Art materials to develop the bulletin board "Disney (Caring) on Parade"

Procedure:

1. Begin by asking children to write down the names of their favorite Disney characters. Discuss why these characters are favorites.
2. Talk about the "caring" characteristics shown by so many Disney characters. If children can't think of any, use the following examples:
   a. Snow White—takes care of the seven dwarfs, cleans their house, treats everyone kindly, and so on.
   b. Mickey Mouse—always looks out for his friends, wants his friends to be happy, shares with others, and is always willing to help.
3. Choose a video from the Disney collection and have children watch it and identify all of the characteristics of "caring" they see in the video.
4. Make a combined list of all of the characteristics that the children were able to identify.
5. Allow small groups of children to choose any Disney character and begin to identify all of the "caring" characteristics they can for that character. (It may be helpful to have

some storybooks, short videos, and so on available to jog
their memories.)

6. Provide an opportunity for children to make a large bulletin
   board display of "Disney (Caring) on Parade." This activity
   can also be extended to a school-wide project by doing the
   bulletin board outside the classroom and by conducting a
   morning announcement of a "caring" Disney character every
   day for a two-week period.

Closure:

Ask your children to choose one caring characteristic that they
would like to practice. Help them to develop their plans to accomplish their goals. Return to this activity in one month to see how
well they have done in becoming more caring.

NOTE: It is pretty apparent that this activity could actually become
a full-blown unit on caring and characters. It could be a lot of fun
for children and adults.

If I Could Be a Genie

Brief Overview of Activity:

In this session, children will have the opportunity to enter the world
of imagination and think about what kinds of things they would like
to have happen in their future life.

Objectives:

1. Children will identify potential positive outcomes of their life
   in the future.
2. Children will begin to think about what they can do besides
   "dream" to make their future as positive as possible.
3. Children will identify at least one realistic action step to reach
   their five-year goal.

Materials Needed:

1. "If I Could be a Genie" worksheet (Figure 7.4)
2. Pencils or pens
3. 3-inch by 5-inch card on which to write an action step

Procedure:

1. Talk briefly with children about the story in which the "genie" comes out of the magic lantern and offers the finder of the lantern the opportunity to have three wishes come true.
2. Discuss what types of wishes one might have for specific time periods in one's life (16 years old, 25 years old, and 50 years old).
3. Give a copy of the worksheet to children. Have them complete the worksheet with wishes for themselves at each age.
4. Place children in groups of four to five and allow time for them to share their three wishes with the small group.

If I Could Be a Genie

At Age 16:

At Age 25:

At Age 50:

Figure 7.4.

5. Bring the class back together and discuss some ideas that came from the small groups. The following questions may be helpful in the discussion:
   a. Were some of the wishes hard to think about?
   b. Did you have trouble thinking of something you may want at age 50?
   c. Did you hear some good ideas from classmates that were different from yours?
6. Ask children to think specifically about the wish they had for age 16. Talk about the kinds of things they can begin to do right now to make that wish come true.
7. Give each child a 3-inch by 5-inch card and have them write down one action step that they need to take now to help assure that their wish will come true.
8. Encourage children to place the card in their room where they will be able to see it often so that it will remind them to keep up their resolve to attain their first wish.

Closure:

Bring closure to the activity by reminding children that hard work can make some wishes come true.

Goal-Setting Activities

Brief Overview of Activity:

During this session, children will become acquainted with things they need to do to set and reach realistic goals. They will also become aware of the intrinsic benefits to one's self-esteem as a result of goal attainment.

Objectives:

1. Children will set a realistic goal and plan the steps needed to attain their goal.
2. Children will keep an ongoing chart to determine progress toward goal attainment.

3. Children will write a brief evaluation of their goal-setting activity at the conclusion of the six-week period.

Materials Needed:

1. "My Goal" worksheet (Figure 7.5)
2. Paper and pencil

Procedure:

1. Share with children a goal you have attained at some time in your life (such as becoming a teacher or counselor). Talk about the things you needed to do to reach your goal.
2. Ask children to think of some realistic goals they may want to achieve. Some possibilities may include:
   a. To become a better basketball scorer.
   b. To bring their math grade up one letter grade.
   c. To make at least one new friend.
   d. To complete homework each night.
   e. To watch little brother at least 30 minutes each day to help mom.
3. Choose one of the goals and talk about action steps that can be taken to reach this goal.
   Goal—bring math grade up one letter grade.
   Possible Action Steps:
   a. Ask mom, dad, or a sibling to use flash cards with you for 5 minutes each night.
   b. Get a "study buddy" in school.
   c. Ask teacher for extra help.
   d. Review math facts at least 10 minutes each night.
   e. Recheck all math problems on tests and homework.
4. Distribute "My Goal" worksheet to children to complete. (At this point it will be important to confer privately with children to assure that they have chosen goals that are attainable.) When they have completed the list of action steps, have them select one choice for each week.
5. Have children implement their weekly action steps.

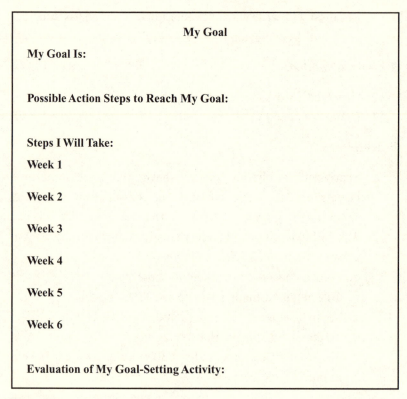

My Goal

My Goal Is:

Possible Action Steps to Reach My Goal:

Steps I Will Take:
Week 1

Week 2

Week 3

Week 4

Week 5

Week 6

Evaluation of My Goal-Setting Activity:

Figure 7.5.

6. Ask children to report weekly on their progress toward achieving their goals.

Closure:

At the conclusion of the initial lesson, remind children that each of them has chosen a goal that is attainable. Remind children that you will be working with them to help them achieve their goal. You will be helping them to revise their plans, if necessary, and guiding them in charting their progress.

At the conclusion of the six-week period, allow time for children to write a personal evaluation of the activity and to talk about the feelings they associate with goal attainment (or the lack of it). They may also want to describe what they could have done differently to reach their goal.

Making Caring Choices to Protect Me and My School

Brief Overview of Activity:

This session will encourage children to think about the kinds of things they can do to foster self-protection and the protection of others.

Objectives:

1. Children will identify the kinds of things that cause threats to school safety.
2. Children will role-play appropriate actions to reduce threats to safety.
3. Children will develop a "Peace Pledge."

Materials Needed:

1. List of situations for role plays
2. Chalkboard or chart paper for brainstorming
3. Poster board for "Peace Pledge"

Procedure:

1. Discuss with children the types of things that threaten the safety of children in our schools. Allow time for children to work in small groups to brainstorm a list of "threats to safety."
2. Review the lists and talk with children about some caring choices they may want to make to deal with each of the "threats."
   a. When is it appropriate to tell the teacher?
   b. Is it ever okay to reveal a "secret" someone has told you?
   c. What's the difference between tattling and responsible telling?
3. Present and role play some situations (use the ones listed below or choose your own) for role plays. Discuss each role-play scenario in terms of what kinds of caring choices were made. Did we do what was necessary to assure that people were safe?
   a. Your best friend Bill shows you what looks like a pen, but then pulls it apart to reveal a knife. Bill tells you that he trusts that you will not tell anyone that he has it in school.

    b. A little girl in your class shows you a large bruise on her arm, but asks you not to tell the teacher about it.

    c. Some children in your class make fun of a new student who is different from your classmates (because of nationality, skin color, clothing, ability). They tell you that if you tell the teacher, they will not be your friend anymore and will tell the other kids to avoid you too.

    d. A first grade girl on the bus shows a gun that she has in her book bag. She tells you that she found it on the way to school. You think it may be a real one. What do you do?

4. Encourage children to get back into their brainstorming groups and develop a "Peace Pledge" for their class. If they have trouble thinking of ideas, present some of the following statements that they may want to incorporate into their pledge: We believe that everyone in the class has a right to be safe and to be respected by everyone. We pledge to be kind and responsible and follow the rules. We pledge to always be fair and caring to each other.

5. When groups are reassembled for follow-up discussion, allow time for sharing of pledges and create a classroom pledge that children say at the beginning of each day.

Closure:

Strongly reinforce the idea that safety and caring for self and others must be central themes of classroom life. Encourage all children to do everything they can to keep the school a warm and caring place. Model this behavior for others—at home, at school, and in the community.

ADDITIONAL IDEAS FOR PERSONAL/EMOTIONAL CARING

I Am . . .

Give children a worksheet with the words "I am . . ." printed at least five times. Children are to identify themselves in five different ways using the sentence stem, "I am . . ." For example: *I am* a sister. *I am* a good math student. *I am* a Girl Scout. *I am* a good friend. *I am* a daughter. After children have completed their worksheet, allow them to work in groups of four or five to share their sentences. This can be a good method for getting acquainted early in the school year.

Feeling Worm (or Feeling Chain)

For each week of the school year, have children identify a specific feeling. Write that feeling word on a segment of a worm (or on a paper chain), which will continue to grow throughout the school year as each new word is added. Place the worm (chain) somewhere in the room where children can watch it grow. Try to focus on the feeling of the week in other curricular areas as well—for example, draw a picture of anger, write a story about a time when you were angry, and so on.

Strengths Puzzle

This activity can be completed on an individual basis or with a group to show "group strengths." To begin the activity, cut a 24-inch by 36-inch sheet of poster paper into jigsaw puzzle–shaped pieces (one for each child). Instruct children to either write a sentence or draw a picture of a strength that they have on the puzzle piece. When each piece has been completed, encourage the children to reassemble the puzzle to show classroom strengths.

Themes of Character

In order to promote caring for each other in the classroom, have a character theme for each month of the school year. Some possible themes could be: caring, kindness, respect, honesty, responsibility, self-discipline, patience, trustworthiness, perseverance, giving, and so on. Many curricular, co-curricular, and service activities can be developed around each of the monthly themes.

Stress Thermometers

As a way of discussing the effect of stress on our lives, have children each develop their personal stress thermometers going from zero (little stress) to 10 (major stress). Allow time for children to color in their thermometers to show how much stress they are experiencing at the current time and to talk about the stress-producing events in their lives. Encourage discussion of ways to cope with these stressful times.

Network of Caring

Utilizing a computer theme, develop a "network of caring" bulletin board for children to show ways they care about themselves and each other. Use the network idea to point out that if one part of the network "goes down," the remainder of the network won't work well either.

Ways to Relax

During an activity in which children have a tendency to become stressed, try playing some soothing music in the background while they are completing the activity. When the activity has been completed, talk about the music—Did it make a difference? Was it annoying to you? Do you think it helped you to relax? and so forth. Talk about things they can do to release their stress. Make a list of possible stress relievers. Post it on the bulletin board for future reference.

Feeling Game

In preparation for this activity, write a variety of feeling words on 3-inch by 5-inch cards. Distribute these cards to the children and have them act out the feeling that is on their card. See if the other members of the class are able to identify the feeling. Provide time for children to share times when they have felt the same way.

Not Everyone Feels the Same Way

This is an excellent activity to help children see that the same comment may not always result in the same feeling. To show this, use the following statements (or others more appropriate to the grade level) to point out that they may create different feelings in different people. "I have to sing a solo in the school play." "I'm going to the movies with my brother." "My dad is taking me fishing with him." "I got a C on my spelling test." Choose one of the sentences and identify different feelings that may occur. Example: *I have to sing a solo in the school play* may evoke a feeling of pride if one is a good singer who feels comfortable in front of an audience or may prompt a feeling of dread for one who would see the event as a major producer of stress. Also use this opportunity to talk about *body language* and *tone of voice* as indicators of how someone may be feeling.

Feelings Booklet

Encourage children to identify at least 10 feelings that they have experienced in their lives. Provide a sheet for each feeling word and allow time for children to develop their personal feelings booklet by writing a brief story or drawing a picture for each feeling. When the pages have been completed, provide time for children to make a cover for their feelings booklet.

Stop, Not Pop!

As a way of helping children learn to control anger, use a balloon to show what happens when anger continues to build (keep filling the balloon with air until it is almost ready to pop). Remind children that, rather than "popping off" and getting into trouble, they need to "Stop—Not Pop." Discuss good ways to diffuse anger (release air) without losing one's cool.

Practice Active Listening

Provide opportunities for children to practice active listening skills. Pair children and give them a topic for discussion. Remind them to maintain eye contact, face the person who is talking, use nonverbal forms of communication, and repeat back the essence of what they have heard as a way to communicate to the other person that they have been listening. This is an excellent "sponge activity" when you have just 5 or 10 minutes left in a class period. Children enjoy this type of activity, and it can help them improve their listening skills.

Feelings Journal

As a way to encourage children to regularly reflect on their feelings, provide time each week for entries into a "Feelings Journal." They will need 10 minutes to do a journal entry to chronicle their feelings. Allow children to keep their journal private if they wish, but encourage them to share it with others if they choose to do so.

Joke Time

Children need to know that a sense of humor can be very helpful in putting daily experiences into perspective. One way to promote a healthy sense of humor is to allow 5 minutes each week (or more often if you choose) for children to share jokes or riddles with the class. Be sure you screen them first!

Mottos for Life

Share with children some basic mottos for life that people have used as guides for living. "Do unto others as you would have them do unto you," "A penny saved is a penny earned," "A bird in the hand is worth two in the bush," and so on. Encourage children to think about what these mottos mean and how they can be used in making their life more caring and responsible.

Mentor Program

Develop a mentoring program that utilizes community members meeting regularly with children to discuss hobbies, promote interests, and share life stories. This type of program helps children to realize the importance of nurturing their strengths and interests and using them to help others and their community.

Magic Wand

Talk about how often we wish we could make changes in our lives. Encourage children to think about what they would do if they had a magic wand and could make their life better and more fulfilling. Once children have identified what would make their life better, begin to work with them on how they can do more than just wish. Tell them that if they are willing to work hard to make their life better, they can achieve much success. Promote the idea that having a plan and working toward an achievable goal is better than having a "magic wand."

Getting Rid of Garbage Thinking

Remind children that many of our bad feelings come from our garbage thinking—those things that we say to ourselves that are guaranteed to make us feel bad. Encourage them to think of comments they use that make them feel angry, sad, lonely, left out, and so forth. Once a series of "garbage thoughts" have been identified, help them to identify self-talk ideas that will help them to get rid of their "garbage thinking."

My Personal Plan for Handling Anger

Since most children have difficulty handling their anger, it may be helpful to assist them in developing a personal plan for handling anger. The personal plan should include three basic sections: things that make me angry, things I need to do to keep from acting inappropriately, and things I can do to deal with my anger in more positive ways. In order for this plan to work most effectively, it is important for children to review their plan on a regular basis so that the anger coping skills they have identified will become habit.

How Are You Smart

Many children see themselves as less than adequate because they are not *school smart*. Present information on Gardner's Multiple Intelligences Theory. Identify and describe the seven areas of intelligence: verbal/linguistic, intrapersonal, interpersonal, visual/spatial, musical/rhythmic, body/kinesthetic, and logic/mathematic. Encourage children to identify the area in which they feel most competent. Develop a bulletin board of the seven areas with the names of children listed under each of the areas to show their perceived strength. It is important for all children to know that each of them has an area of strength.

BIBLIOGRAPHY

Akin, T., Cowan, D., Dunne, G., Palomares, S., Schilling, D., & Shuster, S. (1990). *The best self-esteem activities: For the elementary grades.* Spring Valley, CA: Innerchoice Publishing.

Akos, P. (2000). Building empathic skills in elementary school children through group work. *Journal for Specialists in Group Work, 25,* 214–224.

The Alliance for Eating Disorders Awareness. Available at http://www.eatingdisorder info.org/.

American Academy of Child and Adolescent Psychiatry (1999). Violence fact sheet. Washington, DC: American Academy of Child and Adolescent Psychiatry.

Aronen, E.T., & Soininen, M. (2000). Childhood depressive symptoms predict psychiatric problems in young adults. *Canadian Journal of Psychiatry, 45,* 465–471.

Barasch, D.S. (2000, October). Help children face their fears. *Family Life,* 35–37.

Bean, R. (1992). *The four conditions of self-esteem: A new approach for elementary and middle school.* Santa Cruz, CA: ETR Associates.

Beland, K. (1992). *Second step: A violence prevention curriculum, grade 1–3* (2nd ed.). Seattle, WA: Committee for Children.

Berg, F. (1998). Views on eating disorders in children. *NEA Today, 16*(7), 22.

Boyer, E.T. (1995). *The basic school: A community for learning.* Princeton, NJ: The Carnegie Foundation for the Advancement of Teaching.

Briggs, D.C. (1975). *Your children's self-esteem.* New York: Dolphin Books.

Brooks, R. (1999–2000). Tips for promoting children's self-esteem. *Reading Today, 17,* 7–9.

Broughton, J. (1978). Development of concepts of self, mind, reality, and knowledge. In W. Damon (ed.), *New directions for child development No. 1. Social cognition* (pp. 75–100). San Francisco, CA: Jossey-Bass.

Chandler, L.A. (1987). *Childhood stress: The teacher's role.* (ERIC Document Reproduction Service No. ED 285367).

Children's Defense Fund. (2002). *Facts on youth, violence and crime: February 2002.* Retrieved September 8, 2002, from *http://www.childrensdefense.org/ss_ ydfs_viocrime.php.*

Dubuque, S.E. (1998). Fighting childhood depression. *Educational Digest, 63*(6), 64–69.

Erikson, E.H. (1963). *Children and society* (2nd ed.). New York: Norton.

Felger, M.A. (1992). Gangs and violence. *Journal of Emotional and Behavioral Problems, 1,* 9–12.

Goleman, D. (1996). On emotional intelligence: A conversation with Daniel Goleman, *Educational Leadership, 6,* 6–11.

Goleman, D. (1995). *Emotional intelligence: Why it can matter more than IQ.* New York: Bantam Books.

Grunbaum, J.A., Kann, L., Kinchen, S.A., Ross, J.G., Gowda, V.R., Collins, J.L., & Kolbe, L.J. (1999). *Youth risk behavior surveillance—national alternative high school youth risk behavior survey, United States, 1998.* Atlanta, GA: U.S. Centers for Disease Control and Prevention (MMWR Surveillance Summaries: October 29, 1999/48(SS07);1–44).

Harter, S. (1998). The development of self representations. In W. Damon (series ed.) and N. Eisenburg (vol. ed.), *Handbook of child psychology: Vol. #3. Social, emotional, and personality development* (5th ed., pp. 533–617). New York: Wiley.

Harvard Eating Disorders Center (2002). *Facts and Findings.* Retrieved September 13, 2002, from *http://www.hedc.org/undrstnd/.*

Harvard Mental Health Letter (2002, February). *Depression in Children—Part I, 18*(8), 3.

Herring, R. (1990). Suicide in the middle school: Who said kids will not? *Elementary School Guidance and Counseling, 25,* 129–137.

Hutter, S. (1999). Teaching kindness, *Good Housekeeping, 229*(2), 80–81.

Jackson, J.T., & Owens, J.L. (1999). A stress management classroom tool for teachers of children with BD. *Interventions in School & Clinic, 35*(2), 74–81.

Kohn, A. (1996). *Beyond discipline: From compliance to community.* Alexandria, VA: Association for Supervision and Curriculum Development.

Kuersten, J. (1999). Healthy young minds: Rx for children's emotional and mental health, *Our Children, 25,* 8–12.

Mann, J. (1993, April 6). Easing up to excel. *The Washington Post,* B.3.

Maslow, H.A. (1954). *Motivation and personality.* New York: Harper & Row.

Meeks, L., Heit, P., & Page, R. (1996). *Comprehensive school health education* (2nd ed.). Blacklick, OH: Meeks Heit Publishing Co.

National Institute of Child Health and Human Development (2000). National Institute of Health News alert on the health behaviors of school aged children (1997–1998 survey).

National Institute of Mental Health (2000). *Depression in children and adolescents: A fact sheet for physicians* (NIH Publication No. 00-4744). Washington, DC: U.S. Government Printing Office.

National School Safety Center (2002). *NSSC review of school safety research.* Retrieved September 13, 2002 from *http://www.nssc1.org/studies/statistic%20resourcespdf.pdf.*

Nazario, S.L. (1991, October 7). Relaxation classes rile many parents. *The Wall Street Journal,* A1, A9.

O'Rourke, K., & Worzbyt, J.C. (1996). *Support groups for children.* Washington, DC: Accelerated Development—A member of Taylor and Francis.

Perls, F. (1969). *Gestalt therapy verbation.* Moab, UT: Real People Press.

Robenson, E.H. (2000). Humanistic education to character education: An ideological journey. *Journal of Humanistic Counseling Education & Development, 39,* 21–26.

Saarni, C., Mumme, D., & Campos, J. (1998). Emotional development: Action, communication, and understanding. In W. Damon (series ed.) and N. Eisenburg (vol. ed.), *Handbook of child psychology: Vol. 3. Social, emotional, and personality development* (5th ed., pp. 237–309). New York: Wiley.

Sapon-Shevin, M. (1999). *Because we can change the world: A practical guide building cooperative, inclusive classroom communities.* Boston, MA: Allyn & Bacon.

Schmidt, T.M. (1993). *Anger management and violence prevention: A group activities manual for middle & high school students.* Minneapolis, MN: Johnson Institute.

Selman, R. (1980). *The growth of interpersonal understanding.* New York: Academic Press.

Stefanowski-Harding, S. (1990). Suicide and the school counselor. *School Counselor, 37,* 328–336.

Stepp, L.S. (1993, January 12). When life's the pits: Adolescents' pessimistic view of America and themselves. *The Washington Post,* A5.

Suicide rates in children: Fact sheet #651. (2000). Available: *http://www.thecarolina channel.com/gs/health/stories/health-20000726–182134.html.*

Thompson, C.L., & Rudolph, L.B. (2000). *Counseling children* (4th ed.). Belmont, CA: Brooks/Cole.

U.S. Department of Health and Human Services (1999). Prevalence of serious emotional disturbances in children and adolescents. *Mental Health, United States, 1996.* Center for Mental Health Services, Substance Abuse and Mental Health Services Administration. U.S. Department of Health and Human Services.

Zigler, E.F., & Stevenson, M.F. (1993). *Children in a changing world: Developmental and social issues* (2nd ed.). Pacific Grove, CA: Brooks/Cole.

CHAPTER 8

Social Caring

Social Caring is a process in which children learn how they should be with others. The Golden Rule, in a simply stated moral imperative, teaches children the value of treating others as they themselves would like to be treated. Stated yet another way, social caring represents the attitudes, information, and skills children learn that enable them to participate in social relations and social service while promoting social justice and responsible social change (Pittman & Cahill, 1992).

SOCIAL DEVELOPMENT

"Socialization is the process by which children learn behaviors that are appropriate for their age, sex, and culture" (Lefrancois, 1989, p. 335). McCandless (1967) defined socialization as ". . . a learning process, that when successful, results in the human organism's moving from its infant state of helplessness, but total egocentricity, to its adult state of semi-conformity coupled with independent creativity" (p. 421). Taking both definitions into consideration, socialization can be described as a process by which human beings become human as they learn the ways of the culture, while at the same time, developing their own sense of individuality.

Social development, in contrast to socialization, emphasizes the lifelong, stage-driven, developmental process that children experience as their social sense of self unfolds. During this process, children begin to recognize that they are intimately tied to other people (Damon & Hart, 1988).

This chapter places emphasis on that developmental process and begins with a brief discussion of the importance of social cognition and how it affects children's relationships. Social cognition relates to children's ability to understand people and to think about social relations (Zigler & Stevenson, 1993). As children grow and develop, they learn to accurately infer other people's thoughts and feelings and recognize that others are equally adept at doing the same. As children begin to develop their social awareness, they become more adept at perspective-taking (role-taking), making it possible for them to understand themselves in relationship to others.

Perspective Taking

Selman (1976, 1980) identified five levels of perspective-taking that occur between the ages of 4 and 12.

Level 0, Egocentric Perspective-Taking (Birth to 6): Children, between birth and age 6, assume that other people's feelings and thoughts are similar to their own.

Level 1, Subjective Perspective-Taking (Ages 6 to 8): Children are becoming more aware that other people may think and feel differently than they do. They also realize that the same event may be viewed in different ways. However, they have little understanding of the reasons that support these differences. Perspective-taking is considered to be one way in that children are unable to consider their point of view and that of others at the same time. Consequently, they are unable to place themselves in another person's "shoes" and experience their thoughts and feelings.

Level 2, Reciprocal Perspective-Taking (Ages 8 to 10): Children develop a realization that others may have a different point of view from their own. They also understand that others can recognize their perspective as well. The major change from level 1 to level 2 is that children are now able to recognize their own perspective while "stepping into the shoes of another" and understand their position as well. At the same time, children are capable of reasoning that points of view other than their own have value. Because of this, they may take other people's points of view into consideration. Children are now capable of thinking about how others may view them and are able to anticipate how others may react to their ideas and actions.

Level 3, Mutual Perspective-Taking (Ages 10 to 12): Children are now capable of seeing their own perspective and their partner's perspective, and are capable of stepping back as a neutral third party and taking a more generalized perspective of the situation. At this level of social cognition, children are able to divest themselves of their original perspective and consider other options that will advance the social situation.

Level 4, Societal Perspective-Taking (Adolescents to Adults): Only at this level do people develop a social awareness that takes into consideration values, laws, and the morality of the larger group (society) when making caring social choices that will affect not only themselves, but others as well.

Social Experience

Selman's research on social cognition is significant because it emphasizes the importance of cognitive development and the role that it plays in developing social relationships. Social experience, however, is of equal importance. No matter how old children become, if they are lacking in opportunities to interact with other children and adults, they will be less skilled in perspective-taking than other children who have had extensive social experiences (Zigler & Stevenson, 1993). Consequently, some researchers have disagreed with Selman's attachment of age levels to his findings (Hoffman, 1976; Maccoby, 1980; Rubin & Pepler, 1980), noting that social experience, or the lack of it, can significantly affect social cognition. The final result, however, is that social interactions do enhance children's perspective-taking skills and enhance their interactions with peers and adults. However, the opposite is also true. Children who have difficulty getting along with their peers and initiating and maintaining friendships are often lacking in perspective-taking skills and effective communication skills, which are dependent on their assessment of social situations.

Perspective-taking enhances children's ability to understand and experience what other children and adults are feeling. Empathy enables children to help others by being sensitive to their situation and making caring choices that support them in their time of need. Perspective-taking, coupled with social interactions, also enhances moral development in that children are constantly being presented with life situations and decisions to be made that shape their moral behavior. As children advance in their social development, the hope is that they will make moral decisions based on right, not wrong; reality, not myth; and responsibility, not immorality. Counselors likewise hope that children will develop sound social relations, participate in social service activities, promote social justice, and advocate in behalf of responsible social change.

Peer Relationships

Peer relationships become increasingly important to children during their middle childhood years. This is particularly true given the fact that children spend much of their school day in social contact with their peers. By age 11, many children are actually spending more time with agemates than they do with their families (Rubin, Bukowski, & Parker, 1998).

Aside from the fact that social contact is a given in most children's lives, it serves a very real and useful purpose in their social development and is an important part of the socialization process. During the fostering of peer relationships, children learn to interact with others; develop complex social skills; learn social control; understand the perspectives, needs, and feelings of others; grasp and practice more complex social rules that foster peer relationships; and become more astute and effective communicators in understanding others and making themselves understood (Boyer, 1995).

According to DeHart, Stroufe, & Cooper (2000), five major developments in peer relations occur during the middle childhood years.

1. Children begin to expect more from friends, including loyalty and understanding.
2. Children start to form networks of friends or peer groups.
3. Children learn to coordinate their allegiances to individual friends with their functioning in a group.
4. Children's adherence to peer group norms becomes increasingly important.
5. Children develop clear boundaries for interaction with members of the opposite sex (p. 418).

To the extent that children become successful in developing peer relationships, they will be prepared to make the transition from family support to peer and self-support, thus achieving their independence. They likewise will achieve success in holding membership in a variety of groups and will understand how social institutions have shaped their lives for the better and how they can help to shape social institutions. There is no escaping the fact that human beings, despite their striving to achieve personal independence, are social animals living in a social world, dependent on the good works of others to afford living quality lives. Ralph Waldo Emerson (1832) stated some one hundred and seventy years ago, "[W]e do not make a world of our own, but fall into institutions already made and have to accommodate ourselves to them" (pp. 318–19). Given this fact, it is imperative that all children possess the needed attributes, information, and skills that will enable them to understand and care for their relationships with others and, in a very real sense, also care for themselves.

THE SOCIALLY HEALTHY CHILD

Children have a need to initiate and maintain positive social interactions with others. They have a need to behave in ways valued by society while benefiting themselves and others. More specifically, socially healthy children have a need to belong, to trust and be trusted, to develop lasting friendships, to receive the approval of others and approve of herself, and to develop all-around social competence. Consequently, the socially healthy and well-adjusted child exhibits the following characteristics:

- is respectful of others;
- forms healthful relationships that are self-esteem enhancing, productive, and free of violence;
- is a socially competent problem-solver who adheres to societal norms;
- treats others fairly;
- exhibits a strong sense of belonging;
- resolves conflicts in nonviolent ways;
- cooperates with and encourages others;
- accepts responsibility for his (her) actions;
- has socially accepted goals;
- has good communication and perspective-taking skills;
- is "we minded" versus "I minded"; and
- has a positive sense of humor and is generally good-natured.

Children who possess these social qualities enjoy healthy, caring relationships with others. They form responsible and long-lasting relationships and honor diversity in their interactions with peers and adults. They also are accepting and valued group members who gain from contributing to the groups to which they belong. Ultimately, these children will become the next generation of peace-makers, community builders, and responsible citizens who will make caring choices in support of humankind.

UNDERSTANDING THE NEED FOR SOCIAL CARING

While many factors contribute to children's social status—includ-ing appearance, intelligence, athletic ability, their names, and other identifiable characteristics—most people also would agree on the importance that perspective-taking, social interactions, and social skills development play in shaping children's level of acceptance among their peers. When factors that contribute to so-cial acceptance are missing or are underdeveloped, children learn a variety of behaviors that contribute to their low social status (Cole, Dodge, & Kupersmidt, 1990).

Characteristics of Low Social-Status Children

Low status (unpopular) children fall into two categories: the unliked and the disliked. Unliked children are socially invisible. They tend to be unassertive, withdrawn, isolated, shy, passive, and lethargic (Coie & Dodge, 1988). In addition to demonstrating signs of depression, loneliness, failing academic grades, negative self-perceptions, and a general loss of control over their social world, they often are victims of teasing, name-calling, ridicule, and social exclusion (Orecklin & Winters, 2000).

In contrast to the unliked child, disliked children are often perceived as being overly aggressive. They lack acceptance by their peers and tend to maintain that status into their adult years. Disliked children are often uncooperative and disruptive. They exhibit social skill deficits that limit their ability to cooperate with others, to make their needs known in socially acceptable ways, to respond appropriately with their peers, and to make friends. Disliked children often openly exhibit their dysfunctions in the form of verbal and physical assaults on others, quarreling, fighting, and violating or ignoring the rights of others (Oliver, Young, & LaSalle, 1994). These children pay a high price for their social ineptness and skill deficiencies in the loss of friendships; in reduced interpersonal contact with others; and in feelings of anger, guilt, worthlessness, and frustration. If not corrected, aggressive (disliked) children, in addition to their obvious loss of popularity, also are at high risk for academic failure, antisocial behavior, psychiatric disturbances, and long-term effects that can include alcoholism, mental problems, and job-performance difficulties caused by an inability to work well with others (Coie & Dodge, 1983; Hepler, 1997; Little, 1988; Mehaffey & Sandberg, 1992).

Once children are labeled as being unliked or disliked by their peers, they tend to receive more negative responses from them when compared with their more popular counterparts. Some high-status or popular chil-

dren, to the contrary belief of many, may be aggressive, bossy, and insti-
gators of bullying behavior, but often do not receive negative responses
from their peers when compared with similar behaviors exhibited by
low-status (disliked) children (Hepler, 1997; Orecklin & Winters, 2000).
Even when low-status children exhibit appropriate social behaviors,
their actions frequently go unnoticed or are ignored. Despite their attempts to change their behaviors in a more positive direction, they continue to receive negative feedback from their peers (Coie & Kupersmidt,
1983; Dodge, Schlundt, Schocken, & Delugach, 1983; Hepler, 1995).
The end result, in the eyes of many peers, is that popular children, despite their inappropriate behaviors, can do no wrong while low-status
children, despite their attempts to do better, can do no right. Low-status
children often receive little or no recognition for improved social behavior and consequently often feel stuck with their label (disliked or unliked) and give up hope in their attempts to change their status.

To recap what has been said about the potential damaging side
effects of low social status, we now know that these children are at
an increased risk of experiencing lives of

- alienation, loneliness, and low self-esteem;
- destructive and unhealthy relationships;
- anger, hostility, and violence;
- truancy and school dropout;
- lowered academic performance;
- delinquency;
- substance abuse;
- depression;
- suicide;
- conduct disorder; and
- long-term side effects (mental, marital, military, and job
  performance).

The Cumulative Effects of Risk

We are social beings by nature. Children want to be of this world, to
develop a personal identity, and to live lives of purpose and mean-

ing. Their success is dependent upon their ability to build satisfying and meaningful interactions with family, peers, acquaintances, and with people they do not know. When children fail in their attempts to love and be loved and to belong, they will experience daily the cumulative and stressful effects that prevent them from establishing a productive and satisfying social life. The side effects of the previously mentioned risk factors are not likely to go away on their own; rather, they demand the attention of a carefully planned program of social caring. This program must provide children with the experiences to learn perspective-taking and social skill development in an environment that seeks to foster caring social interactions. Elementary school counseling programs are mission oriented in their desire to help children enhance their social well-being through social caring.

ENHANCING SOCIAL WELL-BEING THROUGH CARING CHOICES

We believe that it is important for all children to possess the needed attitudes, skills, and knowledge that will enable them to understand and care for their relationships with others. We want our children to develop healthful and caring relationships that will enhance their self-esteem and happiness. We want our children to achieve self-worth, earn the respect of others, and express positive feelings toward others and themselves. We want our children to recognize harmful relationships and how to respond to them. We want our children to build healthful family relationships, form responsible friendships, and honor and respect diversity in their interactions with others. We want our children to understand the nature of groups and how they affect their lives. We want them to consider the value and benefits of group membership, the forces that groups can exert on their members, why people form and join groups, and what contributions they can make to the groups to which they belong. And lastly, we want our children to learn what it means to be peacemakers, community builders, and good citizens with rights and responsibilities to care for the welfare of all human beings.

Elementary school counseling programs are in the people-building business and therefore are challenged to promote social caring with a wellness focus. In particular, elementary school counseling programs want children to become able and motivated learners and principled caring human beings. This goal cannot be achieved through a limited single approach that focuses only on academic achievement. To do so is to negate the fact that social development and caring are closely linked with the cognitive, personal/emotional, physical, and career and societal development of children. Children do not learn in a vacuum. They must be connected to their school, teachers, and peers if they are to feel safe, secure, loved, and experience a sense of belonging. Social caring occurs when schools commit themselves to teaching and giving children opportunities to practice

- relationship building skills,
- respect for diversity,
- conflict resolution and peer mediation,
- healthful family relationships,
- responsible friendship building, and
- healthful community building.

Relationship Building and Caring

Children, throughout their lives, will be developing connections with many people and groups. These relationships can be healthful or harmful. We want children to develop healthy relationships that will enhance their own personal well-being while they in turn contribute to the healthy well-being of others.

Caring relationships are a source of personal happiness and are energy enhancing. They promote self-esteem; enhance productivity; foster mutual respect; enhance self-worth; and engender feelings of safety, security, love, and belonging. Caring relationships encourage personal growth and development through responsible decision-making in an environment that respects individual freedoms and is free of violence, bullying, and drug misuse and abuse.

Children need to develop those social skills that will help them to foster healthful and caring relationships with others. We believe that an effective elementary school counseling program should promote the teaching of social skills and the development of social relationships throughout the school day (cafeteria, playground, school buses, hallways, classroom, and guidance office). The learning of social skills will go a long way in helping children to develop caring relationships. Some social skills that we advocate teaching are the following:

- using manners (thank you, please, may I),
- sharing,
- taking turns,
- giving and receiving compliments,
- giving and receiving feedback,
- expressing feelings in a caring manner,
- asking for help,
- greeting others,
- starting a conversation,
- asking to be included in an activity,
- following group rules,
- empathizing with others,
- responding to the feelings of others,
- problem-solving, and
- offering assistance to others.

The practice of these social skills, through interactions with others, will lead to social competence and an understanding of how to cultivate caring, meaningful, and responsible relationships.

Diversity and Caring

Children live in a world of human diversity. Those differences represent their uniqueness, contribute to their humanness, and help to shape their identity. Children are members of a world culture, a geographical culture, a national culture, a regional culture, and lastly, a racial-ethnic culture, according to Clemmont E. Vontress (Lee, 1994). All children are thus multicultural and diverse in all aspects of their being, which accounts for differences in language, skin color, race, religion, dress, physical ability, customs, beliefs, behaviors, genetic make-up, and in other ways not mentioned.

While diversity is a fact of life for all children, it also is a source of pain, anger, loneliness, and despair for many. Children are quick to notice individual differences in themselves and others. In their quest to be accepted, many children will find themselves the objects of discriminatory behavior and prejudice. Cruel teasing, name-calling, physical aggression, and shunning are common practices exhibited by peers against those who are different. Physical attractiveness, athletic ability, dress, academic ability, handicaps, level of popularity, and many other factors are often the focus of attention by children who feel justified in striking out against those who are different.

Elementary school counseling programs can play a significant role in helping children to make caring choices in their relationships with family and friends, acquaintances, and distant others (people they do not know). Children are likely to care for others when children are functioning at their personal best. Thus, the power of diversity can be realized when children are taught to (Meeks, Heit, & Page, 1996)

1. challenge stereotypes,
2. create synergy through diversity,
3. show empathy for all people,
4. avoid [making] discriminatory comments,
5. ask others to stop discriminatory behavior, and
6. learn about people who are different (p. 170).

Children should be asked to answer questions like the following that will help them to connect with a caring future they can help to create (O'Rourke & Worzbyt, 1996):

- What would the world be like if we all got along with each other?
- How would the world be different from the way it is now?

- What can I do to help bring peace [caring] and cooperation into my home, school, and community?
- How does a peaceful community look and act?
- How do people relate to one another peacefully?
- How do you want others to treat you?
- What are some things that you would see people doing for each other in a caring community?
- What kind of home, school [classroom], and community do you want?
- What are some things that you and others can start doing now to make peace (p. 506)?

We believe that diversity and caring choices can best be promoted through a curriculum and school-based activities that will (O'Rourke & Worzbyt, 1996):

- assist children in accepting and understanding differences in themselves and others;
- help children to appreciate and value themselves and others;
- teach children about stereotypes, prejudices, and biases and how they affect people's lives;
- encourage children to explore their own misinformation concerning issues of diversity;
- provide children with reality-based information regarding human differences;
- help children to explore a range of differences among themselves in addition to cultural differences;
- explore with children a variety of ways in which they can improve communication with their peers and others;
- provide children with experiential opportunities to explore and appreciate diversity in others (e.g., celebrations, foods, dress, beliefs, and disabilities);
- give children an opportunity to work together in building a sense of community amongst themselves;
- assist children in understanding and developing the qualities of peacemakers; and

- help children collaboratively create a "Declaration of Peace" (p. 513).

Racial, gender, cultural, religious, and physical differences do exist among people. And yet in addition to these differences, there is a common ground of similarities on which a caring platform for mutual understanding can be built. All people, despite their differences, share needs for safety, security, love and belonging, loyalty, respect, kindness, justice, and forgiveness. On these values, and others like them, elementary school counseling programs can begin to forge a community of caring that embraces diversity as a common force that can bring people together rather than create a great divide.

Conflict Management and Caring

Conflict is a part of life and occurs in all relationships. "Conflict represents a state of opposition that occurs between two partners (individuals or groups) who are at odds with each other in their attempts to secure their wants and needs. Conflict management is a process that brings conflicting parties together in search of a peaceful settlement in attaining their respective goals" (O'Rourke & Worzbyt, 1996, p. 259).

Conflict is neither good nor bad, nor is it right or wrong. Like so many things in life, conflict is a force (wind, water, sun, fire) that can have either destructive or constructive outcomes. Therefore, conflict must be respected and harnessed in a manner that brings out its constructive possibilities. Conflict is beneficial when it (O'Rourke & Worzbyt, 1996)

- clarifies both sides of an important issue;
- results in both parties being heard in a spirit of cooperation;
- focuses on problem identification and a win-win resolution;
- serves as a safe release of pent-up anxiety, stress, and emotion;
- helps children to resolve their conflicts and invest in their relationship with each other; and
- becomes a learning experience providing opportunity for responsible conflict management.

Conflict is destructive when it

- promotes name-calling, labeling of others, and fighting;
- diverts attention away from the problem and a cooperative, win-win solution;
- destroys children's sense of self-worth;
- polarizes individuals and groups and widens gaps between the parties in conflict; and
- promotes a win-lose competition fueled by deception and manipulation (pp. 261–262).

Thompson and Rudolph (2000) have indicated that the source of most problems that bring children into the counselor's office is in the form of unresolved conflicts that children experience, as noted in the following examples:

- *Interpersonal Conflict.* Children have relationship problems with their peers, siblings, teachers, and parents.
- *Intrapersonal Conflict.* Children experience internal conflict in response to making difficult choices that affect their needs, wants, and values in their quest for self-preservation.
- *Intergroup Conflict.* Children, as members of groups, experience conflict with other groups in their quest to preserve their identity. Thus conflicts exist between families, schools, gangs, racial groups, religious affiliations, and nations.
- *Intragroup Conflicts.* Children experience conflict with other children who belong to the same group as they do. Consequently, disagreements exist between members of playgroups, sports teams, and study groups.

The focus of elementary school counseling programs is to teach children how to live in harmony with each other. This can best be achieved by teaching children caring attitudes, knowledge, and skills that will help them to learn constructive ways of managing conflict. More specifically, we believe that for children to be truly effective managers of conflict, they must

- understand the nature of conflict;
- identify examples of conflict in their own lives; and
- practice caring strategies to prevent the preventable and peace-fully resolve the seemingly unresolvable.

Nature of Conflict

Conflict occurs over resources, needs, and values (Kreidler, 1984).

- *Conflict over Resources.* When two or more children want the same thing(s) and the supply is limited, conflict can occur in the absence of sharing, taking turns, or other conflict prevention strategies.
- *Conflict of Needs.* Children have many needs, including needs for safety, security, love and belonging, self-esteem, etc. Conflict can arise between children or groups of children when they try to satisfy their needs in ways that threaten the need satisfaction of their peers.
- *Conflict of Values.* Children learn their beliefs and values from those closest to them. Because no two people share the exact same values, conflict can arise between children and groups of children based on the expression of these differences.

Identify Examples of Personal Conflict

Children are asked to describe examples of conflict in their own lives as they relate to conflicts over resources, needs, and values. As children identify with their own life conflicts, they can be taught caring strategies to prevent conflict where possible and learn from and resolve conflict constructively when it does occur.

Conflict Prevention and Resolution

Children need to understand that many conflicts are preventable through the effective use of caring interpersonal skills, many of which have been discussed in this chapter. Children can learn to share resources, meet their needs and the needs of others, and express their values and beliefs in socially acceptable and responsible ways. However, when the inevitable happens, and it will, children need to know how to resolve conflict in a caring manner. What follows are the essential components of most successful conflict resolution plans (O'Rourke & Worzbyt, 1996).

- Give each disputant a chance to present his or her feelings and the problem as he or she sees it using "I messages."
- Children are to refrain from attacking each other physically or verbally. They are to stay focused and give each other a chance to be heard.
- Each disputant restates the problem from the other's perspective and does so to the other's satisfaction.
- When the problem has been clearly stated, the disputants look for common ground on which to build a solution.
- The disputants brainstorm together a list of possible solutions.
- The disputants look for ways in which they can change their own behaviors to achieve a win-win solution to their conflict.
- The disputants affirm each other for their efforts in resolving their conflict.

When children learn how to resolve conflict in their own lives, with the help of teachers, parents, and counselors, many may choose to become peer mediators themselves. Children can be taught, through peer mediation training, the information and skills necessary to facilitate the resolution of conflict among their peers (Deutsch, 1993; Lane & McWhirter, 1992; Meeks et al., 1996).

O'Rourke and Worzbyt (1996) have reported the following literature review findings pertaining to the value of school-based conflict prevention and resolution programs:

- drop in school discipline;
- decrease in self-reported aggressive conflicts;
- more prosocial attitude toward conflict;
- increased use of the peer mediation process to settle disputes;

- positive improvement in the school climate;
- school-to-home transfer of conflict-management skills used in resolving siblings disputes;
- improved peer status, self-esteem, self-discipline, and responsibility of mediators; and
- improved self-esteem and respect for peer mediators by disputants (pp. 266–267).

We encourage all elementary school counselors to work with teachers, parents, and administrators in developing school-wide conflict management programs for children. Children can learn the value of practicing caring strategies in preventing and managing conflict in their lives. There is no better way to reduce the risk of conflict while learning from it than practicing a caring approach in seeking to resolve it.

Healthful Family Relationships and Caring

While elementary school counseling programs primarily strive to promote social caring in schools, they can have a limited, yet important, role to play in promoting social caring in the family. Counselors can provide parents with information, skills, and ideas to promote the importance and development of caring connections between and among family members. This can begin by discussing some of the attributes of healthful families. For example, healthful families

- spend time together;
- demonstrate respect for each other;
- share ideas, concerns, and feelings in caring ways;
- trust each other;
- give praise and constructive feedback;
- set rules for responsible behavior;
- resolve conflicts openly and nonviolently; and
- use caring words and practice caring deeds in support of building family connectedness.

Children likewise can be taught ways to care for family members. They can be taught to identify with their interpersonal strengths and to practice them at home with family members. Children have a lot to give and should be encouraged to do so on a daily basis. Children can give family members their

- hugs,
- smiles,
- kind words and actions,
- compliments,
- time,
- helping hands,
- caring ideas and suggestions,
- listening attention,
- respect, and
- kindness.

The list of ways to build caring connections is endless. When children and family members realize and practice all the things they can do to contribute to the well-being of all family members, they will never run out of caring ideas. Children can practice these same ideas with peers at school and extend their gifts of caring to community members who will likewise learn from and appreciate what children have to offer.

Elementary school counselors are in the "family-building" business too. Elementary school counseling programs have much to offer in strengthening the family through promoting social caring.

Responsible Friendship Building and Caring

Being a friend and making friends require children to exhibit effective and responsible social skills in their interactions with others. During the middle childhood years, children are gradually investing more time and energy in cultivating special and meaningful relationships with peers whom they like.

Good friends play a significant role in children's lives. They listen to their problems, offer assistance when needed, and provide companionship during and after school. Friendships validate one's likeability, acceptance, and sense of belonging.

During this time in their lives, children begin to realize that to have a friend, they must be a friend. Learning to be a friend and developing meaningful relationships takes time, effort, and the practice of social skills that increase one's likability. Meeks et al. (1996) have stated that the following skills help children to become good friends:

- listening carefully and keeping confidences;
- avoiding gossip;
- telling the truth;
- being able to say, "I am sorry";
- being a good companion;
- sharing with the other person;
- accepting mistakes the other person makes;
- praising the other person when he does something well; and
- helping the other person when she needs assistance.

Elementary school counseling programs have a significant role to play in helping children to be a friend and to make friends. Counselors can guide parents, teachers, and children in exploring the dynamics of friendships, beginning relationships, understanding and responding to peer pressure, making healthful caring choices with friends, recognizing the differences between harmful and healthful relationships, and ending relationships that encourage a violation of personal values.

Children need to recognize the importance of making caring choices for themselves and the impact of caring choices in relationship building. Children likewise need to understand that caring choices should always be made in the context of being careful. Caring is not without risk. Children must learn self-protection strategies and how to use them. Elementary school counseling programs can teach children to identify risk (danger), assess the danger, judge the severity of the situation, and act in ways to prevent, avoid, or reduce risks to themselves and others. We want our children to practice social caring in ways that enhance responsible peer relationships while making those tough choices that promote social justice and responsible social change. Relationships that reduce self-esteem and foster disrespect; threaten health; and cause people to feel unimportant, worthless, isolated, and frustrated serve no useful purpose. Harmful relationships need to be dissolved and the children involved in them helped to regain their social well-being.

Healthful Community Building and Caring

Children have a vested interest in caring for those who care for them. They want to be accepted and loved, and therefore are more apt to see the value of caring for those people in the inner circle (family and friends) when compared with caring for acquaintances and distant others. However, caring for people whom children do not know is necessary if they are to strengthen communities and address the social problems that exist when people of diversity occupy and share the same planet. Problems of prejudice, domestic and foreign violence, drug and alcohol abuse, poverty, racial tension, overpopulation, war, environmental pollution, disease, depletion of our natural resources, and the effects of natural disasters are but a few of the many societal factors that affect a community's well-being. Nonetheless, when people work together in the spirit of cooperation and caring, they can accomplish great things.

Elementary school counseling programs can help teachers and parents explore the vast array of caring choices that children can make in and out of school to strengthen the human bond between and among all people. This can be accomplished by helping children to

- identify their caring attitudes, skills, and knowledge;
- explore areas of school and community interest where they can make caring choices; and
- select, design, and implement caring activities that will benefit their school and community.

Children can explore participating in activities that will improve the lives of senior citizens, strengthen health care practices, promote home and school safety, and participate in social service and community projects designed to improve the quality of life for all.

The message that we want to communicate to children is that caring is a choice. As caring choices increase in our schools and communities, more people will be affected by and benefit from these acts of caring. When children are involved in acts of caring, they experience an outpouring of warmth, kindness, and respect from others. Equally important, they experience the joy of life and living that comes through caring and giving. They likewise come to understand that caring is what gives life meaning, direction, and a purpose for being.

THE COUNSELOR'S ROLE

Social caring is an important dimension of the elementary school counseling program. It is concerned with teaching children information, shaping attitudes, and developing caring social skills that will enable young people to function successfully in a variety of groups in which they hold membership. Elementary school counselors have a major role to play in support of helping children to discover the importance of developing meaningful and satisfying social connections in the family, classroom, small work and play groups, clubs, religious groups, and other groups to which they will belong.

As we have discussed throughout this chapter, children's social well-being has a significant impact on their physical, personal/emotional, and cognitive health. The evidence is clear. When children feel they belong and receive support from their parents, teachers, and peers, they experience improved academic success, enhanced self-esteem, and generally feel healthier. In addition to the personal benefits of being socially adept are the benefits experienced by the recipients of those who choose to care.

Noddings (1992) has stated that to care and be cared for are fundamental human needs. *Social caring is at the core of our existence. The ability to care and be cared for is what makes us human and gives life meaning and purpose. ". . . without caring, individual human beings cannot thrive, communities become violent battlegrounds, the Ameri-can democratic experiment must ultimately fail, and the planet will not be able to support life"* (Lipsitz, 1995, p. 65).

Elementary school counselors must convey to their social com-munities that children do have the capacity to care, heal, and grow. Pittman and Cahill (1992) have stated that "caring is something that needs to be conveyed to young people through relationships (nurturing) and environments (structure and setting). It is a way of approaching self, group, and community/society that should be explicitly promoted through example, teaching, and practice. It is something, ultimately, that should be demonstrated by youth through ongoing attitudes and behaviors that transcend the bound-aries of specific programs and events" (p. 4).

Teaching children how to give and receive social care are actions that run counter to violence, loneliness, and human suffering and encourage thoughtfulness, community building, peacemaking, re-sponsibility, freedom, self-confidence, and self-esteem. *Families, classrooms, and communities become caring and safe places when the people in them become responsible and generous caregivers.*

When it comes to social caring, elementary school counselors must first become conveyors of a simple, yet powerful, guiding prin-ciple: Treat others as you would like to be treated. This statement becomes the seed from which all caring relationships can emerge and flourish. For the golden rule to become a reality, counselors must help their schools to design and promote social skill development programs that include the following components (Hepler, 1994):

1. Teach all children positive social skills. Too often, only the children with low social status receive social skill training, and the results are discouraging, because other children have not learned how to care for those with low social skills.

2. Encourage popular children to develop a more positive and accepting attitude toward children of low social status.

3. Work with entire classrooms to bring about positive changes in social interaction patterns. This can be accomplished by

changing children's social networks, using sociometric test data results to form peer groups with a distribution of high, medium, and low social status children.

4. Continue to focus on the importance of developing and practicing social caring choices throughout the school day, every day, all year long. Too many social skill programs have had limited success because they were restricted in scope to a few weeks during the school year and then were dropped.

5. Integrate social caring ideas and practices into the school curriculum. Much of what children learn in language arts, social sciences, and health classes relates to developing skills that will improve social relationships. Demonstrate the importance of social caring using curriculum-taught skills and by showing how they can be used to strengthen peer and family relationships, build friendships, and unite acquaintances and distant others in improving community and global relationships.

6. Teach children social perspective-taking, decision-making, and problem-solving skills as tools that can be used to improve social relationships.

7. Help children to understand the value and purpose of being a caregiver and volunteer. Help them to explore caring actions they can take in support of humankind (family, peers, school, community).

School counselors who create social-skill development programs that address these components will be well on their way to improving the social culture in their schools, enhancing the social status of children, and developing a sense of social responsibility in children that will be demonstrated through their caring choices.

The pages that follow contain activities and ideas that are designed to facilitate social caring. Use these ideas and the material in this chapter to develop a social-caring program for children. Help children to experience the positive effect of being a caregiver and the joy that comes from knowing that life takes on purpose and meaning through giving and through graciously receiving from others.

SOCIAL CARING ACTIVITIES

Making Friends

Brief Overview of Activity:

In this session children will explore the ways people make and keep friends and will begin to understand the effects of cliques on friendships.

Objectives:

1. Children will utilize brainstorming techniques to identify ways people make and keep friends.
2. Children will identify the positive and negative aspects of cliques.
3. Children will identify ways to include all persons in groups and activities.

Materials Needed:

1. Chart paper for each group
2. Markers

Procedures:

1. Divide children into small groups and encourage them to make a list of all the things people can do to make new friends. Some examples are introducing new children to school, inviting someone to your house to watch a video or play a game, share crayons or other art materials, etc. Give the groups about 10–12 minutes to come up with their list.
2. Allow time for groups to share their lists. Compare lists for similarities and differences.
3. Write the word "clique" on the chalkboard and define it.
4. Encourage discussion of the positive and negative aspects of cliques.

Positives	Negatives
Belonging to a group.	Some people feel left out.
Always having friends.	Not everyone can belong.
Feeling popular, accepted.	Sometimes feeling pressured to go along with the group, even though you may not agree.

Talk about the kinds of things that can be done in the classroom to assure that no one feels left out of activities. Challenge children to do everything they can to assure that no one is left out.

5. Remind children that during the next week they will be looking for examples of inclusion and invitation skills. Children who are "caught being friendly" will have their names listed on the "Friendship Honor Roll" at the end of the week.

Closure:

Talk briefly with children about reaching out to others in friendship and including others, when possible, in all activities. Encourage them to make one new friend during the next week.

Friendship

Brief Overview of Session:

In this session, children will explore the many different qualities of friendship in forming and maintaining lasting friendships.

Objective:

• Children will understand that all qualities (sharing, reliability, loyalty, sympathy, and caring) are equally important at one time or another in the course of building friendships.

Materials Needed:

1. Movable desks
2. 3-inch by 5-inch cards

Procedure:

1. List five qualities (sharing, reliability, loyalty, sympathy, and caring) and ask children to vote on a 3-inch by 5-inch card for the quality they feel is most important in a friendship. Then divide children into groups based on the friendship quality they felt was most critical in making friends.
2. Have children (in small groups) discuss why their friendship quality is important. Allow approximately 10 minutes for discussion.
3. Allow children to choose a spokesperson for their group who will advocate in behalf of their group's chosen quality.
4. Now hand back the cards and ask children to vote again on what they feel is the most important quality in a friendship.
5. Collect the cards again to see if anyone changed their mind as a result of the discussions.
6. Discuss the results of the second vote and process the children's ideas about friendship qualities.

Closure:

Remind children that all qualities of friendships are important. As friendships change and grow, different qualities will emerge as being important.

As a homework assignment, give children 3-inch by 5-inch cards and ask them to write a brief note to a friend explaining why they appreciate their friendship. Ask them to share this information with their friend and then ask their friend to write down his/her reaction on the back of the same 3-inch by 5-inch card.

Want Ad for a Friend

Brief Overview of Session:

In this session, children will identify the characteristics they look for in choosing a friend.

Objectives:

Children will list qualities they value in friends (e.g., sharing, reliability, loyalty, sympathy, caring, etc.).

Materials Needed:

1. Want Ad worksheet (Figure 8.1)
2. Chalkboard/markers
3. Numbered 3-inch by 5-inch cards (cards are numbered in duplicate so that there are 2 ones, 2 twos, 2 threes, 2 fours, and so on, so that each class member gets a number).

Procedure:

1. As children enter the class, each child receives a 3-inch by 5-inch card with a number on it.
2. Instruct children to find the other person in the room whose number is the same as theirs and sit with that person.
3. Tell them that this is now their best friend.
4. Ask children if they can think of a better way to obtain a best friend.
5. Give a copy of the "Want Ad" worksheet to each child to complete. Have them list the qualities they are looking for in a friend. Then have them again pair up with their partner and discuss the qualities they have listed.
6. Write the most common qualities on the board. You will probably list such qualities as sharing, reliable, dependable, loyal, caring, sympathetic, etc.

**Want Ad
for a Friend**

I am looking for a friend who is:

Figure 8.1. Want Ad Worksheet.

Closure:

Remind children that they look for certain qualities when choosing a friend. If children wish to make more friends, they will want to practice the qualities most common to friendship building.

Stereotypes

Brief Overview of Session:

In this session, children will have an opportunity to look at their own personal stereotypes as well as become aware of many common stereotypes that are held by others. They will also begin to discuss how they can do their part in trying to eliminate stereotyping.

Objective:

1. Children will identify common stereotypes that many people currently hold.
2. Children will evaluate their own personal stereotypes.
3. Children will discuss ways to overcome stereotyping behaviors.

Materials Needed:

1. A variety of pictures for display, for example, an elderly person, a business or professional person, an athlete, a punk rocker, a clergyperson, a small child, and so on.
2. Chart paper (at least three pieces)
3. Markers

Procedure:

1. Begin by directing children's attention to pictures that you have placed around the room. Tell them that you are going to ask them some questions about these people to see how they view each of them. They will demonstrate their choices by voting for the people they think best fit the description.
2. Ask the following questions, providing time for voting and discussion.

      a. Which person is the richest?

      b. Which person is the friendliest?

      c. Which person would you fear?

      d. Which person has the most friends?

      e. Which person likes rock music?

      f. Which person is the most successful?

      g. Which person is the most religious?

3. Following the discussion, ask children to think about their choices. Why did they choose as they did? What are some of the stereotypes children hold?

4. Explain the concept of stereotyping. Ask children how they may have been using stereotyping when answering the earlier questions based on the pictures they viewed.

5. Ask children to identify some of the stereotypes that they can refute. Talk about the fact that we should get to know people rather than stereotyping them.

Closure:

Bring closure to this session by reminding children that we can make school and community more peaceful places by resisting stereotyping behavior and getting to know people rather than judging them. Children should be challenged to make a concerted effort to get to know others who are different from themselves during the next week.

Dots for Diversity

Brief Overview of Session:

In this session, children will experience how it feels to be a member of a minority group.

Objective:

- Children will demonstrate their understanding of diversity issues. (Classification systems and discrimination.)

Materials:

Colored dots (at least six colors)—one per child.

Procedure:

1. Begin this session by stating that there is to be absolutely no talking while the activity is taking place.
2. Ask children to shut their eyes while placing a dot on each forehead. Make sure two to three children have no color dot matches in the room (select popular children).
3. When all children have been given a dot, ask them to find a way to form groups based on the color of the dots on their foreheads. They are not allowed to talk. They are to form into groups in absolute silence. They may not remove their dot to see what color it is. They must rely on others' nonverbal feedback. Give children about 5 minutes to form their groups.
4. After children have formed into groups, discuss the following:
   a. How were groups formed without discussion?
   b. How did children figure out what color dot they had?
   c. What class leaders developed?
   d. Were any children left out? How did they feel?

   Relate this activity to real life. How does this occur in school (specific groups—jocks, band members, academic, general, etc.)?

Closure:

Bring closure to this activity by asking children to write a personal reflection on this activity.

Diversity in Physical/Mental Capacity

Brief Overview of Session:

In this section, children will begin to identify things other than culture that make them different. They will consider differences in physical and mental abilities and how these differences affect how people are treated.

Objectives:

1. Children will identify differences other than culture that can be found in their school or community.
2. Children will begin to identify ways in which they can promote better communication among all people.

Materials:

1. Pictures of people who are disabled
2. A braille book
3. Sign alphabet cards
4. If possible, a visitor from the local Easter Seal Community to talk with the children about disabilities

Procedures:

NOTE: Prior to doing this activity, ask children to get to know someone different from themselves.

1. Begin by asking children to share with the group their experiences from their "homework" assignment on getting to know someone different. What were some of the positives of their experience? Allow a brief time for discussion from each group member.
2. Ask if any children had the opportunity to get to know someone who was different in a way other than culturally.
3. Discuss some other "differences" children encounter each day. Provide time for brainstorming about these differences.
   a. Disabilities
   b. Differences in school attitude or aptitude
   c. Differences in athletic abilities
   d. Differences in beliefs

4. Show the braille book, the signing alphabet, and pictures of people who are disabled. Provide time for discussion regarding these and other differences among people.

5. Introduce the resource person from Easter Seals and allow time for her to talk with the children. Be sure to save time for children to ask questions.

6. Encourage a discussion of how children can develop a friendship with a child who is a client of the Easter Seals Society. Discuss some things children can do to volunteer their services to children with special needs.

Closure:

Bring closure to this session by providing a little "thinking time" for each group member. Ask children to discuss their feelings about today's discussion. As a homework assignment, ask children to spend some time thinking about what it might be like if they were blind, deaf, or confined to a wheelchair. Encourage children to write down their thoughts on a piece of paper and bring it to the next class.

Friendship Goals

Brief Overview of Session:

In this session, children will identify a personal goal for friendship and will have an opportunity to develop an action plan for reaching that goal.

Objectives:

1. Children will identify a personal friendship goal that they hope to attain.

2. Children will develop an action plan for attaining their friendship goal.

Material Needed:

Friendship Goal Worksheet (Figure 8.2)

Friendship Goal

My Goal:

Steps I Will Need to Take to Reach My Goal:

How I Will Know If I've Reached My Goal

I Will Discuss My Goal with _____
in Two Weeks.

Figure 8.2.

Procedure:

1. Discuss the term "goal." Identify some academic goals that children have reached in the past. Allow time for sharing. Then ask, "Have you ever thought of developing a goal for friendship?"

2. Discuss with the children some friendship goals that children their age may have:

   a. Learn to feel more comfortable initiating conversations.

   b. Teach someone a new skill.

   c. Help someone study for a test.

   d. Invite someone to eat lunch with you.

   e. Be kinder to new students.

   f. Work on a school project with someone you haven't worked with before.

3. Ask children to name one friendship goal that they would like to attain.

4. Give children a copy of the *Friendship Goal Worksheet* and demonstrate how to complete it using a friendship goal of your choosing (introducing oneself to a new child).
5. Using their selected friendship goal, help children to complete the *Friendship Goal Worksheet*. Once completed, encourage and assist children in achieving their goal.

Closure:

Provide time for children to talk briefly about their individual friendship goals and to share their goals with classmates, if they wish to do so.

What Is Conflict?

Brief Overview of Session:

In this session, children will begin to identify their definitions of conflict and explore how people deal with conflict.

Objectives:

1. Children will draw a picture of conflict.
2. Children will begin to understand what conflict is and how people deal with it.

Materials Needed:

1. 12-inch by 18-inch sheet of paper for each child
2. Chart paper or blank overhead transparencies for brainstorming
3. Crayons or markers

Procedure:

1. Briefly discuss conflict. Give children a piece of paper and ask them to draw a picture to represent their idea of conflict (5 minutes).
2. Provide time for children to share their pictures. Discuss the types of conflict that were identified. Post their ideas about conflict around the room.

3. Brainstorm with children the words that come to mind when they think of conflict. List their ideas on the chalkboard or overhead transparency.

4. Discuss the kinds of words that were shared. Some ideas are anger, hostility, violence, hate, eye rolling, staring, laughing, and ignoring.

5. Have children rate the words as Positive, Neutral, or Negative. You will probably have very few positive words at this point. Talk briefly about the fact that conflict can be positive in that it can move people to action. Many times action causes positive changes.

6. Ask children to think of additional positive words, such as solution, learning, choices, and peaceful.

7. Define conflict. Conflict is seen as a disagreement between people. Conflict is a normal and natural part of life and can be positive in that children can learn more about themselves and others.

Closure:

Ask children to identify some ways to prevent conflicts from happening and, when they do happen, things they can do to resolve conflicts peacefully.

ADDITIONAL IDEAS FOR SOCIAL CARING

Game Day

As a special reward for achieving a goal, encourage children to bring in a variety of board games. Set aside time for them to socialize and engage in game playing.

Scavenger Hunt

Develop a list of 5 to 10 facts that children do not know about each other. Give children a copy of this list. Some items for the hunt could be: Who plays on the school football team? Who has a newspaper delivery route? Who has a birthday closest to yours? Who has one older brother and one younger sister? Let children circulate and talk to each other as a way of identifying and collecting the names of children that go with the scavenger hunt items.

New Friend for the Day or Week

At the beginning of the day, have half of the children draw, by lottery, the name of a classmate (class roster) who will be their friend for the day or week. During the specified time, the children will eat together, work in groups together, and so on. At the end of the day or week, children will give a brief oral report titled "Five Neat Things I Learned About My New Friend."

My Younger Friend

Make arrangements with a primary teacher to have children from an intermediate class be paired with a child from a lower grade. During the week, provide opportunities for children to work together on a specific assignment, for example, read a book together, write a letter or a story, complete an art project, and so forth. At the completion of the activity, provide time for the younger and older children to describe what was fun about this activity.

My Older Friend

Have children become pen pals to people in nursing homes or hospitals. Allow time for letter writing at least every other week to maintain interest. After several months of corresponding by letter, schedule times for children to visit their older friends.

Make the World (Your School) a More Friendly Place

Develop a poster contest in which children design posters around the theme of making the world/school friendlier. When the posters are completed, have them displayed in an area that is visible to all.

Smile—It's Contagious

Choose a week when the class will consciously try to smile more often and be friendlier to those they meet. This includes classmates, people in the grocery store, neighbors, and so on. At the end of the week, ask children to write a brief synopsis of what happened as a result of their experiment.

"Thank You" Awareness

Help children to understand the importance of saying *thank you* to those who have done something for them. Have children make and mail *thank you* cards to those special people in their lives.

Acts of Friendship

Purchase a number of disposable cameras for children to use to take pictures of people who are doing friendly acts. If the activity is to be done in school, announce to the school that Mr. Brown's class will be on the lookout for persons who are committing "acts of friendship." Tell children not to be surprised if they see their pictures (photos) on the "Acts of Friendship" bulletin board. Allow each child to have the camera and take five pictures of "acts of friendship." Post the photos on a bulletin board that is accessible to the school community, for example, near the cafeteria.

Friendship Chain

Give children a 1-inch by 6-inch piece of paper on which to write their names and something that makes them a good friend. After each class member has completed a link, staple the pieces together to form a classroom *friendship chain*. The chain also can be expanded to make a school-wide friendship chain to be hung in the cafeteria. Don't forget to add names such as those of teachers, principal, cafeteria workers, librarians, maintenance people, counselor, and nurse to the chain.

Showing Caring Behaviors

Write the following behaviors on a slip of paper: asking for help, being empathetic, offering assistance, providing feedback, taking turns, sharing, giving compliments, and so on. Then divide the class into pairs and give each pair a slip of paper with one of the caring behaviors listed on it. Have children role-play their caring behaviors.

Conflict Box

Ask children to write on slips of paper conflicts they are currently experiencing. Have them place these slips into a decorated shoebox with a mail slot at the top. Once a week, selected children are to remove a slip from the box and, with the assistance of their classmates, arrive at possible solutions to the conflict.

Win-Win/Win-Lose/Lose-Lose

Divide children into three groups. Each group is given a different set of directions as to how to deal with the box of "goodies" that has been placed in the center of their table. (The goodies should be something that can be easily damaged (small bags of potato chips). The directions are as follows:

Group 1—Share the chips so that each person gets the same amount.

Group 2—The girls get the "goodies."

Group 3—The strongest member wins the "goodies."

In Group 1, all members share the snack (win-win). In Group 2 (Win-Lose) the girls get the snack (win-lose). In Group 3, children put their hands on the snack and pull. The snack is destroyed in the process (lose-lose). Discuss the value of working together to solve problems so that everyone comes out a winner, rather than having winners and losers. Complete the experience by giving snacks to children in Groups 2 and 3 as they did not receive any during the activity.

Labeling

Ask children to identify the labels that kids sometimes use for each other (e.g., nerds, jocks, geeks, druggies, etc). Write the labels on pieces of masking tape and put one label on each child's forehead (without letting the child know what their label says). Encourage children to walk around the room and respond to children they see based on what is written on their label. Talk about the negative feelings that arise as a result of labeling.

Tower Building

Form groups of four to six children. Give each group a stack of old newspapers and a roll of masking tape. Allow 20 minutes for each group to build the tallest, "free-standing" tower they can build. When they have completed their activity, talk about the co-operative behaviors that are needed to achieve group success in reaching their goal. Discuss the various roles that children played in completing their tower. Was anyone excluded? Did the group have a leader? How did cooperation enter into this project?

I Like You Because . . .

Give children a sheet of paper and have them write their names in large letters across the top. In turn, the children will pass their paper to the person nearest them who will complete the sentence "I like you because . . ." Each child will write a comment on every other child's paper. When each sheet has been completed, laminate the sheets and encourage children to take them home and display them in a prominent place in their room to remind them of all the good things people like about them.

Care Quilt

Purchase enough heavy cotton material for each person to make a 12-inch by 12-inch square. On the square, children will indicate how they personally show caring for family, pets, classmates, friends, community, and so on. When the squares have been completed, sew them all together to make a classroom "Quilt of Caring." Display the quilt in a prominent place in the school for all to see.

BIBLIOGRAPHY

Boyer, E.L. (1995). *The basic school: A community for learning.* Princeton, NJ: Carnegie Foundation.

Coie, J., & Dodge, K. (1988). Aggression and antisocial behavior. In W. Damon (series ed.) and N. Eisenburg (vol. ed.), *Handbook of child psychology: Vol 3. Social, emotional, and personality development* (5th ed., pp. 779–862). New York: Wiley.

Coie, J., & Dodge, K. (1983). Continuities and change in children's social status: A five-year longitudinal study. *Merrill-Palmer Quarterly, 29,* 621–681.

Coie, J.D., Dodge, K.A., & Kupersmidt, J.B. (1990). Peer group behavior and social status. In S. Asher & J. Coie (eds.), *Peer rejection in childhood* (pp. 17–59). New York: Cambridge University Press.

Coie, J.D., & Kupersmidt, J.B. (1983). A behavioral analysis of emergency social status in boys groups. *Child Development, 54,* 1400–1416.

Damon, W., & Hart, D. (1988). *Self-understanding in childhood and adolescents.* Cambridge, England: Cambridge University Press.

DeHart, G.B., Stroufe, L.A., & Cooper, R.G. (2000). *Child development: Its natures and course* (4th ed.). Boston, MA: McGraw-Hill.

Deutsch, M. (1993). Educating for a peaceful world. *American Psychologist, 48*(5), 510–517.

Dodge, K., Schlundt, D., Schocken, I., & Delugach, J. (1983). Social competence and children's sociometric status: The role of peer groups' entry strategies. *Merrill-Palmer Quarterly, 29,* 309–336.

Emerson, R.W. (1832). Journals and miscellaneous notebooks. Ralph Waldo Emerson. In W.H. Gilman et al. (vol. ed.), *Vol. 3* (pp. 318–319). Cambridge, MA: Harvard University Press, 1960.

Hepler, J.B. (1997). Social development of children: The role of peers. *Social Work in Education, 19*(4), 242–256.

Hepler, J.B. (1995). Social skills training. In R.L. Edwards (ed.-in-chief), *Encyclopedia of social work* (19th ed., vol. 2, pp. 2196–2205). Washington, DC: NASW Press.

Hepler, J.B. (1994). Evaluating the effectiveness of a social skills programs for preadolescents. *Research on Social Work Practice, 4,* 411–435.

Hoffman, M.L. (1976). Empathy, role-taking, guilt, and development of altrusive motives. In T. Lickona (ed.), *Moral Development and Behavior.* New York: Holt, Rinehart, & Winston.

Kreidler, W.J. (1984). *Creative conflict resolution: More than 200 activities for keeping peace in the classroom.* Glenview, IL: Scott, Foresman.

Lane, P.S., & McWhirter, J.J. (1992). A peer mediation model: Conflict resolution for elementary and middle school children. *Elementary School Guidance & Counseling, 27,* 15–23.

Lee, C.C. (1994). Pioneers of multicultural counseling: A conversation with Clemmont E. Vontress. *Journal of Multicultural Counseling and Development, 22,* 66–78.

LeFrancois, G.R. (1989). *Of children: An introduction to child development* (6th ed.). Belmont, CA: Wadsworth Publishing Co.

Lipsitz, J. (1995). Prologue: Why we should care about caring. *Phi Delta Kappan, 76*(9), 665–666.

Little, R. (1988, November). Skills for growing: A new K–5 program. *Principal,* 19–21.

Maccoby, E. (1980). *Social development: Psychological growth and the parent-child relationship.* New York: Harcourt Brace Jovanovich.

McCandless, B.R. (1967). *Children: Behavior and development.* New York: Holt, Rinehart & Winston.

Meeks, L., Heit, P., & Page, R. (1996). *Comprehensive school health education* (2nd ed.). Blacklick, OH: Meeks Heit Publishing Co.

Mehaffey, J.I., & Sandberg, S.K. (1992). Conducting social skills training groups with elementary school children. *The School Counselor, 40,* 61–67.

Noddings, N. (1992). *The challenge to care in school: An alternate approach to education.* New York, NY: Teachers College Press.

Oliver, R.L., Young, T.A., & LaSalle, S.M. (1994). Early lessons in bullying and victimization: The help and kindness of children's literature. *The School Counselor, 42*(2), 137–146.

Orecklin, M., & Winters, R. (2000). Beware of the in-crowd. *Time, 156*(8), 69.

O'Rourke, K., & Worzbyt, J.C. (1996). *Support groups for children.* Washington, DC: Accelerated Development.

Pittman, K.J., & Cahill, M. (1992). Youth and caring: The role of youth programs in the development of caring (Draft-Research Paper #2). Commissioned Paper for Lilly Endowment Youth and Caring Conference (February 26–27, 1992). Miami, FL: Center for Youth Development & Policy Research.

Rubin, K.H., Bukowski, W., & Parker, J.G. (1998). Peer interactions, relationships, and groups. In W. Damon (series ed.) and N. Eisenburg (vol. ed.), *Handbook of child psychology: Vol 3. Social, emotional, and personality development* (5th ed., pp. 619–700). New York: Wiley.

Rubin, K.H., & Pepler, D.J. (1980). The relationship of child's play to social-cognitive growth and development. In H. Foot, A. Chapman, & J. Smith (eds.), *Friendship and childhood relationships.* New York: Wiley.

Selman, R.L. (1980). *The growth of interpersonal understanding.* New York: Academic Press.

Selman, R.L. (1976). Social cognitive understanding: A guide to educational and clinical practice. In T. Lickona (ed.), *Theory, research, and social issues.* New York: Holt, Rinehart, & Winston.

Thompson, C.L., & Rudolph L.B. (2000). *Counseling children* (5th ed.). Belmont, CA: Brooks/Cole.

Zigler, E.F., & Stevenson, M.F. (1993). *Children in a changing world: Developmental and social issues* (2nd ed.). Pacific Grove, CA: Brooks/Cole.

CHAPTER 9

Cognitive Caring

Cognitive Caring is a process of self-care in which children learn, practice, and use cognitive skills to perceive reality as it is, to respond successfully to its challenges, and to live a life of purpose and meaning grounded in reason.

COGNITIVE DEVELOPMENT

Cognitive health is achieved through a developmental process that includes exercising and conditioning of the mind. The process is developmental in nature. Children experience longitudinal periods of growth in which they not only acquire more cognitive skills, but undergo a series of quantitative and qualitative changes in the way they think, learn, and understand the world.

In studying cognitive functioning in children, three basic approaches will be briefly examined, namely:

- *Piaget's Theory of Cognitive Development,* which examines the development of children's logical reasoning abilities and the qualitative changes that occur with age in how children think, learn, and understand their world.
- *Information Processing Theory,* which studies human thought by comparing it with the workings of a computer in which children input information from the environment, process it, and draw upon information stored in memory to make life decisions.

- *Sociocultural Theory,* which investigates the impact that social interactions and specific cultural practices have on shaping the development of children's cognitive skills.

Piaget's Theory of Cognitive Development

Piaget, the Swiss-born developmental psychologist, formulated the first comprehensive theory of cognitive development (1970). He believed that all normal, healthy children go through the same major periods of development, in the same sequence, at approximately the same time (age), and that this developmental process cannot be significantly accelerated through training. Cognitive development, he stated, occurs in stages, and children's understanding of the world is limited by their cognitive structures, which change as they develop, becoming increasingly more abstract and complex. Piaget identified four stages of development:

- *Sensorimotor Period (ages 0–2),* in which a child's world is limited to sensory awareness and motor acts.
- *Preoperational Period (ages 2–7),* in which children are not yet capable of logical or systematic reasoning, but are able to deal with the world symbolically or representationally using language, mental images, and their imagination.
- *Concrete Operational Period (ages 7–11),* in which children begin to demonstrate a greater capacity for logical reasoning at a very concrete level regarding those areas of life in which they have had direct personal experience.
- *Formal Operational Period (ages 11 years and older),* in which older children, adolescents, and adults are capable of reasoning logically and systematically about abstract issues and hypothetical situations.

Middle childhood (ages 7–11) is a time when children are facing major challenges in their lives, the most significant of which is adapting to the rigors of a formal education that places high demands on their cognitive abilities. The cognitive changes from early to middle childhood are not to be considered dramatic or revolutionary, but rather represent a refinement in skills that begin to evolve during the preschool years (DeHart, Stroufe, & Cooper, 2000).

Somewhere between the ages of 5 and 7, children begin to be treated differently with respect to observable changes in their cognitive skills. Many cultures, including our own, believe that children by this stage in their development have begun to enter the "age of reason" and are often held to higher standards of conduct and accountability for their actions when compared with their preschool years (Sameroff & Haith, 1996).

While children, during the latter years of the preoperational development period, are becoming more responsible and growing in their cognitive abilities, they are still experiencing a number of cognitive blocks common to this age group, namely (De Hart, et al., 2000):

- **Egocentrism Block.** Children experiencing this block have difficulty seeing another person's point of view. They are incapable of perspective-taking, even in the face of conflicting evidence to the contrary. These children would have difficulty empathizing with others' feelings because they are convinced that everyone should think, feel, and behave as they do.
- **Centration Block.** Children experiencing this block are unable to focus on more than one thing at a time even though multiple pieces of information are relevant to solving the problem. Children watching a ventriloquist give voice to a puppet believe that the puppet is speaking and moving by itself even though additional data is present that would lead to a different conclusion by someone not experiencing this block. Children with a centration block have a difficult time in distinguishing between appearance and reality.
- **Reversibility Block.** Children experiencing this block have difficulty with reversible thinking. They would find it difficult to order a sequence of events or operations from front to back and back to front. A child with a reversibility block would

have difficulty ordering the sequence of events that led to his being in a fight on the playground.

- **Transformation Block.** Children experiencing this block are unable to see the dynamic changes that occur in a situation as it unfolds. They are unable to relate to cause-and-effect reasoning or to explain a process of change.

As children enter the concrete operational period (ages 7–11), some important improvements in the following areas are noteworthy (DeHart, et al., 2000):

- Children's capacity for logical and systematic thinking, using multiple pieces of information, has increased due to a decline in centration.
- Children's ability to perceive underlying reality, despite a superficial appearance to the contrary, has advanced.
- Children have shown growth in their domain-specific knowledge or expertise; information-processing capacity; and control over their attention (concentration) and memory.
- Children have demonstrated improvement in their ability to think about their own knowledge and processes of thought. This capacity to think about the way one thinks is called metacognition.
- Children have demonstrated an improved capacity in their ability to overcome the cognitive blocks that were present as they transitioned into the concrete operational period of their development.

Despite all the improvements that children make in the concrete operational stage of development, they still lag behind in their ability to display adultlike competencies in the following areas (Zigler & Stevenson, 1993):

- Children, while possessing an increased knowledge base, still lack the breadth and depth of knowledge possessed by adults. This lack of information often diminishes mature reasoning ability. For example, Bob and his friend decided to build a fort in the woods. They had wood, nails, and tools to do the job, but their fort did not materialize as they had envisioned. Because they were lacking in knowledge and understanding of building design and construction, they were unable to perform as planned.

- Children in middle childhood, while learning many new thinking skills, are not always capable of using their abilities and applying them together in the context of a larger problem-solving system. Many times cognitive skills have been learned, but are not used, or when used, are applied in isolation. For example, Susan, when faced with being teased on the playground, hits her teaser rather than applying a decision-making model that she had learned in class that would have helped her to explore other options in addition to the one she used.

- Children in middle childhood still have difficulty with abstract reasoning and hypothetical problem-solving. Their reasoning abilities are limited to concrete and here-and-now situations. For example, when asked to consider packing for a weekend camping trip, Tom was unable to demonstrate an organized, comprehensive, and systematic approach in response to this hypothetical situation.

These limitations will be addressed with the passage of time as children undergo the necessary maturational changes that will transform them into young and more capable adults.

Information Processing Theory

The Information Processing Theory views human thought processes in relationship to the workings of a computer. This theory describes the way children obtain information, remember it, retrieve it, and use it in solving problems (Rice, 1992). Children first input information from their environment, process it, and draw on information already stored in memory when completing cognitive tasks.

Information Processing theorists (Klahr & MacWhinney, 1998; Siegler, 1998) view cognitive development in terms of quantitative changes (gradual improvements) in attention, memory, and thinking that result in improved ability to interpret life events and to use a wider range of problem-solving strategies. These theorists thus seek to analyze the steps that children take in performing various mental tasks and in examining the cognitive changes that occur with age. They likewise believe that improvements in attention, memory, and thinking can be enhanced within the confines of human potential through environmental manipulation (teaching), which helps to explain some variations in cognitive processing abilities in children of the same age.

Attention Abilities

Six- to 11-year-olds demonstrate significant improvement in their ability to increase their attention (concentration) when compared with preschoolers. They are capable of selecting information to attend to, of staying focused on it, and of ignoring irrelevant and competing stimuli (Flavell, Miller, & Miller, 1993). They have become more systematic, organized, and selective in directing their attention than their preschool counterparts (Flavell et al., 1993). This increase in children's attention is in large part due to their development and consistent use of more sophisticated and effective strategies for staying focused in the presence of internal and environmental distractions.

Attention improves with age, as does the consistent application of learned strategies that can be applied in reducing distractibility. Not all children are equally successful in staying focused on tasks and information that hold little value for them. As children progress through middle childhood, individual differences in attention and levels of concentration become more evident, as does the diagnosis of attention deficit disorders. Recognition of variations in attention capabilities become more noticeable at this time because of the increasing demand placed on children in addressing academic challenges that require greater attentional abilities. Specific techniques for developing attention capabilities will be discussed later in this chapter.

Memory Abilities

In addition to having effective attention strategies, the ability to remember is basic to all learning. "Without memory, we would never be able to recall or recognize what we have already experienced. We would not be able to accumulate a body of knowledge, to learn from past mistakes, or to think and reason intelligently" (Rice, 1992, pp. 154–155). During the middle childhood years, children become better at using their memory capabilities and increasing their understanding of memory, how it works, and what they can do to improve it.

The process of remembering is often viewed as a three-stage process consisting of sensory storage, short-term storage, and long-term storage (Flavell, Miller, & Miller, 1993; Schneider & Bjork-lund, 1998). The capacity for long-term storage of information is virtually unlimited, whereas sensory storage and short-term storage capacities are limited, but continue to expand from early to middle childhood.

In sensory storage, information is first retrieved by the senses and is held for less than one second before it begins to decay or is obliterated by other incoming sensory information. Any information remaining in sensory storage is passed on to short-term storage (conscious mind), where it remains for up to 30 seconds before it too is lost. Information to be passed on to relatively permanent, long-term storage must first be rehearsed in short-term storage so that it can be preserved long enough for transference to long-term storage.

While very little processing of information occurs in sensory or short-term storage, long-term memory contains information that has been processed deeply until it is thoroughly familiar and stored on a rather permanent basis. Unlike short-term memory, long-term memory continues to increase quite rapidly throughout middle and late childhood on into young adulthood (Price & Goodman, 1990). In the process of information retrieval, stored information is obtained by searching the database, finding, and remembering through recall (without the use of cues) or recognition (use of cues). Increases in functional capacity with respect to memory are most likely due to continued neurological development and practice in processing information (Kail, 1991; Schneider & Bjorklund, 1998).

Metamemory is an aspect of memory that develops during middle childhood and involves children's knowledge and understanding of memory and memory processes. Children thus recognize the need to remember and how to go about increasing their capacity to remember using metamemory strategies. They are likewise able to identify their memory strengths and weaknesses and are able to monitor their own memory performance (DeHart, Stroufe, & Cooper, 2000). There are a number of memory-aiding strategies that children can use to learn and remember information. Some of these strategies will be discussed later in this chapter.

While most children in middle childhood tend to have some ideas as to how they can expand their memory capacity and knowledge through the use of intentional goal-directed strategies, others may experience, in varying degrees, three types of deficiencies in their use of memory strategies (Schneider & Bjorklund, 1998).

- *Mediation deficiencies* occur when children are unable to use a strategy even when adults suggest it.
- *Production deficiencies* occur when children do not use (produce) a strategy spontaneously, but can use it when instructed to do so.
- *Utilization deficiencies* occur when children use a strategy spontaneously, but with no benefit to their memory performance.

These types of deficiencies help to explain that while younger and less mature children are capable of increasing their memory, they are still deficient in their understanding of memory strategies and of how they can be used to learn and remember information. Kail and Hagen (1982) summarized the development of children's mnemonic strategies (behaviors designed to improve memory) as follows:

- Five- and 6-year-olds do not spontaneously use mnemonic strategies often. They may feel it is important to remember something, but they seldom turn this motivation into a deliberate effort to improve memory.

- The period between 7 and 10 years of age seems to be a transitional stage during which the use of mnemonic devices expands. Exactly when a particular strategy emerges depends on both its nature and the context in which it is used.

- Beginning at about age 10, children show signs of using mnemonic devices consistently and effectively. This tendency increases over the next several years, until by adolescence, youngsters are quite good at using deliberate strategies to help themselves remember (DeHart et al., 2000, pp. 393–394).

Children's attentional and memory abilities improve significantly during middle childhood. These improvements are due in part to an increased speed in processing information supported by continued neurological development. Ever increasing control and flexibility in information processing also is attributed to expanded metacognitive understanding and to a growing knowledge and utilization of attentional and memory strategies.

Social Interaction and Cognitive Development

Children's cognitive development is greatly influenced by social interactions of peers and adults (Rogoff, 1998). They are influenced by *didactic learning* experiences, in which adults and peers pass on their knowledge and skills to children during teachable moments both at home and in school. Learning how to set a table, eat properly, do household chores, solve homework problems, and practice family and cultural traditions are examples of didactic learning experiences.

In addition to didactic learning, children often enhance their cognitive development through *cooperative learning* experiences, in which learners of approximately the same knowledge level, age, and skill development share ideas and discover solutions to problems on their own. Both types of learning experiences can foster cognitive growth and expand cultural understandings in children commensurate with their intellectual capacity and stage of development.

Cooperative learning experiences, according to Piaget (1970), facilitate cognitive development within children through social interaction and provide experiences that help children to construct their understanding of reality. This process occurs as children are challenged to notice and resolve discrepancies between their own thoughts and ideas and those of their peers. This process in itself is a reality-attaining experience in that children gradually draw their own conclusions as to how the world really works.

In contrast to Piaget, Vygotsky (1978) viewed cognitive development from a sociocultural perspective in which children first learn cognitive skills in social situations and only later internalize them. Children gradually learn to plan and regulate their own behavior based on directions that they received from adults in social situations (didactic learning).

With respect to the power of didactic learning experiences in shaping cognitive development, Vygotsky introduced the concept of *Zone of Proximal Development*. This term was used to explain the existence of a gap between children's current performance and their potential performance within each stage of cognitive development. He believed that if given guidance by someone more skilled (teacher, parent, peer), that gap could be closed or reduced in accordance with the child's developmental potential, the skill level of the teacher, and the child's readiness to learn. Essentially, Vygotsky's approach to cognitive development applies more to didactic learning situations. He viewed it as a sociocultural process in which children internalize knowledge and skills that are shared among people in their culture. Again, in contrast to Piaget, Vygotsky believed that children do not have to create their understanding of reality on their own, but rather can benefit from what they learn from those around them. Vygotsky's theory is based on the premise that a more knowledgeable adult provides guidance and instruction to less knowledgeable learners operating within the *Zone of Proximal Development*.

The good news concerning cognitive development from a social interaction perspective is that it can be greatly influenced and enhanced through *didactic* and *cooperative* learning experiences. Parents, teachers, counselors, and other adults shaping children's lives need to consider the impact of these two learning strategies and use them in ways that will enhance children's learning potential.

THE COGNITIVE HEALTHY CHILD

Children's minds need care and conditioning, as do their bodies if they are to perform in caring and helpful ways. When children enjoy cognitive health, they are able to use their cognitive skills and understandings "to perceive reality as it is, to respond to its challenges, and to develop rational strategies for living" (Hales, 1992, p. 25). *The development of sound cognitive health is a prerequisite to attaining and maintaining peace and balance in life.* With the mastery of thought and reason comes an internal guidance system that helps children to navigate through a lifetime of routine and challenging choices.

While the qualities associated with physical, personal/emotional, and social health are quite clear to most people, defining the qualities of cognitive health is a bit more elusive. Children who follow a heart-healthy diet, exercise regularly, get plenty of sleep and relaxation, and adhere to sound health practices can generally expect to enjoy a healthy life. Unfortunately, there is no uniform easy prescription to follow in attaining cognitive health. However, the following statements provide a point of reference in discussing cognitive health in children ages 7 to 11. These children

- demonstrate an ability to perform concrete operations (classification, serialization, and conservation);
- demonstrate an increased capacity for logical, systematic thinking at a concrete level;
- recognize reality in most situations despite appearances to the contrary;

- demonstrate increased information-processing capabilities due in part to metacognitive understandings, a growing knowledge base, and greater use of attentional and memory-enhancing strategies;
- demonstrate an increased capacity for self-introspection and insightfulness regarding their conduct;
- demonstrate their ability to solve problems and make decisions;
- demonstrate their ability to use cognitive strategies in meeting the daily academic challenges of school life;
- demonstrate their willingness to accept responsibility for their actions;
- understand and accept their limitations, but strive to self-improve in those areas of life in which self-improvement is possible; and
- like and care for themselves in responsible ways.

By the age of 12, children have come a long way in their cognitive development. Middle childhood is a time when children face new demands and need to draw upon their cognitive abilities in making caring and careful choices (risk management) in relationship to self, others, and society. Children who attain cognitive health possess feelings of positive self-worth, make sound decisions that are in harmony with their values and the law, and cope responsibly with life's challenges while shaping a life of joy, meaning, and purpose.

UNDERSTANDING THE NEED FOR COGNITIVE CARING

To care and be careful are fundamental human needs. Some have described caring as the ultimate reality of life, for it is at the core of what makes us human beings. To care is to show concern and interest in oneself, others, and the environment. Children who care and make caring choices seek to preserve all that is good about themselves and the world. In learning to make caring choices, they also appreciate and value being cared for by others. Caring, in many ways, is a reciprocal process. Unless there are givers and receivers of care, human connections can never be realized and the value of caring can never be experienced.

Caring is a cognitive, thought-based process with emotional and behavioral outcomes. Children who care must make caring choices that are based on right (not wrong), reality (not myth), and responsibility (not careless action). The purpose of an education (Chapter 1) is to provide children ". . . with a coherent curriculum, a climate for learning, and a commitment to character that will develop in children the capacity to judge wisely and act responsibly in matters of life and conduct" (Boyer, 1995, p. 192). We must develop in them a capacity to think, reason, and make responsible caring choices that can channel their knowledge to humane ends. In doing so, they will be able to cultivate for themselves a life of dignity and purpose.

When children fail to make responsible caring choices in meeting their developmental, variant, societal, and academic needs to succeed in school and life, they and others are at risk of engaging in behaviors (actions) that are devoid of thought. Children who are lacking in cognitive capabilities (information-processing, thinking skills, goal setting, and decision-making/problem-solving) are at risk of exhibiting the following:

Learned Helplessness

When children experience repeated failure in life and living, they feel helpless and believe that they have no control over life's circumstances. When this happens, these children often give up on themselves and become dependent upon others. They entice others to do for them what they believe they can no longer do for themselves. They become helpless victims in need of being rescued. These discouraged children are easy prey and are often taken advantage of by those who show them "kindness."

Irrational Thinking

When children fail to develop healthy and responsible cognitive skills, they are likely to harbor and act on irrational thoughts about themselves, others, and the world. Irrational thoughts and beliefs are not supported by evidence. They represent myths or distortions of reality that appear to be based on truth. Walters (1982) provided the following detailed list of some of the most common irrational beliefs held by children.

1. It's awful if others don't like me.
2. I'm bad if I make a mistake.
3. Everything should go my way; I should always get what I want.
4. Things should come easy to me.
5. The world should be fair and bad people should be punished.
6. I shouldn't show my feelings.
7. Adults should be perfect.
8. There's only one right answer.
9. I must win.
10. I shouldn't have to wait for anyone (p. 572).

While harboring these irrational thoughts (beliefs) has the potential for eliciting emotional and behavioral problems in children, four factors play a significant role in determining the likelihood and severity of their effect. They include

1. the number of irrational beliefs the child holds,
2. the range of situations in which the child applies her ideas (school, home, peers, adults, work, play),
3. the strength of the child's beliefs, and
4. the extent to which the child tends to distort reality as observed in errors of inference about what has happened or what will happen (Bernard & Joyce, 1984, p. 128).

Most children during the middle childhood years possess some irrational beliefs (I must be perfect. You must be perfect. The world must be perfect.). Some irrational thought is developmentally based as children are just now developing the cognitive attributes needed to test the reality of conclusions they have drawn. However, children lacking in cognitive skill development are incapable of examining their thoughts and are likely to be guided by irrational thinking and respondent behaviors triggered by environmental stimuli (reactive behaviors).

Defense Mechanisms

Children who are lacking in cognitive skills in dealing with difficult life situations often resort to using defense mechanisms as a way of avoiding or escaping from stressful encounters. While defense mechanisms are useful stress reducers and used by most people for that purpose, an over-reliance on them can create a dependency and hinder the use of responsible decision-making and related cognitive skills in addressing life's challenges. Some examples of defense mechanisms commonly used by children are daydreaming, projection, rationalization, regression, and repression.

Stress

Children who lack in or fail to use cognitive skills place themselves at a real disadvantage when it comes to managing life situations and events. When children lack the models, attributes, and power to build connections in their lives, they are likely to become fearful, angry, and overwhelmed. Unpleasant and negative stress, commonly referred to as distress, is usually counterproductive, and if left unchecked can have a negative and debilitating effect on health (emotional difficulties, cardiovascular problems, psychosomatic illness, injury proneness, low self-esteem, lack of concentration, a disrupted capacity to process information, lowered academic achievement, etc.).

Responders

Responders are people whose behaviors are triggered by environmental stimuli. These people are sometimes referred to as reactors. Responders fail to view life situations from a decision-making perspective in which there is a goal to be attained and a problem to be solved. For example, moving down a school hallway is a life situation. The goal is to navigate the hallway in a safe and caring manner for self and other hallway users. The problem posed is, "How to accomplish this goal?" Choices are generated and examined as either being helpful or hurtful in attaining the goal. Multiple caring ideas can emerge from this process that can be used to navigate the hallway safely. A responder fails to recognize life situations and the choices they hold. They act without thinking about the consequences of their actions. Their behaviors are predicated on what is happening around them and the desire to satisfy their own needs without regard for others. Children lacking in cognitive skill development cannot use what they don't have. They are a detriment to themselves and those affected by their failure to think before they act.

The Cumulative Effects of Risk

Children who are cognitively disadvantaged have a difficult time meeting their needs in caring and responsible ways. They are the children (and adults) in our society who think that others control their lives or that their own lives are out of control. They feel powerless, have poor self-images, make negative self statements, exhibit low self-confidence, avoid the difficult, experience interpersonal conflict, appear depressed and unhappy, are overly influenced by peers, have poor refusal skills, are unable to concentrate, and are often inattentive (Goodwin, Goodwin, & Cantrell, 1988). These children do poorly in school, struggle to develop satisfying peer relationships, and are more prone to school dropout, teen pregnancy, acts of violence, depression, illicit drug use, and suicide when compared with children who possess and use their cognitive skills and attributes to meet life's challenges.

Despite the cumulative risks associated with stalled cognitive development, children can learn to develop their cognitive potential and make wise and caring choices in all areas pertaining to their health and wellness. They likewise can contribute to society's betterment by making caring choices that support humankind and a healthy, protected environment. These ends can be met to the extent that we enhance the cognitive well-being of children and teach them ". . . to perceive reality as it is, to respond to its challenges, and to develop strategies for living" (Hales, 1992, p. 25).

ENHANCING COGNITIVE WELL-BEING THROUGH CARING CHOICES

In the domain of cognitive caring, children are taught the cognitive skills and abilities that will serve them well in making responsible choices that will preserve their health and wellness, achieve success in school, and contribute to the betterment of society.

When discussing cognitive health and caring, it is difficult to separate this domain from all others, for cognitive well-being is at the core of what makes children who they are and what they become. Making caring choices requires the use of children's cognitive abilities in processing information and making life decisions. Cognition affects the way children feel and is often a good predictor of the behaviors they will exhibit. While not always visible, thinking, feeling, and doing are inseparable elements of the whole that separate human beings from all other species on the planet. When it comes to cognitive health and caring choices, we want our children to (Anspaugh & Ezell, 1995)

- like themselves and discover their unique qualities, skills, and talents;
- be introspective, examine the motives for their behaviors, and become insightful regarding their own conduct;
- accept their limitations and think in terms of goal-directed self-improvement rather than being a success or failure;
- deal with life problems and challenges as they arise rather than put them off or avoid them altogether;
- establish realistic goals (short and long term) and work toward their accomplishment;
- understand their thoughts and emotions, and manage them responsibly;

- involve themselves in a variety of life experiences and cultivate many interests as a way of bringing balance into their
lives;
- develop a sense of humor, laugh, and enjoy life; and
- develop an optimistic attitude toward life.

*When children learn how to develop and care for their cog-
nitive attributes, their cognitive attributes will take care of them.*
They will achieve a sense of industry that characterizes children's
movement from a state of dependence and egocentricity to one of
independence, openness, and creativity. As children grow in their
cognitive development, they experience the freedom that life has
to offer and assume the responsibility for defining themselves and
their purpose through the caring choices they make for themselves,
others, and the planet. Only then will life take on personal meaning
and provide children with the joy and excitement that comes from
responsible risk-taking.

*Cognitive health is attained through learning and using cogni-
tive skills that help children to stretch and grow and attain a reality-
bound sense of self that comes from making caring choices based
on right, reality, and responsibility.* Elementary school counseling
programs, being in the people-building business, seek to achieve
this end through the caring actions of teachers, parents, children,
counselors, administrators, and community supporters, working together, to help children love themselves, gain acceptance of others,
and develop lifestyles with a "service to others" focus. Thus the primary goal of elementary school counseling programs is to promote
excellence in living and learning (Boyer, 1995). This can best be accomplished by meeting children's developmental and unique needs
in a safe and supportive teaching-learning environment through an
integrated curriculum with coherence that applies the lessons of
the classroom to life. Thus elementary school counseling programs
have a vital role to play in helping children to develop in all areas of
their being and especially in the cognitive health area, which is the
focus of this chapter.

While there are a number of cognitive strategies that children can learn that will help them to communicate more effectively, acquire a core of essential knowledge, become disciplined and motivated learners, live more responsibly, and attain a sense of well-being (Boyer, 1995), we have selected eight core cognitive attributes that we believe every child should develop.

- Attentional skills
- Memory skills
- Thinking skills
- Decision-making
- Study skills
- Cognitive restructuring
- Self-instruction training
- Thought-stopping

Attention and Caring

Children's ability to process information successfully is closely linked to their ability to pay attention (concentrate). They must be able to connect with the stimuli being received through their senses if they are to move this data (information) into short-term memory and later into long-term memory, where it can be retrieved in making thoughtful, caring choices.

To pay attention (concentrate) means to stay focused, engage in penetrating thought, and maintain a degree of interest over a sustained period of time. Most children, with practice, can enhance and sharpen their ability to attend by addressing the variables that interfere with this process. Two major causes of concentration problems are physical and environmental. Children with severe concentration problems may be experiencing a physical disorder caused by a specific brain dysfunction known as attention-deficit-hyperactivity disorder (ADHD). This brain abnormality effects 3 percent to 5 percent of all children (Dehart et al., 2000). These children are very easily distracted and therefore find it difficult to stay focused long enough to benefit from what is being taught. Once diagnosed, medication, behavior modification, and therapy are used to help children to sustain their attention for longer periods of time. Usually a team of specialists to include teachers, psychologists, counselors, physicians, and behavioral specialists is required to help alleviate the symptoms that interfere with concentration and learning.

Environmental factors, the second major cause of distraction, seem to be the root cause of most concentration problems experienced by children. Children are often bombarded by stimuli coming from every direction. They need assistance in determining what information is important, how to stay focused on it, and how to ignore irrelevant and distracting data competing for their attention. With practice, most children can learn to become more systematic, organized, and selective in directing their attention.

What follows are a few suggestions that elementary school counseling programs can offer children that will enhance their ability to concentrate more effectively.

Eliminate Distractions

Concentration will increase when *visual, auditory, environmental, and internal* distractions are reduced or eliminated. Visual distractions for children might be television, toys, games, other people, windows, anything that can divert their attention away from what they are trying to accomplish. Auditory distractions, like visual distractions, can interfere with children's attention. Slamming doors, ringing phones, blaring radios, noisy heating systems, and talking are examples of auditory distractions.

Environmental factors such as cluttered desks, study areas devoid of needed tools and materials, poor lighting, uncomfortable room temperatures, and overcrowded classrooms can cause children to reduce or lose their attention as well. When these distractions occur, children can either be relocated to other areas, or actions can be taken to reduce or eliminate the distractions.

Also, internal distractions exist within children and compete for their attention to concentrate on their schoolwork. Internal factors consist of such things as hunger, fatigue, illness, stress, and personal problems that can cause children to daydream or shift their attention to areas of discomfort.

Elementary school counseling programs can help children to increase their attention by preventing distractions from occurring and by reducing or eliminating external and internal distractions when they occur. Conducting environmental and internal (children) audits designed to identify distractions is perhaps a first place to begin in helping children to improve their attention span.

Set Goals

When children understand what they are to do, how to do it, and why it is important for them to do it, their attention (focus) will improve. Children need to receive clear directions, detailed feedback (coaching), and positive reinforcement if they are to maintain a high level of concentration in staying on task.

Take Breaks

Children are unable to hold their attention for extended periods of time. Periodic breaks are needed to reduce stress and fatigue and energize children's batteries. Planned periodic breaks of varying lengths can involve exercise, games, story time, and other diversionary activities designed to revitalize the body, mind, and spirit.

Focus on One Task at a Time

Children lose their ability to focus when they try to do too many things at one time. A boxing structure is a great technique to improve attention and concentration. Have children identify the tasks they want to complete. Help them to order their activities and the amount of time to be given to each. Now children can box their activities and follow their schedule, taking periodic breaks between activities.

Stimulate the Senses

Concentration increases when children are fully involved in a task or life situation. When the learning event involves all or most of their senses, children's attention (level of concentration) will increase. They will be able to stay focused for a longer period of time. When children are taught attention-enhancing techniques to increase their attention span and their ability to concentrate, they will be able to connect more readily with what they are being taught. Helping children to strengthen their ability to attend (self, others, and the environment) is a prerequisite to caring and being careful.

Memory and Caring

Another ability closely linked to information processing is the ability to recall information and experiences from the past—to reconstruct what one has heard, seen, learned, or experienced. Memory allows children to draw upon what they already know and build on this knowledge through problem-solving and acquisition of new information (Zigler & Stevenson, 1993). A good memory (recollection and understanding) is a prerequisite to learning and living and improves children's chances of doing well in school.

Memory can be improved through the use of memory aids (mnemonic strategies), which are designed to enhance remembering and decrease forgetting. Direct personal experience, learning to distinguish between the important and the unimportant, using self-talk, writing things down, overlearning, focusing, and visualization, when used effectively, will increase memory capabilities.

Direct Personal Experience

Firsthand experiences and direct application of newly learned material will help children to remember what they have learned. Visits to a zoo, caring for an animal, solving a problem, conducting an experiment, or participating in an exercise or demonstration are all good examples of firsthand experiences. Helping children to apply what they have learned from these experiences speaks to direct application. When experience and application are combined, memory improves, as does learning.

Focus on What Is Important

Helping children to distinguish between the important and the unimportant improves memory. This can be accomplished by asking children to identify the most important ideas they learned from a lesson, book, or experience. Teaching children to highlight important concepts by repeating, underlining, and color-coding them can increase memory.

Self-Talk

Teaching children to recite out loud, or to themselves, important ideas and concepts will help to drive these new learnings into their long-term memory bank for later recall and understanding when needed.

Writing Things Down

Teaching children to record (write) what they want to remember is a great way to enhance recall (memory). The act of writing things down is similar to self-talk and has a similar effect. Also, writing things down preserves the information for later review and recall. Grocery lists, addresses, homework assignments, names, birth dates, and special events are best remembered when recorded.

Overlearning

Overlearning occurs when children continue to immerse themselves in the same information over time. Practice, repetition, and drill on things that children know and can do preserves these learnings in long-term memory. Overlearning results in automatic recall and confidence in oneself. Activities that are often overlearned are ones like bicycle riding, tying shoes, swimming, and remembering phone numbers, birthdays, and addresses. These are actions that children and adults seldom forget even during extended periods of delayed use. For example, many adults can still recall the names of grade school teachers and classmates years after leaving school.

Focus Questions

Children can increase remembering and decrease forgetting by focusing on what they read, hear, and see. They can accomplish this by raising five questions in reviewing what they have just experienced. What? When? Where? Why? and How?

Visualization

Another helpful way to increase memory and recall is to form mental pictures of past experiences. By focusing on such details as people present, objects, actions, sounds, and smells, children will be able to recall scenes from their lives and remember the past with clarity and purpose.

Other Memory Aids

Among the hundreds of techniques that can be used to improve memory are the following five methods that children can learn.

1. *Notebook:* Children can keep their own diaries as a way of preserving the past.
2. *Cues:* Alarm clocks, Post-It notes, string around the finger, and calendars help children to remember important things to do.
3. *Chunking:* Organize long lists of things by categories. Example: A grocery list can be organized according to drinks, vegetables, meats, household products, and so on. Long lists can be broken into smaller chunks. Phone numbers are easy to remember using this method.
4. *Stimuli:* Use letters, sayings, and rhymes to remember important information. Roy G. Biv can be used to remember the

colors of the rainbow (**R**ed, **O**range, **Y**ellow, **G**reen, **B**lue, **I**ndigo, **V**iolet).

5. *Relating:* Connect new information with what is already known.

Developing a good memory is important in helping children to make caring choices for themselves, others, and the environment. Helping children to explore ways in which they depend upon their memories to make caring choices is a good exercise to emphasize the importance of a healthy and well-functioning mind.

Thinking and Caring

While attention and memory skills are important for retrieval of past information, thinking skills are critical for processing information. Knowing how to think is a necessary prerequisite to making caring choices.

Children must be able to reason, figure out things, question, organize, classify, compare, hypothesize, solve problems, and evaluate. Thinking is more difficult than memorizing because it requires additional energy and effort. Thinking stimulates learning and helps children to become more independent, responsible, and self-directed.

Children, by nature, are inquisitive human beings. They watch the way things work, ask lots of questions, challenge, and experiment on their own. These same behaviors are viewed by some as annoying and showing disrespect. In reality, these behaviors are signs of cognitive growth that should be encouraged and stimulated through activity.

Elementary school counseling programs can play a significant role in helping teachers and parents to develop children's thinking skills through formal instruction and by creating stimulating learning environments, opportunities, and experiences that challenge their intellect. While there are many different thinking skills that children can learn, we have selected ten operations that are consistently mentioned in the literature (Bann, 1993; Butler & Hope, 1995; Raths, Wassermann, Jonas, & Rothstein, 1986).

Thinking Skill	**Teaching Suggestion**
1. *Observing* You look carefully at the details and make a record of what you see and/or hear.	Ask children to observe objects, pictures, and life situations. Have them describe what they observe.
2. *Comparing* You use your observation skills to examine two things and then name their similarities and differences.	Ask children to compare two apples, two children, or two role plays of the same situation.
3. *Classifying* You use your observing and comparing skills to sort things, situations, or ideas into specific groupings using different categories or identifiers (size, shape, color, and so on).	Ask children to classify objects by size, shape, or color. Ask children to classify ideas as either being helpful or hurtful to themselves or others. Have children think of other things to classify and ways to do it.
4. *Assumptions* You identify statements that are not supported by facts (observable). Assumptions, treated as facts, can be misleading and potentially harmful.	Ask children to make a statement of fact and then an assumption. For example: The sun is shining right now is a fact because the sun is visible. The sun will be shining this afternoon is an assumption because no evidence exists to support this statement. "People who have red hair have bad tem-

pers." Is this a statement or an assumption? Explain!

5. *Hypothesizing*

You make an educated guess to explain an outcome from the facts you are given.

Ask children "what if" questions. What if you were mean to everyone, what do you think would happen?

6. *Feedback*

You let others know what you like and dislike about something by providing specific information (details) to support your perspective.

Ask children to provide feedback on their favorite food, a vacation they took, a school subject they are taking, or a character in a reading book.

7. *Interpreting*

You are asked to examine a body of information and then to make statements about the information in response to questions that are asked.

Ask children to look at a picture and observe what they see. Then make statements about the picture, some of which will be true, false, and inconclusive. Have children interpret from the pictures which of your statements are true, false, or inconclusive and why this is so.

8. *Imagining*

You are to use your mind to create ideas, pictures, and feeling in response to directions that you are given. You are to place no parameters on your imagination. Become as creative as possible in what you create.

Ask children to imagine that they are a piece of furniture, a tree, or a bicycle. Have them tell or write a story about their lives and what it is like to be this object. Ask them how they and the object are alike and different. "What if" questions work well to stimulate children's imagination. What if you didn't have any worries, what would life be like for you?

9. **Summarizing**

You are to listen to a story and identify what you believe are the most important points to remember. You can use other thinking skills (observing, comparing, classifying, and so on) to help you sort the important from the unimportant.

Ask children to summarize a short story that you read to them. As they listen to the story, ask them to consider the most important facts they will include in their summary. Questions like who, what, where, when, and how can help children summarize the main points to be remembered. Children can compare their summaries.

10. **Predicting**

You are to decide what you think will happen next based on information that you already have about something.

Show children pictures of adults or children involved in an activity. Ask them to observe the picture and interpret what is going on in the scene. Then ask them to tell you what they think will happen next (predicting) and why. Example: A picture shows a boy standing on a frozen pond next to a sign that says, "Keep off the pond—Thin Ice." The children are to predict what may happen next.

Thinking skills can and should be used in all areas of children's lives. The elementary school counseling program can help teachers and parents explore the value of their use in the classroom, on field trips, during discussions, and on the playground. Thinking skills encourage children to fully explore life situations and to develop the perspective-taking skills that can enhance their ability to make responsible caring choices.

Decision-Making and Caring

The process of decision-making begins when children realize they have choices to make in every dimension of their lives. Decision-making, as with any process, must be taught and practiced if it is to be used effectively.

Effective Decision-Makers

Researchers (Bann, 1993; Butler & Hope, 1995; O'Rourke & Worzbyt, 1996; Worzbyt, 1991) have suggested that those children who become effective decision-makers know what is important to them (values), are capable of generating relevant choices in response to satisfying their needs and wants, and are skilled at ranking their choices based on predicted safe and caring outcomes. When these steps are taken, effective decision-makers choose what seemingly are the most responsible courses of action to take and then act.

Ineffective Decision-Makers

In contrast, ineffective decision-makers either do not possess the prerequisite skills (attention, memory, and thinking skills) or possessing them, are inhibited or are thwarted in some way from acting. A failure on the part of children to think or act in response to any life situation reduces the odds for success in achieving safe, caring, and desirable outcomes. What follows is a very teachable model for helping children to make responsible and caring decisions.

STOP, THINK & GO Decision-Making

We have selected an easy-to-use and simplistically designed decision-making model to teach children. **STOP, THINK, & GO Decision-Making** functions similar to a traffic light and helps children to exercise care and caution in the choices that they make in response to life situations (Worzbyt, 1991). While traffic signal lights regulate the safe flow of pedestrian and vehicular traffic through busy and potentially dangerous intersections, the same model (**STOP, THINK, & GO Decision-Making**) can help children to exercise a degree of caution in making caring decisions as they negotiate the many intersections of life (see Figure 9.1).

The Traffic Signal Light Model first instructs children to *STOP* and clarify the life situation before them and then to identify their

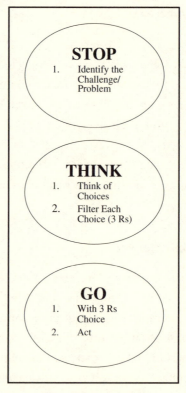

Figure 9.1. A Winning Signal.

goal and the problem to be solved. Next they are instructed to proceed, with caution, to *THINK* of the potential choices open to them in solving their problem and attaining their goal. With these choices in mind, children are taught how to filter (Right, Reality, and Responsibility) each choice in search of caring and safe choices designed to address their challenge. The last step in the process requires children to identify their 3 Rs choices (Right, Reality, and Responsibility) and *GO* with the one(s) they favor in reaching their goal.

3 Rs Filters

The three filters of Right, Reality, and Responsibility are key components of the *THINK* stage of decision-making. They work in the same manner as coffee, fuel, and human body filters. Their purpose is to protect children from making harmful choices by removing them from further consideration. Figure 9.2 illustrates how the three filters function.

The Right, Reality, and Responsibility filters are applied as described in the following paragraphs.

1. **Right Filter**

   Helpful choices that are based on Right (not wrong) will pass through this filter. A choice is considered to be Right if it is legal (based on law), ethical (meets acceptable societal standards of conduct), and moral (meets personal rules of conduct and basic goodness). Next, children are asked to consider how this choice will affect themselves, others, or property (help or hurt). If a choice is believed to be a Right thing to do (legal, ethical, and moral) and will be helpful, not hurtful, to those affected by the choice, that choice will pass through the Right filter to the Reality filter. When working with 5- to 9-year-olds, *we recommend that these children determine the suitability of a Right choice based on whether it is helpful or hurtful to themselves and others.*

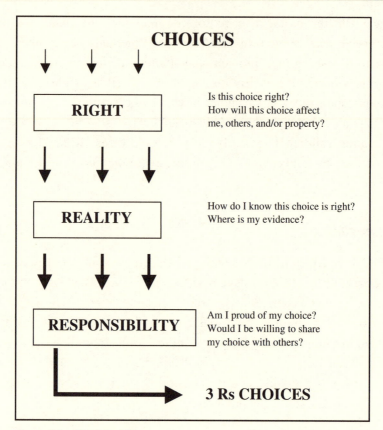

Figure 9.2. The 3 Rs Filters.

2. **Reality Filter**

   This filter emphasizes the importance of reality testing. Children must provide evidence (facts, observational data, proof) to validate the "Rightness" of this choice. Only by challenging the accuracy and reasonableness of this choice can children legitimately endorse it. If after a review of the evidence, this choice fails the "reality check," it will be discarded from further consideration. Any choice that meets the "reality check" will pass through the Reality filter on to the Responsibility filter.

3. **Responsibility Filter**

   At the third and final filter, children consider the potential consequences of this choice (level of risk) in solving their problem and meeting their goal. Only when children are proud of this choice and are willing to publicly affirm it in the presence of knowledgeable and caring people who can attest to its soundness will this choice pass through the Responsibility filter.

The **STOP, THINK & GO Decision-Making** model provides children with an opportunity to apply what they have learned (information, skills, and attitudes) in response to simulated and real life situations. Only when children see the value of using their knowledge and skills to solve life problems and challenges will they truly understand the power of knowledge.

Now that **STOP, THINK & GO Decision-Making** has been explained, the following life situation (see Figure 9.3) will be processed through the model (see Figure 9.4).

After reading Bill's life situation, the children are asked to summarize his dilemma. "Bill, after getting into the back seat of the car, is not able to close the seat belt latch." Next, the children are asked to consider Bill's goal. Using the decision-making model, the goal is always the same—to meet the life situation in a caring and safe way for everyone who will be affected by the decision. Bill's goal is for himself and the occupants of the car to get to the movies safely. His problem is stated simply as an open-ended question to be solved. Bill's problem is "What can I do to help us arrive at the movies safely?" Children are now ready to *THINK* about what choices Bill has available to solve his dilemma and reach his goal. The choices should be kept to a few

---

Bill's Dilemma

One afternoon Bill's friend, Tom, invited him to the movies. Bill accepted the invitation. Tom's mother picked up Bill at his house. When Bill got into the backseat to buckle up, he could not get the seat belt to latch. The ride to the movies would last about 5 minutes.

Figure 9.3. Bill's Dilemma.

STOP

    A. Summarize Bill's Life Situation. _____

    _____

    B. State Bill's Goal.

    _____

    C. State Bill's Problem. _____

THINK

    D. State Bill's Choices.

    _____

    _____

    E. Filter Each Choice.

Right

    1. Is this choice a Right thing to do? _____ yes _____ no Explain!
    2. How will this choice affect Bill, others, and property (Help/Hurt)? Explain!

Reality

    3. How does Bill know this choice is Right? What evidence (proof) does Bill have to support his choice as a Right thing to do?

Responsibility

    4. Bill has reason to be proud of this choice? _____ yes _____ no
    5. People that love Bill will support this choice? _____ yes _____ no
    6. This choice will solve Bill's problem safely? _____ yes _____ no

GO

    F. Bill selects and acts on a 3 Rs (caring) choice.

Figure 9.4. *STOP, THINK & GO* Decision-Making Worksheet.

while students are learning how to make decisions. In Bill's situation, there are two obvious choices.

    1. Bill could ride to the movies without a seat belt.
    2. Bill could tell Tom's mother about his situation and ask for assistance.

Now that two choices have been identified, they can be individually processed through the three filters. The value of this model is that it generates a lot of discussion during the filtering process. When discussion on a choice has ended, children get to decide individually if that choice should or should not pass through the filter being discussed. Additional choices can be generated if none of the existing choices pass through all three filters. Another alternative is to identify several choices and have children select ones they think will pass through all three filters. This option speeds up the process by reducing the number of choices to be filtered through the system. Children should be informed that there is no right answer for using this model. Many choices may pass through all three filters. These choices can be applied in combination, in some preferred sequence, or one at a time depending on the life-situation goal and what one chooses to do. Now, filter each of Bill's choices (Figure 9.4) and select a caring choice that Bill can make.

The value of **STOP, THINK & GO Decision-Making** is that children are forced to pause long enough between **STOP** and **GO** to **THINK** about their options before acting. They are thus forced to consider if their choices are based on *Right* versus wrong, *Reality* versus myth, and *Responsibility* versus actions that are harmful to themselves and others. When children learn how to use this decision-making model effectively, they will make wise and caring choices in response to the life situations they will face.

Study Skills and Caring

Study skills encompass a wide range of cognitive skills and abilities that enable children to systematically organize, plan, and encode information that they need to learn (Rafoth and Defabo, 1990). When study skills are combined to solve problems, children are said to have developed a strategy for learning. Learning strategies thus enable children to complete plans for accomplishing learning goals. Some of the basic study skills that affect academic improvement and school success are:

- **Creating a Beneficial Study Environment**

  Such factors as proper lighting, a comfortable room temperature, a manageable noise level, few external distractions, and a properly equipped study center (books, paper, pens, pencils, computer, and so on) all contribute to a user-friendly and supportive learning environment.

- **Developing a Positive Attitude**

  Children can enhance their academic success to the extent that they develop a positive relationship with teachers, maintain an open mind, put forth the effort to connect with their subject matter, and come to school prepared to do their best (participate in class activities, ask questions, complete work assignments, and so on).

- **Time Management**

  Children are likely to succeed in school to the extent that they are able to manage their time responsibly, are skilled in estimating how long it will take to complete assignments, and are adept at using a daily activity schedule to track their progress toward goal attainment. Creating a daily planner and sticking with it helps to improve academic and life successes.

- **Stress Management**

  Children must monitor and manage those internal stressors that will affect their academic record. Fear, anxiety, fatigue, poor nutrition, illness, and tightly held irrational beliefs serve to create distress, distraction, and discouragement. Children should be taught about the nature of stress, its positive and negative effects, and how to harness its potential.

  Proper eating habits, exercise, rest, relaxation, positive thinking, and preparation are some of the keys to stress reduction. Elementary school counseling programs can help by encouraging schools to provide healthy lunch programs, opportunities to relax, times to exercise, available counseling services, and a pleasant and caring school environment.

- **Academic Techniques and Self-Assessment**
  Children can further enhance their learning potential and school
  success by learning techniques that will help them to listen
  more attentively, read with comprehension, take meaningful
  class notes, write legible and well-planned papers, and successfully manage their ability to prepare and take exams with mini-
  mal stress and quality results.

The successful application of study skills and learning strategies increases children's ability to commit what they have learned to long-
term memory, where it can be retrieved for future use. Study skills
also improve with increased attention, memory, and information-
processing skills. When children apply study skills effectively, they
grow in knowledge, self-understanding, and in their ability to solve
problems and make caring choices in behalf of themselves, others,
and their environment.

Cognitive Restructuring and Caring

Ellis (1987, 1997) stated that human beings, by nature, are prone to
think irrational, self-defeating thoughts. Irrational thoughts are
ideas that human beings harbor that simply are not true (not supported by facts). Children, like adults, according to Ellis, hold irrational beliefs in three areas.

1. I must be perfect.
2. You must be perfect.
3. The world must be a perfect place in which to live.

Because irrational beliefs are unattainable in action, they lead
to discouragement, self-condemnation, low self-esteem, and feelings of worthlessness. The goal of cognitive restructuring is to teach
children how to detect irrational thinking and correct it before it can
adversely affect their emotional and behavioral stability (ability to
self-manage).

Teaching Cognitive Restructuring

Children are first taught to write down their upsetting thoughts in response to a particular life situation. Next, they learn to examine and challenge their thoughts. Is there evidence (facts) to support these thoughts? Thoughts that cannot be supported with evidence are considered to be untrue (myths) and must either be eliminated or corrected. With practice, children can learn how to examine their thoughts and feelings and correct those thoughts that are needlessly self-defeating. They will learn to recognize that rational thoughts tend to produce reasonable, responsible, and manageable emotional responses and actions that are rooted in self-improvement rather than unreasonable perfectionistic demands.

Richard's Irrational Dilemma

Richard, age 11, in his quest to make friends, *believes* that everyone should like him and if they don't, he somehow is a worthless failure and an unlikable person. Richard, as hard as he tries, is unable to get everyone in his class to like him. Because he has fallen short of his perfectionistic mark, he experiences a heavy heart and feels defeated and broken. Using cognitive restructuring techniques, Richard would write his thoughts down on paper. He would then be challenged to examine the logic of his thinking and asked to provide evidence (facts) to support his belief that everyone must like him or else he is a failure. Finding no evidence, Richard would reframe his goal and expectations. Richard's new goal is that he wants to be a friend to others with the expectation that some children will like him in return. Rather than define success in terms of changing others, Richard now decides to change himself by examining what he can do to become a friend to others. He decides that he will be satisfied with each new friend that he makes.

The goal of cognitive restructuring is to help children understand that they choose their own thoughts and that irrational thoughts trigger emotional disturbances and unsuccessful goal attainment. The making of caring choices is rooted in rational thought and actions based on Right, Reality, and Responsibility.

Self-Instruction Training and Caring

Self-instruction is a form of self-talk in which children learn how to verbally guide themselves through complex and often stressful life situations. Self-instruction training involves the use of goal-setting, mental rehearsal, and coping statements that can provide direction and counter self-defeating thought patterns that interfere with goal attainment. The following incident involving Eric, age 7, and his fear of dogs provides one example of how self-instruction training can be used in making a caring decision.

Eric is afraid of dogs. When he sees a dog, he becomes anxious and very fearful. However, using self-instruction training, Eric has set a goal to remain calm and not run when approached by a dog. He has mentally rehearsed, several times, what he will do and say to himself the next time he encounters a dog. As a dog approaches, Eric tells himself to "Take it easy. Remain calm. Take slow deep breaths. The dog is curious about me, but will eventually leave. Remember to keep facing the dog and slowly back away. I'm doing a good job. Keep cool." Eric concentrates on achieving his goal and succeeds. While slightly tense, Eric did not panic and achieved his goal.

Self-instruction training can be used by children to guide themselves through exams, social situations, stressful events, and new learning experiences. Self-instruction training is a powerful cognitive skill that can help children to make caring choices. Other techniques that can support self-instruction training are visual imagery, relaxation training, and cognitive restructuring.

Thought-Stopping and Caring

Thought-stopping is used to "short circuit" invasive and counter-productive thoughts. For example, negative self-talk, if not addressed, can lower children's self-esteem and weaken their resolve in coping with stressful life situations. As devastating as invasive thoughts can be, children can learn to cope with them using a cognitive strategy referred to as thought-stopping. Thought-stopping is designed to interrupt counterproductive messages. This can be done by teaching children to yell out STOP (verbally or mentally) in the presence of an unwanted thought. Other thought-stopping techniques include snapping oneself with a rubber band around the wrist, counting to 10, shifting one's focus to something more pleasant, or writing the negative thought on a piece of paper and throwing it away. Any one of these methods, or some combination of them, can be used to extinguish a painful thought that just won't go away.

Ann learned to use thought-stopping as a way of breaking loose from a negative reoccurring thought that would invade her mind days before she would take an exam. Although a good student, she kept telling herself that she would forget everything she learned when she sat down to take the test. In order to reduce her anxiety, Ann began to practice yelling out STOP every time the negative thought occurred. She then pictured herself in a calm state and used self-instruction training to tell herself that she should remain calm and that she had prepared well for her exam. Gradually, over time, the negative thought subsided. Ann found that thought-stopping, visualization, and self-instruction training helped her to make a caring choice in managing her self-defeating thought.

The cognitive strategies presented in this chapter are designed to help children develop the "I can" conscious and the "I will" state of mind in achieving academic, personal/emotional, and social success. Children who work toward enhancing their cognitive abilities are able to make caring choices in thinking their way through life's most complex challenges. They possess a positive view of the future and achieve happiness in all that they do, especially when they experience happiness in the following manner.

Happiness requires problems plus a mental attitude that is ready to meet distress with action toward solution.

THE COUNSELOR'S ROLE

Few people would disagree that the development of cognitive health is second to none in helping children to become fully functioning and healthy self-managers. The ability to think and decide represents information-processing skills that give power to knowledge so that it can be put to good use in making caring choices in all areas of life and living.

Elementary school counselors have an important role to play in helping teachers and parents to understand that a relevant education teaches children how to apply the lessons of the classroom to life. This also means recognizing that children's lives do not revolve around subject matter labels (math, science, social studies, language arts, physical activities, and so on), but rather around themes of caring (see Chapter 1), in which daily choices are made and lives are lived.

In order for children to care for themselves, others, and society (environment), they must become responsible thinkers and doers. They must be able to process information, form goals, and make decisions if they are to make caring choices and become responsible risk managers. Elementary school counselors can help parents and teachers to recognize the importance of making cognitive skill development the centerpiece of their teaching. Information should always be taught in the context of helping children to understand how they can apply what they have learned in making caring decisions in response to daily life situations (seven themes of caring).

While there are many things that counselors can do to strengthen children's cognitive skills, here are but a few that will enhance their ability to make caring and careful choices in all that they do.

- Help children to understand that it is not how much they know that counts, but rather being able to count on what they know to make effective decisions.
- Encourage teachers to use activities, games, and problem situations that facilitate children's understanding and application of new learnings.
- Use thinking skills in your work with children (classroom guidance, individual counseling, and group counseling).

- Organize in-service training sessions for teachers and parents that focus on the application of cognitive techniques that can be used at home and in the classroom (attentional skills, memory skills, thinking skills, study skills, cognitive restructuring, self-instruction training, and thought-stopping).
- Work with teachers and parents in helping them to assess and monitor in-school and at-home cognitive activities that are developmentally appropriate.
- Work with teachers and parents in helping children to learn skills they need to survive and thrive and that are valued by the culture.
- Help parents and teachers to assist children in discovering ways in which they can use their cognitive skills to solve social, personal/emotional, and physical challenges in their pursuit of a wellness lifestyle.
- Help children to examine ways in which they can use their cognitive skills in service-learning projects to tackle community challenges that need to be addressed.
- Expose teachers and parents to Gardner's (1983) theory of multiple intelligences and the development of cognitive strengths that can be applied in each area (logical-mathematical, linguistic, spatial, musical, body-kinesthetic, and personal/emotional intelligence).

Elementary school counselors can help to create school and community environments that showcase the importance of cognitive health and its impact in every area of a child's life. The ability to manage time and stress, enhance self-esteem, communicate effectively, manage emotions responsibly, develop and maintain satisfying peer relationships, and develop a healthy lifestyle requires the utilization of cognitive strategies in making caring choices. There are two types of failures in this world: The failures of those who think and never do, and the failures of those who do and never think. This chapter has been about teaching children to become logical and rational thinkers and doers. In the pages that follow, there are a number of activities and ideas that are designed to facilitate cognitive caring.

COGNITIVE CARING ACTIVITIES

Reducing Stress through Laughter

Brief Overview of Activity:

This activity will help children to realize the value of humor in their lives as a way of reducing stressful situations. They also will be able to identify persons whom they can be around who are good at helping them to have fun and reduce stress through humor.

Objectives:

1. Children will identify at least three times in their life when they were able to use humor as a way to reduce stress.
2. Children will be able to name at least one person in their life who uses fun and laughter to help them cope with stress.

Materials Needed:

1. Chalkboard or chart paper
2. Chalk or markers

Procedure:

1. Begin the activity by telling a funny joke or riddle. When children have finished laughing, talk with them about the value of humor in their lives. Provide a few minutes for them to share amusing anecdotes.
2. Divide the group into smaller groups of four to five children and instruct the groups to discuss the following five questions:
   a. What is the funniest thing that has ever happened to you?
   b. What is your favorite comedy show on TV?
   c. Who is your favorite funny cartoon character?
   d. Did anything make you laugh today? What?
   e. Who is one of the funniest people you know?
3. Before bringing the group back together for discussion, ask each child to share with the group at least three times in their life when they used humor to reduce stress.

4. When groups have completed their discussions, bring them back together and remind them that they can benefit from humor as a way of reducing stress. Ask children to identify some ways that humor can help them in their daily lives. Make a list of their responses on the chalkboard or on a piece of chart paper. Leave it posted for a week or so as a reminder to the children.

5. Ask children to privately identify someone in their life who uses humor as a way to help them deal with stress. Remind them to seek out that person in times of stress.

6. Have children identify some things they can do to bring more humor into their lives (read funny stories, collect jokes, go to humorous movies, watch for humor in everyday situations, and so on).

Closure:

Reiterate the fact that humor can be a valuable resource to assist children in times of stress. Remind children that demeaning humor can cause stress in others and should not be used.

Using Time Wisely

Brief Overview of Activity:

This activity will provide an opportunity for children to look critically at how they are spending their time each week and to determine the best use of their free time.

Objectives:

1. Children will account for the amount of time each week they spend on various activities.

2. Children will be able to determine how much free time they have each week.

3. Children will make a basic plan for the best use of their free time.

Materials Needed:

1. Time Management Worksheet (Figure 9.5)
2. Pencils

Procedure:

1. Talk briefly with children about the amount of time they have each week. See if they can determine how much time they actually have in a week. (7 days × 24 hrs. = 168 hrs.)

Time Management Worksheet

NUMBER OF HOURS IN A WEEK—168

Time Spent:

_____ Sleeping
_____ Eating
_____ Taking care of personal needs (bathing, dressing, etc.)
_____ In school
_____ Doing chores
_____ In extracurricular activities (clubs, sports, etc.)
_____ Traveling to and from school
_____ Working (delivering newspapers, yard work, etc.)
_____ Doing homework

_____ **TOTAL TIME SPENT**

Total amount of time in a week **168 hours**
Total amount of planned time in a week _____
Amount of free time left _____ (total time subtracted from hours in a week)

MY FREE TIME PLAN

Three things I can do in my free time.

1.

2.

3.

Figure 9.5.

2. Ask children to estimate the amount of free time they feel they have each week and have them jot their estimates down on a piece of scratch paper.

3. Discuss their estimates concerning the amount of time they spend in sleep, school, eating, doing chores, and so on.

4. Provide a time management worksheet for children so they can determine the amounts of time they spend in each category.

5. When children have completed their worksheet and have determined the amount of free time they have each week, encourage them to make a plan using that time to schedule "fun" things they want to do.

6. Remind children if they practice time management as young people, it will be easier for them to maintain this routine as they get older.

7. Provide time for children to share their free time plans with the class.

Closure:

In order to bring closure to the activity, stress the importance of using time wisely and making the most of every minute of one's life.

Stressed Out

Brief Overview of Activity:

In this activity, children will begin to identify the things (or people) that cause them to "lose their cool" in certain situations. Once they identify what these things are, they can develop an action plan to deal with them.

Objectives:

1. Children will identify the top five stressors in their life and their reactions to them.

2. Children will get feedback from classmates regarding appropriate ways to deal with their stressors.

Materials Needed:

1. Copy of "Stressed Out" Checklist (Figure 9.6) for each child
2. Pencil
3. Chart paper and markers (or chalkboard)

Procedure:

1. Brainstorm with children some things that cause them to be stressed out. Make a list of these stressors on the chart paper or chalkboard.
2. Provide children with a copy of the "Stressed Out" worksheet and ask them to identify their top five stressors numbering them from one to five.
3. Allow time for children to work in groups of four to five to share their "top five" list of stressors.
4. After everyone has had an opportunity to share, encourage children to work together to identify things they can do to reduce their stress in these situations. For example, if giving a report in class is a major stressor, one could
   a. present the speech to a parent or group of friends;
   b. practice giving the report in front of a mirror; or
   c. make an outline of major points and keep it on a 3-inch by 5-inch card.
5. Bring the large group back together and give them a brief opportunity to share some of their best ideas for managing stress.

Closure:

Remind children that identifying their stressors can help lessen their effect on them. Help children to realize that although all people have stress in their life, it's possible to develop appropriate skills to deal more effectively with it.

Stressed-Out Checklist

Directions:

From the list below, identify your top five stressors and put them in order, with number 1 being the most stressful for you. Remember, there are some blank spaces at the bottom of the sheet for you to add your own stressors if they are not on this list.

_____ having too much homework

_____ tests

_____ being late for school

_____ giving a report to the class

_____ a special school subject—identify the subject _____

_____ people who are mean

_____ bossy people

_____ not getting enough sleep

_____ chores

_____ not having enough money

_____ arguing with friends

_____ playing video games

_____ going to the doctor/dentist

_____ losing something important

_____ going to physical education class

_____ when parents argue

_____ being punished

_____ getting detention/or suspension

_____ being interrupted

Add your own personal stressors here if they are not on the list.

_____

_____

_____

_____

_____

Identify one thing you can do to reduce stress in your life.

Figure 9.6.

Signs of Success

Brief Overview of Activity:

This activity will provide children with an opportunity to focus on their successes and look at the additional positive feelings that were generated as a result of those successes. They will then determine what qualities they possess that enabled them to be successful.

Objectives:

1. Children will identify at least twelve successes they have had to this point in their life.
2. Children will identify at least two qualities they possess that have helped them to achieve success.

Materials Needed:

1. Copy of "My Dozen Successes" (Figure 9.7) for each child
2. Pencil

Procedure:

1. Talk briefly with children about successes they have had to this point in their lives. Ask a couple of children to share some successes they have had and to think about what qualities they possess that have helped them to achieve success. For example: Billy may indicate that when he was 10 years old, he scored 15 goals for his soccer team. The quality that helped him to achieve this feat was perseverance. Ann indicated that she volunteered at a nursing home and read to the elderly residents. The qualities that helped her to succeed were caring about others and good communication skills.
2. Talk about success as something that one does that creates a feeling of pride. It doesn't necessarily have to involve "being the best" or "winning something." It may mean just doing one's best on a project, or having perfect attendance for one marking period at school, or being a friend to someone who doesn't have many friends.

3. Provide children with a copy of "My Dozen Successes" worksheet and provide ample time for them to complete the worksheet. Remind them to be particularly diligent about completing the section that describes a quality they have that helped them to be successful.

4. Allow time for children to share at least one of their successes with the class and describe the quality of which they are most proud. Post the sheets on the bulletin board for a period of time for others to view.

My Dozen Successes

Think carefully about some successes you have had in your life. On the chart below, describe your successes. List your age at the time of the success and describe the quality you possess that enabled you to be successful.

When you have completed this activity, list your top two personal qualities for success.

My Success	**Age**	**Quality**
1. _____		
2. _____		
3. _____		
4. _____		
5. _____		
6. _____		
7. _____		
8. _____		
9. _____		
10. _____		
11. _____		
12. _____		

My Top Two Personal Qualities for Success!

1. _____

2. _____

Figure 9.7.

Closure:

Remind children that they have had many successes in their daily lives. They also have many personal qualities that help them to be successful. Encourage children to cultivate these special qualities as a way of increasing their daily successes.

Self-Talk

Brief Overview of Activity:

In this activity, children will begin to look at statements they make to themselves. They will learn to change negative statements to more positive ones through positive self-talk.

Objectives:

1. Children will learn to identify their negative self-talk and the self-defeating thoughts that accompany such statements.
2. Children will be able to identify an appropriate positive self-talk statement to replace a negative statement.

Materials Needed:

1. "Changing My Thoughts" worksheet for each child (Figure 9. 8)
2. Pencils

Procedure:

1. Begin by sharing a comment that one often overhears from children, for example, "Nobody likes me." Talk about this statement in terms of what it may really mean. For example, the person who is saying this may believe that:
   a. I should be liked by everyone.
   b. Since I didn't get picked first for the game, that means nobody likes me.
2. Ask children if they can think of a more accurate statement they could make in this situation, one that is more realistic and emotionally supportive. For example, a more accurate state-

ment might be, "I really shouldn't expect everyone to like me. No one is liked by everyone."

3. Discuss the self-fulfilling prophecy idea—"If we always go around thinking negative thoughts and making negative statements, people will not want to be around us."

4. Remind children that they are in charge of their own thoughts and can, with practice, learn to make more accurate self-statements. This, in turn, will help them to feel better about themselves.

5. Give children a copy of "Changing My Thoughts" worksheet and allow time for them to change negative self-talk statements into more accurate statements.

Changing My Thoughts

Directions:

See if you can change the negative statements listed below into more accurate (true) statements.

1. If I can't solve all of my problems, I must be really bad.
   Accurate (true) Statement:

2. If everyone doesn't like me, I must be a bad person.
   Accurate (true) Statement:

3. I can't face all my problems and responsibilities, so I'll just avoid them.
   Accurate (true) Statement:

4. There should be a reward for everything or else there's no use doing the work.
   Accurate (true) Statement:

5. That person doesn't like me and I know he will never change.
   Accurate (true) Statement:

6. I just know it won't work out. That's why I need to be so worried about it.
   Accurate (true) Statement:

Figure 9.8.

6. When children have completed their worksheet, provide time for them to share some of their accurate self-talk statements.

Closure:

Encourage children to take what they have learned from this exercise and apply it to their daily lives. They may soon find that they will be happier and more successful in their day-to-day activities.

Things I Like to Do

Brief Overview of Activity:

This activity will encourage children to begin to think about the types of things they enjoy doing and to classify these things into various categories.

Objectives:

1. Children will identify at least 10 things they enjoy doing.
2. Children will determine the primary category of their enjoyable activities.
3. Children will write a brief story to identify what they learned about themselves as a result of this activity.

Materials Needed:

1. "Things I Like to Do" worksheet (Figure 9.9)
2. Pencils

Procedure:

1. Spend 1–2 minutes helping children to brainstorm a list of things children their age enjoy doing.
2. Provide a copy of the "Things I Like to Do" worksheet for all children and have them make a list of their 10 favorite things to do.
3. After the activities have been identified, ask children to code the activities in the following manner.

If the activity has a cost, put a $ after it.

If the activity is done outdoors, put an *0*.

If the activity is done with friends, put an *F.*

If the activity is done with family, put an *Fa.*

If the activity is physical in nature, put a *P.*

If the activity is done alone, put an *A.*

4. Remind children that an activity can have more than one letter after it. For example "going to the roller rink with friends" would have a $ and an *F.*

5. When children have completed this activity, provide time for silent reflection on the types of things they like to do. Pose some of the following questions to help them in their reflection.

   a. Do most of your activities have a cost?

   b. Are your favorite activities done alone or with friends?

   c. Are many of your activities physical in nature?

Things I Like to Do

1.

2.

3.

4.

5.

6.

7.

8.

9.

10.

Figure 9.9.

    d. Are you involved in family activities?

    e. In which category do most of your activities fall?

6. Ask them to write a brief story about what they discovered about themselves and their interests as a result of this activity.

Closure:

Encourage children to think about what they learned about themselves as a result of this activity. If they found that all of their favorite things fell into one category, they may want to set a goal to become more well-rounded by participating in some different kinds of activities.

Lifting Burdens

Brief Overview of Activity:

In this activity, children will have the opportunity to think of others in a compassionate manner. They will also begin to realize that they are not the only ones who have some burdens or challenges with which to deal.

Objectives:

1. Children will identify at least three persons in their life who are dealing with difficult situations.

2. Children will gain a realization of the value of someone who cares about them and who helps them deal with their burdens.

Materials Needed:

1. Copy of "Everyone has Burdens" worksheet (Figure 9. 10)

2. Pencil

Procedure:

1. Talk with children about the kinds of stressful burdens that people deal with every day. As they discuss these burdens, make a list of them on the chalkboard.

    a. Not having enough money to pay bills

    b. Serious illness

    c. Loss of one's job

    d. An accident that causes injury

    e. Loss of something important to them

    f. Death of a family member

2. Ask children to think of three people in their life with burdens. If they could help these people, what are some things they could do? Talk briefly about the value of being compassionate with others rather than always focusing on their own needs.

3. Give children a copy of the worksheet ("Everyone Has Burdens") to fill out.

4. Have children discuss ways they can help others. For example, if an older neighbor is sick and can't get around well, they could:

    a. Visit that person.

    b. Do some chores.

    c. Run errands.

5. Ask children to choose one person from their list and something they can do to ease that person's burden. Have them write their response on their worksheet.

Closure:

Encourage children to reach out to others who are in need. Share a time when you did so and the positive results that you received as a result of your action. Remind children that similar acts of compassion can be demonstrated daily. Encourage them to care for people who can use their help.

Everyone Has Burdens

Three people and their burdens:

1.

2.

3.

Something I can do to help:

Figure 9.10.

In My Head

Brief Overview of Activity:

This activity will help children to explore their thoughts and to realize that they are unique.

Objectives:

1. Children will identify 10 thoughts (things to think about).
2. Children will understand that everyone is unique.

Materials Needed:

1. *What's in My Head?* worksheet for each child (Figure 9.11).
2. Pencil

Procedure:

1. Begin discussion by asking the following question, "When you have spare time, what kinds of things do you think about?" Allow time for several children to share their thoughts.

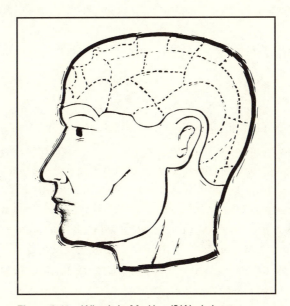

Figure 9.11. What's in My Head? Worksheet.

2. Point out to children that each of them is unique in that their thoughts (and interests) may be very different from those of their classmates.

3. Give children a copy of the *What's in My Head* worksheet to complete. Tell children to choose 10 spaces on the worksheet and write their responses to the question, "What kind of things do I think about?"

4. When children have completed their worksheet, ask them to pair up with a partner and discuss their sheets. Encourage them to discuss similarities and differences and to identify at least one similarity and one difference they discovered between themselves and their partners.

5. Allow a few minutes for discussion. Discuss the fact that their class is special. Everyone is unique and has much to contribute to class discussion and problem-solving.

Closure:

Spend a few minutes reminding children that each child is a valued class member and that their unique characteristics make them special. Encourage acceptance and appreciation of such differences.

ADDITIONAL IDEAS FOR COGNITIVE CARING

Memory Game

Play the "memory game" to increase retention skills. This may be done by having children share a favorite food. Each child says his or her name and favorite food after reciting the names of the children and their favorite foods in proper sequence. The sequence continues until every child has been added to the list. The last child must remember all the children's names and their favorite foods. Be sure to place the children who will be most successful remembering at the end of the line. Before playing the memory game, discuss and practice various memory techniques that children can use to increase their memory. Try these ideas when playing the memory game.

"I Can" Folder

A great way to help children focus on their successes is to have them decorate a folder that describes all of the skills they have learned. As they master a new skill, have them write the skill on the inside of the folder. Examples would include, "I can name all of the states and capitals, I can do long division, I can use the computer to write a story, and so on." Have children explore ways in which they can use their thinking skills (things they can do) to care for themselves, others, and the environment.

Irrational Thoughts

Take 5–10 minutes at the end of the week and ask children to write down one irrational thought they had during the week and identify how they refuted that thought. For example, "I thought nobody liked me because I was picked last for the game, but then Jenny asked me to work with her on an art project." This activity can also be done orally in small groups if children are comfortable with it.

What Are My Cues?

Divide children into groups of four or five and ask them to share some "cues" to their behavior. Remind them to share both negative and positive cues to their actions. Examples of this might be, "When I see someone who looks sad (cue), I try to cheer them up;" or "When someone says something (cue) that makes me angry, I yell at them." Follow up with a discussion of coping skills children can use to neutralize cues that result in their behaving in a hurtful manner. For example, "When someone says something that makes me angry, I can hit that person, or I can _____ (helpful-caring response)."

Power"full" or Power"less"?

Brainstorm with children a list of things that make them feel power "full" and a list of things that make them feel power "less." Then work together to develop coping strategies that can help them to deal with their power "less" feelings.

Why Do I Do That?

Ask children to think of behaviors that people do that result in others avoiding them (tattling on others, talking about people in a mean way, bullying, and so on). Then make a list of these behaviors and label them "Things I Don't Want to Have People Say About Me." Display the list in a place where children see them regularly.

"Learn Something New" Week

Invite persons to class who have interesting hobbies and ask them to give demonstrations of their hobbies. Then allow time for children to select one hobby or new skill they would like to learn. Challenge them to learn the new hobby or skill. Discuss plans for getting started and where they can obtain help if needed. Schedule a time in the future so that children can share their newfound skill or hobby with the class.

What Can I Do with a . . .

As a fun way to help children develop their thinking skills, take 10–15 minutes and allow them to think of 10 creative things they can do with an object. Children will have lots of fun with this activity, and it stretches their thinking skills and creativity. For example, what can one do with a paper cup?

1. Plant seeds in it.
2. Turn it upside down, put a ribbon through the bottom, add greenery, and make a Christmas decoration.
3. Decorate it and use it as a container for buttons, paper clips, etc.
4. Make a hat for a puppet. And so on.

Skill for the Week

Introduce a new study skill each week. Provide assignments in which children can practice the skill in school and in their homework assignments. By adding a new study skill each week, children will soon become more adept at studying and learning.

Cleanup Day

In conjunction with an environmental theme or classroom routine, have children go through their desks or lockers and do some "house-cleaning." Make sure to stress the importance of keeping things neat and orderly as a way of keeping themselves better organized. Discuss strategies that can be used to enhance children's ability to organize. Practice some of these ideas. Ask children to share the organizational strategies that work best for them.

Boxing My Time

As a way of managing one's time, give each child a list of three things that need to be done within a specified time period. Show children how they can box activities and times so they can focus on one thing at a time and complete what they set out to do. Boxing is used to schedule important activities and tasks.

My Fondest Memory

Have children write a story about their fondest memory, telling why this particular event was important to them. If children wish to do so, allow time for them to share their memories with the class. Follow up with a discussion on memory. Help children to explore the value of being able to remember and strategies they can practice to increase their memory.

Caring for My Community

Allow children to work in groups and think of five things they can do to help their community. This brief activity has the added bonus of stimulating children's skills and making them more conscious of things they can do to serve their community. Based upon children's suggestions, choose one project to pursue.

My Perfect Day

This activity can help children begin to look at time management as it applies to their own personal life. Instruct children that they have a total of 4 hours in which to do whatever they would like to do. Remind them that they must plan the time in such a way as to make the most of the activity or experience that they have chosen.

My Goal for the Month

As a way of introducing the topic of setting attainable goals, have a goal for the month in the classroom. Start off with something that is very attainable early on in the year (attendance). Make a chart or graph to show children how their attendance is increasing (or decreasing) during the month. Encourage children to identify other goals that they would like to accomplish (at home, at school, or in sports).

A Choice I Made That Worked Well for Me

Helping children to think about positive choices they have made is one way to help them think about wise decisions and the effects that such decisions have on their life. Use the title of this activity as a prompt for a creative writing exercise. When children have completed their papers, those willing to do so may share their stories with the class.

A Choice I Made That Didn't Work Well

As a follow-up to the *Choices That Worked Well* exercise, ask children to share with the class a choice that they made that didn't work well for them. This serves two purposes. First, it provides children with the opportunity to think about poor decisions and how they might have handled them differently. Second, it gives children an opportunity to learn from other's mistakes. Teach children how to make **STOP, THINK, & GO Decisions.**

Strengths Bombardment

Provide time for each child to sit in front of the class and be bombarded with positive comments from classmates. This is an excellent way to help children realize that everyone has strengths and that everyone is good at something. This also might be a good time to discuss Gardner's Multiple Intelligence Theory, which emphasizes that it's not "how smart you are" but "how are you smart."

This Is How You . . . !!

To reinforce the idea that all of us are able to do something well, provide time for each child to teach something to the class. This activity gives every child an opportunity to be in the spotlight and to share a personal skill or strength with the class. Strengths that can be shared relate to the many cognitive strengths addressed in this chapter (memory, concentration, thinking skills, decision-making, study skills, thought stopping, rational thinking, and so on).

BIBLIOGRAPHY

Anspaugh, D.J., & Ezell, G. (1995). *Teaching today's health* (4th ed.). Needham Heights, MA: Allyn & Bacon.

Bann, J.R. (1993). *Parents assuring student success: Achievement made easy by learning together.* Bloomington, IN: National Educational Service.

Bernard, M.E., & Joyce, M.R. (1984). *Rational emotive therapy with children and adolescents: Theory, treatment, prevention methods.* New York: John Wiley & Son.

Boyer, E.T. (1995). *The basic school: A community for learning.* Princeton, NJ: The Carnegie Foundation for the Advancement of Teaching.

Butler, G., & Hope, T. (1995). *Managing your mind: The mental fitness guide.* New York: Oxford University Press.

DeHart, G.B., Stroufe, L.A., & Cooper, R.G. (2000). *Child development: Its nature and course* (4th ed.). New York: McGraw-Hill.

Ellis, A. (1997). Must musterbation and demandingness lead to emotional disorders? *Psychotherapy, 34*(1), 95–98.

Ellis, A. (1987). The impossibility of achieving consistently good mental health. *American Psychologist, 42,* 364–375.

Flavell, J.H., Miller, P.H., & Miller, S.A. (1993). *Cognitive development* (3rd ed.). Englewood Cliffs, NJ: Prentice-Hall.

Gardner, H. (1983). *Frames of mind: The theory of multiple intelligences.* New York: Basic Books.

Goodwin, L.W., Goodwin, T., & Cantrell, J. (1988). The mental health needs of elementary school children. *Journal of School Health, 58*(7), 282–287.

Hales, D. (1992). *An invitation to health.* Redwood City, CA: The Benjamin/Cummings Publishing Co.

Kail, R. (1991). Development of processing speed in childhood and adolescence. In W. Reese (ed.), *Advance in child development and behavior* (vol. 23, pp. 151–185). San Diego, CA: Academic Press.

Kail, R., & Hagen, J. (1982). Memory in childhood. In B.B. Wolman (ed.), *Handbook of developmental psychology* (pp. 350–363), Englewood Cliffs, NJ: Prentice-Hall.

Klahr, D., & MacWhinney, B. (1998). Information Processing. In W. Damon (series eds.), *Handbook of child psychology: Vol. 2. Cognition, perception and language* (5th ed., pp. 631–678). New York: Wiley.

O'Rourke, K., & Worzbyt, J.C. (1996). *Support groups for children.* Washington, DC: Accelerated Development—A member of the Taylor & Francis Group.

Piaget, J. (1970). Piaget's theory. In P.H. Mussen (ed.), *Carmichael's manual of child psychology.* New York: Wiley.

Price, D.W.W., & Goodman, G.S. (1990). Visiting the wizard: Children's memory for a recurring event. *Child Development, 61,* 664–680.

Rafoth, M.A., & DeFabo, L. (1990). *Study skills. What research says to the teacher.* West Haven, CT: NEA Professional Library (ED 323 184).

Raths, L.E., Wassermann, S., Jonas, A., & Rothstein, A. (1986). *Teaching for thinking: Theory, strategies, and activities for the classroom* (2nd ed.). New York: Teachers College, Columbia University.

Rice, F.P. (1992). *Human development: A life-span approach.* New York: Macmillan.

Rogoff, B. (1998). Cognition as a collaborative process. In W. Damon (series eds.), D. Kuhn, & R.S. Siegler (vol. eds.), *Handbook of child psychology: Vol. 2. Cognition, perception and language* (5th ed., pp. 631–678). New York: Wiley.

Sameroff, A.J., & Haith, M.M. (eds.) (1996). *The five to seven year shift: The age of reason and responsibility.* Chicago, IL: University of Chicago Press.

Schneider, W., & Bjorklund, D.F. (1998). Memory. In W. Damon (series eds.), D. Kuhn & R.S. Siegler (vol. eds.), *Handbook of child psychology: Vol. 2. Cognition, perception, and language* (5th ed., pp. 467–521). New York: Wiley.

Siegler, R.S. (1998). *Children's thinking* (3rd ed.). Englewood Cliffs, NJ: Prentice-Hall.

Taylor, E. (1994). Syndromes of attention deficit and overactivity. In M. Rutter, E. Taylor, & L. Hersou (eds.), *Child and adolescent psychiatry* (pp. 285–307). London: Blackwell.

Vygotsky, L.S. (1978). *Mind and society.* Cambridge, MA: Harvard University Press.

Walters, V. (1982). Therapies for children: Rational emotive therapy. In C.R. Reynolds & T.B. Gutkin (eds.). *Handbook of school psychology.* New York: John Wiley & Sons.

Worzbyt, J.C. (1991). *Beating the odds.* Altoona, PA: R.J.S. Films.

Zigler, E.F., & Stevenson, M.F. (1993). *Children in a changing world: Development and social issues* (2nd ed.). Pacific Grove, CA: Brooks/Cole.

CHAPTER 10

Career and Societal Caring

Career and Societal Caring is a mutually interdependent process in which children develop a comprehensive understanding and utilization of self (life career caring) leading to a lifestyle based on social interest in which they learn to belong, cooperate, and work with others for the common good of all (societal caring).

LIFE CAREER DEVELOPMENT

Gyspers and Henderson (2001) defined life career development as self-development that occurs over people's life span and involves the integration of life roles, settings, and events that shape their lives. One's life is thus one's career and entails all life experiences that affect the growth and development of human beings.

Throughout the course of their lives, children experience a variety of roles (son, daughter, friend, consumer, worker, spouse, parent, and citizen), function in a multitude of settings (home, school, community), and participate in numerous life events (class plays, sporting events, graduation, job entry, marriage, etc.), all of which will contribute to their development and identity as caregivers and receivers of care. Thus, life career development is an all-encompassing concept that unites the previous chapters on physical caring, personal/emotional caring, social caring, and cognitive caring into a unified whole in helping children to develop a collective and comprehensive understanding of themselves and to acquire the competencies needed to make responsible life choices.

The concept of societal caring is strongly linked to career development caring in that children are shaped by the society in which they live and in turn help to shape it. As social beings living in a social world, children are motivated to find their place in the world. They strive to achieve a sense of belonging, meaning, and purpose in their lives. This developmental process follows a somewhat predictable path based on the research of developmental theorists (Havighurst, 1972; Maslow, 1954; Erikson, 1963; and others) who believe that if children's natures are nurtured along developmental lines, they will develop according to nature's plan and become responsible and fully functioning human beings caring for themselves and the communities in which they live.

Counselors, parents, teachers, administrators, and community supporters are responsible for helping children to believe in themselves, to develop a sense of industry, and to participate in life roles, settings, and events that will have a positive effect on their present and future life career development. Children and adults have a psychological need to participate in life roles, settings, and events in which they engage in meaningful work in support of themselves, others, and their communities. "When a person's career [life] involves work that contributes to the greater society, there is greater self-esteem, higher satisfaction with life and enhanced personal meaningfulness, and social connection" (McIntosh, 2000, p. 621).

CAREER AND SOCIETAL CARING: THE HEALTHY CHILD

Children who engage in career and societal caring learn that the two concepts are inseparable. Human life and societal life are born from the same seed. They must be nurtured and strengthened together if both are to flourish and grow. The healthy, caring child functions as a total organism and learns from life roles, settings, and events the importance of making and receiving caring choices and of how those choices contribute to their own personal growth and development and to a stronger and more caring society.

Healthy, caring children understand that despite everything they do to care for themselves, they can never do enough, for they also must depend on the care given to them by others. Healthy, caring children are career and societally minded in that they seek to develop certain characteristics that will help them to care for others and for society. Children who are career and societally minded

- respect the rights of others;
- cooperate with others;
- possess a realistic and positive self-concept;
- feel as though they belong and are socially useful;
- practice socially acceptable goals;
- understand their personal strengths and limitations;
- know their specific interests and talents;
- demonstrate effective interpersonal skills;
- function effectively in their roles as student, family member, friend, worker, volunteer, and so forth;
- contribute to the life of their home, school, and community;
- seek out life events in which they can make a caring contribution in support of others;
- understand the nature of work and why people work;
- understand that it takes the collective contribution of all people to sustain a fully functioning and caring society;
- understand the relationship of classroom learning in shaping their life experiences and future adult roles;
- recognize the wide variety of interdependent and caring occupations needed to nurture healthy people and build strong communities;
- enjoy greater freedom and expanded opportunity to explore occupations previously limited by such stereotyping as gender, physical characteristics, and race; and
- possess and use good work habits and decision-making skills when participating in current life roles, settings, and events.

UNDERSTANDING THE NEED FOR CAREER AND
SOCIETAL CARING

Children, like adults, are looking for meaning and purpose in their lives. The socialization process, which begins in early childhood, involves children acquiring an awareness of themselves and their surroundings and a sense of what it takes to belong, to contribute, and to secure a meaningful place in society.

Mosak (1995), in Corey (2001), stated that all human beings must master five life tasks that involve (1) relating to others (friendships), (2) making a contribution (work), (3) achieving intimacy (love and family relationships), (4) getting along with self (self-acceptance), and (5) developing a spiritual dimension (including values, meaning, life goals, and a relationship with the universe). These five life tasks are interconnected and evolve developmentally over a lifetime (life career development). These same life tasks are referenced in the literature of Havighurst (1972) (developmental tasks), Maslow (1954) (needs hierarchy), Erikson (1963) (psychosocial stages of development) and in the preceding four chapters (6–9) of this text. Children's lives are thus shaped by the people, places, and events they experience and the perceptions they draw from their life experiences. Thus the extent to which children will become caring children and builders of caring communities will largely be determined by the caring (nurturing) choices that adults make in shaping their life career development.

Human development and career development theorists speak to the developmental stage process that children go through as they mature into caring and responsible adults. They likewise speak to the need of nurturing that process so that children will be exposed to the most conducive teaching-learning environments and life experiences that will best meet their developmental and unique needs through the most appropriate behaviors to be learned.

Human and career development theorists are in general agreement that childhood development cannot be left to chance. Learning is always taking place, for good or bad, and what children learn or fail to learn will either contribute to their forming a healthy and successful identity or lead to their living a life of confusion, frustration, and pain. Devoid of having developed a constructive sense of social interest and a life of giving, these children are likely to remain self-centered and live adult lives lacking in meaning and purpose.

The need for life career education in the elementary school grades is most evident and substantiated when one considers that what children learn or fail to learn about life, living, and the pursuit of happiness will be played out in the life choices they make or fail to make. If educators fail to provide children with a balanced education that teaches them how to give and receive care and to become builders of caring communities, the circle of caring (Chapter 12) will be forever compromised, and caring choices in support of self, others, and society will be diminished. What follows are a few simple truths that crystallize the risks that children and society are likely to encounter in the absence of career and societal caring.

- *Failure to develop reality-based beliefs and goals.* Children live in a rapidly changing society and are exposed to a multitude of people, life settings, and events that influence their beliefs about themselves, others, and the world of work. To the extent that children are exposed to inaccurate, stereotypical, and mythical life experiences, they are likely to develop faulty cognitions and misguided goals that will influence their impressions of the world of work and their life career options well into adulthood (Ginzberg, Ginsburg, Axelrad, & Herma, 1951). Thus, children are likely to prematurely restrict their understanding of work and their rightful place in it. Personal, social, stereotypical, and cultural biases that are formed during childhood—in the absence of reality-based role models, accurate information, and settings and events that portray the truth—place children and society at risk unless addressed (Ginzberg, 1972; Gottfredson, 1981; Gunn, 1964).

  A well-designed life career education program (balanced education) involving home, school, and community can expose children to role models, life settings, and events that enhance their life career awareness and exploration of work, leisure time, and volunteer activities that will contribute to their life career and societal caring.

• *Failure to understand the relevancy of school.* Throughout this text, we have made it abundantly clear that children who fail to understand the value of what they are learning are more likely to lose interest in school and, more tragically, begin to develop physical, personal/emotional, and social problems that will carry over into adulthood. Lacking in self-understanding and the skills necessary to live and to make a living, these young people will be unable to care for themselves or their families or to make a positive contribution to society.

Children are more likely to enjoy and stay in school if they receive a balanced education (life career education) that is coherent, integrated, applicable, and timely; one that relates classroom learning to life and living. A balanced education relates academic curriculum understanding to the seven themes of caring and the world of work (both paid and volunteer). For example, children can be taught how numbers will help them to make caring choices when caring for family and friends (a caring theme). They can explore caring occupations (medical, scientific, and others) involving workers who use numbers to care for others. They can also explore hobbies and volunteer and leisure-time activities in which numbers can help them to care for themselves, others, and society. When these kinds of connections are made, children find school a fun place to be and enjoy the love of learning that will stay with them beyond their childhood years.

• *Failure to develop caring and responsible lifelong work habits.* Work has been defined in many ways, but simply stated, it involves people engaged in useful pursuits (paid and volunteer) that contribute to personal, social, and societal caring. Children's work is done at home, in school, and in their communities. Through work, children develop social interests and a lifestyle that enhances their personal health and wellness and helps them to secure their place in society as responsible producers and consumers of goodwill and caring.

As children pursue their work (home, school, and society), they learn the importance of being a team player, being punctual, following directions, producing quality work, developing effective interpersonal skills, and respecting all people of diversity. These are the very same traits and abilities that the workplace demands, expects, and rewards. Children first begin to develop lifelong work habits at home and in school. Elementary schools that foster inclusion, cooperation, and people-building in the context of a caring community give children the opportunity to engage in career and societal caring practices that foster sound work habits.

The research is clear (Chapters 6–9) that children who fail to develop responsible and caring work habits become adults who experience a number of life adjustment problems, which include a high incidence of divorce, addictions (alcohol, drug, etc.), job dissatisfaction and frustration, depression, a high rate of absenteeism from work, illness, rejection by coworkers and management, and so on.

Leaving the development of sound work habits to chance guarantees that children and society will suffer needless losses in a world that depends on caring choices. One answer to solving this dilemma is an elementary school counseling program that supports a balanced education (life career education) that advocates on behalf of life career and societal caring.

- *Failure to develop an awareness and mastery of life career tasks.* Life career tasks are behaviors that children are expected to master at each stage in their development. As children accomplish these tasks, they develop a sense of industry and begin to form an identity based on self-assessment.

Children who are successful in mastering life tasks develop healthy self-concepts and emotional well-being, foster caring relationships, make useful contributions (home, school, and community), and develop lifestyles of purpose and meaning. They understand their likes and dislikes, strengths and weaknesses, and what they can do to self-improve.

The successful mastery of life tasks has a direct bearing on the world of work and on life career choices, as children will gravitate toward those life tasks in which they believe they possess strengths and avoid those in which they feel inadequate. How children relate to life task development will thus have an impact on how they define themselves in relationship to all life experiences. Will they see themselves as being successful or unsuccessful, fearful or outgoing, capable or incapable, dependent or independent, fully functioning or diminished in their capacity to act? The answers to these questions will be found in the caring choices that adults make in helping children to explore their roles in career and societal caring.

Life career and societal caring can best be accomplished in career education programs (through balanced education) that teach children life tasks in the context of daily life situations that reflect the world of work and community building. We need to help children connect with such daily life tasks as thinking on their feet, attending to detail, working under pressure, learning how things work, following directions, working with people, expressing themselves through writing, and so on. As new life tasks are presented, we can help children to identify with them using a Likert-type scale developed by Munson and Gockley (1973). The scale contains five positions that reflect emotionality (like-dislike) and directionality (seek-avoid) when personally evaluating life tasks (see Figure 10.1).

As children examine various life tasks in which they participate, they can rate themselves on a continuum. They also can explore various life settings, events, and occupations that require the use of these life tasks and decide if they would like to explore ways in which they can change their ranking. For example, Billy does not like talking in class (life task). This is a task that he *dislikes* and

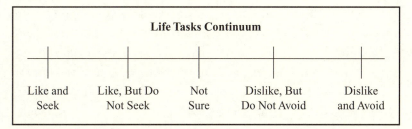

Figure 10.1. Life Tasks Continuum.

avoids. However, he realizes that talking in front of people is a skill that he needs to develop if he wishes to do better in school and to pursue after-school work opportunities with people in his community. Billy asks for help and learns ways to feel more comfortable when talking with people. He now rates this task as something that he still *dislikes*, but *does not avoid*.

With practice, children will become more aware of the life tasks they can perform and become more astute in examining the various life events, settings, and occupations in which these tasks can be used. Thus, children will become more effective in making caring life choices that will lead to their own personal fulfillment and to a stronger, more compassionate, and caring society.

The Cumulative Effects of Risk

In the absence of a life career education program, academic subjects are often taught in isolation with emphasis being placed on the mastery of disconnected information, skills, and attitudes learned through repetition and tested through meaningless recall. These memorized and often isolated bits of information and seemingly unimportant skills, lacking in relevancy and purpose, are seldom given meaning in the context of their usefulness (learning to live, learn, and work). When children are subjected to this type of an education, they fail to develop an awareness of themselves, of how they are changing, of what they would like to be, of what they would like to do, of what they would like to have, and of what they would like to give. They fail to understand the people-building mission of the school, to use what they are learning in order to make caring choices in the seven themes of caring, and to find a purposeful and meaningful place in the world of work (home, school, and community). Career and societal caring practices become null and void in elementary schools that unknowingly nurture the cumulative effects of risk rather than support a balanced education rooted in people-building and career and societal caring.

ENHANCING CAREER AND SOCIETAL CARING THROUGH CARING CHOICES

Career development cannot be separated from human development. Life career education cannot be separated from a balanced education. Subject matter learning cannot be separated from life learning, nor can life choices be separated from career choices. The goal of career and societal caring during the elementary school years is to help children realize how what they are learning in school is contributing to their evolvement as caring human beings and builders of caring communities.

Enhancing career and societal caring can best be accomplished through an education that connects school academic subjects with the seven themes of caring and relates both of these areas to the world of work and a wide variety of occupations. To the extent that this is accomplished during the elementary school years, children will develop an awareness of self leading toward a more effective understanding and utilization of self in relation to others and work. As children learn more about themselves in relation to work and society, they will make caring choices in support of themselves, others, and the society-at-large.

The Concept of Work

Hoyt (2001) stated that "Work is clearly the bedrock of career education" (p. 327). In order to understand career education (*basic education*), work must be clearly defined as well. Hoyt (2001) defined work ". . . as intentional effort, other than that whose primary purpose is either coping or relaxation, aimed at producing benefits for oneself and others" (p. 327). In dissecting this definition, Hoyt stated that *intentional* means that the activity is something that has been freely chosen by an individual versus being the object of force. *Effort* signifies that some degree of difficulty is involved in the activity versus an accidental event. *Producing* implies that some outcome is sought, and *benefits* suggests that some people are better off in some way after the work has been completed (the worker benefits as do others).

People value work (paid and unpaid) in that it contributes to their identity, represents a way of being helpful to others, can improve the world order by making it a better place to live, provides an avenue through which to excel at something, opens up opportunities to do things of interest, encourages identification and interaction with others of similar interests, and becomes a source for achieving economic benefits (Hoyt, 2001). These work values not only explain why people work, but also provide the impetus to improve upon the quantity and quality of people's work efforts.

Occupations, in contrast to work, speak to the vast number of specific jobs in which work is performed. People choose specific occupations based on such variables as personal interest in the skills required for success, an aptitude for performing these skills, geographic location, ease of access, influence of family members and friends, good job security, attractive fringe benefits, opportunities for promotion, and high entry-level salary.

Hoyt has suggested that the best workers are those whose work and occupational values are closely aligned to their work assignments. They understand the nature of work and their own work values and how they relate to a number of occupations. Career education programs seek to develop workers who understand the broad concept of work in relationship to making caring choices that will benefit themselves, others, and society.

Career education is not new in that it was first promoted as the answer to educational reform in the 1970s by Sidney Marland, Jr. (1974) as a way of bringing relevancy to education by helping students to connect classroom life and work with life and work out-side the classroom. The aim was to make work (paid and unpaid) possible, meaningful, and satisfactory for each individual. Career education remained a top federal program for educational reform throughout the 1970s and received $130 million in appropriated funding for that period (Hoyt, 2001).

The Career Education Incentive Act was repealed in 1981, and with it came a decline in organized career education programs, es-pecially at the elementary school level. While career education ini-tiatives are still being carried out in some school districts by some teachers, the results are uneven at best with career days, isolated ca-reer activities, and stand-alone career units being the focal point of hit-and-miss programs that often lack a systematic, developmental, collaborative, and fully integrated approach to meeting children's life career needs. The good news is that even after 30 years of no funding, ". . . career education is still the most widely demonstrated and best validated proposal for educational reform" (Hoyt, 2001, p. 327).

According to Hoyt, the best hope for career education is for teachers and children to embrace the definition of work provided earlier and to view themselves as workers with the classroom and school as their workplace. Indeed, Hoyt has stated that the goal of career education as an educational reform proposal is to increase the number of teachers and children who consider what they do as work. When teachers view themselves and their children as workers, they will approach what they teach from the perspective of helping children to understand and perform their work roles as students, family members, classmates, community members, and volunteers.

We begin from a very simple premise that states that work is the bedrock of career education and that the purpose of work is rooted in teaching children how to care. We believe that all subject matter learnings serve to help children become caring people and builders of caring communities.

Children learn how to care and to be careful through reading, writing, math, science, language arts, social studies, health, physical education, music, and art. When children are taught caring from this perspective, they make the connection between caring and work. They learn how their subject matter disciplines can help them to make caring choices and how they can carry out their life's work through their hobbies, interests, leisure time activities, volunteer experiences, and paid service (home, school, and community). They also learn how occupations, and the people who work in them, rely on the same subject matter learnings as they do to provide caring goods and services in support of caring workplaces and communities throughout our nation and world.

When children understand the relationship among academic subject matter disciplines, caring choices, and the world of work, they will develop an understanding and utilization of self leading to a life of purpose and meaning because they can see the value in what they have learned. Children are less likely to question, "Why do I have to learn this?" when they see how it can be directly applied to work inside and outside the classroom.

Elementary school counseling programs have a significant role to play in helping children and teachers to view themselves as workers and their classrooms and schools as workplaces. They likewise have an important mission to communicate, which emphasizes children attaining the following life career tasks (Hoffman & McDaniels, 1991, p. 164):

a. Develop self-understanding and a realistic, positive self-concept.

b. Acquire the knowledge, understanding, attitudes, and competencies to function effectively in their current life roles, such as son, daughter, family member, sibling, student, classmate, worker at home and at school, friend, peer group member, team member in sports and games, and "leisurite."

c. Develop an awareness of the career development options available to them in school and the community.

These same life career tasks are similar to the national career goals for children in kindergarten through grade six as published by the

National Occupational Information Coordinating Committee (1989). These goals are addressed according to Self-Knowledge, Educational and Occupational Exploration, and Career Planning.

Self-Knowledge

Knowledge of the importance of self-concept
Skills to interact with others
Awareness of the importance of growth and change

Educational and Occupational Exploration

Awareness of the benefits of educational achievement
Awareness of the relationship between work and learning
Skills to understand and use career information
Awareness of the importance of personal responsibility and good work habits
Awareness of how work relates to the needs and functions of society

Career Planning

Understanding how to make decisions
Awareness of the interrelationship of life roles
Awareness of different occupations and changing male and female roles
Awareness of the career planning process (National Occupational Information Coordinating Committee, 1989)

The American School Counselor Association (Campbell & Dahir, 1997) also published national standards for school counseling programs in grades K–12 with respect to personal/social development, academic development, and career development. In the area of career development, three general standards were stated, which are in keeping with the previous tasks and goals for career programming at the elementary school level. Those standards are as follows:

Standard A: Students will acquire the skills to investigate the world of work in relation to knowledge of self and to make informed career decisions.

Standard B: Students will employ strategies to achieve future career goals with success and satisfaction.

Standard C: Students will understand the relationship among personal qualities, education, training, and the world of work (p. 24).

A close examination of life career standards, goals, and tasks suggest, as we have indicated throughout this text, that career education is life education. More simply stated, it is a balanced education in which children learn how to learn, live, and work and make caring choices in support of themselves, others, and communities, small and large.

Elementary school academic-instructional and counseling programs, with home and community support, can provide children with a life career education (balanced education) that will embrace career and societal caring to the extent that these programs focus on three innerconnected themes that unite the concepts of education, work, and caring.

1. Self-understanding and caring
2. Education and work connections and caring
3. Career planning and caring

An education provides children with an understanding and utilization of self and the information, skills, and attitudes to engage in useful and meaningful work in caring for themselves, others, and the society, which has in turn cared for them. Work is a central condition to career (life) and societal caring, for it is what gives life purpose and meaning and maintains and enhances a caring community.

Self-Understanding and Caring

Caring for self is the first of the seven themes of caring (Chapters 1 and 2). From the time children are born, parents begin the process of teaching children how to care for themselves and to be careful. That process continues today and well into adulthood, with children and adults developing healthy attitudes, acquiring useful information, and learning appropriate life skills that will enable them to make caring life choices in all that they do.

Elementary school counseling programs can help to facilitate self-understanding and caring by engaging teachers, parents, children, and community supporters in people-building experiences (Chapters 6–10) that will increase children's awareness and utilization of themselves in kind and caring ways. Children need to become physically, personally/emotionally, socially, and cognitively aware of their development and know their personal assets, strengths, likes, dislikes, interests, and limitations. They must learn how to care for themselves and others and build positive self-concepts, healthy self-esteems, wellness lifestyles, and a sense of social interest that encourage them to pass on to others the very best of what they have to give.

Some of the following strategies have proven to be useful in helping children to gain in self-awareness, self-understanding, and a more effective and caring utilization of self:

- Teach children a caring vocabulary, and have them practice these words with others (thank you, please, may I, can I help you, etc.).
- Have children name feeling words and explore their meaning in relation to self and others. Words like happy, sad, and angry can be explored, understood, and practiced in safe and caring ways.
- Teach children a variety of social skills, the benefits derived from their use, and how to use them in building social connections.
- Assist children in learning about various character (caring) traits, identifying the traits that they possess and those that they most admire in others.

Additional ideas for helping children to become more self-aware and to exercise caring choices on behalf of themselves, others, and their communities can be found in Chapters 6–9.

Educational and Work Connections and Caring

A balanced education (career education) focuses on school as community, a curriculum with coherence, a climate for learning, and a commitment to character (Chapter 1). A balanced education connects academic instruction, caring, people-building, and work. Children and teachers are viewed as workers living and working in a community of workers. Classrooms and schools become workplaces where children learn information, develop skills, and acquire attitudes that will help them to make caring choices (work choices) in support of themselves, their classrooms, and their school communities.

A balanced education helps children to learn about the world of work and various occupations by relating "school work" to useful forms of work performed at home, in school, and in their communities. As children become more aware of themselves and develop self- and work-related understandings, they will experience the education-work connection and discover a curriculum with coherence and relevancy. In this kind of environment, teachers can

1. help student workers understand the importance of the task they are being asked to perform,
2. reward the use of productive work habits,
3. ensure variety in the work tasks,
4. give special rewards for excellent work,
5. establish and use systems of teamwork to produce better products,
6. evaluate students in ways that will motivate them to do better, and
7. establish goals that can reasonably be met by those who are motivated to work (Hoyt, 2001, p. 328).

The outcome of a meaningful education and work connections is that children will come to understand that what they are being taught in school is being used by workers in a variety of occupations. And because they possess many of the same learnings, they too can become valued workers when they use those learnings to benefit themselves and humankind in caring ways.

What follows are some useful strategies that will help to facilitate the education-work connection.

- Help children to relate how information, skills, and attitudes learned in various subjects can be used to make caring choices (decisions) in the seven themes of caring. For example, explore ways in which reading can help children to care for themselves, family and friends, distant others, plants and the environment, and so on. Reading is a caring attribute that can help young people to care and to be careful.
- Help children to explore and understand how the same subject matter information, skills, and attitudes relate to their work and to various occupations in the home, school, and community. For example, ask children to name occupations and workers that rely on their ability to read when performing their work. Ask children to identify times when reading was beneficial to them when working at home, in school, and in their communities.
- Challenge children to identify the seven themes of caring and the occupational connections that exist between and among the various caring themes. For example, ask children to identify all of the occupations they can that relate to "caring for plants and the environment." Help children to understand that when they care for plants and the environment, they too are engaged in useful and meaningful work.
- Ask children to identify caring work experiences in which they have participated (home, school, and community) and the various subject matter information, skills, and attitudes that they utilized in doing so.
- Have children identify the various life roles they play (son, daughter, family member, student, classmate, group member, volunteer, etc.) and the work they have performed in each role.
- Ask children to identify and practice what they believe to be good work habits required of all workers who do their best

performing acts of caring (work) at home, in school, and in their communities.

- Help children to explore how all forms of work (occupations) help communities (families, classrooms, schools, villages, towns, cities) to function more effectively.
- Have children explore the value of work and the importance that work plays in people's lives. This can be accomplished by having children interview their parents and the adults they know, as well as by bringing people in from the community to discuss the role that work plays in their lives.
- Encourage children to discuss the value of their work and what they gain through their acts of caring.

When children are given the opportunity to connect with themselves and with what they are learning in fun and meaningful ways, they will see the relevancy of school and how it relates to their various roles as caring workers and builders of caring communities.

Career Planning and Caring

As children develop an understanding of self in relation to education and work, they will begin to develop impressions about themselves and the world of work. Left to chance, this process can have devastating effects in the formulation of faulty attitudes, beliefs, and actions that can evolve from prejudices, myths, stereotypes, and all forms of discrimination, resulting in a long-lasting impact on future career exploration, understanding, and planning. And, while the focus of career education during the elementary school years is not on occupational choice, it does address career planning in a more general way. Because children are developing as human beings, what they are exposed to will help to shape what they become. Consequently, career education at the elementary school level is concerned with enhancing children's self-awareness and the learning of basic life skills, all of which will help children to develop a positive attitude toward themselves, work, and career life planning. Chapters 6 through 9 provide useful information and activities that will help children to explore and experience career-planning strategies in keeping with their stage of development. Some additional, age-appropriate, career-planning strategies to consider are the following:

- Ask children to write a short paragraph describing the person they would like to be and some of the things they would do. Help them to relate their writings to various work roles, settings, and events addressed in their paragraph.
- Have children break into boy and girl groups and brainstorm a list of occupations that men and women can do. Discuss the lists and help children to challenge any gender-biased stereotypes they may have developed.
- Similar to the previous activity, encourage children to explore people's faulty beliefs, prejudices, stereotypes, and examples of discrimination (race, religion, age, handicaps, etc.) and how these factors affect occupational choice. Help children to challenge their thinking about occupational choice and the value of all kinds of work in contributing to a strong and healthy society.
- Ask children to consider various occupations that they would find difficult to choose for themselves and their reasons for thinking that way. Help them to explore their thoughts and feelings and to reality-test their beliefs.
- Have children explore their interests, hobbies, strengths, limitations, and personality attributes. Ask them to identify work-related activities and occupations that they think they would like and might seek.
- Ask children to identify work responsibilities at school and in the classroom. Discuss the attitudes, skills, and information needed to do a good job in each work area.
- Teach children how to write job descriptions and ads similar to those found in the newspaper. The ads can be posted, and children can be taught how to apply for various positions based on job particulars and on their strengths and interests. Job interviewing can be incorporated into this activity as well.

- Help children to identify various occupations that interest them. Tell them to select one occupation that they think they would like and to say why. Teach your children how to research their occupation, and after they have done so, ask whether that occupation still appeals to them.
- Help children to explore the various factors that affect job selection (geographic location, climate, inside versus outside work, skill requirements, aptitude for the job, fringe benefits, salary, years of education required, etc.). Ask them to consider what factors would be most important for them and why.
- Have children explore the needs of their home, school, and community. Ask them to identify what they could do to help address some of these needs. Help children to examine their skills, interests, and strengths and select a work experience (paid or unpaid) they could perform by themselves or in partnership with a family member, peers, or community volunteers. Have them perform the work experience and share what it was like to be a caregiver (worker) in support of others.

Activities, like the ones mentioned, can help children to engage in meaningful career planning experiences. Older elementary school children can explore various work opportunities using their decision-making skills as presented in Chapter 9. Regardless of the strategies utilized, children need experiences that will help them to view themselves as workers and the classroom as their workplace, where they will learn how to become caring workers making caring choices in behalf of themselves, family and friends, acquaintances, and distant others in support of caring communities where they live.

THE COUNSELOR'S ROLE

Elementary school counselors will have their greatest and most significant impact on career and societal caring in their roles as consultants, coordinators, collaborators, and trainers and developers. Elementary school counselors must provide the leadership and managerial skills that provide children with a balanced education (career education) that will infuse academic instruction, work, and caring in ways that will help children to understand that what they are taught will help them to live, learn, and work in their homes, classrooms, and communities.

While creating and implementing a systematic and comprehensive life career education program can easily become a frightening and overwhelming task, this need not be the case. Hoyt (2001) has stated that career education, or what we refer to as a balanced education, can truly reform education to the extent that such a proposal contains several important components relating to changes that must

- involve activities that most teachers are capable of performing and that both teachers and their pupils find interesting and enjoy doing;
- be inexpensive to carry out;
- provide teachers with a sense of ownership of the project;
- yield increases in student achievement;
- involve communities, including parents; and
- result in some kind of credit or award for the teachers who participate in the project.

In addition to addressing these components, we believe that, for career and societal caring to grow, it needs a simple, yet comprehensive focal point. Thus the size or magnitude of the program is second to its purpose, which is to develop caring children and builders of caring communities (career and societal caring). We believe that this end can be achieved on behalf of elementary school counselors helping parents, teachers, and community supporters to explore four basic questions that are central to life, living, and work (focal point). These questions are as follows (see Chapter 4):

1. What do we want our children to *Be?*
2. What do we want our children to *Do?*
3. What do we want our children to *Have?*
4. What do we want our children to *Give?*

First parents, teachers, administrators, and community members must decide what they want their children to *Be*. Child and career development theorists provide useful information supported by research that states we would like our children to *Be* caring human beings and builders of caring communities. We want our children to become capable human beings who can care for themselves, for others, and for the environment in responsible ways. We also want them to become aware of the fact that nearly all human beings contribute to a caring and functioning home, classroom, community, and world based on what they have to give (work). And, we want our children to realize that they are significant and valued family, classroom, community, and world members who have much to give as paid and volunteer workers in support of the various groups in which they hold membership.

The second question, "What do we want our children to *Do?*", evolves from the first question in that *Doing* leads to *Being*. Counselors are to help teachers, parents, administrators, and community members to examine what children must learn to *Do* if they are to become caring human beings and builders of caring communities.

Doing relates to the specific behaviors, thoughts, and feelings that we want to teach our children. *Doing* defines the curriculum that will provide children with the information, skills, and attributes they will need to care for themselves, intimate others, acquaintances and distant others, nonhuman animals, plants and the environment, objects and instruments, and ideas. *Doing* also defines the actions of school personnel in their relationships with each other and with children. The goal must be to determine what caring role model actions a caring community wishes to teach its children and then to support these teachings in practice.

In the context of *Doing,* children, with adult guidance, will learn how to make caring and careful choices that will have a positive and significant impact on the home, school, community, and world. Through *Doing,* children will develop social interests and begin to formulate a lifestyle of service (work). *Doing* helps children to become aware of their strengths, limitations, and interests. It helps them to develop hobbies, leisure-time pursuits, a desire to help others, and work and occupational interests.

The third question, "What do we want children to *Have?*", relates to questions one and two. What children *Have* is based on what they *Do* and *Become*. Doing leads to *Having*. We want children to *Have* the information, skills, and attitudes necessary to become caring people and builders of caring communities. Once learning has taken place, children take ownership of what they have learned and it becomes theirs.

The last question is a most significant one because it focuses on what we want our children to *Give*. *Giving* stems from what children *Have*. Consequently, children *Give* both the best and worst of themselves depending on what they *Have*. If children *Have* caring and community-building skills, that is what they will *Give*. If they *Have* stereotypes, prejudices, and discrimination tendencies, that is what they will *Give*.

Home, school, and community experiences shape children's lives for good or bad and will determine what they *Become, Do, Have,* and *Give*. Unfortunately, in far too many instances, what children learn or fail to learn (*Do*) will have a significant impact on what they *Have* to *Give*. Children who *become* violent *give* violence. Children, who *become* manipulators manipulate others. Children who *become* prejudiced act in prejudicial ways. Consequently, teachers, parents, administrators, and community members cannot afford to leave to chance what they want their children to learn about themselves, others, their communities, and the world of work. Elementary school counselors must help administrators, teachers, parents, and community members to decide what they would like their children to *Be, Do, Have,* and *Give* and offer consultation, collaboration, coordination, and training assistance in achieving their goals. If schools are to be successful in creating caring children and builders of caring communities, they will need to focus on career and societal caring in the home, classroom, and community.

Career Education and the Home

Parents have primary influence in the career development of their children. They play a key role in shaping their children's perceptions of themselves: what it takes to belong as a family member, the development of social interest, and their view of work and various occupations. These factors and others will have a significant impact on children's life career development and on their future occupational choices (Birk & Blimline, 1984; Seligman, Weinstock, & Heflin, 1991).

For all the reasons given, we believe that parents need to be involved in teaching their children to care and to become builders of caring communities very early in their development. Utilizing the four key questions (*Be, Do, Have,* and *Give*), counselors can guide parents in providing life experiences that will help their children to:

- Care for themselves
- Care for intimate others (family and friends)
- Care for acquaintances and distant others
- Care for nonhuman animals (domestic and wild)
- Care for plants and the environment
- Care for the human-made world of objects and instruments
- Care for ideas (Chapters 1, 2, and 6–10)

As children develop the skills and understandings needed to make caring choices in the seven themes of caring, they can begin to explore their own strengths, interests, and hobbies as they pertain to acts of caring and being careful. Counselors can assist parents in helping their children to identify with the importance of becoming a *Giving* person and providing them with opportunities to volunteer their time, treasure (allowance), and talents (skills) in support of a caring home, school, and community life.

As children connect with what they *Have* to *Give* and the appreciation from others for having done so, they will begin to develop a sense of initiative and industry giving way to a lifestyle grounded in purpose and meaning. They will, with parental guidance, come to realize the importance of developing a good work ethic and the need for a wide range of occupations and volunteer activities to support and maintain a circle of caring that includes all people.

Counselors can best serve the needs of all parents in the area of career and societal caring by offering parents

- training in the seven themes of caring;
- activities for teaching caring;
- ideas for involving their children in work experiences at home and in their community; and
- opportunities to consult and interact with teachers and community members in monthly idea-sharing sessions on career and community caring.

The goal is to involve parents in teaching their children how to become caregivers, receivers of care, and builders of caring communities.

Career Education and the Classroom

A balanced education (career education) focuses on helping children to become caring and responsible self-managers and people who are capable of living in society and contributing to its betterment. This goal can be achieved when teachers and children view themselves as workers and their classrooms and school as work settings. In this environment, children and teachers can work together, with teachers performing three basic duties: (1) transmitting knowledge to children, (2) motivating children to learn what the teacher is trying to teach, and (3) helping children learn to learn on their own (Hoyt, 2001). In the context of this framework, teachers are encouraged to teach subject matter content and skills from a caring perspective, thereby helping children to understand and apply what they are learning by making caring choices that will benefit themselves, others, and society (work). Making caring choices is children's work and their responsibility for helping to create a better today and shape a better tomorrow.

Children are learning to *Be* good citizens and caring human beings. Their work setting (classroom and school) provides them with the skills, understandings, sound work habits and attitudes, and the opportunity to practice *Doing* the work of good citizens building caring classrooms and school communities.

Elementary school counselors have the responsibility of helping teachers to understand that their primary responsibility is helping children to become caring human beings and builders of caring communities and that everything they teach is designed to support that process. For example, children must learn the importance that numbers play in their lives and how numbers help them to make caring choices and to be careful. They must learn of the many workers and occupations that rely on the use of numbers in support of the people and communities they serve. Children must likewise learn the value of reading and writing from a caring perspective and how these skills can help them to make caring and careful choices as workers and community builders.

As teachers make the connection between the academic curriculum and caring, they will be able to help their children make the same connection. Once this has been accomplished, teachers can easily integrate this new perspective into their teaching so that children can readily see and experience how what they are learning can be used as caring tools to benefit themselves and society. Counselors can help teachers to understand that the act of making caring choices to improve people's lives is work whether paid or unpaid and gives purpose and meaning to life. Once children understand that they are workers and that their work has a caring focus, teachers, with the assistance of elementary school counselors, can help children to explore the caring nature of all responsible occupations and the caring skills (subject matter learnings) that these workers use to make life better for others.

Counselors can assist teachers in integrating career and societal caring into their academic curriculum by following five simple steps.

Step 1: Subject Matter Identification

Identify a subject content area to address. *Example:* math.

Step 2: Decide What to Teach

Determine what information, skills, and attitudes are to be taught. *Example:* Children will be taught to count from 1 to 20. They will learn how this skill can help them to care and be careful.

Step 3: Identify Caring Value

Explore the caring value of this skill as it relates to the seven themes of caring. *Example:* How can counting help children to care for themselves? How can counting help children to care for family and friends? How can counting help children to care for plants and the environment?

Step 4: Relate to Work/Occupations

Explore the world of work and various occupations in which workers depend on counting to make caring and careful work choices. *Example:* Teachers use counting when children get on and off the school bus during field trip days to be sure that no child is left behind. Pharmacists count pills to make sure patients receive the correct amount of medication.

Step 5: Putting It All Together

Create a plan to teach children how to count from 1 to 20 using ideas developed in steps 2 through 4. Help children to understand the value of being able to count and how counting can be used as a caring skill (seven themes of caring). Assist children in exploring the world of work and various occupations that require workers to be able to count. Involve children in classroom, school, and home activities that require counting as a caring skill.

Using this five-step process, teachers can think about and develop a plan for relating subject matter content to caring and work. In so doing, children's career development will be affected in a positive manner. They will learn about their various life roles, the different settings (home, school, and community) in which they function, and the many life events in which they participate. And, they will understand and appreciate the value of what they have learned in helping them to become caring human beings and builders of caring communities.

In addition to curriculum integration, elementary school counselors can help teachers to develop special career education units, coordinate career days and field trips to local businesses and industry, teach occasional classroom guidance lessons with a career focus, and help teachers develop career portfolios for children that will track changes in their life career development. Counselors also can coordinate home and school career-related ventures that bring teachers and parents together in support of children's career development. For example, Parent-Teacher Association meetings can be used to present programs on career education and to involve parents in career-related activities that they can do at home with their children. And, parents and teachers can brainstorm ways in which they can support home, classroom, and school-wide career awareness programs that instill acts of caring.

Career Education and the Community

A balanced education would not be complete nor would career and societal caring be fully achieved in the absence of a career education and community connection. Communities have always had a significant impact on children's career development, whether by design or chance. Exposure to the media, children's experiences, and parental impact all unite in shaping children's perceptions of their world and the people in it. Because life career development begins to evolve at a very early age, it behooves communities to take a more active and responsible role in helping children to develop a sense of belonging, cooperation, and inclusion with respect to experiencing and participating in an enriching community life.

Elementary school counselors can visit local community social service agencies, religious and spiritual organizations, businesses and industry, chambers of commerce, community action leagues, law enforcement and the courts, and political action groups to discuss what impact the community wishes to have in helping to shape the views that children will have of their communities. What counselors must convey to these various groups is that children are already living in the community and are learning in school how to become caring people and builders of caring communities. These children are ready to become active citizens and caring community members who are eager to give of themselves.

Community leaders must decide what they want to teach their new citizens about their community with respect to its strengths, weaknesses, opportunities, and threats. Children need to hear about the people who work together in their community and the vast array of occupations that are needed to make life safe and comfortable for all. They likewise deserve to know of the weaknesses that plague their community with respect to such factors as cost of living, health care, poverty, availability of low-income housing, prejudice, discrimination, unemployment, racial tension, and crime and the degree of threat that these social ills pose to community caring.

Children likewise deserve to know about the exciting opportunities that exist for those who care and who are ready to meet the challenge as community builders. Here is where community leaders, teachers, administrations, parents, and counselors must come together and explore what they want to teach their children about community life and find ways to draw them into the life of their community. Children have much to give to their communities but need some direction, and communities need to involve their new citizens in community life but need a plan detailing ways in which they can become involved.

Homes and schools have a role to play in developing a community plan that involves the participation of caring children. Homes and schools must teach children ways to care and be careful, the value of giving and receiving care, and the skills needed to be caregivers and builders of caring communities. Homes and schools must become builders of this new workforce, and communities must find ways to involve children in meaningful acts of giving care through work. When this happens, communities will reap the benefits of a caring citizenry, and children will understand the value of an education in learning to live and make a living. And home, school, and community will understand the value of working together to provide children with a balanced education that builds caring children and strong communities.

Chapters 11 and 12, in addition to this chapter, provide a number of suggestions for elementary school counselors to consider that are designed to involve the participation of children in career and community caring. Community-based service learning projects, job shadowing, and model community betterment projects sponsored by various community groups provide opportunities for children to become caregivers and builders of caring communities.

Regardless of the approaches taken to involve children in community life, communities have much to give to their small citizens, and given the opportunity, the children have much to give in return. The seeds of career and community caring must be planted early if children and communities are to benefit from what each has to give. What follows are a number of activities and suggestions that can facilitate growing caring children and caring communities.

CAREER AND SOCIETAL CARING ACTIVITIES

Now and in the Future

Brief Overview of Activity:

This activity will assist children in making the connection between current "jobs" and potential careers for the future.

Objectives:

1. Children will identify current chores and relate those chores to potential adult career fields.
2. Children will relate interests to future career fields.

Materials Needed:

1. Paper
2. Pencil or pen
3. Chalkboard or chart paper

Procedure:

1. Ask children to identify current "jobs" they have at home and in school that may be related to potential future careers. List all of the jobs children have currently. Examples may include:
   a. caring for pets
   b. delivering newspapers
   c. helping with household chores
   d. mowing lawns
   e. watching younger siblings
2. Relate current jobs to future career options:
   a. watching younger siblings—running a day care center
   b. mowing lawns—working as a horticulturist
   c. caring for pets—veterinarian
3. Provide time for children to develop a matching game in which they are asked to match current jobs with future careers. This activity could be completed in small groups. The groups could then compare their matches with other groups.

4. Conclude the activity by discussing the relevance of children's current jobs to future careers. Encourage them to begin thinking about their interests and skills and how these will be an asset to them as they choose a future career.

Closure:

Bring closure to this activity by asking children to list four to five skills they have that help them in their current "job."

JobsThat Help Us Have Fun

Brief Overview of Activity:

In this activity, children will begin to think about all of the people who have jobs that entertain us and identify why such jobs are an important part of our life.

Objectives:

1. Children will identify at least three jobs directly aimed at creating entertainment.
2. Children will recognize the importance of developing leisure time activities.

Materials Needed:

1. A variety of pictures that show persons whose jobs provide entertainment.
2. Copy of worksheet *"What I Like to Do for Fun and Fun Jobs I Could Do"* (Figure 10.2).

Procedure:

1. Begin by discussing leisure activities. What are some things children do to have fun?
2. Ask children to think about persons who have jobs in the entertainment industry. Brainstorm a list of some of the people who entertain us. Their list might include some of the follow-

ing: amusement park workers, Disney characters, television personalities, sports figures.

3. Discuss the fact that many people have jobs that we would consider "just having fun" and they get paid for doing these jobs.

4. Discuss interests and strengths as being major factors in helping people choose their careers.

5. Provide a copy of the worksheet for each child and allow time for children to complete the worksheet.

6. When all worksheets have been completed, have children exchange papers with another child and discuss the "fun" jobs they have identified.

Closure:

Use this activity as a springboard for discussing the importance of choosing a career that is enjoyable. Remind children that jobs are

---

What I Like to Do for Fun and Fun Jobs I Could Do

Fun: *Play with my dog.*

Jobs: Dog trainer, dog groomer, dog show judge

Fun: _____

Jobs: _____

Fun: _____

Jobs: _____

Fun: _____

Jobs: _____

Fun: _____

Jobs: _____

Fun: _____

Jobs: _____

Figure 10.2.

not always fun, but if one has an interest in a specific area, it is good to consider a future career that will include that interest.

Occupation Shield

Brief Overview of Activity:

In this activity, children will choose a specific occupation or interest and develop a shield or coat of arms depicting many of the things they would need to understand about their topic.

Objectives:

1. Children will choose a specific career for in-depth study.
2. Children will create a shield to show all of the specifics of their chosen occupation.

Materials Needed:

1. Large sheet of poster paper for each child
2. Crayons or markers

Procedure:

1. Talk briefly with children about shields or coats of arms. Show some specific designs and shapes. Give each child a piece of poster paper, and direct the children to draw a large shield on their paper. It may be helpful to have some shield patterns available for those who will need some assistance.
2. Explain that each child will be developing a shield for his or her chosen occupation.
3. Instruct children to divide their shield into six sections. Suggest that the six sections be used for descriptions and/or pictures in the following areas related to their chosen occupation:
   a. a description of the job
   b. skills needed
   c. education necessary to obtain the job
   d. any tools that are needed

    e. special dress or uniform needed

    f. location of the job

4. When children have completed their shields, ask them to display them on the bulletin board for a short time before taking them home to share with their parents.

Closure:

Bring closure to this activity by posing the following questions for discussion:

    a. Did you learn anything that you didn't know about your chosen occupation?

    b. Did you see any other occupation shields that "piqued" your interest?

    c. What was the most interesting part of completing this activity?

    d. Does your occupational choice match your current interests?

Jobs We See on TV

Brief Overview of Activity:

Children will begin to identify the large number of occupations they are exposed to each time they watch TV.

Objectives:

1. Children will identify at least three occupations identified on their favorite TV programs.

2. Children will spend one-half hour per night for at least three nights to identify as many occupations as they can that are portrayed on various TV shows.

Materials Needed:

1. Pencil or pen

2. Paper

3. Access to TV

Procedure:

1. Spend a brief amount of time discussing the children's favorite TV programs. Choose one of the programs you are most familiar with, and make a list of the occupations portrayed by the characters on the program.
2. Ask children if they think the jobs portrayed on the shows are realistic. Why or why not? Talk about the fact that sometimes, for entertainment value, the jobs may be exaggerated a bit on TV shows.
3. Tell children that they are going to have a TV-watching homework assignment. For the next three nights, they are to watch at least one-half hour of television and write down all of the jobs or occupations that are portrayed on the show they watch.
4. When children share their information after the three nights, tally the results to see how many different occupations were represented.

Closure:

Bring closure to the activity by talking with children about the fact that occupations are all around them. Even when they are being entertained, they will become aware of people doing a variety of jobs.

Jobs Needed to Make a . . .

Brief Overview of Activity:

In this activity, children will become aware of the inter-relatedness of occupations and how many different jobs may be needed to make some everyday items that we take for granted.

Objectives:

1. Children will identify at least three jobs that are needed to create a household item.
2. Children will work with a small group of their peers to develop simple charts to identify the jobs involved in the production of a specific item.

Materials Needed:

1. Chart paper
2. Markers or crayons

Procedure:

1. Place an object, such as a wooden chair, in front of the class, and ask children to think of all of the jobs that are necessary to create the chair. Remind them that it begins with the lumbering process and ends with the purchase of the chair. Talk briefly about all of the jobs that are involved in the production of that chair and moving it to market.
2. Divide the class into groups of three to four and give each group an object that they are to use in their group. Some examples of things may be: a loaf of bread, a box of cereal, a football, or a book.
3. Ask each group to develop a chart to identify all of the jobs that may be involved in the production of that particular object.
4. When children have completed their charts, allow time for sharing and discussion of additional jobs or tasks that may have been involved in its production and in moving it to market.
5. Ask children to share their reactions to this activity. Did they realize how interdependent jobs can be? Were they surprised at what they learned through this activity?

Closure:

Remind children to think about the everyday things they take for granted and to use what they have learned to broaden their awareness of careers.

Job Posters

Brief Overview of Activity:

In this activity, children will focus on a specific interest area as a potential occupational choice. They will begin to investigate that occupation.

Objectives:

1. Children will choose a specific occupation and investigate it.
2. Children will develop a poster illustrating their chosen occupation and write a one-page report to describe it.

Materials Needed:

1. 24-inch by 36-inch poster paper for each child
2. Markers, old magazines, scissors, and paste
3. Pens, letter patterns, and stencils

Procedure:

1. Talk with children about choosing a specific occupation or interest area that they would like to explore in depth. This task should take place about 1 to 2 weeks prior to the actual poster-making activity.
2. Encourage children to begin to collect pictures and other information about their chosen occupation. Remind them that they will be using the collected materials to develop an occupation poster and write a one-page report.
3. Provide each child with a piece of poster paper and the instructions to develop a poster about their chosen occupation. The poster should contain the following:
   a. The name of the occupation.
   b. Several pictures showing persons working in the occupation.
   c. A one-page report describing the occupation.
4. Set a time limit of two to three weeks for completion of the poster-report.
5. When the posters have all been completed, allow time for children to give an oral report on their chosen occupation.
6. Display the posters in the hall for all to see.

NOTE: It may be helpful to do this activity in small groups so that children can utilize their strengths to the greatest advantage. For example:

The good artist can do the lettering, the strong writer can write the report, the verbal member of the group can do the oral report, and so on.

Closure:

Remind children that it is never too early to begin thinking about one's occupational choice. Early opportunities to explore specific occupations help in this process.

My Family Occupation Tree

Brief Overview of Activity:

This activity will give children the opportunity to explore, the types of occupations that are represented in their family.

Objectives:

1. Children will trace their family tree back at least three generations to determine which types of occupations are represented. (Note: Children who are unable to trace their family tree back three generations can chart the occupations of aunts, uncles, cousins, parents, and grandparents.)
2. Children will develop an "Occupation" Family Tree.

Materials Needed:

1. 12-inch by 18-inch construction paper for each child
2. Fine-line markers

Procedure:

1. Provide a piece of construction paper to children, and give them instructions to draw a large tree with many branches on it. Have them write their name on the trunk of the tree.
2. Allow time for children to complete their family tree in the following manner:
   a. On the first level of branches, write the names of parents.
   b. On the second level of branches, write the names of grandparents.

    c. On the third level of branches, write the names of great-grandparents.

3. Discuss with the children the occupations of the persons on their family tree. Instruct them to write the occupation of each person on their "tree" directly below that person's name.

4. Provide time for sharing and displaying of family "occupation" trees.

5. Invite parents in to see the display.

Closure:

In closing this activity, remind children that they may find their interests to be similar to their parents and grandparents or they may not. Stimulate discussion, encouraging everyone to choose a career path based on interests and aptitudes.

Organize a "Big Event" Party

Brief Overview of Activity:

This activity will introduce children to the "interconnections" of jobs and how one job often is dependent upon others.

Objectives:

1. Children will gain an increased awareness of the inter-relatedness of tasks involved in planning a special activity.

2. Children will become more acutely aware of the need for careful planning.

Materials Needed:

1. Pencil

2. Paper

Procedure:

1. Discuss with children how special sporting events are accompanied by parties at which neighbors get together in homes of friends to watch these events and celebrate the outcome. Examples of these events include the Super Bowl, the World Series, March Madness basketball tournaments, and NASCAR racing.

2. Talk briefly with children about the jobs involved in these events. The Super Bowl, for example, involves not only the athletes and coaches, but also souvenir salespersons, ticket vendors, food vendors, TV camera operators, analysts, newspaper writers, photographers, security staff, and others.

3. Tell the class that they are going to be organizing their own special event and that they will each have a special task to perform.

4. Divide the group into special committees: Publicity, Teams, Food, Entertainment, Souvenirs, Preparation of Field, Cleanup, and so on.

5. Allow each group time to write a plan for their committee, indicating all of the tasks that their group will have to complete in order for the event to run smoothly.

6. Provide time for plans to be shared with the group, and permit additional suggestions from children in other groups.

7. Stage an event so that children will have an opportunity to carry out their plans and evaluate the outcome.

Closure:

Following the event, evaluate it from start to finish and make a list of the "Things that went well," "Things that would need to be changed," and "Other suggestions" to make such a future event runs more smoothly. Again, remind children of the necessity for careful planning.

ADDITIONAL IDEAS FOR CAREER AND SOCIETAL CARING

Work Roles I Play in My Life

Provide a paper plate for each child. Ask them to divide the plate into segments to show the work roles in their life at this time. Some of these work roles may be: child, athlete, newspaper carrier, and so on. Provide time for children to share their plates with the class and talk about the roles they have now and how these may influence a future career choice.

ABCs of Careers

Give each child a letter of the alphabet or give a group of children a series of four to five letters. Have them think of as many careers as they can beginning with each letter. For example: A for airline attendant, artist, attorney, art teacher, architect, actuary, actor, athlete, and so on.

"The Career of My Dreams"

Direct each child to write an essay titled "The Career of My Dreams." Have children research career tasks, earnings, training necessary, working conditions, etc. Encourage children to interview someone who is working in the career of their dreams.

Career Day

Spend a day in which parents, grandparents, and other significant adults in children's lives come into school to talk about their careers.

Popcorn Factory

To give children a chance to experience making and selling an item, start them off with $20 to purchase the raw materials to go into the business of making and selling popcorn. Assign tasks to class members and see if they can make money on their venture. Also use this time as a way to identify all of the jobs that are necessary to make and market a product.

Nontraditional Occupation

To make children aware of the nontraditional occupations, invite some persons, who are in nontraditional occupations, to talk with children about how they chose their work, what they like about it, some of the difficulties they have encountered, and so on.

Occupation Sponge Activities

When you have 5–10 minutes available, encourage children to make a list of all of the occupations they can think of that require math (reading, speaking, etc.). Provide opportunities for children to share their lists with their classmates.

Tools of the Trade

Encourage children to bring in a tool used by one parent in his/her occupation. Provide time for children to see if they can determine the occupation based upon the tool provided. This experience will also give children an opportunity to note that the same tool could be used in many different occupations.

Occupational Interviews

Encourage each child to find someone with an interesting occupation and interview that person. Provide a sample list of interview questions such as the following:

a. Do you need any special schooling or training to do your job?
b. How much money do persons who have this job make?
c. What are the advantages and disadvantages of this job?
d. Are there any special tools or equipment needed for your job?
e. What do you like best about your job?
f. What do you spend most of your day doing in this job?

Seasonal Jobs

To help children think about jobs that are seasonal in nature, pose the following questions:

a. What do ski instructors do in the summer?
b. What do summer amusement park workers do in a winter climate?
c. What do department store Santas do in July?

Occupation Game

A quick activity for the end of the day is to name a business in the area (such as McDonald's). Ask children to think of all of the jobs that are involved in the operation of the McDonald's franchise. This can cover everything from the people who build the restaurant to the persons who clean and prepare food. This activity provides some breadth and depth to occupational awareness and yet is a fun activity that takes very little time.

In the Year 2030

Ask children to think about where they will be in the year 2030. To get them in the appropriate frame of mind for discussion, pose the following questions:

1. How old will you be?
2. What kind of job do you think you will have?
3. How will you spend your free time?
4. Will you have accomplished most of your goals by this time?
5. What will be your greatest accomplishment to this point?

Discussions such as this can be very helpful in getting children to think long term about their future. It also helps to bring up the subject of leisure time and the importance of developing lifelong hobbies and interests.

Career Collage

As an art activity, ask children to choose a specific interest area and develop a career collage based upon the specific interest area. They may want to include a variety of jobs within a special field, show different aspects of one job, or describe the path they may need to take to obtain the job. When the collages are completed, develop a bulletin board using the career collages.

Job Reference

In order to give children an opportunity to see what it's like to need a job reference, encourage them to review the want ads and decide upon a job that they feel they would qualify for based upon the stated skills. Ask children to get three persons to write a letter of recommendation for them based upon their knowledge of the child's skills.

Career Awareness Week

Identify a specific week as a "Career Awareness Week." Begin the week by discussing careers in the child's home, followed by careers in the school, careers in our town (city). Help children to see the wide range of careers that may be available to them in the future. Culminate the week by having a "Career Dress-Up Day," in which children come to school dressed in the outfit of someone working in a specific career.

Career Pictures

Obtain several cameras for children to use to take pictures of different career fields. The disposable cameras are great for this activity. Encourage children to take pictures of at least five different careers. Use the pictures to develop a bulletin board showing all of the careers they were able to identify.

(Note: Children love the freedom they have when you turn them loose with a camera. It seems to make them feel very grown up.)

Jobs in Our School

As a way of getting children involved in the career education mindset, give each child a 3-inch by 5-inch card, and ask them to write down all of the careers they observe in the school during a school day. This includes people who make deliveries to the school as well as those who work there every day. The children may be surprised at the length of their lists at the end of the school day.

Career Clusters

Help children to understand that a special interest area (for example, sports) may take many different paths. Encourage children to choose an interest area and then find as many different jobs as they can that would involve that interest. It may be necessary to give children some help to get them started. For example, interest in sports may involve jobs such as coach, sports announcer, sports writer, sports medicine, teacher of physical education, equipment manager.

Riddles about Careers

Children can get very involved in career education by making up riddles about specific careers. To get them started, share the following: "Every morning when you come to school, I'm on the job. I try to make sure you're safe so that you can do your job in school. Who am I?" (school crossing guard)? "I wear floppy feet and I like to fool around. You can find me in the circus. I am a _____" (clown)!

In My Crystal Ball

This activity will help children to look into their career future by predicting what they will be doing in 5, 10 or 15 years. In doing so, children will have a chance to realistically think about what their future goals are and whether or not they are attainable and reasonable. This is a good activity to share with parents to get them involved in the career education process. In a follow-up activity to this project, children can take their crystal ball picture home and share it with their parents.

BIBLIOGRAPHY

Birk, J., & Blimline, C. (1984). Parents as career development facilitators: An untapped resource for the counselors. *The School Counselor, 31,* 310–317.

Campbell, C.A., & Dahir, C.A. (1997). *Sharing the vision: The national standards for school counseling programs.* Alexandria, VA: American School Counselor Association.

Corey, G. (2001). *Theory and practice of counseling and psychotherapy* (6th ed). Belmont, CA: Brooks/Cole.

Erikson, E. H. (1963). Children and Society (2nd ed.). New York: Norton.

Ginzberg, E. (1972). Toward a theory of occupational choice: A restatement. *Vocational Guidance Quarterly, 20,* 169–176.

Ginzberg, E., Ginsburg, S.W., Axelrad, S., & Herma, J.L. (1951). *Occupational choice: An approach to general theory.* New York: Columbia University Press.

Gottfredson, L.S. (1981). Circumscription and compromise: A developmental theory of occupational aspirations. *Journal of Counseling Psychology, 28,* 545–579.

Gunn, B. (1964). Children's conception of occupational prestige. *Personnel and Guidance Journal, 42,* 538–563.

Gysbers, N., & Henderson, P. (2001). Comprehensive guidance and counseling programs: A rich history and a bright future. *Professional School Counseling, 4,* 246–256.

Havighurst, R.J. (1972). Developmental tasks and education (3rd. ed.). New York: McKay.

Hoffman, L., & McDaniels, C. (1991). Career development in the elementary schools: A perspective for the 1990s. *Elementary School Guidance and Counseling, 25,* 163–171.

Hoyt, K.B. (2001). Career education and education reform: Time for a rebirth. *Kappan, 83,* 327–332.

Marland, Jr., S.P. (1974). *Career education: A proposal for reform.* New York: McGraw-Hill.

Maslow, H. A. (1954). Motivation and personality. New York: Harper & Row.

McIntosh, P.I. (2000). Life career development: Implications for school counselors. *Education, 120,* 621–626.

Mosak, H.H. (1995). Adlerian psychology. In R.J. Corisini & D. Wedding (eds.), *Current psychotherapies* (5th ed., pp. 51–94). Itasca, IL: F.E. Peacock.

Munson, H.L., & Gockley, G.C. (1973). *Career insights & self awareness games.* Boston, MA: Houghton Mifflin Company.

National Occupational Information Coordinating Committee (1989). *The national career development guidelines.* Washington, DC: U.S. Department of Labor.

Seligman, L., Weinstock, L., & Heflin, E. (1991). The career development of 10-year-olds. *Elementary School Guidance and Counseling, 25,* 172–181.

PART IV

CHALLENGING
THE FUTURE

CHAPTER 11

Caring for School Counseling Programs Today and Tomorrow

Elementary school counseling programs require care and attention to be progressive and proactive, and to display a sense of vitality through purposeful activity that is responsive to the ever-changing needs of children, school districts, and communities. There is an emerging spirit and a sense of enthusiasm that surrounds programs that are fueled by creativity and imagination.

Elementary school counseling programs, and the counselors that lead the way, must monitor their programs daily in order to assure that what they do in practice today is consistent with where they hope to be tomorrow (vision and mission). They must continue to breathe new life into their programs to keep pace with daily challenges while keeping an eye on the future. What counselors do today will surely have an impact on tomorrow.

Elementary school counselors can keep their programs progressive, proactive, and vital to the extent that they practice good leadership strategies (see Chapter 3), engage in strategic planning (see Chapter 4), and make programmatic decisions using the Ternary Decision-Making Model (see Chapter 5). We believe that if elementary school counseling programs are to be truly successful, they must receive care before they can give care in helping children to become caregivers and builders of caring communities.

In the pages that follow, we have identified a number of primary, secondary, and tertiary activities and strategies (see Chapter 5) that will breathe new life into existing elementary school counseling programs. These strategies also are futuristic in nature and reflect current societal trends affecting children's lives today and tomorrow. Before implementing any of these suggestions, we offer a word of caution. Counselors are encouraged to review their current strategic plan, strategies, and activities, and the societal trends affecting children's lives, before selecting primary, secondary, and tertiary interventions to use in their counseling program.

The strategies and activities included in this chapter

- support the vision and mission of caring elementary school counseling programs;
- represent current societal trends (economic, sociological, medical, demographic, multicultural/ethnic, political, legal, technological, and educational) that affect the development of caring children building caring communities;
- affect all children and are developmental in focus and comprehensive in nature; and
- reflect the three types of program interventions (primary, secondary, tertiary) described in the Ternary Decision-Making Model.

Counselors who are diligent in controlling their program offerings in the manner suggested throughout this book (see Chapter 4) will have viable and relevant programs that meet children's needs and reflect school and community values.

PRIMARY INTERVENTION INITIATIVES

The primary intervention level focuses on four main areas: curriculum integration, classroom guidance, and peer and parent-helping programs. Primary initiatives emphasize channeling energy into programs and activities that benefit the whole and responding to trends that have the greatest promise for the future. They are designed to increase involvement and participation by everyone in both the school and the community. Due to the all-encompassing nature of primary level intervention strategies, there is a wide range of options for counselors to be creative and innovative and thus help their programs in proactive ways. The Ternary Decision-Making Model places the greatest emphasis on the primary intervention level and delivery systems as they provide for the most efficient and effective overall services to meet the developmental needs of all children. It is obvious then that the best and most efficient manner to vitalize an elementary school counseling program and to plan for the future is with primary intervention strategies. As counselors look toward the future, the most critical information for them to consider is the relevant societal issues affecting and influencing the future, including economical, sociological, medical, demographic, multicultural/ethnic, political, legal, technological, and/or educational issues. Counselors can use this information to guide their primary intervention planning or revitalization efforts. To illustrate this, we have chosen several primary initiatives that showcase how primary interventions can be responsive to societal evidence and trends (see Figure 11.1).

Primary Initiatives	Programs	Societal Focal Areas
School-Wide Programs	Diversity	Sociological, Multicultural/ Ethnic, Demographic
	Conflict Resolution & Violence Prevention	Sociological & Legal
	Childhood Obesity	Medical
Volunteer Programs	Parent/Grandparent Programs	Sociological & Demographical
	Adult Mentoring Programs	Demographical & Economical
School & Community Partnerships	Service Learning	Sociological, Political, Economical

Figure 11.1. Primary Initiatives, Programs, and Societal Focal Areas.

For each delivery system within the primary intervention level, we provided the evidence or trends that were used to inform these futuristic planning and revitalization ideas, listed several suggested activities for implementation, and identified helpful resources (books and periodicals, innovative programs, and relevant organizations) for counselors. These are but a few selected ideas to bring attention to programs and services at the primary intervention initiative level. School counselors might consider implementing one of these ideas or developing one of their own primary intervention–level initiatives. Because it is important to affirm that since the primary intervention strategies are the most efficient and have a wider range of effect than secondary and tertiary interventions, we have placed emphasis in the following primary initiatives.

School-Wide Programs

There is no more effective way to create a sense of caring and community within the school than to implement school-wide initiatives (MacGregor, Nelson, & Wesch, 1997; Slavin & Fashola, 1998). This focus serves the purpose of getting everyone "on the same page" in terms of commitment to a concept, theme, program, or activity. It creates a sense of purpose for the entire school community. By using school-wide initiatives, the counselor can also facilitate a directed response to an emergent issue or trend.

There are numerous areas that would be appropriate for school-wide initiatives. We have chosen to highlight diversity, conflict resolution, and violence prevention and to address childhood obesity because of the evidence and data that suggest their importance as societal issues and trends. Each of these topics can be addressed by implementing developmentally appropriate activities by grade level throughout the school. There are many ways to address these items through curriculum integration and by developing helping programs with a focus on these critical areas.

Diversity

Our personal awareness that the culture is changing and evolving to one of a more diverse nature is most definitely supported by recent reports. For example, a report from the Federal Interagency Forum on Child and Family Statistics (2001) indicates that the percentage of children who are white, non-Hispanic has decreased from 74 percent in 1980 to 64 percent in 2000 and that the number of Hispanic children has increased faster than that of any other racial and ethnic group, growing from 9 percent of the child population in 1980 to 16 percent in 2000. By 2020, it is projected that more than one in five children in the United States will be of Hispanic origin.

This change and evolution has not come without a social price. The *2000 Annual Report on School Safety* by the Department of Education and Department of Justice reports that among students nationwide, 13 percent reported being called a hate-related word or name. These reports also varied somewhat by racial-ethnic group, from a low of 12 percent for Hispanic students to a high of 17 percent for black students.

Given our awareness and the relevant data, it is apparent that a primary initiative in this area would help schools, children, parents, and community move to a place of appreciation for diversity.

Suggested Activities:

Diversity Groups—These groups meet on a regular basis to plan activities and displays within the school to help all students respect and appreciate others. The group is composed of a diverse population (cultural, academic, social, physical, etc.) who, through participation in the group, learn to appreciate those different from themselves.

CARE Week—Develop a series of activities aimed at the following topics: **C**ultures **A**re All Special; **A**ppreciate Our Differences; **R**each Out with Respect, **E**mpathize with Others. Utilize one day for each of the slogans, and plan a culminating celebratory activity for the final day of the week.

Speakers Bureau—Many communities have Multicultural Panels or other types of speakers bureaus to acquaint students, at their level, with the cultures and customs of a variety of people. Help children to grow and develop a healthy respect for all people.

International Days in the Lunchroom—This would require some assistance from food service staff, but could have very positive results. It might even make going to the cafeteria an adventure!

"Walk a Mile in My Shoes" Day—With assistance from a local rehab center or health care facility, one could allow students to experience being in a wheelchair for a day, being blind or deaf for a day, and so on. This experience creates a whole new respect for the disabled.

Some Helpful Resources:

Books and Periodicals

- LaBelle, Thomas (1994). *Multiculturalism and education: Diversity and its impact on school and society.* Albany: State University of New York Press.
- Lynch, J., Modgel, S., & Modgel, C. (eds.) (1992). *Cultural diversity and the schools.* Philadelphia: Taylor and Francis.
- Manning, M. L. (1995). *Celebrating diversity: Multicultural education in middle level schools.* Westerville, OH: National Middle School Association.

Programs

- A World of Difference—*http://www.adl.org/awod/classroom.html*
- Teach Tolerance—*http://splcenter.org/teachingtolerance/tt-index.html*
- Puzzle Peace—*http://main.nc.us/diversity/puzzlepeace.html*

Organizations

- Association for Multicultural Counseling and Development P.O. Box 791006, Baltimore, MD 21279-1006 *http://www.amcd-aca.org/*

Conflict Resolution and Violence Prevention

Teachers, parents, and administrators as well as children are aware that schools are not always safe places. Children can be both the victims of such things as bullying and other more serious crimes and the aggressors, engaging in such behaviors as vandalism, theft, and even physical assaults. *The 2000 Annual Report on School Safety* by the Department of Education and Department of Justice indicated that younger students, ages 12 through 14, were more likely than older students, ages 15 through 18, to be victims of crime at school. In 1998, 125 per 1,000 of the younger students were victimized, and 83 per 1,000 of the older students were victimized. Additionally, the National Center for Education Statistics *Report on Violence and Discipline in U.S. Public Schools: 1996–1997* shows that 45 percent of elementary schools reported one or more violent incidents. And, in a report titled *Indicators of School Crime and Safety* by the National Center for Education Statistics and Bureau of Justice Statistics (1998), there is data that indicate that from 1993–1994, secondary school teachers were more likely than elementary school teachers to have been threatened with injury by a student from their school (15 percent versus 9 percent). However, elementary school teachers *were more likely* than secondary school teachers to have been physically attacked by a student (5 percent versus 3 percent).

Caring communities by their very nature should be void of violence. In caring communities, individuals are able to express emotions and resolve differences in positive ways. For learning to occur within schools, children must feel safe there, it must be seen as a caring community, and teachers must be able to work in caring threat-free environments. Primary intervention initiatives that target conflict resolution and violence prevention can facilitate a school-wide response to these critical issues and go a long way in developing a safe and caring community for all children.

Suggested Activities:

Peacemaking Classroom Guidance Lessons—Develop classroom lessons around the theme of "Peacemaking" and assist children of all ages and grade levels to learn the skills of conflict resolution.

Create School and Classroom Peacemaker Awards and Recognition Assemblies—Give recognition to the "Peacemaker of the Week" in each classroom, the "Most Peaceful Classroom (or grade) Award" (based upon disciplinary data), and have an assembly in which each classroom could present skits, songs, or artwork on the theme of peacemaking.

Implement a Curriculum Designed to Teach Conflict Resolution Skills—There are numerous "canned" programs (see program section) that provide developmentally appropriate instruction to students on ways to solve problems, or one can develop a program specifically aimed at the needs of the particular school.

Some Helpful Resources:

Books and Periodicals
- Teolis, Beth (1999). *Ready-to-use conflict-resolution activities for elementary students.* Center for Applied Research in Education.
- Hollenbeck, Kathleen M. (2001). *Conflict resolution activities that work!* New York: Scholastic Professional Book Division Programs.
- Don't Laugh at Me Project—*http://www.dontlaugh.org/*
- Creating the Peaceable School: A Comprehensive Program for Teaching Conflict Resolution—*http://www.nccre.org/programs/peaceable.html*
- Program for Young Negotiators—*http://www.pyn.org/*

Organizations
- Association for Conflict Resolution
  1527 New Hampshire Avenue, NW
  Third Floor
  Washington, DC 20036
  Phone: (202) 667-9700
  Fax: (202) 265-1968
  http://acresolution.org/

- U.S. Department of Education
Office of Elementary and Secondary Education
Safe and Drug-Free Schools Program
400 Maryland Avenue, SW
Washington, D.C., 20202-6123
Telephone: (202) 260-3954
Web site: *www.ed.gov/offices/OESE/SDFS*

Childhood Obesity

There can be no doubt that as a culture we are increasingly reliant on fast food, have developed poor eating habits, and are not likely to engage in physical activity on a regular basis. This cultural trend is having a tremendous impact on our children. The National Center for Health Statistics news release, "Prevalence of Overweight among Children and Adolescents: United States, 1999," indicates "over the past two decades that the number of overweight children and teens nearly doubled. The initial results for 1999 show 13 percent of children ages 6–11 years are overweight, up from 11 percent."

In a recent review article by Wing et al. in Diabetes Care (2001), it was noted that childhood obesity is particularly common in minority groups, such as African Americans and Hispanics. It also confirms that this increasing prevalence of childhood obesity has led to a marked increase in type 2 diabetes in adolescents and young adults.

While an integrated curriculum focuses on the need for wellness that includes physical health, it may be necessary to institute a more targeted primary initiative to address this important medical issue.

Suggested Activities (see Chapter 6 for additional physical caring activities):

Harvest Fun—Counselors work with teachers to celebrate healthy eating by focusing on seasonal fruits and vegetables.

Healthy Snack Tasting Day—Cut up fresh fruits and vegetables for children to sample.

Healthy Role Models—Have a group of high school athletes work with children to teach and provide helpful ways for them to become and stay healthy.

Stop, Think, and Go Decision-Making for Nutrition—Have children apply the stop, think, and go decision-making model (Chapter 9) to nutrition. Give children three cereals to choose from and have them do so using this model.

Some Helpful Resources:

Books and Periodicals

- Ikeda, J. (1990). *If my child is too fat, what should I do about it?* Publication #21455. Available from the Cooperative Extension, University of California, Division of Agriculture and Natural Resources; telephone (415) 642-2431.
- Smith, J. Clinton (1999). *Understanding childhood obesity.* Jackson, MS: University Press of Mississippi.
- Hardouin, Benny (1998). *Cumulus the puffy cloud: A story about dealing with childhood obesity.*

Programs

- The Healthy Choices for Kids—*http://www.healthychoices.org /toc.html*

Organizations

- Food and Nutrition Information Center (http://www.nal.usda. gov/fnic/)
- The American Diabetes Association
  1701 North Beauregard Street
  Alexandria, VA 22311
  1-800-DIABETES (1-800-342-2383)
  http://www.diabetes.org

Volunteer Programs

Previous chapters (see Chapters 3 and 5) have highlighted the importance of volunteers and how they can assist counselors by becoming service providers for the counseling program. As counselors plan for the future and prepare to revitalize their programs, they can infuse a tremendous amount of energy and vitality into their elementary school counseling program by rallying these volunteers in support of the counseling program and of their planful and timely primary initiatives. While many different community volunteers can be identified and many different types of programs can be implemented to help support the elementary school counseling program, we have chosen to highlight parent/grandparents and adult mentoring programs.

Parent and Grandparent Programs

The structure and composition of the family has undoubtedly been changing, and schools have worked to respond to changes in children's family structure. Schools struggle with responding to the needs of children from a wide range of family constellations from traditional families, blended families, single-parent families, same-sex families, and interracial families.

Data released by the Federal Interagency Forum on Child and Family Statistics in their report *America's Children: Key National Indicators of Well-Being* (2001), indicates that "The family structures of children have become more varied. The percentage of children living with one parent increased from 20 percent in 1980 to 27 percent in 1999. Most children living with single parents live with a single mother. However, the proportion of children living with single fathers doubled over this time period, from 2 percent in 1980 to 4 percent in 1999. Some children live with a single parent who has a cohabiting partner: 16 percent of children living with single fathers and 9 percent of children living with single mothers also lived with their parents' partners. And, in 1999, 54 percent of children from birth through third grade received some form of child care on a regular basis from persons other than their parents, up from 51 percent in 1995. This same report provides data that indicates that for the 2.6 million children (4 percent) not living with either parent in 1996, half (1.3 million) lived with grandparents.

With respect to parental involvement in the schools, *The Condition of Education* (2001), a mandated annual report submitted by the National Center for Education Statistics to Congress, indicated that in 1999, 88 percent of children in grades K–5 had parents who reported that they had attended a scheduled meeting with a teacher. In contrast, among children in grades 6–8 and 9–12, about 70 percent and 51 percent, respectively, had parents who reported attendance at such a meeting. Additional, parental involvement was least likely for those activities requiring the most time, such as volunteering or serving on a committee.

The challenge for schools and school counseling programs is not only to recognize and appreciate the various family structures and social and environmental variables that affect them, but also to utilize the families to help foster and develop caring school communities. While parents seem to be invested in attending meetings at the school, creative and resourceful primary intervention initiatives can "pull them" into the school counseling program and help them become full participants in the caring community.

Suggested Activities:

Counseling Newsletters and Brochure Assistance—Many parents and grandparents have writing skills, word processing skills, and artistic ability. They could form a volunteer team, guided by the school counselor, to write a monthly newsletter and to develop brochures and audiotapes on counseling program topics of interest that could be loaned to children and parents.

Classroom Counseling Aids—Counselors are always in need of props to use in small- and large-group counseling sessions with children. Parents or grandparents who like to sew can make puppets, stuffed animals, and masks. Others can assist the counselor in developing a picture file. Pictures can be drawn or clipped out of magazines, and photographs can be taken to illustrate and support various teachings in the seven themes of caring.

School Advocates—We know how important it is to promote involvement of parents in the education of their child. Possibly one of the most effective methods to accomplish this is through "parent-to-parent" contact. A parent who has had a positive experience with the school can be an advocate for other parents to become involved. Such a parent can promote a positive communication with other parents, recruit new parent volunteers, and provide an "inside" look at why other parents should be more knowledgeable about their child's school.

Strength Sharing—Many parents or grandparents have skills that can be shared with children. Sharing one's strengths is not only a rewarding experience for parents, grandparents, and children alike, but it is also a form of modeling worthy of emulation. Children could also be given an opportunity to share their strengths with parents or grandparents.

Special Interest Programs—Parents or grandparents can coordinate a variety of worthwhile skill-building programs for children. Babysitting certification programs, latchkey safety training, fire safety, making a safe home, children's rights, and caring for a younger sibling are but a few of the many types of programs that could be staffed by parents or grandparents that can benefit children.

Room Parents or Grandparents—Most schools have a room-parent program in the primary grades. This could be expanded to include grandparents. Parents and grandparents can assist teachers in planning and conducting parties and other related classroom activities.

Parents as Partners—Some school districts have a club or organization called Parents as Partners. This is a group for parents that have both a professional and social purpose. Parents have an opportunity to socialize with each other and to perform a useful function in working closely with the elementary counselor by providing a variety of direct services to the program. These parents meet with the counselor throughout the school year and provide support services as needed. These parents or grandparents also can be valuable members of school councils and curriculum committees.

Some Helpful Resources:

Books and Periodicals
- *The Apple of Your Eye* (1996)—*How Grandparents Can Help Their Grandchildren Succeed in School.* A booklet and video available from the National Association of Elementary School Principals.
- Coulombe, Gerard (1995, January). *Parental involvement: A key to successful schools.* NASSP Bulletin 71–75.
- National PTA (2000). *Building successful partnerships: A guide to developing parent and family involvement programs.*

National Educational Service Programs
- Project Appleseed—*http://www.projectappleseed.org/npid.html*
- Partnering with Parents to Foster Learning at Home—*http://eric-web.tc.columbia.edu/families/partnering/*
- Building Successful Partnerships—*http://pta.org/parentinvolvement/bsp/*
- Partnership for Family Involvement in Education—*http://pfie.ed.gov/*

Organizations
- National Coalition for Parent Involvement in Education (NCPIE)
3929 Old Lee Highway, Suite 91-A
Fairfax, VA 22030-2401
Voice: (703) 359-8973
http://www.ncpie.org/
- American Association of Retired Persons
Grandparent Information Center
601 E Street, NW
Washington, DC 20049
(202) 434-2296
http://www.aarp.org/confacts/programs/gic.html

- National PTA
  330 North Wabash Avenue
  Suite 2100
  Chicago, IL 60611
  Phone: (312) 670-6782
  Toll-free: (800) 307-4PTA (4782)
  http://pta.org/

Adult Mentoring Programs

Undeniably, we are rapidly becoming a "gray" nation as the population shifts as the "baby boomer" generation grows older. The fact that there is a demographic change looming has been addressed within many political arenas and has also been actively covered by the media. From this we have developed an awareness that this change will have both an economic and social impact on our culture. The Federal Interagency Forum on Aging-Related Statistics (2000) confirms this reality. The data indicate "In 2011, the 'baby boom' generation will begin to turn 65, and by 2030, it is projected that one in five people will be age 65 or older. The size of the older population is projected to double over the next 30 years, growing to 70 million by 2030." Of those individuals, only 16–17 percent are projected to remain in the workforce (Purcell, 2000).

The sheer volume of adults who will be leaving the work force suggests that they will be an untapped resource for schools and school counselors. Thus, futuristic counselors can create plans that will capture this resource and also find ways to channel the energies of this population into service for children.

Suggested Activities:

Academic Mentor/Tutor—Many students are sorely in need of a significant adult to oversee their academic work, to support them in their efforts, to explain things more fully to them, and to help them prepare for tests.

Fine Arts Mentors—Mentors with specific fine arts talents can be paired with talented youth to encourage their continued efforts toward achievement in the arts.

Mentors for At-Risk Students—At-risk students face many barriers in their lives. Destructive relationships, lack of consistency in their homes, a sense of irresponsibility, and defiant or rebellious behavior are just a few of the issues they deal with on a daily basis. A caring mentor can provide a supportive role model, a warm and personal relationship, a sense of purpose, and assistance with decision-making skills to help the at-risk student be successful.

Hobby Programs—Many older adults have developed wonderful hobbies that they can share with children. A program such as this can have a dual benefit as the adult achieves a sense of purpose in sharing his or her skills with the mentee.

Friday Friend Programs—This type of innovative program provides an opportunity for a once-per-week contact with the mentor and mentee. It can be held within the school and closely monitored for success. It is very rewarding for the counselor to observe the caring relationships that develop in such a program.

Some Helpful Resources:

Books and Periodicals
- Fletcher, Sarah (2000). *Mentoring in schools: A handbook of good practice.* London: Kogan Page.
- Herrera, Carla (1999). *School based mentoring: A first look into its potential.* Philadelphia: Public/Private Ventures.
- Jucovy, Linda (2000). *The ABCs of school-based mentoring.* National Mentoring Center. Philadelphia: Public/Private Ventures.
- Jucovy, Linda (2001). *Recruiting mentors: A guide to finding volunteers.* Portland, OR: National Mentoring Center.

Programs

- The Foster Grandparent Program administered by the Corporation for National Service—*http://www.seniorcorps.org/joining/fgp/*
- Governor's Mentoring Initiative—*http://www.flmentoring.org*
- Delaware Mentoring Council—*http://www.delawarementoring.org.*
- SMART Program—*http://www.thesmartprogram.org*
- Big Brothers/Big Sisters of America—*http://www.bbbsa.org/*

Organizations

- Corporation for National and Community Service—Senior-Corps
  1201 New York Avenue, NW
  Washington, DC 20525
  Phone: (202) 606-5000
  http://www.seniorcorps.org/
- The National Mentoring Partnership
  1600 Duke Street, Suite 300
  Alexandria, VA 22314
  Main phone: (703) 224-2200
  http://www.mentoring.org/
- America's Promise—The Alliance for Youth
  909 North Washington Street, Suite 400
  Alexandria, VA 22314-1556
  http://www.americaspromise.org/

School and Community Partnerships

School and community partnerships are designed to provide opportunities for the school and community to work together for the betterment of each other. Children learn about their communities and how they can participate in making them a better place to live. Likewise, community members are encouraged to become involved with their schools to learn about ways in which they can contribute to helping develop caring and productive citizens (see previous section). School and community partnerships involve the full participation of the school and community in identifying and addressing each others' needs. Community and school partnerships can serve as the mechanism for encouraging necessary dialogue between the elementary school counseling program and the public. The process can become a key strategy for mobilizing resources in search of excellence in education and in breathing new life into the school's counseling program. This partnership process must also utilize the children. Our children represent a vast untapped resource as problem-solvers, service providers, and humanitarian advocates. What better way is there for children to become fully involved caring citizens than to contribute, in meaningful ways, to the growth and development of their communities? After all, children are not merely preparing for citizenship; they are citizens and need opportunities to be recognized as community supporters.

While there is a wealth of ways to formulate school and community partnerships, we have chosen to focus this section on the involvement of children in the caring connection with the community through service learning activities. Not only can these activities facilitate this citizenship process, they are also a vital part of a balanced education. Children engaged in *service learning* experience the ultimate application of the caring school community—caring children themselves building caring communities!

When selecting community service learning projects, counselors should look for activities that develop life skills, decision-making skills, and personal management skills. Look for activities that will help children mature, grow, and develop individually and socially; learn group processes and experience group involvement; and develop healthy attitudes and wholesome values. Community service learning projects can accomplish these attributes by helping children to utilize and extend their interests, talents, networks, and feelings of self-worth and personal power in the interest of caring for others and for their community.

Service Learning

The joy that comes from giving and caring for something outside ourselves is a common human experience and awareness. The seven themes of caring provide a template to show that as individuals we care not only for ourselves, but we care for intimate others, distant others and acquaintances, plants and the environment, nonhuman animals, objects and instruments, and ideas. Thus, caring involves choices and actions. Service learning is simply the application of caring choices in the fulfillment of educational objectives.

Data to support these caring initiatives are provided in the book, *The Complete Guide to Learning through Community Service, Grades K–9* (Stephens, 1995). The book provides the following data regarding service learning:

- Students in elementary and middle school service-learning programs showed reduced levels of alienation and behavioral problems.
- Middle and elementary school students who participated in service learning were better able to trust and be trusted by others, to be reliable and to accept responsibility.
- Elementary and middle schools students who participated in service learning developed a greater sense of civic responsibility and ethic of service.
- Elementary and middle school students who participated in service learning had improved problem-solving skills and increased interest in academics.

Suggested Activities:

Develop Service Clubs—While it would be best to integrate service learning directly into the curriculum, it may take some time to do so. In the meantime, counselors can work with teachers to form various clubs like an Adopt a Grandparent Club, Clean the Local Park Club, Helping Hands and Eyes (an outreach to people with disabilities club), Caring for Those

Who Care for Us (an outreach to support police officers, fire fighters, and other public servants).

Have a "Caring for the Community" Teacher In-Service Day—Counselors can present the concept of service learning to the teachers and have them engage in a brainstorming process as to how they can enhance students' learning through service activities.

"I Care" Day—Set aside one day a month for caring. Each student and all school service providers are asked to, either as individuals or groups (classrooms, sports teams, teams of teachers, or groups of parents), devote time on the chosen day to act within one of the themes of caring. Disposable cameras can be used to document these activities, and these pictures can be used to create posters for a "wall of caring" in the school.

Reaching Out to the Local Food Bank (from the State Education Agency K–12 Service-Learning Network, 2001)—As a lesson in weights and measurements, first grade students sort large quantities of rice and dry beans into smaller portion-size bags for a local food bank. In addition to actively using and practicing their mathematical knowledge and skills, students learn that they are performing a valuable service for the food bank in their community, which is primarily staffed by volunteers and is not able to spend the time sorting their donations into individual- and family-serving sizes. At the end of the project, the class creates a group chart that captures both quantitative data (e.g., weights, measurements, number of individuals and families served) and qualitative reflections of their service-learning experience.

Some Helpful Resources:

Books and Periodicals
- Stephens, L.S. (1995). *The complete guide to learning through community service: Grades K–9.* Upper Saddle River, NJ: Prentice Hall.

- Schukar, R., Johnson, J., & Singleton, L.R. (1996). *Service learning in the middle school curriculum: A resource book.* Boulder, CO: Social Science Education Consortium.
- Council of Chief State School Officers (1994). *Service learning planning and resource guide.* Washington, DC: Council of State School Officers.

Programs

- Kids Around Town—*http://pa.lwv.org/kat/*
- Innovation in Community and Youth Development Project. Also known as the Community Leadership Council (CLC) Project—*http://www.nylc.org/3m_index.cfm*
- Adopt-a-Watershed—*http://www.adopt-a-watershed.org*
- Do Something!—*http://coach.dosomething.org*
- Peace Corps World-Wise Schools—*http://www.peacecorps.gov/wws/*

Organizations

- National Service-Learning Clearinghouse
  ETR Associates
  PO Box 1830
  Santa Cruz, CA 95061
  Phone: 1-866-245-SERV (7378)
  http://www.servicelearning.org/
- State Education Agency K–12 Service-Learning Network (SEANet)
  One Massachusetts Avenue, NW
  Suite 700
  Washington, DC 20001
  Phone (202) 336-7031
- National Helpers Network Inc.
  875 Sixth Avenue, Suite 206
  New York, NY 10001
  http://www.nationalhelpers.org/

SECONDARY INTERVENTION INITIATIVES

The secondary intervention level includes collaboration, consultation, and counseling (both individual and group). These processes are designed to respond to children's needs and provide individualized interventions to meet those needs. They also provide ways to enhance the child's learning and development. Planning for the future and breathing new life into the secondary intervention levels involves energizing the personnel who provide these important services, facilitating a more integrative team approach to service provision, and utilizing networks or creating new ones to enhance movement toward counseling program goals. The processes for gaining more integration of services and developing networks for broadening program support are presented in the following sections.

Secondary Integrative Service Teams

The various personnel that provide the services of the secondary intervention area are critical individual providers of service. Typically, such professionals have chosen to work in isolation from one another. They at times can even get so caught up in the same day-in-and-day-out routine that they begin to lose some enthusiasm for their work and find themselves getting stale. They may even come to lack the very drive and dedication they once had for providing services to children. We are proposing that the future of counseling programs and their very vitality lies in the development of a synergistic Secondary Integrative Service Team (SIST) for the counseling program. Such a team can help professionals view themselves as a unit, an entity that works collaboratively to meet the needs of all students. The purpose of this section on the SIST is to suggest ways in which members of such a service team, in cooperation with one another, can plan for the future and "help to breathe new life" into an elementary school counseling program. Our intent is not to discuss the services management issues of such a team or to go into an in-depth description of the role and function of each of the key players on the team. While we recognize the importance of this topic, space simply does not allow us the opportunity to do so.

The basic purpose for SIST is thus facilitating the process of secondary intervention and insuring that all children have an equal opportunity to be educated. The individual members of the SIST are trained professionals who all bring high levels of expertise to the functioning of the elementary school counseling program and the subsequent secondary interventions. They are experts in their own discipline. Individual expertise, channeled into a team that has synergy, in which the actions of the whole are greater than the individual will undoubtedly improve secondary services to children.

In order to assist the elementary school counseling program SIST to become more synergistic, we have provided some suggestions for team building activities.

Suggested Activities:

It Is All in the Name—Teams function best when they have a purpose and an identity. A school-wide contest can be used to establish a name for the SIST, or the team can brainstorm creative names for their group.

Retreat—Plan a time devoted solely for the SIST; a time when the team can focus on getting to know one another, creating personal and professional connections, and have some fun in using their creative potential to develop exciting, stimulating, and enthusiastic plans to facilitate secondary interventions.

The Plan—A team without a game plan or a direction is lost. Drawing upon the mission and vision statement for the elementary school counseling program, the collective energies of the SIST can be utilized to develop creative plans to provide the collaborative, consultative, and counseling services of the secondary intervention level. The plan will help them to work more synergistically.

Time—As service providers, the members of the SIST will find that most of their time and efforts are directed to the provision

of the actual services of collaboration, consultation, and counseling. However, there should be biweekly devoted team time
when no one schedules activities and the team gathers to:

- Connect and care for each other
- Connect and care for the children
- Care for the counseling program

Practice What We Preach—Good interpersonal skills and interactions are the cornerstone of service provision. The SIST must
endeavor to create an environment where those skills are included in the team process. The team should develop positive
ways to maintain the highest of interpersonal skills in their interactions with each other.

Getting Consultation—Sometimes teams need help to maintain
their vitality and to enhance their current modes of functioning.
Bring in an outside professional to conduct a team-building
workshop/in-service for the SIST.

Remember the main purpose of service integration is to create
an organized, coordinated, and well-developed services team that
functions as a system in providing services to all children in the
school district.

Networking to Broaden Support

The Secondary Integrative Services Team provides the foundation
for secondary service implementation. Networking is an excellent
way to breathe new life into an existing program and to further enhance the work and planning of the SIST. Fresh ideas, new faces,
the availability of multimedia resources, and an opportunity to interact with other experts in the field serve to stimulate a renewed interest in the elementary school counseling program. Like the
intricate interlocking root system of a stand of giant sequoia trees,
networking provides the means through which an elementary counseling program can be nurtured, grow stronger, and maintain its

strength because of the depth, breadth, and diversity of its support systems.

A network is, as the title implies, a series of interconnecting lines like the fabric of a net, which link people, places, and information centers. Networks exist because they serve to bring people, places, ideas, and resources together for the benefit of those who use them. Our transportation networks (road, rail system, air routes, and nautical navigation routes) are designed to move people, needed goods, medical supplies, and produce rapidly, efficiently, and safely to their destinations. Our tele- and audio communications links (telephone, radio, television, satellites, and computers) exist for the purpose of collecting, organizing, maintaining, and releasing needed information in the most expedient, systematic, and efficient manner possible to sources whose very survival may depend on that information.

People networks exist among individuals who share common interests, who wish to promote specific causes, and who may be collectively contributing to the growth of a common body of knowledge. Networking has made a significant difference in the quality of life that we all enjoy. We are able to access a variety of services quickly and manage our time more effectively, and we have been able to expand out resources significantly. Networking can be viewed in terms of the people to be served and the nature of the services to be provided. Networks tend to be rather fluid and free of the structure associated with organizations. Their boundaries are not well defined nor should they be. Networks may be short-lived, and many form rapidly as the need dictates. As the needs of people and programs vary and tasks to be accomplished shift, so do the shared values, interests, goals, and objectives. The strength of the network lies in the deep commitment of its members to a shared position or common cause.

Elementary school counseling programs can make effective use of different types of networks. Here are several examples of network use for the counseling program.

Suggested Networking Activities:

Speakers Bureau—In-service programming can be costly. However, there are many groups and organizations that would be
willing to provide such a service for little or no cost to the district because of the free advertising for the organization. Also,
many social service agencies would be willing to do training
in school districts because it is a part of their agency's mission. Other groups might be willing to trade services. Members of the SIST need to interact with the community and let
various support groups learn about their work. When given the
opportunity, various community specialists can conduct training sessions for each other at no cost or at very limited cost,
thereby contributing to each other's knowledge and upgrading
the availability of high-quality professional services.

Topic Networks—Topic networks consist of people who have
an interest in a specific area and want to exchange ideas, material, and expertise in that area (such as self-esteem, stress
management in children, parenting, children of alcoholics,
divorce, etc.).

A Child Advocacy Network—School districts are dependent
upon a number of social service agencies to meet the special
needs of children. Accessing these services as quickly as the
need arises is often difficult because the school SIST and the
various social service agencies have not developed a close
working relationship. A child advocacy network can open the
lines of communication more quickly and speed up the delivery of services.

Electronic Networks—Internet-based networks on practically
every topic imaginable can be accessed by the SIST. These professional networks can provide a valuable resource for counselors. We, however, recommend a slight caution because, in
most cases, these networks are not restricted nor moderated
and provide some anonymity for the persons sharing information. Therefore, the information could be suspect.

We have stressed that networks can be valuable resources to be utilized and tapped to facilitate secondary interventions and the functions of the SIST. It is important to note that applications of networking can and should exist in both the primary and tertiary intervention levels. They are emphasized in this section because they clearly and directly support collaboration, consultation, and counseling services.

TERTIARY-LEVEL INITIATIVES

The tertiary intervention level, by definition, brings together the resources of the community to address those student needs that are beyond what the school counseling program can offer. Breathing new life and planning into this intervention level can focus on either creating better understanding of community resources and services or on reintegration programs to facilitate the assimilation of students back into the school.

Community Resources and Services Identification

Many communities have established human services councils or task forces designed to facilitate interagency collaboration and cooperation. In many cases, they also produce an agency directory of local services. However, these councils and task forces tend to meet on a limited basis and are not designed to facilitate referral and placement; their goal typically is to increase awareness across agencies. As counselors and SIST move to the tertiary intervention level, it is imperative that they are not only aware of the services, but can also tap into those resources to meet the needs of the child. The networking done in the secondary intervention level now becomes critical.

Additionally, it is important that counselors work to normalize the referral and placement process and dispel the beliefs that only "really bad" children are in need of outside resources. The counselor can take an active role in helping the school community understand that all of us, at one time or another, may need additional help and that getting that targeted help is a good thing and should be celebrated as such.

Suggested Activities:

Referral Handbook—Many communities have general resources handbooks. School counselors should collaborate to develop a referral handbook for school counselors and SIST to use. This handbook expands the general resource handbook to include type of treatment issues handled by the agency/service, typical length of services (number of sessions or days in placement), cost of services, insurance payment provisions, intake and discharge procedures, and any other special notations about the agency/service provider that would be helpful for placement. Include a flowchart that explains how the various agencies and systems work to provide services to children and families.

Counselor as "Client"—Many counselors do not have firsthand information about residential treatment service facilities. It is helpful for the counselor and or members of the SIST to spend a day at a residential facility and become fully immersed in the experience so that they gain a greater appreciation and understanding of what children and families experience as they go through the process.

Pamphlet for Parents—Design a pamphlet for parents to explain community resources and explain how they are a part of the tertiary intervention level of the school counseling program.

Plan an In-Service School Workshop "Agency/Human Services Day"—Invite members from the various community agencies to come and explain their purposes, roles, and processes to the school counseling program's "service providers." This also can be done in coordination with the school's student council. In this case, it might be called, "How we help to care for your friend," where the various agencies share the caring resources they offer children.

Host a Coffeehouse—Develop a monthly gathering time at the school for various personnel to informally connect and share new initiatives and services with each other.

Parent's Support Group—Create a support group for parents whose children are involved with tertiary interventions.

There is often a stigma attached to those children needing specialized tertiary services. Counselors and SIST need to actively work to dispel those beliefs through education and awareness. Such efforts will serve to promote caring and healing for those children who are most in need of compassion and empathy.

Reintegration

All too often, tertiary interventions focus solely on the referral and placement aspect and not on the ongoing support for the child who is involved with outside services or on the important aspects of the assimilation and readjustment of the child back into the school community postplacement. Counselors, as well they should, must endeavor to maintain the privacy and confidentiality of the child and not draw undo attention to the child's referral or return from placement. While we applaud the ethical behavior of counselors, we are asking them to consider requesting consent to share some information and build community support for that child. Why? It is quite simple; the school community and service providers cannot provide extra care for someone who is in need when no one is aware of that need. The "secrecy" surrounding referral and placement thus tends to minimize the child receiving support or caring from anyone other than the school counselor.

However, if the counselor seeks consent to share some information, then the counselor may be able to rally the resources of the service providers to assist the child and enhance caring for the child. For example, a young 6-year-old child, Rashid, was recently placed in foster care because his parents were neglectful and not providing for his physical needs. While in placement, Rashid attended a different school. Rashid was in placement for six months. He then returned to his "old" school, and the school counselor was informed that the social service agency now reports that Rashid's home life has stabilized and his mother and father have worked to address the concerns identified by the social service agency. With consent from the parents, the school counselor can work with the school counseling program service providers to celebrate Rashid's return to school and the classroom. The students may plan a welcome-back party for him, or he may be given a classroom buddy to help him get readjusted to the class and school. The teacher might conduct a classroom meeting prior to Rashid's return and discuss the importance of respect and appreciation for Rashid's situation. With appropriate informed consent, support, and assistance, the full resources of the school counseling program can be marshaled to assist Rashid and others like him.

Here are several activities designed to assist counselors in planning future tertiary interventions for breathing new life into meeting children's needs (referral, placement, follow-up, and reintegration).

Suggested Activities:

Tracking Notebook—Create a notebook to track and follow up with children who are receiving outside services or who are placed outside the school. Keep a record of the service provider, when the services began, and all follow-up contacts with the provider.

Reintegration Plan—Develop a plan for reintegration for students back into the school community. Become familiar with the exit procedures for the various placements.

School Caring Teams—Create a *School Caring Team* (made up of the various service providers) that has a reintegration focus. Team responsibilities could include, but would not be limited to, planning and conducting welcome-back celebrations, training reintegration buddies, sending "were thinking of you" cards, and developing special activities to help all children understand that "we all need extra help sometimes."

> *Build a MODEL Caring Community*—Build a model of an actual caring community with building blocks. Have the children identify "outside the school" agencies that would need to be a part of this caring community. Include such things as foster homes, hospitals, social service agencies, and so on.

OVERALL INITIATIVE: PUBLIC RELATIONS

This overall initiative is designed to infuse energy into the total school counseling program. Public relations (PR) is not a topic that is new to elementary school counseling. Over the past several years, it has received a great deal of attention from the American Counseling Association and more specifically from the American School Counselor Association (ASCA). Each year, for the past several years, ASCA also has published a public relations kit for school counselors that has provided the counseling profession with much technical assistance and many effective ideas for promoting school counseling. There is also a network website for elementary counselors to share information, participate in chats, and have questions answered.

Public relations programs, if handled effectively, can do much to breathe new life into an existing program. As an energizer and forum for cooperative planning and interaction, PR activities are second to none. Public relations is a process that conveys responsible activity on the part of the school counseling program to make the public aware of and understand its planned educational efforts. As a process, it is not only designed to let people know about the elementary school counseling program, but to engender community participation and support whenever and wherever possible. That participation can come in the form of a kind word, financial support, and volunteer efforts in school.

Because we believe that effective public relations is central to successful counseling programming, we have included it as a way of breathing new life into an existing program. As space is limited and as there is a wealth of available materials, we will highlight a few activities key to implementing a PR program.

Suggested Activities:

Identify the "Key" Publics—Select the key publics to be reached. Public relations is a two-way communications process and must touch those publics who will be most influential in determining the success of the school counseling program. Some key people who can either help or hinder the school counseling program are

a. opinion and power leaders in the community,

b. senior citizen leaders and families who no longer have children in school,

c. teachers and staff,

d. parents and families of enrolled children,

e. elected and appointed officials,

f. children in school,

g. business and industry,

h. local media, and

i. service clubs and organizations.

Take a Pulse of the Current Public Perception—Before engaging resources in PR efforts, the school counseling program needs to assess its current communication effectiveness. By assessing the public's perceptions of school counseling, program strengths and liabilities can be targeted. Assessing perceptions is critical, for school counseling will be judged like any other program, not as it is, but as it is perceived to be by those who will be doing the judging. Opinion surveys and attitude assessment devices are very effective tools for obtaining a quick pulse on the public's assessment of school counseling programs.

Employ Multiple Channels—Select a variety of communication channels. Successful PR programs not only know the various public sectors, but also know how best to influence or inform them about counseling program issues. The frequency with which specific channels are used also will be determined by such variables as time, cost, availability of talent, and the nature of the message to be conveyed.

Develop PR Ambassadors—Public relations is everybody's business and needs to be broad-based and continuous in terms of its involvement. Parents, teachers, school board members, administrators, and community supporters need to understand their PR responsibilities and how they all are literally daily PR ambassadors for the school counseling program. Public relations activities also can be extended to children through a Little Ambassadors program. Have children write personal letters to their parents, to senior citizens, and to community members telling them about their school counseling program and how they can help.

Welcome Letter and Packet—Provide new children, parents, and visitors with a welcome letter and informational packet about the school counseling program.

A "Good Idea" Box—Establish a box to gather parent and teacher suggestions and opinions regarding ways to improve the school counseling program. Parents will need to be given varying opportunities to share their suggestions (phone, newsletter, tear-offs, conferences, etc.) with the counselor. As ideas and opinions are shared, the sender should be supported and when suggestions are implemented, the person making the suggestion should be duly recognized.

Remember that the primary focus of any effective counseling program is to initiate ideas and actions rather than respond defensively to criticism. We also must be realistic and recognize that people evaluate counseling programs based on their perceptions of them and not on a rational, organized accounting of the facts or on the program's success or relevance.

While school counselors and service providers in counseling programs must first be concerned with how well they do their jobs, they also must establish ongoing PR practices that encourage daily discussions between and among friends and neighbors. These low-keyed and less sophisticated PR practices can often be more influential than those that require much time and costly resources to implement.

BIBLIOGRAPHY

Department of Education and Department of Justice (2000). The 2000 annual report on school safety. Washington, DC: U.S. Government Printing Office.

Federal Interagency Forum on Aging-Related Statistics (2000). Older Americans 2000: Key indicators of well-being. Washington, DC: U.S. Government Printing Office.

Federal Interagency Forum on Child and Family Statistics. America's children: Key national indicators of well-being, 2001. Washington, DC: U.S. Government Printing Office.

MacGregor, R.R., Nelson, J.R., & Wesch, D. (1997). Creating positive learning environments: The school-wide student management program. *Professional School Counseling, 1,* 33–35.

National Center for Education Statistics (2001). The condition of education. Washington, DC: U.S. Government Printing Office.

National Center for Education Statistics and Bureau of Justice Statistics (1998). Indicators of school crime and safety. Washington, DC: U.S. Government Printing Office.

National Center for Health Statistics (1999). Prevalence of overweight among children and adolescents: United States, 1999. Washington, DC: U.S. Government Printing Office.

Purcell, P.J. (2000, October). Older workers: Employment and retirement trends report. *Monthly Labor Review, 123* (10), 19.

Slavin, R.E., & Fashola, O.S. (1998). Schoolwide reform models: What works? *Phi Delta Kappan, 79,* 370–379.

State Education Agency K–12 Service Learning Network (2001). Service-learning in action. Retrieved March 21, 2002, from *http://seanetonline.org/sl-in-action.cfm.*

Stephens, L.S. (1995). *The complete guide to learning through community service, grades K–9.* Boston MA: Allyn and Bacon.

U.S. Department of Education, National Center for Education Statistics, *The Condition of Education 2001,* NCES 2001–072, Washington, DC: U.S. Government Printing Office, 2001.

Wing, R.R., Goldstein, M.O., Acton, K.J., Birch, L.L., Jakicic, J.M., Sallis, J.F., Smith-West, D., Jeffery, R.W., & Surwit, R.S. (2001). Behavioral Science Research in Diabetes. *Diabetes Care, 24,* 117–123.

CHAPTER 12

A Circle of Caring

We end where we began by focusing on the real purpose of an education, which is to teach children how to live a life of purpose and meaning. At the heart and soul of this mission is helping children to build caring connections. Being connected to self, others, and the environment is a fundamental human need, and it is the single most important driving force in children's quest to be accepted by others.

At the very heart of teaching children to make caring connections is people-building. People-building is a lifelong process during which children are taught skills and experiences, develop caring attitudes, and acquire the needed information that enables them to care for themselves, humankind, and the planet. Because elementary school counseling programs are in the people-building business, they share a major responsibility in helping all educators (all people who work with children) to form caring relationships with each other and with the children they serve.

Children must be taught the value of caring and how to give and receive care, and must learn various ways in which to express it. They must likewise learn to recognize and exercise due care in a world that is not always kind and caring. Elementary school counselors, through their counseling programs, can help to accomplish this end by communicating and demonstrating that teaching is a people-building process in which caring concepts and understandings are passed on to children so that they can become responsible givers and receivers of care. What children give in the way of making caring choices is based on what they learn and how they use those learnings to build caring and responsible connections.

Caring represents "the activities, relationships, examples, and services offered to young people which support their development and the attitudes, values, and behaviors that young people develop that in turn positions them to value and participate in social service, social justice, and social change" (Pittman & Cahill, 1992, p. 39). Thus, caring becomes an energizing and life-shaping force in which children first experience being cared for and then learn how to care for themselves and others. The lesson learned by children is that despite all they do to care for themselves, they can never fully attain happiness and peace of mind in a world that ceases to care for them.

We live in a world community that when viewed from space is a beautiful green-and-blue-colored sphere with no beginning or ending and no artificial country boundaries. Life is sustained through a delicately balanced ecosystem that is maintained by a circle of caring. To the extent that human beings make caring choices in the seven themes of caring (see Chapter 1), they help to sustain that delicate life-enhancing balance. When that balance is threatened through poverty, war, divorce, all forms of abuse, unwise use of our natural resources, disease, political unrest, oppression (sexism, racism, classism, handicapism, etc.), and inequities of all kind, the lack of caring choices sets a chain reaction in motion. That chain reaction first threatens the safety and security of individuals and eventually harms the world community.

Two simple truths represent the cornerstone of maintaining and strengthening a global circle of caring. These truths, when practiced, will result in caring children building caring communities. These very simple truths communicate the following:

1. What you care for will in turn care for you.
2. Treat others as you wish to be treated.

When these truths are practiced, a network of caring prevails, connecting the seven themes of caring into one circle of caring. A circle of caring thus contributes to the development of caring people and a caring world order. It fosters a climate of belonging and acceptance, and instills the belief that all people are of value and that everyone counts, including people whom we do not know, in establishing a network of care.

After writing this text, we are more convinced than ever that elementary school counseling programs with their people-building mission have a significant role to play in fostering a circle of caring that connects children to themselves, to other human beings, and to caring communities. It is our hope that children who experience and contribute to the caring circle will one day find a life of purpose and meaning as full participants in the same circle that nurtured them.

As we bring this text to a close, we would like to emphasize that children learn how to give and receive care by living, learning, and working in a circle of caring. That caring circle consists of a caring physical environment, a caring interpersonal climate, a caring curriculum, and a caring school and community partnership. Each of these building blocks cares for children and is cared for by them. Collectively, each dimension of care connects to form a circle of caring in which care is freely given and received. This simultaneous, mutual interaction process thus serves to strengthen the circle of caring and life itself.

A CARING PHYSICAL ENVIRONMENT

For children to grow into caring human beings, they need to experience a caring and warm physical climate. Caring physical environments are safe, secure, and comfortable and offer a sense of predictability. Children feel connected to environments that contribute to their health and wellness.

Caring physical environments do not occur by chance. They are developed through the caring choices that people make. When people care for their physical environments, their physical environments will care for them. Children need opportunities to explore and understand their physical surroundings and need to learn how those surroundings affect their quality of life.

Activities

Perhaps the first place to begin is to have children identify observable and unobservable factors that make up their physical environment. Such things as water quality, air quality and temperature, lighting, money, and highway signs and road markings affect people's lives. Have children explain how these physical factors and others can contribute to or detract from their physical caring and what caring choices they can make to enhance the physical environment.

We encourage teachers and children to explore ways in which they can create a caring physical classroom climate. What caring choices can they make using color, decorations, artwork, literature, sayings, and pictures to create a caring physical environment? Some ideas that schools have practiced are to

1. conduct a safety check of the classroom, school, and playground for potential dangers and correct them;
2. hang pictures on the wall depicting acts of caring;
3. create a caring word wall in the classroom and use these words often (thank you, may I, please, etc.);
4. create a caring corner in the classroom where children can go to relax;
5. play soft calming music during reading time; and
6. identify objects and instruments that children use and ways they can care for them so that these objects and instruments will care for the children (books, pencils, chairs, computers etc.).

Help children to understand how the physical environment affects their lives and what they can do to make caring choices to create a more caring physical environment. Children can learn ways to conserve the earth's natural resources, plant gardens, keep parks and recreation areas clean, and become politically active in trying to save endangered plants and species that may one day have the potential to protect them from disease and illness. Explore with children how they can use subject matter skills like reading, writing, math, scientific understandings, and language arts to promote a caring physical environment. Help children to understand that their health and well-being depend on a caring physical environment that they can shape through their caring choices.

A CARING INTERPERSONAL CLIMATE

The main focus of a balanced education should be to produce competent, caring, loving, and lovable people (McInnis, 1998). As children explore and understand their individual capacity to care for themselves, they should be challenged to consider what their homes, classrooms, and communities would be like if the entire human species drew upon its collective capacity to care for one another.

A caring interpersonal climate is best accomplished in a caring physical environment, in which children experience a sense of safety, security, and predictability in their lives because their physical and educational needs have been met through physical resources provided by the school. Although having a caring physical environment is important in support of a caring interpersonal climate, the nature of the interactions between and among people also must be addressed if the circle of caring is to become a reality.

A caring interpersonal climate will develop in classrooms where children are taught to care. Gilligan (1982) stated some 30 years ago that classrooms must promote a "web of relationships" that weaves together everything that teachers, parents, and children do to create a learning community that promotes the ethic of caring. Based on the research of Battistich et al. (1995), Noddings (1992), and Schaps (1998), teaching children how to care for themselves and others and to build caring communities is at the core of what makes us human, binds us together as a people, and provides the stepping-stone to becoming productive members of other communities.

Throughout this book, we have provided evidence that a caring interpersonal climate is strongly linked to a variety of significant child-related outcomes to include their greater liking for school, enhanced concern for others, better conflict resolution skills, stronger commitment to key democratic values, higher sense of efficacy, and more frequent altruistic behavior. These outcomes become a reality in schools that are functional, aesthetically appealing, visually inviting, and educationally exciting (Boyer, 1995). Beyond a caring physical environment, elementary schools can strive to build a caring interpersonal climate in which children experience the support, helpfulness, and concern of their fellow classmates and become active participants in shaping classroom plans, activities, and decisions (Solomon et al., 1996).

Caring interpersonal climates in classrooms and in schools that foster learning and community building are ones that embrace and encourage open communication, promote emotional and physical security, instill mutual liking between and among all people, encourage the development of shared goals, and support connectedness and trust (Sapon-Shevin, 1999). In a caring interpersonal climate, children experience a sense of cooperation and inclusion while seeking to identify and eliminate a climatic culture of educational practices that tend to foster competition and exclusion.

Activities

A variety of activities and experiences can be implemented to create a caring interpersonal climate. Because children learn what they live, living in a caring interpersonal climate will produce caring children and builders of caring communities. One of the most significant ways in which children develop a sense of interpersonal caring is to function in an interpersonal climate in which children share themselves with others, know others well, feel a sense of belonging, set goals and give support to others, work together in learning, speak the truth, and act powerfully in support of caring causes (Sapon-Shevin, 1999). Some specific activities that teachers and counselor might consider in fostering a caring interpersonal climate are to (Sapon-Shevin, 1999; Schaps & Lewis, 1997; Worzbyt, 2002)

1. send children welcoming notes before the school year starts;
2. greet children with a warm hello at the beginning of each day;

3. teach children how to give compliments and practice compliment giving throughout the day;

4. celebrate children's successes, acts of courage, and caring ways;

5. involve children in brainstorming, problem-solving, and decision-making activities that foster community building in classrooms and throughout the school;

6. conduct daily classroom meetings in which children discuss "What kind of classroom do we want to be?" Conduct class meetings to brainstorm caring community-building ideas to practice in the classroom. Give children an opportunity to implement their ideas, assess their progress, identify issues that need to be addressed, and enjoy their successes;

7. provide opportunities for children to participate in cooperative learning ventures in which the process of cooperation takes on as much importance as the task to be completed;

8. help children to connect with their strengths and interests and the strengths and interest of their peers and other members of the school community; and

9. downplay competition and exclusion by celebrating everyone's accomplishments, playing games and activities in which everyone wins, providing classroom jobs for all children that can be rotated throughout the year, and challenging practices in and out of school that promote competition, exclusion, and injustices that run counter to caring and community building.

Elementary schools need to examine the nature of their child-based activities and programs through caring and community-building filters to determine if what they are doing is supporting or undermining a balanced education. Some areas to examine are school policies and practices designed to motivate children's interest in school through the use of competition, awards, achievement-based grouping, gifted programs, and grade-based report cards.

Elementary school counselors, in their quest to help teachers and administrators create a caring interpersonal climate, would be well advised to contact the Development Studies Center, 200 Embarcadero, Suite 305, Oakland, CA 94606, and seek permission to use their field-tested questionnaire that measures a "sense of community" in grades 3 through 6. This instrument consists of two subscales that measure the degree to which children feel their classmates are supportive, helpful, and mutually concerned (14 statements) and the degree to which children feel they are able to participate in classroom planning and decision-making (10 statements).

Sample questions from the Classroom Supportiveness scale are:

1. Students in my class are willing to go out of their way to help someone.
2. Students in my class treat each other with respect.
3. When someone in my class does well, everyone in the class feels good.
4. Students in my class are mean to each other.

Sample questions from the Student Autonomy and Influence in the Classroom scale are:

1. In my class the teacher and students together plan what we will do.
2. In my class the teacher and students decide together what the rules will be.

Both subscales utilize a Likert-style evaluation process in recording children's responses.

We strongly believe in the need for a caring interpersonal climate in support of a circle of caring. A strong interpersonal caring climate contributes to positive child outcomes. Children who experience this climate do better than those who do not, and teachers who create and support a caring interpersonal climate are better at helping their children to grow ethically, socially, and academically (Schaps & Lewis, 1997).

A CARING CURRICULUM WITH COHERENCE

A circle of caring would not be complete in the absence of a caring curriculum that provides children with the information, skills, and caring attitudes needed to make responsible and caring life decisions. The caring curriculum teaches children how to care and to be careful in the context of having to make daily life choices in response to daily life situations. Thus, a caring curriculum is a people-building curriculum that helps ". . . children to become caring adults, builders of caring communities, sharers of learning, lovers of the printed word, and nurturers of nature" (Teeter, 1995, p. 360). It is through a caring curriculum that children understand the relevancy of subject matter learnings and their application to life and living.

A caring curriculum with coherence focuses on the teaching of traditional subject matter material in relationship to universal human experiences that are shared by all people and give meaning to their lives (Boyer, 1995; Noddings, 1995). We believe that a caring curriculum with coherence that best meets the needs of children and society is one that addresses seven themes of caring as expressed by Noddings (1995) and addressed in Chapter 1 of this book. It is in the context of the following seven theme areas that children will make responsible and caring choices and live their lives:

1. Caring for self
2. Caring for intimate others
3. Caring for acquaintances and distant others
4. Caring for nonhuman animals
5. Caring for plants and the physical environment
6. Caring for the human-made world of objects and instruments
7. Caring for ideas

Elementary school curriculums that connect subject matter learnings (information, skills, and attitudes) to the seven themes of caring will be able to help children understand how what they are learning prepares them to make responsible and caring life choices.

The seven themes of caring have a significant place in the circle of caring in that children first learn what it is like to be cared for, then to care for themselves, and finally to extend their care to family, friends, and distant others. They soon learn to recognize that they are part of a complex circle of caring in which they are benefactors and providers of care in a master plan that supports an everdelicate balance of living, loving, and caring.

Activities

A caring curriculum with coherence built around the seven themes of caring will help children to understand how what they are learning in their subject matter disciplines relates to making caring responsible life choices. As we have stated, a caring curriculum is a people-building curriculum that helps children to understand the relevancy of classroom learnings and how to apply them in caring for themselves, others, and the planet (seven themes of caring). The following suggestions are offered to teachers and counselors who wish to develop a caring curriculum with coherence:

1. Write each subject matter discipline at the top of a separate sheet of paper.
2. Identify key concepts, skills, and attitudes to be taught for each academic area.
3. Ask the following question: (a) How can each academic area (key concepts, skills, and attitudes) help children to care and be careful (risk management)? (b) How can children use what they learn to make caring and careful choices in the seven themes of caring?
4. Select one subject matter discipline and a skill/concept to teach.
5. Teach the skill/concept in a way that helps children to understand how it relates to caring. For example, a teacher may wish to explore the importance that numbers play in children's lives. Begin by asking children to identify numbers and where they see them (road signs, mailboxes, thermome-

ters, pressure gauges, their age, height, weight, etc.). Discuss how numbers help them to make caring choices and to be careful. Numbers are used to play games, keep score, locate people's homes, keep people safe (telephones, thermometers, highway speed-limit signs), and make life decisions (weight management, inflating bicycle tires, following directions on medicine labels).

6. Relate the skill/concept to the seven themes of caring. For example, help children to explore how numbers can help them to care for themselves, family, friends, acquaintances, and distant others; nonhuman animals, plants, and the environment; human-made world of objects and instruments; and ideas. Ask children to consider what life would be like for them and others in the absence of numbers.

7. Engage children in life experiences in which they have to use numbers in helping them to make caring and careful life decisions. For example, present children with the following life situation. You and your family decide to go ice-skating at the local pond. The outside temperature is ten degrees Fahrenheit. How will you use this number in preparing for your family outing? Your goal is to have fun in a caring and safe manner. Your problem is how to accomplish this goal.

These seven steps will help teachers and elementary school counselors relate subject matter teachings to caring and being careful. As children acquire skills, concepts, and understanding and learn how to apply them from a caring perspective, they will recognize the value of a balanced education and its relevancy to life and living. A caring curriculum with coherence gives children the assets they need to build caring physical environments, caring interpersonal climates, and caring school-community partnerships.

Many activities, ideas, and suggestions for building a caring curriculum with coherence can be found in Chapters 1, 2, 6, 7, 8, 9, and 10. We recommend that parents, teachers, counselors, and administrators meet periodically to brainstorm and discuss ways in which they can bring coherence and relevancy to their curriculum through caring strategies that link classroom to life experiences. Start slowly, accept the challenge of doing more each year, and share ideas and suggestions that relate subject matter skills to people-building strategies.

A CARING COMMUNITY BEYOND THE SCHOOLHOUSE DOORS

"Community is important not just as a place where we feel connected and supported, but as a solid base from which we move into the world" (Sapon-Shevin, 1999, p. 17). Children are members of the school community, a fact that often goes unrecognized. Caring cannot stop at the schoolhouse door if the circle of caring is to be complete. Children's lives are affected by their families, neighbors, friends, distant others, private associations, social service agencies, public institutions, youth organizations, the media, religious denominations, and business and industry. A caring community must seek to develop a web of relationships that connects people and institutions together in support of children and family life. That same network also must provide opportunities for children to become active participants in their communities, thus completing the circle of caring.

Many schools across America have embraced service-learning programs as a way for children and teenagers to become involved in improving their communities and stimulating classroom learning by providing rich and meaningful educational experiences for children at all grade levels. The intended focus of service learning has been to involve young people in service projects that respond to community needs while furthering the academic goals of the school. Such projects were thought to instill human caring; connect classroom learnings to real life experiences; and promote volunteerism, democracy, and citizenship.

We believe in service learning (see Chapter 11) and its potential for helping children to become caring human beings and builders of caring communities. However, we also believe that becoming a good citizen goes beyond participating in service-learning activities that emphasize giving and charity in the absence of developing a caring relationship with those who benefit from the services provided. Our goal must be to reduce the distance between those giving the care and those receiving it. Children are encouraged to see those they care for not as clients or objects, but as resources from whom they can learn. Nell Noddings (1984) stated that when I care "the others' reality becomes a real possibility for me" (p. 14). And when this happens, good citizenship and caring escalates beyond kindness and decency toward people. Children for the first time begin to understand ways in which they are connected to other people, the importance of developing caring relationships, how they draw upon the strengths of others, and how others draw upon their strengths. They realize that they are members of many different communities and a member of the worldwide community. They realize that a circle of caring requires the support of all human beings in maintaining a strong sense of community.

Elementary school counseling programs and elementary school counselors are encouraged to foster school and community partnerships that will help children and all community members discover their collective power and how to use it in building cooperative and inclusive communities, large and small, in which people are valued, supported, work together, and experience an abundance of love and friendship.

Activities

When children are enveloped in a circle of caring, they will experience an outpouring of warmth, kindness, and respect shown to them by others. But equally important, they will personally experience the joy of life and living that comes through caring and giving. Children will come to understand and appreciate the value of life and the significance of being a caring person making caring choices on behalf of themselves, others, and the environment. They will likewise come to understand that caring is what gives life meaning, direction, and a purpose for being.

We hope that everything that elementary school counselors and their programs do will help children to develop the attitudes, values, behaviors, and personal commitment they need to become involved citizens in promoting social service, social justice, and social change. We want our children to connect with what they are learning and then to use those learnings to make caring choices at home, in school, and in their communities. We believe that children would like to be helpers, caregivers, kind-hearted people, and forces of positive change. We believe that they would like to do things that can help their classmates, loved ones, and people in their community. We also believe that children would like to have kind and caring people around them, a clean environment, and a peaceful and caring school and community in which to live. And lastly, we believe that children are eager to seek opportunities to give their time and talents in support of causes that are dear to them. What follows is a partial list of caring service activities in which children can participate and become involved in the life of their community and truly participate in the caring circle.

1. *Caring for animals.* Children can become involved with local animal shelter projects, raise money for animal care, adopt a pet, and become actively involved in animal rights activities locally and nationally.

2. *Community development and beautification.* Children can support community cleanup days; identify community hazards and dangers and report them to the proper authorities; help community members rake leaves, shovel snow, paint fences, and so on; organize a *caring community club* and work with local organizations to improve the community's physical appearance; and work with community service groups (hospitals, fire companies, and police departments) to improve community safety.

3. *Caring for acquaintances and distant others.* Children can volunteer to work for soup kitchens, meals-on-wheels, religious groups, welcome wagon, and other social service groups that seek to offer support to people in their communities.

4. *Intergenerational caring.* Children can provide entertainment to nursing homes, bring flowers to the elderly, write letters and read books and newspapers to those who are no longer able to perform these tasks for themselves, take walks and share stories, play board games, and help with simple chores.

Additional topics to consider when advocating on behalf of community caring are projects that relate to the seven themes of caring. Counselors and teachers can help children to explore ways in which they can

1. care for plants and the environment;
2. care for family, friends, and loved ones;
3. care for acquaintances and distant others in areas related to health, homelessness, hunger, literacy, safety, transportation, and so on;
4. care for objects and instruments; and
5. care for ideas by becoming involved in causes that support the ideas for which children care (animals, environment, safety, health, etc.).

Caring beyond the schoolhouse door has many possibilities for children and adults alike. Many acts of caring are waiting to be developed, and many potential caregivers are waiting to be discovered.

When children recognize that the circle of caring begins with them and that the caring choices they make define themselves and the world, they will one day experience a kinder and more compassionate society with fewer personal, social, political, economic, and environmental ills because they cared.

BIBLIOGRAPHY

Battistich, V., Solomon, D., Kim, D., Watson, M., & Schaps, E. (1995). School as communities, poverty levels of student populations, and students' attitudes, motives and performance: A multilevel analysis. *American Educational Research Journal, 32,* 627–658.

Boyer, E.T. (1995). *The basic school: A community for learning.* Princeton, NJ: The Carnegie Foundation for the Advancement of Learning.

Gilligan, C. (1982). *In a different voice.* Cambridge, MA: Harvard University Press.

McInnis, D.J. (1998). Caring communication in its language classroom. *Peace Review, 10,* 539–544.

Noddings, N. (1995). Teaching themes of caring. *Kappan, 7,* 675–679.

Noddings, N. (1992). *The challenge to care in schools: An alternative approach to education.* New York: Teachers College Press.

Noddings, N. (1984). *Caring: A feminine approach to ethics and moral education.* Berkeley, CA: University of California Press.

Pittman, K.J., & Cahill, M. (1992). Youth and caring: The role of youth programs in the development of caring (Draft-Research Paper #2). Commissioned Paper for Lilly Endowment Youth and Caring Conference (February 26–27, 1992). Miami, FL: Center for Youth Development & Policy Research.

Sapon-Shevin, M. (1999). *Because we can change the world: A practical guide to building cooperative inclusive classroom communities.* Boston, MA: Allyn & Bacon.

Schaps, E. (1998). Risks and rewards of community building. *Thrust for Educational Leadership, 28,* 6–10.

Schaps, E., & Lewis, C. (1997). Building classroom communities. *Thrust for Educational Leadership, 27,* 14–19.

Solomon, D., Watson, M., Battistich, V., Schaps, E., & Delucchi, K. (1996). Creating classrooms that students experience as communities. *American Journal of Community Psychology, 24,* 719–748.

Teeter, A.M. (1995). Learning about teaching. *Kappan, 76,* 360–679.

Worzbyt, J.C. (2002). *Caring children make caring choices.* Unpublished book manuscript.

Index

About the Authors

JOHN C. WORZBYT, ED.D.

Dr. John C. Worzbyt is a professor and coordinator of school counseling certification studies in the department of counseling at Indiana University of Pennsylvania. He received his doctoral degree in counseling from the University of Rochester in 1971.

John has more than 35 years of experience in education, having worked as an elementary and middle school teacher, elementary school counselor, and counselor educator. He is a state licensed and nationally certified counselor and holds memberships in the American Counseling Association, the American School Counselor Association, and the Association for Counselor Education and Supervision.

A writer, John has coauthored four previous textbooks and three monographs, and has written articles on school counseling–related topics. He is currently completing two additional books on caring and community building.

John is a registrant of the National Distinguished Registry for Counseling and Development, listed in *Who's Who in the World, American Education, Directory of American Scholars,* and *Who's Who in Medicine and Healthcare.* Two of his publications received national writing awards from the American School Counselor Association and the American Counseling Association (American Personal and Guidance Association). He coauthored the United States Congressional Medal of Honor Society Youth Program, *Beating the Odds* (1995) and is the recipient of the 2001 Counselor Educator of the Year Award from the Pennsylvania School Counselor Association. He also received the 1997 Eminent Practitioner Award from the Pennsylvania Counseling Association and Indiana University of Pennsylvania's College of Education Faculty Recognition Award for Outstanding Accomplishments as Teacher-Scholar.

For the past several years, John has been a consultant, keynote speaker, and workshop presenter at state, regional, and national conferences and has worked with school districts, hospitals, social service agencies, and mental health clinics presenting programs on caring, community building, the human side of leadership, and the development of human potential.

John and Jean, his wife of 35 years, are looking forward to retirement next year and spending more time at their lake home in the Finger Lakes in upstate New York.

KATHLEEN O'ROURKE, ED.D.

Dr. Kathleen O'Rourke retired in June 2001 from the Altoona Area School District, where she spent 38 years as a teacher, elementary school counselor, counseling department chair, and coordinator of prevention/intervention programs. She has had a wide range of experiences in the areas of career education, support groups, working with parents, collaboration and teaming for quality schools, and working with at-risk students. She also taught master's- and doctoral-level students in the Counselor Education program at Indiana University of Pennsylvania for 16 years. During her 33 years as a counselor, Kathy became convinced that comprehensive school counseling programs are more important than ever in the lives of children. Since retiring, she has conducted numerous workshops and counselor trainings across Pennsylvania in diversity, conflict resolution, creating caring communities, and group counseling.

Many awards have been presented to Kathy during her educational career, including the Pennsylvania Counseling Association Eminent Practitioner Award, the Altoona Area School District CARE Award, the Distinguished Dissertation Award from the Epsilon Chapter of Phi Delta Kappa, the YWCA Woman Educator of the Year, and the Altoona Hospital D/A Education Award. Kathy has been active in both school and community and serves on the boards of Big Brothers/Big Sisters, Youth Outreach, Celebrate Diversity, Blair County Student Assistance Program District Council, and Balanced and Restorative Justice Advisory Committee.

Dr. O'Rourke and Dr. Worzbyt have co-authored two previous books: *Elementary School Counseling: A Blueprint for Today and Tomorrow* (1989) and *Support Groups for Children* (1996).

CLAIRE J. DANDENEAU, PH.D.

Dr. Claire J. Dandeneau is an associate professor and chairperson of the counseling department at Indiana University of Pennsylvania. Claire has nearly 20 years of counseling and administrative experience. These experiences are wide and varied.

After receiving her masters in counseling from Purdue University, she worked as a therapeutic wilderness counselor and group work supervisor for the Fairfield Wilderness Camp of the Texas Youth Commission. She was honored for her work in this program and was named the Outstanding Employee of the Year for 1985. Building upon her experiences in Texas, Claire moved to South Carolina to help develop a therapeutic wilderness camping program for emotionally handicapped adolescent boys for the John de la Howe School. She began her tenure there as the assistant director for the therapeutic camping program, was subsequently promoted to

director of that program, and then was ultimately promoted to the director of residential and treatment service for the entire agency.

Claire left the John de la Howe School in 1990 to pursue her doctoral studies. She completed her doctorate in counselor education at Purdue University in 1994. While at Purdue, she was the coordinator of their clinical training facilities. Since receiving her degree, Claire has been working as a counselor educator. She taught for one year at Purdue University as a visiting professor and has taught at Indiana University of Pennsylvania in the counseling department since 1995. She has been chairperson of the department since 1996 and took a one-year appointment as interim dean of the graduate school and research during the 1998–1999 academic year. The College of Education and Educational Technology of Indiana University of Pennsylvania recently honored Claire with the Faculty Recognition Award for outstanding leadership, service, and teaching.

Claire is a Nationally Certified Counselor and a Licensed Professional Counselor in Pennsylvania.